D1044696

Opera and the
Morbidity of Music

Opera and the Morbidity of Music

Joseph Kerman

NEW YORK REVIEW BOOKS

New York

THIS IS A NEW YORK REVIEW BOOK

PUBLISHED BY THE NEW YORK REVIEW OF BOOKS

OPERA AND THE MORBIDITY OF MUSIC
by Joseph Kerman

Copyright © 2008 by Joseph Kerman
Copyright © 2008 by NYREV, Inc.
All rights reserved.

This edition published in 2008
in the United States of America by
The New York Review of Books
435 Hudson Street
New York, NY 10014
www.nyrb.com

Library of Congress Cataloging-in-Publication Data

Kerman, Joseph, 1924—
    Opera and the morbidity of music / by Joseph Kerman.
        p. cm. — (New York Review books collections)
    ISBN-13: 978-1-59017-265-0 (alk. paper)
    ISBN-10: 1-59017-265-5 (alk. paper)
    1. Music—Book reviews. 2. Musical criticism. 3. Concerts—Reviews. I. Title.
ML60.K37O64 2008
780.9—dc22

2007046478

ISBN 978-1-59017-265-0
Printed in the United States of America on acid-free paper.
1 3 5 7 9 10 8 6 4 2

To the memory of Vivian Kerman,
who vetted every one of these writings

Contents

PREFACE   *ix*

1 Classical Music: Rise and Fall, and Rise   *1*
2 Opera and the Morbidity of Music   *7*
3 Two Cheers for Rach 3   *21*

4 Labyrinth Music   *27*
5 William Byrd and the Catholics   *41*
6 The Operas of Monteverdi   *57*

7 Bach: A Short Life   *69*
8 A Guide to *The Well-Tempered Clavier*   *79*
9 Wilfrid Mellers on Bach   *87*

10 Mozart: Four Biographies   *99*
11 Mozart's Last Year   *115*
12 Playing Mozart: The Piano Concertos   *123*
13 *The Magic Flute*   *137*

14 Sonata Forms   *151*
15 Beethoven: Works and Life   *161*
16 Beethoven Hero   *173*
17 Text and Act: Beethoven's Concertos   *185*
18 Three Riffs on the Ninth   *201*

19 The Romantic Generation   *205*
20 Schubert's Songs   *221*
21 Berlioz: A Life   *231*

22 Reading Opera   *243*
23 Verdi: A Life   *255*
24 Verdi: The Late Operas   *267*
25 Wagner and Wagnerism   *281*
26 A *Ring* for San Francisco   *307*
27 Bayreuth, 2001   *319*

28 The Art of the Program Note   333
29 Maria Callas (1923–1977)   345
30 Carlos Kleiber (1930–2004)   351

SOURCES   356

INDEX   358

Preface

THIS BOOK BELONGS to a familiar genre: the retrospective collection of an author's essays and reviews, in this case drawn with few exceptions from *The New York Review of Books* over the last thirty years. They mainly treat music of the traditional classical canon. The title, plucked from the latest of the essays included, is not meant for the book's contents as a whole (though there is plenty about opera here, God knows, a long-term preoccupation of mine). Mozart, the very synecdoche for classical music in our time, figures in more articles— that is, in more chapters of this book—than any other composer: four and a third if you care to tally them, edging out even Beethoven the inexorable, with four and a quarter.

A specification of the Mozartian topics will give a general idea of what to expect in the chapters ahead. One piece is indeed a freestanding essay on an opera, *The Magic Flute*, answering the call of the anniversary of his birth in 2006. Another is a review of recordings of his piano concertos, occasioned by the historic (as I think) performances on fortepiano by Malcolm Bilson in the 1980s, and also taking account of interpretations by Artur Schnabel, Vladimir Ashkenazy, and Murray Perahia. Two others are reviews of biographies and other books on Mozart. Chapter 28, "The Art of the Program Note," contains relatively brief accounts of three works: the *War Requiem* of

Benjamin Britten, the Verdi Requiem, and the Mozart Requiem—which parts are inauthentic, and what to do about it.

Of the items in this collection that were written for *The New York Review of Books*, about two thirds take the form, unsurprisingly, of book reviews; the others are performance reviews, obituary essays, and a few freestanding essays like Chapter 13, on *The Magic Flute*. The book reviews tend to slip their moorings to drift over wider waters, as reviews are wont to do. Chapter 1 appeared in the *Los Angeles Times Book Review*, the articles on Berlioz and Verdi in *The New Republic*, and "Three Riffs on the Ninth" goes back to a program note for a performance of Beethoven's Ninth Symphony at Berkeley, by the University Symphony Orchestra, in 2003. The printed program for that concert has become a collectors' item, since it gave the composer's name as Johann von Beethoven.

In a collection of this kind some repetition and redundancy is inevitable, but I hope it is only really annoying if Chapters 25–27, on Wagner, are read at one sitting. All I can do is plead indulgence on account of the subject matter. Chapter 2, "Opera and the Morbidity of Music," written for this volume, draws on a recent review in the *Los Angeles Times Book Review*, "Classical Music: Rise and Fall, and Rise," which stands next to it here, as Chapter 1. The supposed death of classical music is treated differently in the article and the review, and in this case what some readers may look upon as redundancy I see as appropriate emphasis. And to those who may complain that I am beating a dead horse, my rejoinder is that whereas happily classical music is not dead, neither, unless I am mistaken, is the horse.

Music, Dryden cautioned, "for a while may all your cares beguile," but the setting of his words by Purcell has lasted for a very long while (and with the music, Dryden's verse with its elegant rhythm and rhyme and his magic word "beguiled"). The same is true of Schubert's "An die Musik" and his friend Franz Schober's less accomplished lyric, with its countless gray hours charmed away by the beloved art of music. *"Du holde Kunst"*: but while pains are eased and gray hours *entrückt* by music sung or heard—and even by scores read silently, as musicians do—reading *about* music does not soothe or console, inspire courage, enrapture, or transport. Still, while everyone in every culture needs music to sing, play, or hear, some people are also driven to talk about music and read about it, just as they read about art, architecture, literature, and everything else under the sun. George Bernard Shaw claimed that there are people who will read about music and nothing else; admittedly, the allegation harks back to his days as a music critic and may not have been entirely disinterested.

A market exists, then, and with it, suppliers—musicologists, critics, biographers, writers of program notes, Amazon reviewers, and publicists. "Critic and musicologist" is what I used to style myself, before the distinction became less and less evident and interesting (pursuant on some efforts of my own, if I may say so—and of many others). Most musicologists come to the academic study of music by way of playing music, conducting music, or composing music. I started out wanting to know music and write about it. (As a pianist, my progress stalled when I found out that the Music Library on 58th Street, next to the BMT transfer to my teacher in Brooklyn, would circulate seven scores a week, treasure troves of song, keyboard music, and opera that I would sight-read avidly, zealously, instead of practicing Brahms's Variations on a Theme by Handel.) There are articles—now expunged from my formal bibliography—written before I even began studying musicology, as a preparation for criticism (a route taken often enough by aspiring writers today, but seldom in earlier times, at least in America). Musicologists write for fellow specialists, who read musical notation and understand—indeed, appreciate—technicalities. I cannot honestly say I prefer this specialized audience to the more general audience addressed here. This is a readership I have always wanted to write for and love writing for.

Yet—and this must be the case with many others—I am very hazy about the actual composition of that readership. Does this "critic and musicologist" speak to concertgoers, opera buffs, academics, musicians, or a mix, and if so, in what proportions? Can Donald Tovey's "naive listener," privy to the aesthetics of double counterpoint at the twelfth, have survived modernism and postmodernism to resurface, more than a little dizzy, in the twenty-first century? Some of the uncertainty comes from a feeling for the fragility of our whole operation, a condition which, if you tend to read accounts of music criticism, you will have read about only too many times. Music critics cannot offer examples of what they are writing about that readers can take in immediately, along with the critical prose, in the way colleagues from literature and art can cite poems and display illustrations. Neither a symphony recording packaged with a pamphlet of commentary nor a book on the symphony packaged with a CD has anything like the immediacy of a coffee-table art book with commentary tucked in among the glowing reproductions. With music lacking a text, it can require considerable effort for a writer to refer to a musical detail, even to a particular moment in the course of a composition, like a turning point or a climax. Musical notation is a last resort; only one of the following chapters has to use it.

Music critics have to work harder, that's all. So, unless we work harder still, do our readers. We write about composers' biographies, music's history and its role in culture and society, its genesis, its multiple meanings in reception, the nuances of particular performances, the demeanor of particular performers. We relay anecdotes that will supposedly light(en) up the music in question. Too often this amounts to little more than potted musicology, footnoted to the latest research, and commentary of an overreaching, general sort, without addressing what everyone agrees is the primary thing: the immediate experience of music —of particular pieces of music, something which cannot be verbalized.

I have been dealing with this situation ever since (indeed for long before) my first contribution to *The New York Review*, Chapter 20 in this book. Note that everything that I say there about Schubert has to be couched in general terms, until I come to a comparison of his setting of Goethe's "Trost an Tränen" (Consolation in Tears) with the setting of the same poem by Brahms. Then I am able to move from generalities ("in its freedom and simplicity, [Schubert's] career as a song-writer contrasts with those of later figures") to specifics—to a telling musical detail. When the major mode cancels the minor in the song's last stanza at the word *weinen*, the final emphasis is not bluntly "on weeping, rather on the ambiguity of weeping." The specific supports the general. "Taking Goethe's title seriously, Schubert responds to his sentiment more directly and also more richly than does the later composer."

A small point, it may seem, but methodologically one that matters. Alex Ross writes that "the music effectively stops moving and the timpanist drums lightly on the note C like a finger tapping on a pane"—this in the Scherzo of Beethoven's Fifth Symphony, of course, the "goblins" movement of *Howards End*. Beethoven has his morbid, obsessive moods; the hyperbolical military march that emerges can sound like "an attempt to forget whatever existential threat the Scherzo poses."[1] The real "theme" of the Fifth is not the iconic motto *da-da-da-DA* at the beginning, Alan Rich maintains, but an entire twenty-second sequence in which the motto storms twice in its bare form, and is then "played off against itself in tense and bristling counterpoint...and brought to a suspenseful half-cadence"; in this passage "the tensions and ultimate relaxations of the symphony as a whole are enacted in microcosm."[2] In a small way, these critics are

---

1. "Cycles," *The New Yorker*, November 20, 2006, p. 98. Is the subtle instability of the opening of the finale, which Ross catches, answered to by the unusual reprise of the lead-in passage prior to the recapitulation, and perhaps even by the notorious reiterated tonic chords at the very end?

2. *So I've Heard* (Amadeus Press, 2006), p. 77. The relaxations are often overlooked, even by conductors!

suggesting unfamiliar avenues into a work that has become so familiar, so fixed in interpretation, and so often pronounced "classic" that
many listeners have become quite exasperated with it and said so: in
public (Virgil Thomson's "editorial symphony") or in private (Wagner, Adorno, you, dear reader, and me). Major–minor, tapping C,
counterpoint, cadence—whether or not these count as "technicalities," everything is easy to hear and we simply accept or reject the
modicum of insight the writer has ventured. The reader is invited to
listen, to extend his or her engagement with the way music works.

"If the music doesn't say it, how can words *say* it for the music?"
asked John Coltrane. One can imagine the sort of writing that pro-
voked this rhetorical question, and sympathize with the many musicians who have asked the same question, or something like it which
likewise, I have to say, would miss the point. Nobody expects words
to say what music says. Music critics do not try to verbalize the
unverbalizable. All we do, sometimes, is what critics of painting,
dance, poetry, and prose have always done, and which poets do in the
face of ineffables like love and nature. Poets use words not to dupli-
cate or describe immediate experience, but to cozy up to it, suggest it,
create an aura about it that heightens sensitivity and feeling. The
tropes and rhythms of critical prose, too, do their good work. Successful critics are those imbued with passion and delight in art, and in
the case of familiar classics, the live memory of their original novelty
and wonder—those scores from the 58th Street Library, with their
unappeasable weekly stamps—and in addition are blessed with or
have developed a rhetoric to communicate some sense of such feelings. If your rhetoric and sensibility are in order, you will get through
to your readership, whatever that is.

The journal that encouraged me to invent myself as a music critic was
The Hudson Review, and this preface provides one more occasion to
register my affection and gratitude to its original troika of editors,

twenty-somethings and poets all. Thanks also to Leon Wieseltier of *The New Republic* and Steve Wasserman of the *Los Angeles Times*. My greatest debt is of course to *The New York Review of Books*, the journal which has reinvented me—wait, we can't quite say that!—the journal whose influence on my writing has probably been more extensive than either of us have given much thought to. It ranges from the culture of the organization and the example of their other contributors to the books they send out for review and their meticulous editing. Robert Silvers, a very special editor, lavishes his attention on every one of the *New York Review* pieces, paragraph by paragraph and word for word. And we have seldom had words. Thanks to Bob Silvers the *NYR* has always felt more like a home for my work than an outlet.

A little new editing has been undertaken, for style, not substance, and a few clarifying notes indicated by "(2007)" have been added. Michael Shae, editor of this book, has been as effective as any I've ever had, and for accommodation, utter patience, tact, and cool, in a class of his own.

J.K.

I

CLASSICAL MUSIC:
RISE AND FALL, AND RISE

THE DECLINE—sometimes called the death—of classical music has long served as a reliable trigger for lamentation or schadenfreude, as the case may be, and an equally reliable filler of newspaper space. It is therefore not surprising that Joseph Horowitz should press his impressive chronicle of classical music in America into a rigid frame of rise and fall.[1] Horowitz began his career as a music critic and continues it as a presenter of concerts and festivals; he is the author of important studies of musical life in New York—on the reception of Wagner in the 1880s and the Toscanini phenomenon of the 1930s and 1940s[2]—which he draws on liberally here.

He's a voluble, often caustic writer, fast-paced, fabulously informed, and always ready with an astonishing fact or factoid. For example, during World War I, the German conductor of the Boston Symphony, Karl Muck, was interned—together with twenty-nine of his players. In the 1920s the New York Philharmonic included no more than twenty native-born members. A hundred years earlier than that, some 150 operas had already been mounted in New Orleans, with slaves seated in the gallery.

---

1. *Classical Music in America: A History of Its Rise and Fall* (Norton, 2005).

2. *Wagner Nights: An American History* (University of California Press, 1994); *Understanding Toscanini* (Knopf, 1987).

Book 1 covers music's "Birth and Growth" up to World War I. It is a tale of two cities well told, and well shaped by the difference (contrast, tension) between Boston, America's cultural bellwether—prudent, patrician, closed, homogeneous (since the Irish were excluded)—and New York, whose newly arrived ethnic mix could be as open and innovative as it was fickle and voracious. Henry Higginson founded the Boston Symphony Orchestra, nurtured it, built its hall, and hired its conductors; Andrew Carnegie built Carnegie Hall, then switched his attention to peace and education. New York eagerly hailed both Dvořák's extended stay in this country and his exemplary "New World" Symphony, with its evocation of Indian and Negro melodies. Boston sneered at such impurities.

In both cities, music in the late nineteenth century was "sacralized," allowing pre-radio, pre-CD listeners to experience the manifold pleasures they found in music as something even more: as uplift. Influential critics led the way in this process, with publicists, marketeers, and musicians themselves close behind. If Beethoven loomed almost godlike in Boston, it was Wagner who truly rocked New York; it took New York just four seasons to première six of his enormous late operas (*Parsifal* came later—the first unauthorized performance outside of Bayreuth). And Wagner hit Brooklyn like a tsunami: audiences of up to three thousand flocked to hear Wagnerian conductor Anton Seidl exert his magic twice a day, seven days a week, for a two-week festival at Brighton Beach, next to Coney Island.

Book 2 ("Decline and Fall") covers music from World War I to the present. This long historical span can't be analyzed along geographic-ideological lines, or anything else as simple and elegant as that. Boston soon left the main action to New York, and music also flourished in what the author calls the "hinterlands" and can only cope with by means of somewhat frantic cameos. Desacralized by wartime hysteria, German music took a long time to recover, if it ever has.

The New York scene was tangled, and dominated, for Horowitz,

2

by the rise of a "culture of performance," which he traces all the way up to André Rieu and the Three Tenors. More and more hype and spin were, and are, devoted to performers rather than to the music performed. Superstars like Kreisler and Heifetz, Caruso and Flagstad, Rachmaninoff and the other Horowitz—or more precisely, the publicity machines that directed and supposedly stultified their careers— are deplored. But the symphony orchestra comes first on this author's scale of musical values, and it is the career of Arturo Toscanini that shows the culture of performance at its most debilitating. Toscanini dominated orchestral life in New York for more than two decades. He was elevated into "an American culture God" by a very consortium of promoters—David Sarnoff of NBC, *The New York Times*, and the purveyors of "music appreciation." He was exposed and excoriated first in various writings by Adorno and then in a whole book— Horowitz's *Understanding Toscanini*.

My advice to Joe Horowitz: get over it. Toscanini was a great conductor who brought music to millions, never mind the massive exertions of his support system. Unlike virtually all his colleagues of the podium, Toscanini in his New York years (he was sixty when he came) played virtually no new music and there can be little doubt that this contributed to his popularity. Meanwhile in hinterland Philadelphia, Leopold Stokowski premièred around two thousand new works, most of them American, and the endless commissions by Serge Koussevitzky for the Boston Symphony (still continuing under the Koussevitzky Foundations) included four symphonies by Roy Harris, Aaron Copland's Third, and Bartók's Concerto for Orchestra, which became one of the last solid additions to the standard repertory, along with Samuel Barber's Adagio for Strings, introduced by Toscanini.

I have not yet mentioned a central postulate behind Horowitz's history, which he treats as an axiom: the impossibility of classical music rooting itself in America without a repertory of American music. The real damage done by the culture of performance was not so much the disregard of music as the stifling of American music. The rise-and-fall narrative of *Classical Music in America* meshes with a cyclical quest story, then, as generation after generation of composers struggles to found a national repertory.

The book's many thumbnail composer biographies hinge on two questions. Is this person's music authentically American, and has it been accepted as such by the public—or, rather, by the promoters and marketeers who manipulate the public? Horowitz has original, perceptive, and often laudatory things to say about individual American compositions, but with the test put this way, it's only too easy to see that his candidates are bound to fail repeatedly (or disqualify themselves, as Charles Ives did by simply shunning the public). The great American symphony that ought to have followed Dvořák's example never did. Durability, let alone greatness, was beyond the reach of the turn-of-the-century Boston composers—a "genuine American school of shared interests, enthusiasms and interests," discussed here at length and with rare sympathy.

It is moving to read of the tireless, multitiered campaigns on behalf of American music run by Aaron Copland after World War I and by Leonard Bernstein, Horowitz's chief witness for the period after World War II. But their symphonies failed—as did Roy Harris's Third Symphony of 1939, for all the fervid hopes it inspired. The grading curve certainly works to the disadvantage of Copland, who wrote *Billy the Kid* and *Appalachian Spring*, said to have achieved "enduring popularity among American listeners," and who established "the tough and spacious sound world of Hollywood Westerns to come."

The candidate for our own time is John Adams, composer of *Harmonielehre*, *The Wound-Dresser*, *Nixon in China*, *On the Transmigration of Souls*, *Doctor Atomic*, even a much-played Violin Concerto. Adams is treated somewhat gingerly in a significant postlapsarian "Postlude" to this book, on music since 1976, the year of Philip Glass's iconic opera *Einstein on the Beach*. For quite some time now

Glass, Steve Reich—both now in their seventies—Adams, and most younger composers have been writing music with ample infusions ranging from rock, Zen, and postmodern thought structures to Asian and South American musics of all varieties. This, we are told, makes them "post-classical"; they are writing for a new nonelite audience in new nonsymphonic formats. A "new American ripeness" is in the air. Increasingly Adams is seen, and sees himself, as America's composer for the current century.

All this—and in addition to composers, Horowitz points to many other good things on classical music's still capacious plate. There are "eclectic" performers like Yo-Yo Ma and the Kronos Quartet, record companies Nonesuch and Naxos, presenters like now-retired Harvey Lichtenstein at the Brooklyn Academy of Music, conductors Esa-Pekka Salonen and Michael Tilson Thomas (yes, California gets a look-in)—and given his unusually high reliance, as a historian, on the work of critics, he might also have added Alan Rich of the *LA Weekly* and Alex Ross of *The New Yorker*.

But of course there's no good reason to set all this apart as a new category called "post-classical" music. Why isn't it simply the latest phase—following several other distinguishable phases—of classical music in America? Horowitz the historian stumbles here, while Horowitz the journalist-chronicler registers more and more occurrences, trends, and tendencies, surfing the centuries and leaving no name undropped. It would take only a few keystrokes to reconfigure this Postlude into a rather upbeat chapter welcoming the latest phase of classical music in America. More keystrokes would be needed to mitigate the dispirited mood imposed more generally on a fascinating and, as this author tells it, ebullient story.

We would also need a new title, maybe something like *Classical Music in America: Keeps on Truckin'*.

—2005

2

OPERA AND THE
MORBIDITY OF MUSIC

THE MORBIDITY OF classical music: a tired, vacuous concept that will
not die. Are we seriously to conceive of classical music as a unitary
thing whose "slow-motion death in the twentieth century" can now
be confirmed, casually enough, by Carolyn Abbate, who should know
better?[1] Abbate is a musicologist-critic recognized for her brilliant
work on voice and opera, which adds special irony to her quip, as I
will hope to show. If now dead, then, at what point would we have to
say classical music was born—or conceived? With Bach and the final
establishment of tonality, as theorist Heinrich Schenker (though not
all of his followers) assumed? With Monteverdi and the invention,
then the inevitable commodification, of opera? When polyphony was
written down to be disseminated during the so-called twelfth-century
Renaissance? When the angel in a famous miniature painting poured
plainchant into the ear of Saint Gregory, out of a jug?

Classical music comprises a series of linked phases, linked musics.
Music is one of the deep universals of culture, or cultures—it has now
been extended back to the Neanderthals—and "classical" is merely a

---

1. In a much-discussed article, "Music—Gnostic or Drastic?," *Critical Inquiry*, Vol. 30
(2004), pp. 505–536; the citation is on p. 515. Classical music's "moribund status" is also
mentioned.

first cut of classification made from one vastly restricted standpoint. Musics change as societies change; the musics fostered by the elites of Western societies change as the elites change—in changing ways. Different phases (rather than a unitary thing called classical music) wax and wane, overlap one another and coexist. We are in a new phase now; the massive overlapping and coexistence have long been generating grief and clamor.

A link between the phases of Western music that is more logistic than sonorous—and therefore favored by academics—is the fact that in one way or another the music exists in a written form. To speak of classical music is to acknowledge its others, popular music and world music—"I hate 'classical music,'" cries Alex Ross, one of its most influential proponents,

> not the thing but the name. It traps a tenaciously living art into a theme-park of the past.... The name is a masterpiece of negative publicity, a tour de force of anti-hype. I wish there were another name.[2]

Not another name, but another phrase: to speak of Western elite music that has been written down and circulated by documents, though also invidious, if less obviously so, has been useful for scholars working to understand the music of the Roman Catholic Church (Gregorian chant), for instance, before a notation for it emerged. Once music was notated, after around 900 CE, the documents could be read—and not only read, also written about. Medievalists speak of an oral paradigm for music preceding a literate paradigm, and then of the two paradigms coexisting as both evolved; at the start and for a long time afterward, music was written not to sing from, but rather to preserve or propagate canonic repertories. Orality did not stop. From

---

2. "Listen to This," *The New Yorker*, February 16–23, 1994, p. 146.

the start, however, the writing of music by musical scribes enabled writing about music by music intellectuals—theorists, critics, historians, musicologists.

It has been suggested that a further grand paradigm for music, predicated on sound recording, started around 1900, a tidy millennium after the appearance of the first neumatic notation of plainchant practiced by the Benedictines of St. Gall.[3] The notion of such a paradigm—a paradigm of audition—has not received much attention or publicity because it seems too obvious, perhaps, or because it has come to pale before the growing realization that significant new music is appearing without the benefit of written notation at all.

That puts new pressure on the paradigm of literacy. So when Richard Taruskin, another foremost musicologist-critic, defines the subject of his *Oxford History of Western Music* not as classical music, of course, but as music that has been disseminated in the West through the medium of writing, of notation, and entitles the first of its six volumes *The Earliest Notations to the Sixteenth Century*, that in itself is hardly new. But there are new anxieties stirring. The basic claim of his formidable, literally awesome study is that

> the literate tradition of Western music is coherent at least insofar as it has a completed shape. Its beginnings are known and explicable, and its end is now foreseeable (and also explicable).... The sheer abundance and the generic heterogeneity of the music so disseminated in "the West" is a truly distinguishing feature—perhaps the West's signal musical distinction. It is deserving of serious study.[4]

---

3. Joseph Kerman, "A Few Canonic Variations," *Critical Inquiry*, Vol. 10 (1983), reprinted in *Write All These Down* (University of California Press, 1994), Chapter 3.

4. Oxford University Press, 2005, Vol. 1, p. xxiii.

What is new, given the millennium in which *The Oxford History* has seen the light, is the confidence with which the end of music's literate tradition can now be foreseen and explained.

Can it? "At present, things remain in motion," Taruskin observes on the last page of his final volume, Volume 5, *The Late Twentieth Century*—which may seem like the sort of amiable truism needed to wind down books of one kind or another.[5] However, Volume 5 has tracked three distinct strands of contemporary music of the last third of the century very closely, over two hundred pages, and the most successful of these strands remains in motion and shows no sign of stopping. While Taruskin as critic does not think much of this music, as historian he identifies it as a genre of multimedia extravaganzas for a modern-day elite named "Bobos" by *New York Times* conservative columnist David Brooks. A subset of the much-discussed baby boomers, "bourgeois bohemians," for all their subsequent affluence, are said to remain nostalgic for their pretensions in the Sixties, still committed to a left-ist ethos, still aching for spirituality. Bobos are wealthy enough individually to buy high-priced tickets, and wealthy enough collectively, we must suppose, to underwrite the entire enterprise. Under subheadings "A New Topicality" and "A New Spirituality," Taruskin cites symphonies, operas, oratorios, and combinations thereof such as John Corigliano's First Symphony in memory of AIDS victims, Philip Glass's cantata-like Fifth Symphony, Jack Heggie's opera *Dead Man Walking*, the four free-form Passions commissioned from international celebrity composers for the 250th anniversary of Bach's death in 2000, and *El Niño*, John Adam's politicized homage to the *Messiah*.

With the Sixties demonized endlessly by the political right, its progeny the Bobo smacks of a left-wing bogeyman rather than a credible demographic. In any case I believe Taruskin is missing the big

---

5. (I have used this ploy myself.) The citation is from *The Oxford History*, Vol. 5, p. 528; all further citations from this source are from this same page.

picture here. *Dead Man Walking, El Niño,* and the more dramatic of the Passions form part of a larger, more general, and more miscellaneous cultural phenomenon: the upsurge of American opera in the last quarter of the twentieth century.

This has been noticed widely enough, and even celebrated (without palliating the mass media's death verdict on classical music as a whole). A surge of conventional opera after World War II—by Gian Carlo Menotti, Douglas Moore, Carlisle Floyd, the later work of Kurt Weill—dropped off, until an altogether fresh stimulus was provided by Philip Glass and Robert Wilson in *Einstein on the Beach,* performed at the Metropolitan Opera House in 1976. Although the mid-Seventies was a period of considerable moment in music history, the iconic event has become *Einstein at the Met* (as I tend to garble it[6]), overshadowing the deaths of Britten and Shostakovich, the century's last truly popular great composers, and the birth of IRCAM (Institut de Recherche et Coordination Musique/Acoustique) at the Pompidou Center in Paris, an important power play by Pierre Boulez. Glass followed *Einstein* with *Satyagráha, Akhnáten,* and more recently the rather tamer *Waiting for the Barbarians* and *Appomattox*; he has composed about thirty works for the stage so far. Only eleven years after *Einstein,* John Adams's entry into the field played in nine different locations around the world in the year of its launch, 1987; *Nixon in China* was followed by *The Death of Klinghoffer,* and more recently the (again) rather tamer *Doctor Atomic.* Even Adams's *I Was Looking at the Ceiling and Then I Saw the Sky,* a much slighter work which premièred in 1996 to little critical acclaim, has nonetheless had at least fifty performances since then. In the last twenty years a long list of operas by well-, little-, and unknown composers of all

---

6. The Metropolitan Opera House was rented for two free (and packed) performances in November 1976. A French commission, *Einstein on the Beach* had premièred at Avignon and toured Europe during the summer.

descriptions have drawn on a whole shelf of classic novels and plays: *Little Women, McTeague, Ethan Frome, An American Tragedy, The Great Gatsby, Our Town, A Streetcar Named Desire, A View from the Bridge*, and more.

Anyone who even knows about these operas knows they have received a mixed press. Writing before *Dead Man Walking* became a hit, Los Angeles critic Alan Rich spoke of the "sudsy libretto set to an appallingly second-rate assemblage of gestures"—I tend to agree—and San Francisco critic Joshua Kosman dubbed Heggie's next libretto "more Oprah than opera." On the other hand the *New Yorker*'s Alex Ross, at the première of *The Greater Good* by Stephen Hartke (based on Guy de Maupassant's *Boule de Suif*), heard "a tightly constructed, vividly imagined piece that may mark the emergence of a major opera composer," and after further hearings (if not viewings) Rich could be more emphatic, claiming to recognize "something we've long awaited, an American opera of genuine musical stature that uses the elements of opera in proper balance to create dramatic ebb and flow consistent with a storyline." Ross marvels at the late-in-life turn to the stage (or something like the stage) by Steve Reich, *Three Tales* in particular: "a major work, a sneaky sort of tragic masterpiece."[7] John Adams's *El Niño* is a work I value for its lyricism, structure, and vivid mix of textures, as well as for its far from perfunctory riff on the *Messiah*. I've found it more than welcome as a substitute every other Christmas or so.

But fortunately for the present argument, stature, quality, and value are not to the point here, not even professionalism. *Hier gilt's dem Leben*, to redirect Eva's atypically sour retort to Sachs in *Die Meistersinger*. If someone is wheeled into emergency and the paramedics

---

7. Alan Rich, *So I've Heard* (Amadeus, 2006), p. 285, and *Los Angeles Weekly*, August 4, 2005; Joshua Kosman, *San Francisco Chronicle*, November 6, 2006; Alex Ross, *The New Yorker*, August 1, 2006, January 6, 2003.

tell you he's dead, you look first for the flicker of his eyelids and the heave of his chest, not the dirt under his fingernails— And the whole matter of literate music is a separate issue, unconnected to the rise of opera. Taruskin speaks of "a small elite of commercially successful caterers to the needs of a newly ascendent class of patrons"; yet the composers of opera, oratorio, and pageant have always been supported by unlikable patrons, easy to pillory: Dukes of Mantua, Kings of France, Jesuits, Georgian aristocrats, proto-Nazi nationalists, captains of commerce. The works have always been multimedia and they have always been written down in order to be passed from theater to theater.[8] They certainly do not spell the demise of literate music (and Taruskin does not say they do); prophesied many times in *The Oxford History*, this outcome remains a task ahead for what the author describes not very hopefully as

> a vastly overpopulated strata of composers, as yet virtually without a nonprofessional audience, who avail themselves of new technologies that presage the dilution and ultimate demise of the literate tradition.

One thinks of the clerisy in Frank Kermode's *The Sense of an Ending*, calculating the date of apocalypse and when it doesn't happen, repeatedly recalculating the date.

According to Joseph Horowitz in *Classical Music in America: A History of Its Rise and Fall*,[9] classical music needs the infusion of new blood, always has—not by transfusion but by hematopoiesis. Our best composers have never succeeded in developing a full-blooded,

---

8. For striking examples from the earliest days of opera, see Ellen Rosand, *Trilogy: The Venetian Operas of Claudio Monteverdi* (University of California Press, 2007).

9. My review is reprinted as Chapter 1 in this book; the citation is on page 5.

authentic American classical music—neither the Boston composers around 1900, nor Ives, nor Roy Harris, nor even Copland or Bernstein. Yet as I wrote in a review of the Horowitz book, by the end of its Postlude (entitled "Post-classical Music") the author has acknowledged that for some time now

> [Philip] Glass, Steve Reich—both now in their seventies—Adams, and most younger composers have been writing music with ample infusions ranging from rock, Zen, and postmodern thought structures to Asian and South American musics of all varieties. This, we are told, makes them "post-classical"; they are writing for a new nonelite audience in new nonsymphonic formats. A "new American ripeness" is in the air. . . .
>
> All this—and in addition to composers, Horowitz points to many other good things on classical music's still-capacious plate. There are "eclectic" performers like Yo-Yo Ma and the Kronos Quartet, record companies Nonesuch and Naxos, presenters like now-retired Harvey Lichtenstein at the Brooklyn Academy of Music, conductors Esa-Pekka Salonen and Michael Tilson Thomas. . . .

A new "ripeness"—what is that if not a new rise, a renewal? For "post-classical" is simply Horowitz's term for what amounts to a third phase of American classical music, a new rise added to the rise and fall phases he has already chronicled as "Birth and Growth" (from around the Civil War to World War I) and "Decline and Fall" (World War I to the inevitable *Einstein*).

Renewal is the key concept here, hardly surprising in a consumer society that depends for its economic security on renewal and obsolescence. Other musics live without any imperative for renewal in this sense, among them musics of high cultures equipped with musical notation. We all know this, though we do not think about it much;

for however freely we can criticize our culture from within—while some music critics and other critics support our culture, explicitly or by default, others make a good thing out of attacking it—we cannot opt out. Leaving the culture with its deepest premises literally, or in spirit, and writing from the outside is not an option if we want to maintain any traction as critics at all. Renewal is a set theme.

And to the most damaging charge that the culture levels at classical music, its inability to renew itself, opera gives the lie. Music must generate an expanded repertory that will arouse critics and attract audiences; opera is doing this. That opera's primacy is seldom brought out in premature wakes for classical music is exasperating, if perhaps understandable as a survival of the long-standing distrust of the stage, traced in a classic study by Jonas Barish, *The Anti-Theatrical Prejudice*. The aspiration of nineteenth-century American musicians was toward orchestral music, rather than opera; Italian opera was impudently touring America along with vaudeville and other inferior entertainments. (One thinks of another classic study, Lawrence Levine's *Highbrow/Lowbrow*.) Opera's ethnic roots, its reliance on vocal virtuosity, and the company it kept marked opera as low class, a brand that even New York's love affair with Wagner could not erase.[10] Later, New York was less disturbed by Virgil's Thomson's *Four Saints in Three Acts*, which it could comfortably accept (or dismiss) as avant-garde, than by George Gershwin's *Porgy and Bess*, with its disconcerting embrace of the musical. What America was looking for was the Great American Symphony, not the Great American Opera. Porgy waited fifty years for its debut at the Metropolitan.

A living body is not the same thing as a body in perfect health, of course, and classical music's ailments have been exposed in literally thousands of articles and books. Many of these ailments result from

---

10. See Joseph Horowitz, *Wagner Nights: An American History* (University of California Press, 1994).

the gradual, century-long evolution of the paradigm of audition mentioned above—or to put it more simply, from the increasing sophistication and prominence, or rather dominance, of sound recording, and with this, changed modes of listening. Which of us, past a certain age, welcomes change, unless we profit from it? A contrarian contribution to the topic was offered recently by the *New York Times* critic Allan Kozinn in a feature article headlined "Classical Music: A Golden Age."[11] Opera is not Kozinn's beat; for him the center of the musical universe counts as the orchestra (as for Horowitz). Symphony orchestras put on 30 percent more concerts than ten years ago. If season ticket sales have plummeted, that's because people prefer more flexibility: "the seats are hardly empty." Talking up the morbidity of classical music is actually good for fund-raising. As major record companies retrench on classical CDs, smaller companies are springing up; Naxos is booming. Record shops are closing but everyone buys CDs on the Internet anyway. On iTunes, classical music accounts for a healthy 12 percent of sales. It may be disappearing from radio, but there is a great deal more of it available on the Internet.

Kozinn leaves a good deal unsaid—beginning with the ongoing shrinkage of classical music coverage in the *Times*: shorter reviews, the dilution of the Saturday and Sunday arts sections, the encroachment of human-interest stories on music criticism. He does not mention the reduction of music instruction in public schools, something which has been deplored and warned about for years, and which by now may well be approaching a point of no return, like global warming. But take what comfort you can from Kozinn's analysis, even if you find much of it specious—for at least it suggests that the ailments are not life-threatening. Classical music is alive and fairly well. Astonishingly, he says not a word about opera, and it is opera that obviates

---

11. *The New York Times Large Print Weekly*, May 29–June 5, 2006, pp. 26–27. The parent article in the *Times* of May 28 was headlined "Music: This Is a Golden Age."

the most deadly of the diagnoses offered to the *moribund imaginaire*, its inability to renew itself. Can American music ever generate an expanded repertory that will excite critics as well as draw audiences? That will control "mainstream performance and dissemination media, insofar as these remain open to elite art," to cite Richard Taruskin one more time, in an acid moment? This the symphony has not done. Opera has.

With renewal foremost in mind, I have passed over everything else about the current opera scene apart from composers and their scores —more and more inventive spectacle and *régie*, to mention the most obvious lacunae, and crossovers and assimilations from the musical. There are more arrivals of important new operas from Europe—by Messaien, Ligeti, Saariaho, Adès—and more older types of opera finding their way onto stages both large and small. Operas from Monteverdi to Handel and Vivaldi to Rossini answer to contemporary taste, not antiquarianism. The whole complex matter of the changing audience that supports opera deserves more attention, not only here but also in general. Lest negligence of the total opera scene be total, though, in a chapter whose title may seem to promise so much, here is a personal account of some changes in the forest bed, over which the giant trees and epiphytes of contemporary opera grow so profusely.

While the population of the San Francisco Bay Area[12] has more than doubled since the 1950s, grassroots music-making of all kinds has expanded much more than that. When I came to the region, fired up for opera, the San Francisco Opera was just entering into one of its strong periods—and that was great. But to put on modest, unconventional total opera was hard to do. A little theater company operating

---

12. "Surely the Bobo capital of the world," according to Taruskin, in "Sacred Entertainments," *Cambridge Opera Journal*, Vol. 15 (2003), p. 117.

out of a store on Berkeley's auto row near the Bay was persuaded to take on *The Barber of Seville* by Giovanni Paisiello (a pleasing work which originally opened in Vienna in 1783, provoking Mozart's sequel, *The Marriage of Figaro*, a few years later. It held the stage until Rossini's *Barber* of 1816). Using an eighteenth-century English version of Beaumarchais's play, spoken, of course, interspersed with Paisiello's arias and ensembles translated and heavily edited, I was able to entice unpaid singers and a band consisting of piano, flute (for Rosina's big aria), and mandolin (for Almaviva's serenade, except we never knew from one day to the next whether the mandolin player would show up). Great as this was, too, it was hardly a tribute to the opera culture of its time.

Today, radiating around a greatly expanded opera scene in San Francisco, local companies are springing up all over the area, offering short seasons of opera, typically performed in English with reduced orchestras. Someone has counted as many as twenty-two of them. Depending on the length of their shoestrings, they rent halls, made-over movie houses, deconsecrated churches, schools, community centers, even a foundry, and are able to draw on a pool of singers attracted to the region by the San Francisco Opera chorus and training programs, as well as by a good supply of openings for waitpersons. While these companies do *Madama Butterfly* and *Carmen* a good deal of the time, they also offer less conventional fare such as Peter Brook's version of the latter, Cavalli's *La Calisto*, Lortzing's *Der Wildschütz*, John Ward's *The Crucible*, and Carlisle Floyd's *Of Mice and Men* (in which our old dog Chloe played a nonbarking but far from inconsequential role). Premières—there are many—are usually of chamber operas by local composers which make no headlines and will probably not figure in tomorrow's histories of music. Still, a storefront theater in downtown Oakland has put on pieces that are relatively recent and on the national circuit, like *Akhnáten* and *Les Enfants terribles* by Glass, *X: The Life and Times of Malcolm X* by

Anthony Davis, and other new works. In 2006 Sonoma Opera did the première of Libby Larson's *Every Man Jack*. Festival Opera of Walnut Creek co-commissioned Ned Rorem's *Our Town*.

Small local companies live with lower expectations than the major companies. It is less than ideal to hear *Eugene Onegin* with an orchestra of twenty-two. The direction may leave a lot to be desired—but it seldom mimics Eurotrash, and it can come up with real delights when talented people work informally on a small stage. Young singers may enthrall; in small halls they may be capable of sustaining extended roles. Or sometimes not. But quality and repertory are not really the issue, as I have already observed. The (non)issue is life or death. Today's opera phenomenon has roots in the pullulating soil of the forest floor, below the gaudy canopy.

It is natural to wonder how long opera's current florescence will last—whether we are witnessing a more or less ephemeral growth of a decade or two, or not. Late as it may be to start an elephant-sized hare at this point, we should take into account music's universality in all cultures, and its absolute implication with other such universals, ritual, narrative, and theater, from time immemorial to the present moment of gospel, rap, and MTV. View opera, the bonding of music and theater, in the broadest terms (*The Persians, The Play of Daniel*, thirty settings of Metastasio's book for *La clemenza di Tito, Parsifal* and *Pelléas, Phantom, Passion*) and the spoken theater is recognized as a golden but passing phase in the long history of drama (the phases, remember, overlap and coexist), just as the classical symphony—music without words or programs—is a passing phase in the history of music. Consider also music and ritual, broadly conceived: worship, commemoration, celebration, procession, and dance.

Of the three strands of contemporary classical composition Richard Taruskin identifies in Volume 5 of *The Oxford History of Western Music*, world history speaks for opera, as it does not speak for his other options, remnant modernism or the musics of postliteracy.

"Though we habitually conceive [operatic history] as a unitary process," Gary Tomlinson has written, it "might rather be rethought as a set of diverse manifestations, differing at fundamental levels of cultural formation, of the older, deeper, and broader impulse to voice an ordering of the world...."[13] His manifestations are my phases. My guess is that opera will continue as the lifeline for classical music unless or until something unpredictable, if not unimaginable, happens to our American economy and culture.

Opera, said Virgil Thomson years ago, "is almost the only door to classical music still ajar."[14]

—2006

⸱

---

13. *Metaphysical Song: An Essay on Opera* (Princeton University Press, 1999), p. 5.

14. *Music with Words: A Composer's View* (Yale University Press, 1989), p. 54.

3

TWO CHEERS FOR RACH 3

IF CLASSICAL MUSIC is dying, as we know must be the case, for *The New York Times* has been telling us so on a regular basis, its death spasms are certainly momentous. First the Four Seasons, then the Three Tenors, the Spanish Monks, the Anonymous Four, Mozart covers by Keith Jarrett and Chick Corea, and in 1996, *Shine*, the film about a true-life piano prodigy driven to mental breakdown. Young David's nemesis in the movie, Rachmaninov's Piano Concerto No. 3 in D Minor, composed for an American tour in 1909, has entered popular culture like Mozart's "Elvira Madigan" Concerto and God reaching out to Man on the Sistine Chapel ceiling. Reviewing a PBS program on intelligent dogs, a television columnist jokes that while some dogs may be smart, his lhasa apso always breaks down in the middle of the "Rach 3."

Worse (I suppose worse), the *Times* critic Bernard Holland then launched an attack on this unfortunate score, on its very substance, not just on its baleful use (and abuse) as a final hurdle in piano competitions. Trashy, says this critic: "a cozy piece of schlock." Are we keeping classical music alive for *this*? and so on and so forth, to fill up 1996's Sunday-before-Christmas leader.[1]

---

1. "Basking in the Glow of the Golden Arches," *The New York Times*, December 22, 1996.

It is asking a lot of the Rachmaninov Third to bear the burden of standing in for classical music *tout court*. But so be it: Bernard Holland to the contrary, it's a strong work, though not without its failures; a work of real distinction, modeling ecstasy and resignation, potency, play, despair, and so on in the ineluctable way of all music, and with the refinement of classical music. It marks, incidentally, a great advance over Rach 2, another concerto that has known the embrace of popular culture, or at least a little hug. Rach 3 must have its day in court, even though the absence of a specified indictment has to make life more difficult for the defense.

Still, the prosecution's case is predictable enough. When concertos are hauled into court one usual charge is indecent exposure, excessive display of virtuosity at the expense of more respectable musical values. Weakness of form is another common accusation—for that is what Donald Tovey, he of the three B's, meant when he referred sniffingly to "fantasia" form in Liszt's concertos and "a lighter art-form" even in Mendelssohn's. Thirdly, complaints are entered about tawdry melodies ("weepy tunes") that are repeated over and over again.

Of these charges the last is the most subjective, hence the hardest to refute, and also the most contingent on the times. Vivaldi was considered vulgar by eighteenth-century English snobs, as were Puccini and Richard Strauss in the mid-twentieth century. Given the conditions of the arts in the here and now, stale critical labels like "vulgar" and "tawdry," "weepy" and "schlock" should be used with the greatest caution, if at all. That said, in Rachmaninov's Third it is presumably the end of the finale that offends the most in this regard: the lush soaring melody, orchestrated to the hilt, that keeps expanding itself in ecstatic gestures of transcendence and release. (The Chaikovsky Piano Concerto No. 1 was an obvious model.) Are these nine last pages of the score an illegitimate response to the preceding 127 pages of intricate, mostly gloomy, and admittedly somewhat overwrought music?

The response is, in fact, more specific: the ending consummates the most original and surprising theme in this concerto. First introduced in the finale at 1:30 or thereabouts on your CD player display, it feels less like a theme than brute energy—a single, cramped, jerky rhythm hammered out insistently by the piano without interruption (and without any real harmonic movement). The music simply ratchets its way up from low to high, soft to loud, and then back down again.

This arresting whiff of the primal, which can perhaps be traced back to Beethoven's "Emperor" Concerto, associates Rachmaninov with certain composers and artists active in 1909 whose orbit he would have been aghast to enter. The theme comes four times, almost mechanically, until the piano softens it into a real melody. It is this melody, greatly amplified, that ends the concerto so deliriously. Before that amplification, the cramped theme and its whole complex have appeared in both section one and section three of the finale in much the same form. The apotheosis has been a long time waiting, then, and it has a right to flaunt its ecstasy.

As for section two of the finale, that brings us to the second charge, weakness of form. Section one, except for the cramped theme, motors along in a rather generic way, until it slows down for what turns out to be an altogether new melody followed by four variations. A most original idea—and the orchestra stays all but static throughout section two, while the piano is quite the reverse: skittery, fantastic, fascinating. In symphonies, sonatas, string quartets, and especially concertos, it is almost always the finale that is the problematic movement, and I believe Rachmaninov has solved the problem of the finale brilliantly here. For section two also reinstates themes from the concerto's opening movement (the second theme more interestingly than the first), and it even goes some way toward rationalizing the stiffness of sections one and three.

Weakness of form in the first movement, if that is one of the charges, brings us also to the third charge, excessive virtuosity. Virtuosity reaches its absolute peak in the enormous first-movement cadenza. Rachmaninov's accomplishment was to incorporate virtuosity into the very pillars of concerto form.

Some version of sonata form was what most concertos relied on up to this time for their first movements: two (or more) contrasting themes, a development section, a recapitulation that effects a reconciliation of the themes, and (Beethoven's contribution) usually some sort of apotheosis at the end. Indeed, even though the admirable opening tune of this concerto—its resignation *à la Russe* distilled out of hushed piano octaves and melodic twists and turns in the minor mode—can hardly be considered apt as a sonata-form first theme, Rachmaninov does adhere to the sonata model up through the development section. This reaches a great climax, whereupon sonata form disintegrates completely.

A superb sixty-bar sinking passage unwinds from this climax, a seemingly endless descent into some kind of entropic state from which emerges, after a sort of shudder, the cadenza. And in this cadenza, after a time, the quiet first theme returns in the tonic key as a frenetic fortissimo, leading directly to an even more forceful statement in—the major mode! Major trumps minor; apotheosis and recapitulation coalesce. (A second, shorter version of the cadenza also authorized by Rachmaninov does things somewhat differently, but joins the ending of the longer cadenza at the high point. The pianist David Helfgott plays the longer cadenza. His playing is generally more stable in the extracts from the soundtrack to *Shine* than in his live recording of the concerto.[2])

Cadenzas are supposed to be supplements—originally, of course, they were random supplements—to the basic structure of concertos, "the very appendicitis of concerto form," in Tovey's testy phrase. On

---

2. With the Copenhagen Philharmonic Orchestra, conducted by Milan Horvat, RCA Victor Red Seal/BMG Classics, 1996. The soundtrack to *Shine* is on Philips, 1996.

the contrary, and not for the first time in concerto history, this cadenza works functionally, as an essential component of the form. It works through virtuosity, and there is nothing excessive about it at all.

This is not the place for more than an inventory of the remaining sequence of events in the first movement—wind instruments trooping in one by one to reproach the piano for its infraction; the piano taking comfort from the concerto's second theme; a full return of the lengthy opening tune, almost ritual in effect; and the sardonic final page. Again, I am not experiencing a sense of weakness here. This transformation of standard form seems to me novel, persuasive, and expressive. For Rachmaninov, virtuosity is a kind of liberation: apotheosis can happen for the soloist only when the orchestra has been sunk out of existence. But virtuosity also means transgression, a transgression that the ending sequence of events manages to repress. The composer has dug himself an interesting hole here, and I wish I could say he has done a good job of climbing out of it.

This would have to had to happen in the second movement, from whose defense team I must recuse myself since I simply do not get it. Two cheers for Rach 3 from this corner of the bench, then, not three. And more than two cheers for classical music. Dying it may be, yet it continues to be chronicled year by year in *The New York Times*. Time passes and it does not die. Now nearly a hundred years old, Rach 3's life expectancy goes up every year, and given the wonders of bioscience, the piece is likely to end up in some dismaying retirement community of the twenty-second century, toothless, creaky, scarcely ecstatic, but still ready to play and above all garrulous. Asked for the secret of its longevity, classical music will reply, "Back around 2000 I stopped reading the papers."[3]

—1997

---

3. Or: "Back around 2000 the papers stopped" (2007).

4

LABYRINTH MUSIC

MOST MUSICOLOGISTS ARE blinkered souls (or whatever the right word might be: earplugged, perhaps), so it was no great surprise that I knew nothing about labyrinths before reading *The Maze and the Warrior* by —and this was the surprise—another musicologist, Craig Wright of Yale University.[1] Since then I have been to San Francisco's Grace Cathedral and walked through the labyrinth in the nave. Inside the church the labyrinth is woven on a large circular carpet; outside the church another labyrinth inlaid in the pavement can accommodate the overflow of seekers after repose and spiritual renewal. While I was there, a man brought candles to light at the labyrinth's center, annoying the verger, and a woman told anyone who would listen about her on-site epiphanies. The walk was strangely agreeable. I could feel an attack coming of what Wright calls maze mania, a condition that has given us labyrinths in churches, hospitals, gymnasiums, airports, and prison yards, interfaith labyrinths, "maize mazes" on corn-lined acres in both America and France, a great deal of inspirational literature, and hundreds of Web sites.

There were numerous brochures to pick up at the cathedral. I already had the comprehensive, endlessly fascinating book that Wright

---

1. *The Maze and the Warrior: Symbols in Architecture, Theology, and Music* (Harvard University Press, 2004).

acknowledges and draws from, *Through the Labyrinth* by Hermann Kern, a book born, according to the prefatory matter, "from sheer enthusiasm within the American labyrinth community," and "a source book for a new generation of labyrinth scholars and enthusiasts."[2] If a picture is worth a thousand words, the six hundred pictures in Kern's book will fund an entire bibliography. There are diagrams, ground plans, and aerial views of walled mazes, hedged mazes, huge Roman mosaic pavement mazes, and delicate Scandinavian mazes that look from the air like skeins of natural-pearl necklaces, marked out on green areas by white stones. We visit dozens of floor labyrinths in churches and cathedrals, old and new. In a stunning twelve-inch color spread, the one in San Francisco looks almost like a mirror image of its much-admired prototype at Chartres, so closely was the one modeled on the other.

Kern's book includes pictures of labyrinths from throughout the world. They range from temple reliefs in India and Native American petroglyphs to stamped gold rings from Indonesia. Stamped on coins from Knossos is the stylized maze that glared at us for years from the cover of the journal *Daedalus*; it was the great inventor Daedalus, of course, who built the primal labyrinth of the Minotaur for Pasiphaë, as well as a "dancing floor" for her daughter Ariadne. An Etruscan wine jug shows Theseus emerging from the first, and a sixth-century Greek vase shows him presiding over the second. At the center of the labyrinths we see the Minotaur being slain by Theseus, or—when Christianity has taken hold of the myth—the Devil, slain again and again by the Christian Warrior in full armor.

"Surprisingly, almost all labyrinths to be seen in the West before the appearance of the Renaissance garden maze are unicursal"—that

---

2. *Through the Labyrinth: Designs and Meanings over 5,000 Years* (Prestel, 2000), originally published in German in 1982. The English edition, edited by Robert Ferré and translated by Abigail Clay, contains additions by Jeff Saward and others, all of whose names are kept reverently in small print, off the title page.

is, they provide a direct path, however tortuously it may turn, to the center and back out again. Unlike garden mazes, such as the maddeningly complex one at Hampton Court, to say nothing of the maze that Theseus could only manage with the aid of Ariadne's golden thread, unicursal labyrinths never lead you astray. "In a labyrinth, you do not lose yourself," the lady told me at Grace Cathedral. "In a labyrinth, you find yourself." Wright wonders why Theseus needed Ariadne's clew. "The Hellenic poets created multicursal mazes, but the architects did not." Kern, who distinguishes strictly between the multicursal maze and the unicursal labyrinth, has the perfect picture to show the difference, an aerial view of the adjacent maze and labyrinth installed at an English country house in 1977.

The Christian maze must be unicursal, and also recursive, for when the Warrior enters the twisting path to slay the Devil he has to be sure it gets him to the center, and it has to get him out again. The maze itself symbolizes an archetypal combat myth:

> The myth of the maze expresses the eternal hope of salvation—that eternal life will be won for all by the actions of one savior. This warrior will defeat the forces of evil lurking in the center of the maze. The central malevolent power may be a bull, the Minotaur, Khumbaba, Typhon, Satan, or, by metaphorical extension, the wicked pharaoh of Egypt, the giant Goliath, or the menacing Turk. As for the hero of the maze, he has assumed many faces over time: those of Theseus, Jason, Gilgamesh, Hercules, Moses, David, Christ, St. Michael, Christian, Tamino, and the Armed Man. The name of this warrior may change, but he is inseparable from the maze. Every myth needs a hero.

Craig Wright surveys the labyrinth over the centuries with ears unplugged, listening for the music it inspired, and his account of this music constitutes his signal contribution to labyrinth lore.

Actually, music does not come up in his book until about a third of the way in. This author does not skimp on detail, which he maneuvers beautifully, piling it on and pulling it back at the next helpful chapter subheading, keeping up the level of fascination until just before the eyes begin to glaze. He leads us almost punctiliously through every one of the sixteen ancient churches in North Africa, Italy, and France that contain or are known to have contained labyrinths. He traces the theology of the labyrinth as it developed from broad outlines laid down by the Church Fathers to an elaborate, point-by-point articulation in a medieval commentary on Ovid. Like any powerful symbolic nexus, the labyrinth proliferates and entwines endlessly, figuring in the chapter subheadings as Symbol of Purgatory, Stage for the Harrowing of Hell, and Metaphor for the Sinful World. Theseus slays the Minotaur, the Warrior slays the Devil, Jesus travels to confront Satan in the wilderness and returns. Then Jesus embarks on his final circuit, Passion and Resurrection.

Hence the strong association of the labyrinth with Easter. The Redeemer is both "victorious warrior and sacrificial lamb." Wright draws into the labyrinth complex the "bellicose" Lamb of God foretold by Isaiah, celebrated in Revelation, and invoked by some of the main Easter plainchants.

An account of Ariadne's dancing floor in Homer is our earliest record of several labyrinth dances known from antiquity. Dancing is predicated on music, and a vase (the François Vase) painted a hundred years after Homer shows Theseus at the post-Minotaur festivities playing a lyre. Dance was adopted by Christianity—the third-century Apocryphal Acts of Saint John has Jesus leading a ring dance of his disciples on Good Friday—and ultimately Christian dances were channeled onto labyrinths, the dancing floors for special Easter celebrations by, principally, cathedral clergy. Why else would labyrinths have been inlaid in the naves of churches from at least the fourth century on (though there is a gap of seven hundred years between the still-surviving maze of St. Remartus in Algeria and the next known examples)?

The most extensive archival record of this practice comes from Auxerre, France, in the fifteenth century, thanks to documents showing complaints about costs run up by the annual dance with its appurtenances and indeed its decency, for the dance also entailed a game with a *pilota*, a soft ball shaped like our football, and things could get out of hand. The organ played, and it would appear that competing clerics maneuvered their way through the labyrinth while also singing "Victimae paschali laudes," one of the great Easter plainchants. Many other ancient hymns and antiphons can be associated with Easter dances.

Other labyrinth-inspired music was specially written, both for use in church and for delectation at court. Among the organa—polyphonic compositions that embellished important plainchants—sung at Notre Dame Cathedral there is one in which a long tenor melody is first sung and then sung backward. While there is no explicit connection with labyrinths here—the chant comes at Christmas, not Easter—we soon accept that retrograde motion, the musical technique applied to the chant in this prototype work, symbolizes the Warrior's journey into the maze and out, and all its accompanying baggage. It may well resonate in Guillaume de Machaut's rondeau "Ma fin est mon commencement," which has generally been taken as a rather dazzling technical demonstration of musical retrograding and not much more. Machaut (1300–1377), a canon of Reims, asked to be buried near the cathedral's labyrinth, and every year at a special Easter ceremony the canons sang about Alpha and Omega, *commencement* and *fin*, beginning and end, in a local antiphon. He modeled his *Remède de Fortune* on the demonstrably (indeed avowedly) labyrinthine *Consolations of Philosophy* of Boethius.

Next to the Machaut mass, "Ma fin est mon commencement" is the most famous composition by this famous poet-musician, but it is only one piece, an isolated example.[3] Wright extends his inquiry substantially when he links the labyrinth to a major phenomenon of music in the later, waning Middle Ages: the widespread composition of *L'Homme armé* masses.

As background: the mass as we know it today, with its conjoined Kyrie, Gloria, Credo, Sanctus, and Agnus Dei, emerged as a major development in music from around 1450 on. It is, Wright might say, a recursive cycle: prayer, hymn, creed, hymn, prayer. The mass became a prototype for imposing, large-scale composition, the first such in music, comparable to the symphony in another age. Of several ways that composers found to "unify" the cycle, the most productive was to base all five mass segments on a single melody of one kind or another, which could be subjected to various technical manipulations. Among the earliest mass cycles, one attributed to Guillaume Dufay (circa 1398–1474) is based on a long, involuted melody extracted from an even longer plainchant, the *Missa Caput*, and this served as a model for *Caput* masses by Johannes Ockeghem and Jacob Obrecht, later masters. Another Dufay mass uses a blindingly simple, seemingly popular song about the military, "L'Homme armé." The song melody itself is transmitted in a far-from-simple chanson that was probably concocted by Antoine Busnoys (circa 1440–1492), a notably intellectual musician favored by Charles the Bold of Burgundy. Dufay was a Beethoven figure for the fifteenth century.

And once "L'homme armé" found religion, as it were, it replicated itself like a virus in masses by more than thirty composers over the next century. On CDs alone one can find examples by Dufay, Busnoys,

---

3. Wright follows the afterlife of Machaut's work from Mary Queen of Scots, who "during her long captivity... passed the hours embroidering *En ma fin est mon commencement* on various royal insignia" to T. S. Eliot's Easter-soaked poem *East Coker*, which opens with the sentence "In my beginning is my end" and closes with its retrograde "In my end is my beginning."

Ockeghem, Johannes Regis, Johannes Tinctoris, Obrecht, Josquin Desprez, Matthaeus Pipelare, Pierre de la Rue, Robert Carver, Cristóbal de Morales, and Palestrina. These are big, big a capella pieces. Josquin wrote two *L'Homme armé* masses, one lasting for thirty-five minutes and the other for thirty-eight. "The Armed Man, the Armed Man, the Armed Man: beware of the Armed Man": Why should this decidedly raucous song have led to a major church-music repertory including, I hasten to say, some very beautiful music?

It is not Craig Wright's mission to explain the astonishing career of the *L'Homme armé* mass, but he has plenty to say about its origins and its symbolism. The Armed Man is the Christian Warrior of the Maze. His recursive journey is symbolized in the Agnus Dei of the *Missa L'Homme armé* of Dufay, where the tune appears in retrograde motion; the Agnus Dei prays to the sacrificial and bellicose Lamb of Easter.[4] The Warrior hovers behind the music of other *L'Homme armé* masses, and one heavily annotated manuscript invokes him directly: Christ is the "potent armorer of man, giver of arms by which man triumphs over the enemy and chases away the Devil," and the Armed Man, "as before he marched forth, [now] he goes backward ... the end corresponds to the beginning." The composer and annotator of this highly unusual manuscript is thought to have been Busnoys.

The Armed Man can also be identified as a knight of the Order of the Golden Fleece, that fantastic brainchild of Philip the Good of Burgundy anatomized memorably by Huizinga in *The Waning of the Middle Ages*. Over the last few decades musicologists have joined and jostled in a determined campaign to lay "L'Homme armé" to rest; a gun smoked for Richard Taruskin when he noted segments of several

---

4. Dufay regarded retrograde motion as a special, rare technique (as did every other composer, up to the time of Schoenberg) and he only employed it on one other occasion, also bound up with Easter and the Lamb: a papal ceremony in 1431 at Santa Maria in Trastevere—a Roman church boasting a labyrinth.

L'Homme armé masses laid out in thirty-one-bar units, thirty-one being the canonical number of knights of the Fleece at that time... and also the number of turns in the canonical labyrinth.[5] As Wright remarks, it can be no coincidence that "the Christian Image of the Armed Man, then nearly fifteen hundred years old, was given musical expression for the first time immediately after the fall of Constantinople"; after that calamity Charles the Bold reconvened the knights at a music-drenched Feast of the Pheasant to launch a new crusade against the Turk. According to Wright, Jason and the Argonauts slip comfortably enough into labyrinth lore. Quest and salvation myths conflate.

The Armed Man is also the priest officiating at mass. Recently it has been pointed out that for centuries priests in that capacity had pictured themselves enthusiastically as Christian warriors. At certain special masses in certain churches, armor was worn and swords brandished by priests, other clerics, and attendant dignitaries.[6]

Although the later proliferation of *L'Homme armé* masses does not fall within the purview of *The Maze and the Warrior*, it has attracted the greatest interest since it came to light in the nineteenth century. There are numerous small complexes like the three *Caput* masses in which composers enlarged on other composers' ideas, competing in "friendly aemulation" (a nice formulation of Henry Peacham, a

---

5. Richard Taruskin, "Antoine Busnoys and the L'Homme armé Tradition," *Journal of the American Musicological Society* (*JAMS*), Vol. 39, No. 2 (1986), pp. 255–293, and see also subsequent correspondence. Craig Wright's first sortie was in 1975, when he discovered Dufay living by the cathedral close at Cambrai near a house called "Maison l'homme armé"; see "Dufay at Cambrai: Discoveries and Revisions," *JAMS*, Vol. 28, No. 2 (1975), pp. 210–211.

6. In papers by Andrew Kirkman at the International and American Musicological Societies in 2002 and 2003, and Flynn Warmington, "The Ceremony of the Armed Man" in *Antoine Busnoys*, edited by Paula Higgins (Clarendon Press, 1999), pp. 89–130. After the Pope named Henry VIII Defender of the Faith in 1521, the King would whip out his sword at the reading of the Gospel when attending Mass.

seventeenth-century musical amateur), but there is only one aggregate like the *L'Homme armé* masses. "L'Homme armé" served as dissertation or *Habilitation* for generations of composers, who outdid themselves with retrogrades, inversions, singing the core melody in different tempos, keys, and modes, breaking it up according to arcane codes, combining it with other melodies, reproducing it (or them) in various canons, and more. These *Künste der Niederländer*, as the early German musicologists called them, these "Netherlandish artifices," astonished, fascinated, awed, and also repelled, for they ran so counter to the Romantic ideal of musical creation. Nineteenth-century scholars had enough trouble deciphering old music, let alone getting anyone to sing it so they could hear it and judge it on its own sonorous merits. They did not have access to CDs.

Finally the *L'Homme armé* masses lost their rationale, but failed to go gracefully. In the sixteenth century there were stragglers from as far away as Scotland, and the seventeenth century witnessed a truly Baroque *coup de grâce* in a twelve-part entry by Giacomo Carissimi, a composer noted otherwise for his oratorios and cantatas. By then the highly developed, esoteric, inbred sense of competition and technical display represented by "L'Homme armé" had also run its course in another musical genre: the English In Nomine, also an outgrowth of the fifteenth-century mass tradition.

In England the last great pinnacle of that tradition was the *Missa Gloria tibi Trinitas* by John Taverner, who may have written it for the meeting of monarchs at the Field of the Cloth of Gold in 1520.[7] Soon enough after that the mass was abolished (or driven underground) in England's Reformation, first under Edward VI and then Elizabeth I, after a few years' reprieve under Queen Mary. Yet the *Missa Gloria*

---

7. Taverner's *Missa Gloria tibi Trinitas* is available on CD, one of the first in the notable Tallis Scholars series (Gimmel, 1984).

tibi Trinitas experienced a ghoulish afterlife starting in just those turbulent years. A fragment of it found its way without the words into
manuscripts of instrumental music, and around this fragment sprang
up over 150 short works for a consort of viols, or other instruments,
all based on Taverner's core melody. Nearly sixty composers were
involved, over a hundred-year period.

That core melody, the antiphon *Gloria tibi Trinitas*—a long plainchant, very much like that of the *Caput* masses—is heard most clearly
in the Taverner mass at the words *"Benedictus qui venit in nomine
Domini"* (in the Sanctus); this explains the name In Nomine. All the
great names in Tudor church music after Taverner composed pieces in
this genre: Christopher Tye, Thomas Tallis, William Byrd, and
Orlando Gibbons. "Friendly aemulation" runs riot; the In Nomines
of William Byrd dilate upon those of his friends Robert Parsons and
Alfonso Ferrabosco, and so on. The In Nomine breathed its last in a
seven-part marvel by Henry Purcell, though in our own time Peter
Maxwell Davies seems determined to resuscitate it (in his opera *Taverner* and other works).

Ariadne: she makes one vivid appearance early in Wright's narrative,
dancing with Theseus on the labyrinth floor of Daedalus. She has no
Christian counterpart in the Easter dances and symbolic masses of the
Middle Ages. But in 1608 the deserted Ariadne bursts onstage again
with a searing lament-cum-deprecation which ignited the emerging
genre of opera. Every music rack in Italy is said to have borne a copy
of "Lasciatemi morire," the lament from Monteverdi's opera *Arianna*, and Monteverdi followed it up with similar set pieces for the
aggrieved women of his later masterworks, Penelope in *Il ritorno
d'Ulisse in patria* and Octavia in *L'incoronazione di Poppea*. He also
wrote a madrigal which qualifies as a dramatic scene, "The Lament of
the Nymph," where the Nymph's quite excruciating song is framed
and interrupted by male voyeurs—a musical analogue to Bernini's

Saint Theresa—and underpinned by an endlessly repeated descending scale pattern in the bass. This hypnotic musical device, often intensified by chromatic steps, became the standard topos, or convention, for musical lamentation operatic and nonoperatic. A well-known example is the Crucifixus from Bach's B-Minor Mass.

So as with *L'Homme armé* masses and In Nomines, if more dramatically as befits the age of the Baroque, there was a musical thread and perhaps a sense of *paragone* (comparison, competition) running through the prima-donna scenes that became staples and indeed epitomes of seventeenth-century opera. Hecuba, Cassandra, Dido, and Alcestis cast a backward glance or two as they keen and vent and warble with these descending basses as their safety net. The most famous of their arias is Dido's lament "When I am laid in earth" from *Dido and Aeneas* by Purcell, who drew on another composer's work for the unusual form of its chromatic bass—unusual, and unusually expressive, by the time Purcell had got through with it.[8]

You can read through *The Maze and the Labyrinth* with reasonable care without picking up on any recursive journeys that turn out badly. But early opera tells it like it is: the final number for Orpheus in Monteverdi's *Orfeo* of 1607 is the lament of a hero of unconfirmed warrior status, armed only with a lyre.

Wright casts his net wide in a final chapter, "Musical Mazes from Moses to Mozart." Through the centuries, he says, musicians have made musical mazes in three ways, by "duplicating a labyrinthine pattern, recreating the psychological states of a labyrinth, or setting part of the myth to music." These are broad criteria, and some of his examples are tendentious. In any case, after the Renaissance the symbolism of the maze mutates, becomes diffused, and loses much of its

---

8. See Robert Klakowich, "*Scocca pur*: Genesis of an English Ground," *Journal of the Royal Musical Association*, Vol. 116, Part 1 (1991), pp. 63–77.

force: "Along with saintly relics and old bishops' bones, the stones of the labyrinth were thrown upon the rubbish pile of Enlightenment disbelief." As compared to the material earlier in the book, Wright's later examples of labyrinth music form a fairly arbitrary sequence.

Still, all of them are—that word again—fascinating, and one item is too good not to mention: an opera by Peter Winter, a contemporary of Mozart, for the theater run by Mozart's friend Emanuel Schikaneder, the instigator, librettist, producer, and original cast member of *The Magic Flute*. Schikaneder could count on that opera's enormous success for years after its première, and his libretto for Winter's *The Labyrinth* brings back the same characters and basically the same story, but with an interminable labyrinth journey substituted for Mozart's Trials of Fire and Water.[9] Mozart's Masonic imagery meets the myth of the labyrinth. Like Orpheus, the hero of *The Magic Flute* casts his lot with music, not might—Schikaneder makes a point of this by starting the opera with Tamino in full flight from a dragon, bow in hand, empty quiver at his side; but at the end of *The Labyrinth* Tamino battles a new character, Tipheus, one-on-one, and "as Christ did to Satan at the end of the Book of Apocalypse, casts him down into a fiery pit." The show was so successful that Schikaneder ran it on alternate nights with *The Magic Flute*.

Craig Wright concludes his study with Winter's opera, around 1800, and one can see why. Modern music of the labyrinth has become dissonant and ravenous; in Michael Tippett's *The Knot Garden*—"knot garden" is an English word for maze—the polymorphous labyrinth myth of salvation takes in sex, identity, forgiveness, psychotherapy, leitmotifs, and the blues. Not a place where a prudent writer wants to go.

The Maze and the Warrior is quite a book. The author wears his great learning with great lightness. Needless to say he has built upon

---

9. "*Durch's Labyrinth? Weh mir! Ich bin verlohren*," moans Pamina—Wright's readers may feel the same way (mine too).

many studies of the labyrinth less glamorous and more specialized than that of Hermann Kern, and has carried out new archival research, as appears from the endnotes.[10] Medievalists are the mandarins of musicology, the highest of the high-powered, but Wright is not the only one of them with an enviable track record as a writer for nonspecialists. Although he has fashioned this book for general readers rather than musicologists and musicians, it has prompted one specialist reviewer to call for nothing less than a "new appraisal of the history and historiography of Western music, one more cognizant of myth, belief, and symbol as generative forces in human creativity."[11] If this appeal to the clerisy can be scaled down a little, it can also become an appeal to the laity. For all the earplug-defying ubiquity of music in modern life, one cannot be sure that most people understand how much there is to it below, or beyond, the sonorous surface.

—2004

---

10. In which he should not have referred (fifty-odd times) to pages in Kern's *Through the Labyrinth* in the original German edition. The English translation came out when his own book was in the press, he informs us. At that stage the conversion could have been made with a few keystrokes.

11. Barbara Haggh, *JAMS*, Vol. 56, No. 2 (2003), p. 478.

5

WILLIAM BYRD AND THE CATHOLICS

UNTIL FAIRLY RECENTLY the history of Catholicism in Elizabethan and Jacobean England was conceived largely in terms of hagiology. From the first history of the English Jesuits, by Father Henry More, grandson of Sir Thomas, in 1635, to the biography of the Blessed Edmund Campion by Evelyn Waugh, written exactly three hundred years later, Catholic historians concerned themselves mainly with saints and martyrs, men of action and men of vision, with the pious great and the pious poor. They said little about poets and even less about artists or musicians; traditional historians have never been much interested in the arts. No doubt if they had found a Shakespeare among the faithful they would have made much of him. But they did not.[1] They found only the Jesuit poet Robert Southwell, and it seemed rather beside the point to award Father Southwell the laurel since God had reserved for him the higher glory of a martyr's crown of thorns.

In fact the English Catholic community had among its members a much more brilliant ornament in the field of the arts. William Byrd,

---

1. But now they have: I have revisited the subject of this article, taking account of a good deal of new information and interpretation brought forward by many scholars, in "Music and Politics: The Case of William Byrd (1540–1623)," *Proceedings of the American Philosophical Society*, Vol. 144 (2000), pp. 274–286. Byrd is now thought to have been born in 1540, not 1543 (2007).

the premier figure of Elizabethan and Jacobean music, was also one of the greatest European composers of the time and arguably the greatest English composer of all time. But the art of music has been slow to acquire the prestige of poetry; when music did gain it (or something like it) Byrd's music was no longer well-known or easy to come by; and when this music at last became more generally available, the key to its interpretation as a Catholic statement was still lacking. And so Catholic historians have paid Byrd almost no attention.

Music historians, though they have paid more attention, have failed or refused until recently to see the composer clearly enough against the background of his religion. It is not that his religious convictions have ever been in the slightest doubt. He wrote quantities of Latin liturgical music for Catholic services, including the three famous masses, and a high proportion of the records of his life that have come down to us concern his Catholic activities and activism. So many, indeed, that in the standard life-and-works by E. H. Fellowes, which has three chapters on the life, one of these chapters is devoted entirely to "Byrd's Association with the Catholics." But as the word "association" in this context already suggests—would one speak of "Milton's Association with the Puritans"?—Byrd's Catholicism was something that Fellowes could never take quite seriously. A decidedly stiff-necked Victorian clergyman, the author of a major work on Anglican cathedral music, he never missed an opportunity to point out that Byrd also wrote admirable music for the Church of England liturgy—though to be sure, there was very much less of this than of Catholic sacred music. In the early part of the twentieth century Fellowes performed wonders in the publishing and publicizing of Byrd's music, but he did this in an ecumenical spirit which seriously obscured its fundamental sectarian nature.

Thanks partly to Fellowes's work, it is now customary, at least in English and American musical writings, to rank Byrd with the main masters of late-sixteenth-century music—with Palestrina, Lassus, and

Victoria. He is so ranked, for example, in Howard Mayer Brown's recent *Music in the Renaissance* (1976). This is not, I think, a case of mere chauvinism on the part of English scholars and critics, and mere superstition on the part of Americans. A study just published, *The Consort and Keyboard Music of William Byrd*, by Oliver Neighbour,[2] illuminates sharply the greatness of Byrd's instrumental music; he was the first major composer to devote a substantial effort to music without words. Getting Byrd's Latin sacred music into correct focus—a Catholic focus—will allow a clearer view of another body of his music that is equally great. And when this music is in its correct focus it also will be seen to illustrate the responses of the Elizabethan Catholic community in a unique way. Resources are available to art and to artists that are not available to the saints and heroes of traditional Catholic history.

The course of Byrd's life and the history of Elizabethan Catholicism intersect most dramatically in 1580–1581, at the time of the fateful Jesuit missionary expedition to England of Fathers Robert Persons and Edmund Campion. These were two very remarkable men, and Campion, especially, who had been the most brilliant figure at Oxford in the 1560s, seemed to have a disquieting success among the country gentry, the clergy, and academics. After about a year Campion was betrayed, apprehended, interrogated with the help of the rack, and finally condemned to die with two other priests at a great public execution in London. He started his final address from the scaffold with words of Saint Paul to the Corinthians, "*Spectaculum facti sumus Deo, angelis, et hominibus*"—"We apostles are made a spectacle unto God, unto His angels, and unto men"—but this was brutally cut short. The three men were hanged, drawn, and quartered, and their dismembered bodies nailed to a gate on Tyburn Hill.

This triple execution rocked England and set off a storm of protests from abroad. There had been nothing like it since the days of

---

2. University of California Press, 1979.

Mary Tudor. Tracts were written back and forth about the event, and stories began to grow up around it. One of these concerned a young Catholic gentleman named Henry Walpole—"Cambridge wit, minor poet, satirist, flaneur, a young man of birth, popular, intelligent, slightly romantic," as Waugh describes him. Standing near the scaffold when Campion's body was being butchered, he saw a drop of blood spurt onto his coat. Profoundly shaken, he went home and sat up that night writing an extremely long, anguished poem about Campion, "Why do I use my paper, ink and pen," which caused a scandal. The printer of it had his ears cut off, and Walpole had to flee the country. Eventually he became a Jesuit himself and returned to England to meet the same fate as Campion.

Byrd set this notorious poem to music, and the setting certainly did not escape notice. Another future Jesuit, Thomas Fitzherbert, remarked that "one of the sonnets [on Campion's death] was presently set forth in music by the best musician in England, which I have often seen and heard," and no doubt Fitzherbert heard it before 1582, when he too left England. Also, at around this same time, Byrd wrote an extended Latin motet, *Deus venerunt gentes*, which must also rage and lament for Campion under the cover of some blameless verses from Psalm 79:

> O God, the heathen have set foot in thy domain, defiled thy holy temple and laid Jerusalem in ruins. They have thrown out the dead bodies of thy servants to feed the birds of the air; they have made thy saints carrion for the wild beasts. Their blood is spilled all around Jerusalem like water, and there was no-one to bury them. We suffer the contempt of our neighbors, the gibes and mockery of all around us.

We have here the unburied bodies nailed to the gate, the blood that spurted on Walpole, the protests from "our neighbors" abroad, and even an allusion to Campion's speech from the scaffold: for the last of the psalm verses selected begins in Latin *"Facti sumus opprobrium vicinis nostris,"* and I do not think it can be a coincidence that this comes so close to Campion's *"Spectaculum facti sumus Deo, angelis, et hominibus."*

It is likely enough, I suppose, that Byrd too stood in the rain and the mud at Tyburn to witness Campion's martyrdom. It seems very likely that this affected him much as it affected Walpole. Not that he ever went abroad to become a missionary; Byrd was one of those who stayed at home, and prospered, and made his uneasy peace with the system. But after 1581 his religious commitment hardened decisively. Whether it is technically correct to speak of a "conversion" in his case, as in Walpole's, is not clear. But with Byrd as with Walpole we cannot fail to detect a profound new sense of devotion to the Catholic faith and the Catholic cause.

Born in 1543, Byrd was just old enough to have been a choirboy under the old religion—the old religion which Mary Tudor restored, between 1553 and 1558, with special zeal. His first position was in the new Anglican disposition; he was appointed organist-choirmaster of Lincoln Cathedral in 1562. The personality that we are able to glimpse from Lincoln records is not distinguished by any unusual spirituality, but rather by a certain contentiousness and a precocious talent for the great Elizabethan art of applying influence—a talent that obviously stood him in very good stead during his later, intransigently Catholic years. Lincoln appointed him at a higher salary than his predecessor, with a lease of land thrown in to sweeten the contract, and when he left for the Chapel Royal in 1572 he pulled strings from London so that he actually continued to draw a salary from Lincoln for nearly ten years more.

In London Byrd's star rose rapidly. He made connections with powerful lords such as the earls of Essex and Northumberland, and acquired more leases. He was appointed joint organist of the Chapel

Royal, sharing the post with his master Thomas Tallis, who was then around seventy years old. With Tallis, too, he secured a patent from the Crown for music printing—a trade with little history in Britain up to this time. The monopolists' debut was a joint publication of Latin motets, the *Cantiones quae ab argumento sacrae vocantur* of 1575, dedicated to Queen Elizabeth and designed to show the world what excellent music Britain could produce. So at least we are told by the elaborate prefatory matter, which goes on for six pages. Influential persons were enlisted to fill these pages: a courtier and dilettante composer named Sir Ferdinando Richardson and the important educator Richard Mulcaster. One has the feeling it was Byrd, not the aging Tallis, who did the enlisting.

So far it had been a worldly career, with scarcely any signs of Catholic leanings. In 1577, however, Byrd's wife was first cited for recusancy, that is, for refusing to attend Church of England services as required by law. It was a common pattern for Catholic wives to stand on principle while their husbands, who had more to lose, attended the required services as "church-papists." After 1580 the signs multiply. Clearly the authorities were now more vigilant, but clearly also Byrd was more engaged. His house was watched and on one occasion searched. His servant was caught in a raid. His one surviving letter, dated 1581, sues on behalf of a beleaguered Catholic family. In 1586 he was one of a small group assembled to welcome two notable Jesuits to England, Fathers Southwell and Henry Garnet. Byrd must have been highly regarded among the Catholics to have been summoned on this occasion. He himself was cited for recusancy in 1585, and bound in recognizance of the staggering sum of £200 for the same crime two years later. (He may never have paid it.) Still to come, in his declining years, was the accusation that he had "seduced" certain servants and neighbors away from the Church of England, but Byrd seems always to have stayed clear of actual arrest or serious harassment.

Byrd's new religious conviction was expressed in music—in a remarkable series of Latin motets composed in a new style and with texts of an entirely new kind. These texts seem to voice prayers and protests, which are sometimes general and sometimes more specific, on behalf of the Elizabethan Catholic community. Some of these motets speak of a "congregation" or "God's people" who await liberation. Thus *Domine praestolamur*:

> O Lord, we await thy coming, that you may at once dissolve the yoke of our captivity. Come, o Lord, do not delay. Break the bonds of your servants, and liberate your people.

Byrd harps on the theme of the coming of God in various moods—supplicatory, as in the text above, or confident, in *Laetentur coeli*:

> Let the heavens rejoice and the earth exult...for the Lord is coming...

or didactic, in *Vigilate*:

> Be wakeful, for you know not when the lord of the house is coming, in the evening, in the middle of the night, at cock-crow, or early dawn; be wakeful, lest when he come suddenly he may find you asleep....

Several impressive motets refer to the Holy City, Jerusalem, and the Babylonian captivity: a transparent metaphor for the Catholic situation in Britain, though of course it could also be turned in other directions. *Ne irascaris Domine*, which is dated 1581 in two independent manuscripts, was and still is the most popular of these "Jerusalem" motets.

Other texts, of which the most sensational is *Deus venerunt gentes*, the Campion lament mentioned above, are more explicit in reference. Two of Byrd's most impressive motets, *Haec dicit Dominus* and *Plorans plorabit*, tell in the one case of the progeny of lamenting Rachel who are promised their patrimony, and in the other of the king and queen who hold the Lord's flock captive—this motet appeared as late as 1605—and whose proud crowns have fallen. Both texts are drawn from Jeremiah; both seem frankly political in intent. Boldest of all, perhaps, is *Circumspice Hierusalem*, a text from the Apocrypha which can only refer to the Jesuit missionaries:

> Look around toward the East, o Jerusalem, and see the joy that is coming to you from God! Behold, your sons are coming, whom you sent away and dispersed; they come gathered together from the East to the West, at the word of the Holy One, rejoicing in the glory of God.

"Whereas I have come out of Germany and Boëmeland," wrote Campion in the document known as Campion's Brag, a powerful open letter to the Privy Council, "being sent by my Superiors, and adventured myself into this noble realm, my dear country, for the glory of God and benefit of souls...."

Interestingly enough, there is a contemporary acknowledgment of Byrd's covert use of Latin motets for personal or political statements. It is a covert acknowledgment, of course. In 1583 a grandiose motet was sent to him by the Netherlandish master Philippe de Monte, chapelmaster to the Holy Roman Emperor. The motet's words are pointedly rearranged from the most famous of the psalms of captivity, "Super flumina Babilonis" (By the rivers of Babylon, Psalm 137):

> By the rivers of Babylon, there we sat down, yea, we wept, when we remembered Zion. There they that carried us away captive

required of us a song. How shall we sing the Lord's song in a strange land?

A year later Byrd sent back a magnificent answering motet, *Quomodo cantabimus*, as though to a challenge:

> How shall we sing the Lord's song in a strange land? If I forget thee, o Jerusalem, let my right hand forget her cunning. If I do not remember thee, let my tongue cleave to the roof of my mouth, if I prefer not Jerusalem above my chief joy....

Quomodo cantabimus includes a three-part canon by inversion: as though to assure Catholic Christendom that he had not hung up his harp, that his faith was firm, and that his hand had lost none of its cunning. Seldom does the murk of underdocumentation allow so sharp an insight into the Elizabethan musical condition as is afforded by this exchange between two great Catholic composers.

Byrd's motets of the 1580s employ a new musical style, on which his whole political endeavor depended. (We should speak more strictly of a maturing of tendencies already evident in the *Cantiones* of 1575—a brilliant, experimental, uneven group of compositions.) There is much that is historically important about this style, as far as the development of English music is concerned: its refinement of the basic medium of imitative polyphony, its command of the subtle distinctions between various homophonic and half-homophonic textures, and in general its superb native reinterpretation of the classical midcentury idiom of Continental Europe.

But perhaps its most important new feature is its new sensitivity to verbal texts. It is only with the Tallis-Byrd *Cantiones* of 1575 and especially with Byrd's motets of the next decade that English music is "framed to the life of the words," as Byrd himself was to express it some time later. This "framing" we usually associate with the madrigal, a secular genre which had served Italian composers since the 1530s as an endlessly fertile field for the investigation of word–music relationships. But madrigals are not known to have been written in England before the 1590s. Ahead of the English madrigalists, starting with his own student, Thomas Morley, Byrd was already practicing the expressive and illustrative rhetoric of Continental music in his sacred motets of the 1580s.

This rhetoric made for their impact. Byrd did more than provide significant texts with beautiful music. It was music of a rhetorical vividness that was all but unprecedented on the English scene, and so it was music of unprecedented power. Again and again, when the motets break into their great supplications—"Have mercy on us, o Lord," "Lord, do not forget thy people," and the like—the music breaks out of the prevailing polyphonic discourse into powerful chordal passages of direct outcry. When the text of *Ne irascaris Domine* says "Zion is a wilderness," Byrd frames these words with harmonies and textures that are unforgettably bleak and hollow. When the Lord is urged to arise (*"Exsurge Domine"*) the melody mounts up the scale in excitement, and when it is promised that he will not delay (*"et non tardabit"*) the rhythm races in frantic double-time note values. And when Saint Mark warns us to be wakeful, lest when the Lord arrive he find us sleeping, Byrd with grim humor writes music that drones or snores and is then cut short by vivid shouts of *"Vigilate! vigilate! vigilate!"*

The stylistic point is important to make because, of course, the expressive style is at the heart of Byrd's unique contribution to these motets. The texts themselves may not have been his personal choice. They could have been given to him by his patrons or his priests (though some I believe he must have chosen himself, because only a musician would have been likely to know their sources). Whoever chose the words, however, Byrd brought them to life in a way that had previously been unknown in English music. These motets must have seemed extraordinarily moving and powerful to their first listeners. They still seem extraordinarily moving and powerful today.

At the end of the 1580s Byrd for the first time began issuing his music in a systematic way. He published two books of English songs and two of Latin motets, and also supervised a beautiful manuscript collection of his virginal music, *My Lady Nevells Booke.* It is hard to escape the impression that the composer was setting his house in order—writing *finis,* as it were, to a chapter of his creative career. And indeed in his fiftieth year, 1593, Byrd obtained a farm in the village of Stondon Massey in Essex and went there to live. After this move, the music that he wrote was of a different kind than he had cultivated before.

Situated between Brentwood and Chelmsford, the county town, Stondon is about twenty-five miles from Westminster—that is, about twice as far as Byrd's previous home (which was at Harlington, near the present Heathrow Airport). The farm was a good-sized one, and it looked as if the composer was going into a semi-prosperous semi-retirement. Though he certainly did not resign his position in the Chapel Royal, it seems he was not often there, for his name is usually missing from the memorials and petitions signed by all the other members. His printing monopoly was not renewed; henceforth he is not much heard of around London. But I believe that this semiretirement was not the prime consideration, but rather a symptom, and that the real significance of the farm at Stondon was not its remoteness from London but its proximity to the manor house at Ingatestone, just a few miles distant.

Ingatestone Hall had been built by Sir William Petre, secretary of state under Henry VIII, Edward VI, Mary, and Elizabeth. His son Sir John was a circumspect Catholic and a patron of Byrd's. (The first document linking their names dates from the fateful year 1581.) Lady Mary was less circumspect. The Petres presided over a Catholic community centered around their Essex estates of Ingatestone and

Thorndon; and what I suspect is that Byrd moved from Harlington expressly to join this community and participate in the Catholic life there. If so, this clearly marks a new deeper commitment by William Byrd to his religion.

The social historian John Bossy has given us a remarkably full picture of Catholic life in England at this time.[3] A large proportion of the Elizabethan gentry retained Catholic sympathies, and those that were really serious about religion found it possible to work out a *modus vivendi* within the system. They had to stay out of public life and retire to their country estates, and they might have to put up with fines and harassment—and they were well advised to stay clear of their inflammatory sons and cousins who went abroad to become Jesuits and returned, like Henry Walpole, to make life difficult for the authorities and for the Catholic minority alike. That was a lot. But if they were prepared to make these sacrifices, the Catholic gentry were pretty much left to supervise the lives of their families, servants, and tenants according to Catholic principles as they saw them.

The main principles, and the main preoccupations, according to Bossy, were three. First, the Catholic gentry were naturally determined to raise their children in the faith. Second, they labored to institutionalize a daily routine in accordance with the elaborate Catholic calendar of those days, with its feast and fast days, its rogation times, and its seasons of abstinence from meat. The daily texture of their lives grew more and more distinct from that of the Anglican majority. Third, they struggled to maintain undercover Catholic services. They set up "Mass-centers" in attics and barns, furnished with the necessary consecrated church furniture, vestments, and the like, and they harbored traveling or circuit priests, even sometimes resident ones. Mass was celebrated strictly according to the Roman liturgy, of course. On occasions such as Christmas and Easter, it was desirable

---

3. In *The English Catholic Community, 1570–1850* (Oxford University Press, 1976).

for Mass to be sung with a choir in as festive and ornate a fashion as one remembered from the days of Henry VIII and Queen Mary. Then the Petres were inclined to seek out the quiet of Ingatestone, away from the main road and less public than their principal seat at Thorndon.

The impression that Byrd entered into a life of this kind rests not only on the fact that he and his family moved to Stondon but also on the kind of music he wrote after the move. Instead of covert political motets and the other types that he had cultivated in the 1580s— mainly settings of penitential texts, which were widely popular in the sixteenth century, with a few didactic homilies and general songs of praise—he now turned almost exclusively to liturgical items for particular Catholic services. And once again, as at the beginning of the 1580s, the change in text repertory was accompanied by a change in musical style.

His three settings of the Ordinary of the Mass date from 1592–1595. They contain the music by which he is probably best known today: direct, concise, eminently "functional," even austere, yet infused with a remarkable quiet fervor. In the next decade he produced his magnum opus, the *Gradualia*, a collection of more than a hundred motets for the Proper of the Mass (those sections of the service which change according to the season: Introits, Graduals, and so on). The entire Church year is covered; one remembers Bossy's point about the Catholics' preoccupation with the Church calendar. There are motets for Christmas, Epiphany, the Purification, Easter, Ascension, Whitsun, Corpus Christi, All Saints, and various feasts of the Blessed Virgin Mary—as well as two feasts of special importance to the Catholics, Saints Peter and Paul and Saint Peter's Chains. Byrd sets the communion of these two feasts, *Tu es Petrus*, with the greatest of verve: "You are Peter, the rock, and on this rock I will build my Church."

Liturgical music is written to be used in a liturgy. Byrd's masses and *Gradualia* motets were written for services held at the clandestine Mass-centers of Catholic England. He says plainly, when dedicating

Book Two of the *Gradualia* to his patron, that its contents "have mostly proceeded from your house, which is most friendly to me and mine"—Ingatestone Hall, where Byrd and his family must have worshipped regularly. "These little flowers are plucked as it were from your gardens and are most rightfully due to you as tithes." But the fact that this music was printed shows that it was destined to be sung elsewhere, too. "We kept Corpus Christi Day with solemnity and music," writes Father Garnet in 1605, "and the day of the Octave made a solemn procession about a garden, the house being watched, which we knew not until the next day." Was the music taken from the Corpus Christi section of the *Gradualia*, published only a few months earlier? A few months later Garnet, who had an "exquisite knowledge of the art of music," was together with Byrd at a musical gathering in London.

And a few months after that, the Gunpowder Plot brought down Garnet and all possible Catholic hopes for a new restoration. It should already have been clear enough after the defeat of the Armada in 1588 that the best that could be hoped for was the maintenance of a Catholic way of life in a minority status. In the 1580s, when many Catholics still regarded the eclipse of their faith as a temporary aberration, Byrd spoke for them in motets of extraordinary power. Then in the 1590s he turned from these motets of anguish and anger to motets and Mass sections celebrating the Catholic rite in perpetuity. In this turn we may see a new acceptance of the inevitable on the part of his essential patrons among the Catholic gentry.

His own acceptance can be seen in the move to Stondon, the withdrawal from artistic life in London, and the establishment of closer ties with the Catholic community under the Petres. There is one nonliturgical motet in the *Gradualia* that deserves special notice—almost the only nonliturgical motet among a hundred that are strictly bound to the liturgy:

> One thing I ask of the Lord, one thing I seek: that I may inhabit the house of the Lord all the days of my life, to gaze upon the beauty of the Lord and seek him in his temple.

These words from Psalm 27 would seem to speak with uncommon directness of Byrd's own condition.

One might say that Byrd had come full circle, in that he was now treating the same Catholic liturgical texts that he had come to know as a choirboy in the time of Queen Mary. But of course the music he wrote for these texts in the 1590s was not like the music he sang in the 1550s. Much as the Catholics may have wished to return to the medieval order, they could not do this in their music any more than they could in their political accommodation. The clandestine masses at Ingatestone, always in danger of exposure by spies, had no leisure for the grandiose, drawn-out, florid music of Tallis and his genera-tion. Byrd's masses are much simpler and more concise. Some of his *Gradualia* motets are positively aphoristic.

There could also be no return to the older Tudor composers' attitude toward the words. For them, the actual *meaning* of the words in a liturgical text mattered less than the *function* of that text as a unit in the ritual. But for Byrd the word was primary. "There is such a profound and hidden power to sacred words," he observes in the dedication to the *Gradualia*—it is a famous and beautiful state-ment—"that to one thinking upon things divine and diligently and earnestly pondering them, the most suitable of all musical measures occur (I know not how) as of themselves, and suggest themselves spontaneously to the mind that is not indolent and inert." The expressive rhetoric that he had developed in the 1580s still illumi-nates the liturgical texts of the *Gradualia*—texts such as *Ave verum corpus, O magnum misterium, Iustorum animae*, and *Tu es Petrus*, to mention only some of the most familiar. It even illuminates the words of the Ordinary of the Mass, which served Catholic composers on the Continent as the commonest of clay for the building of one purely musical construction after another. But Byrd was a Catholic composer who could not and did not take the Mass for granted.

His late Latin sacred music was, in short, Catholic liturgical music in a new manifestation. Communities such as Ingatestone were not really a continuation of the old late-medieval order, as Bossy explains, but the beginning of a new regime of Catholic life that would, in fact, continue with relatively minor modifications until the nineteenth century.

Anyone who knows anything of the *Gradualia* will remember the luminous "alleluia" sections in *Sacerdotes Domini, Non vos relinquam orphanos, Constitues eos,* and many other pieces. Byrd's treatment of these alleluias—there are nearly eighty examples—can be taken as emblematic of his whole endeavor in the late sacred music. He never thought to cut corners by writing a *da capo* indication for one of these alleluias, though in many cases the liturgical rubrics would have made this perfectly appropriate. He seems to have been fascinated by the problem of setting the same word in dozens of different ways, as though absorbed in the mystery of the inexhaustible renewal of praise. The language of the Seven Penitential Psalms and the Book of Jeremiah echoes through the texts of Byrd's earlier motets. What stays in the mind from the *Gradualia* is the endlessly repeated, endlessly varied acclamation "alleluia" and the act of ritual celebration which it embodies.

—1979

6

THE OPERAS OF MONTEVERDI

IT WAS A BRILLIANT IDEA, and must have required a managerial tour de force, for the Brooklyn Academy of Music to bring together the three surviving operas of Claudio Monteverdi in productions from Amsterdam, Aix-en-Provence, and Chicago, dating from 1993, 2000, and 2001 respectively. Attending all three in a row (this was in 2002) was a wonderful experience, vertiginous even for the seasoned opera-goer, and would have been so even if the three productions had not been so very different.

The works themselves belong to two early phases of operatic history, the famous "birth of opera" in the late Renaissance courts of northern Italy and then the weaning of opera from court life—phases separated by thirty years and a total change of social milieu, but held together (and this makes the story so satisfying) by the same great composer. Opera was developed by a revisionist and highly out-spoken group of Florentine courtiers, scholars, and singers, as the outgrowth of a long tradition of princely entertainments, the masque-like *intermedi*. It was only institutionalized much later, when the great families of Venice transformed it into a potent draw for the free city's especially free carnival season. To say that the story is held together by Monteverdi is no historical abstraction, for one of the Venetian commercial theaters that went over to opera, the Teatro San

Moisè, owned by the Zane family, marked its new course in 1640 by reviving his *Arianna*, composed for the Gonzaga court of Mantua in 1608.[1]

This BAM could not give us, for the music of *Arianna* has disappeared except for its hit number, Ariadne's lament, which was widely copied and published in various forms, and said to be in the library of every mid-seventeenth-century music lover. In any case, the *Arianna* revival must have been a very strange occasion, for toddler opera was quite unlike the newborn babe. Monteverdi's *Orfeo* of 1607, the masterpiece of early court opera, casts the Orpheus myth into eight simple scenes (by my count) with minimal dialogue. Orpheus remains onstage almost continuously, with the other characters as walk-ons who never appear in more than a single scene, except for Eurydice, who appears in two scenes in which she sings for less than two minutes. The librettos of its counterparts from the 1640s, *Il ritorno d'Ulisse in patria* and *L'incoronazione di Poppea*, both first performed in Venetian theaters, are long, elaborately plotted plays drawn from epic or history, in which we follow more than a dozen characters through nearly two dozen scenes. Early court opera behaves much of the time less like a drama than like a masque or a ritual. Venetian opera was already racing on what Jane Glover has called "the ferocious treadmill of operatic show business."[2]

Ritorno, in fact, is quite a show. Monteverdi had moved to Venice from Mantua in 1613 to become *maestro di capella* at San Marco, and little is known about any operas he wrote or may have written in the interim. Certainly none was conceived under such a spotlight, and in this work (also produced in 1640) by the seventy-three-year-old

---

1. I am drawing on the major study by Ellen Rosand, *Opera in Seventeenth-Century Venice: The Creation of a Genre* (University of California Press, 1991). Beyond this, Ellen and David Rosand have helped me with this essay in more ways than I care to list.

2. *Claudio Monteverdi: Orfeo*, edited by John Whenham (Cambridge University Press, 1986), p. 138.

composer one senses the release of operatic energies that have been bottled up for a long time. There are scenes of high pathos, low comedy, dalliance, vengeance, slaughter, and stupendous parlays between gods in the machines. There are vocal pyrotechnics and a stream of catchy little songs. Minerva, who masterminds the action, is also the showstopper, turning up again and again on various machines in various guises and disguises: a disingenuous shepherd boy on the coast of Ithaca, a conjuror making Ulysses over as an old beggar, Telemachus' charioteer on the way home from Sparta, the architect of the plan to kill the suitors—even more sanguinary in Minerva's foretelling than in the event, over which she presides *in maesta*—and finally Ulysses' advocate at the court of Jove. The only well-known operatic extravaganza like *Ritorno* that I can think of is *The Magic Flute*, though *Ritorno* has a much harder edge.

The success of all this depended on Monteverdi's music, of course, and *Ritorno* positively flaunts his musical resources, two in particular. One is the affective recitative style of Ariadne's lament, still enormously powerful today, especially if you follow it word by word, in Italian. The other is a certain kind of melody, which I will attempt to characterize in a moment. (Supertitles are hardly adequate for the recitative, and hardly necessary for the melodies.) After starting with a lament in recitative for Penelope that occupies an entire scene, the opera finds time for extensive solo numbers in much the same style for Ulysses, Telemachus, Minerva, and even Penelope's maid Melanto. The series is capped by an astonishing parody lament for the comic character Iro—a suicide scene which, unlike Papageno's in *The Magic Flute*, does not have a happy ending.

The next scene after the opera's magnificent opening lament, equally static, has Melanto and her boyfriend making love, and now affective recitative gives way to almost continuous melody. Melanto belongs in the opera as a foil to Penelope, and later she will do what maids and nurses always do in these situations, urge her mistress to console herself with a lover. Yet she does not so much as mention Penelope here.[3] Whereas Penelope's scene drags on, symbolizing her endless waiting and the constancy that will sustain her through the drama to come, Melanto's goes far beyond dramatic necessities. Its scattershot of little songs and duos feels like a manifesto, the display of an old master's musical fecundity. Ulysses' return to his homeland was also Monteverdi's return to the theater.[4]

Little songs and duos: Venetian operas are teeming with these. They are short and gay and move in clear, delicately balanced phrases, mostly in triple meter. While sometimes they run to several strophes, punctuated by brief instrumental passages, sometimes they emerge seamlessly out of the recitative and disappear almost before one can take them in. This—to say nothing of the lack of instrumental accompaniment—can be puzzling to audiences used to the melodic opulence of Handel, Mozart, Verdi, and Puccini. Monteverdi's melodies tickle the ear but do not stick, as it were, to the ribs.

What do they do for the drama? There was already at the time much agonizing about the proper place for song in musical drama, that is, when the use of song could be justified dramatically. A famous bit of musico-dramatic strategy shows how sensitive one composer could be to this. After Penelope has launched the opera with her affective recitative (musically heightened speech unconstrained by orchestral backing), hours go by before she breaks into melody—at the moment, of course, when she acknowledges the formidable beggar as her husband. Song should be reserved for heightened mental conditions—Penelope's moment of rapture here, and elsewhere madness,

---

3. There are a few lines referring to her in the libretto, but they do not appear in the surviving score. Although most performances put back the lines, with some made-up recitative music, Monteverdi could certainly have cut them out deliberately. He was famous, even in his own time, for altering librettos when he set them to music.

4. An analogy that was drawn at the time; see Ellen Rosand, "The Bow of Ulysses," *Journal of Musicology*, Vol. 12 (1994), pp. 393–395.

anger, laughter, sexual transport, and indeed plain ebullience, which seems to be a natural state for the shepherd Eumete (a gentle parody of the Arcadian staples of court opera, it seems—Homer's Eumaios was a swineherd).

And in *L'incoronazione di Poppea* the natural state of the heroine is in heat. Poppea, the most single-minded seductress in all of opera, slips in and out of recitative and melody the way she slips in and out of her Roman lingerie. For an opera composer to find characters drawn to affective recitative was not hard—the empress Ottavia in *Poppea*, deserted and then banished by Nero, serves as well as Penelope. It was much harder to find characters driven to song. Nero and Poppea are such characters. In *Poppea*, as in certain operas of later years—*Wozzeck*, *Pelléas et Mélisande*, *The Bartered Bride*—one feels that the composer has found his ideal subject matter. He has found the ideal dramatis personae to bring out his best musical powers.

"*The Coronation of Poppea* is first of all a scandal," wrote a surprised drama critic when this opera was first becoming known again. "It is also a masterpiece in the musical transformation of drama, a conventional 'triumph of love' allegory with flashes of profundity, and a garland of Monteverdi's most inventive pieces. But its matter is scandal...."[5]—the scandal of female eroticism triumphing over reason, morality, and empire.

The dramaturgy supporting this subversive theme is as involuted and sophisticated as that of *Ritorno* is transparent. The librettist, Giovanni Francesco Busenello, who also wrote novels, discourses, and even a patriotic epic, built his plot on shifting sands, pitting stability against instability. Scene after scene for Nero and Poppea confirms the erotic engagement that already precedes the action—like *Der Rosenkavalier*, *Poppea* begins on a postcoital morning—and will

---

5. James Kerans, liner note to the first "early music" recording of *L'incoronazione di Poppea*, directed by Alan Curtis (Cambridge Records, 1966).

remain unchecked at the end. It is true that some of these scenes advance the plot—Poppea persuading Nero with ridiculous ease to do away with the Stoic philosopher Seneca, who disapproves of their affair; Poppea reminding Nero of what he already knows, that Ottavia's treachery sanctions him to get her out of the way too—but it is hard for this part of the plot, given its foregone conclusion, to compete for attention with the vivid lovemaking on view. The ravishing duet "Pur ti miro" ("I Behold Thee") that concludes the opera, with its baby-talk text and its continuous chain of musical caresses, is simply dropped in, an emblem of the eternity of sexual ardor. This final scene has no dramatic context and contains not a word of recitative.[6]

Busenello deemed sex the only constant in a world (indeed a cosmos) dangerously in flux. All the other characters change over the course of the action (none does in *Ritorno*, with the clearly necessary exception of Penelope). Seneca opposes Nero and accepts his death sentence with nobility and Stoic gravitas; yet when we first hear of him he is being abused as a windbag and a hypocrite by "the street," represented by a pair of Nero's guards, and when we first meet him he is delivering a perfectly fatuous speech of supposed consolation to Ottavia—as she herself remarks briskly, before turning him over to her page for another round of abuse, this time to his face. The music of the speech is itself fatuous, a travesty of Monteverdi's and indeed Seneca's normal mode of expression.[7]

---

6. The duet was added to *Poppea* at a late stage, and its authenticity has been doubted . . . though nobody really wants to take "Pur ti miro" away from Monteverdi. See *Claudio Monteverdi: L'incoronazione di Poppea*, edited by Alan Curtis (Novello, 1989), pp. v–ix, and Anthony Pryer, "Authentic Performance, Authentic Experience, and 'Pur ti miro' from Poppea," in *Performing Practice in Monteverdi's Music*, edited by Raffaello Monterosso (Cremona: Fondazione Claudio Monteverdi, 1995), pp. 191–214. The first true scholarly edition of *Ritorno*, also by Curtis with Novello, appeared in 2002.

7. See Wendy Heller, "Tacitus Incognito: Opera as History in *L'incoronazione di Poppea*," *Journal of the American Musicological Society*, Vol. 52 (1999), pp. 39–96. Tacitus was the main source for the *Poppea* libretto. Though I have reservations about some of her conclusions, Heller sheds new light on the libretto by analyzing texts issuing from the leading

Of the disputants in the opera's prologue, Fortune, Virtue, and Love, only Love remains at the end to crow *ex machina*. Virtue never shows her face again after her delegate Seneca dies and the moral bottom drops out of the opera entirely. Ottavia, originally so pathetic, forces Ottone into a plot to kill his former love Poppea. Ottone, originally disconsolate, pretends to love Drusilla, originally a mere ingenue, until she eagerly collaborates in his murder attempt. Even the page changes, from a spiteful loudmouth to a Cherubino figure flirting with an unnamed girl. The macabre edge to this lovely little scene, which follows directly after Seneca's suicide, is honed by its very abstractness. The death of virtue announces an initiation into love.

Following this scene comes a fully explicit reaction to Seneca's death and all it means. "Now that Seneca is dead," says Nero, "let us sing," and he delivers a rapturous song about Poppea, accompanied or rather prompted by Lucano, the poet Lucan. (Nero, we remember, was famous for his music.) Their brilliant duet sends homoerotic signals hard to miss. The death of virtue announces an initiation into unnatural love, for which Nero was also famous.

Pierre Audi, the director of the Dutch National Opera's *Poppea*, did not underplay Nero's apparent orgasm with Lucan, though their scene was vitiated by dry singing and by staging that I found wooden here as elsewhere in the production. What he underplayed was the heterosexual action between Nero and Poppea. Nero had trouble getting his hands on Poppea all evening, either because she held him off or because of clearly mimed neurotic withdrawal. There was a real idea here, one that was more conventionally "dramatic" than my own more voyeuristic reading—Nero only gets what he wants over

---

Venetian academy of the time, the Incogniti, of which Busenello was a member. Heller also writes at length about the Nero-Lucan scene. See also Rosand, *Opera in Seventeenth-Century Venice*, pp. 37–40 and 88–91, and—for a different take on Tacitus and Seneca as seen by the Incogniti—Iain Fenlon and Peter Miller, *The Song of the Soul: Understanding "Poppea"* (Royal Musical Association, 1992).

the course of the action, rather than before it starts—and up to a point support for it can be found in the libretto. But not, I think, in the music. Not, certainly, in "Pur ti miro"—where Audi placed Nero and Poppea thirty feet apart singing the words "Only gaze on you to desire you, only caress you to consume you, I am yours, you are mine," and so on, directly out to the audience. Even when he moved them shoulder to shoulder there was never a kiss, embrace, or even eye contact. Shared words like these, once they are entwined by Monteverdi's music, signal erotic engagement as clearly as do the moans of "Oh God, oh God, oh God" in the Nero-Lucan scene, carved out of the libretto text by the composer, and so suggestively set to music.[8]

Characters in this production were isolated and estranged. Ottone and Drusilla declared their love back to back, ten feet apart. The two nurses (Poppea's and Ottavia's) were suppressed or suffocated by hyperbolical costumes. Audi's concept did, however, put an interesting construction on one of the opera's most memorable scenes, in which Seneca tells of his impending suicide and his Stoic welcome of death as a release. The opera's ambivalence about Seneca, and about Virtue by way of Seneca, is underlined by the chorus of Famigliari that addresses him; "famigliari" may be taken to mean Seneca's students, students who choose this moment to say exactly what they think of their master's teaching. *We* would not welcome death, they say, and then go on at some length about life's pleasures—in music, incidentally, that recalls the hero of *Orfeo* when, early in that opera, he is congratulating himself for winning Eurydice. As the Famigliari sing and stare in different directions, once again widely separated on the stage, Seneca goes to his bath without support or sympathy. I found this unsentimental reading of the scene quite convincing.

---

8. The actual words are "*ahi, destin,*" carved out of the *endecasillabo* line "*Bocca, ahi destin, che se ragiona o ride.*"

In spite of its ambivalences and back currents, or perhaps because of them, I would guess that *Poppea* presents fewer problems to a director today than does *Ritorno*. Penelope's suitors, who dominate three scenes, are one problem. Getting them killed onstage by the disguised Ulysses is the least of it. From the start in this opera they inhabit a third plane of being, stick figures distinct from the humans and the gods. The original audience would have found them comical; the brief trios that Monteverdi wrote for the three suitors evoke a type of Venetian carnival song, the *giustiniana*, sung by three old men eager for sex without the capacity to do much about it. (This genre found its way to England as the Freemen's Song—probably a corruption of Three Men's Song: "We be soldiers three/Pardonnez-moi, je vous en prie," and the like.) To accommodate the suitors to a contemporary sense of humor for any length of time is hard, perhaps impossible.

Another problem is the time it takes for Penelope to acknowledge Ulysses, after he kills the suitors. In the opera's libretto, 250 lines of the *Odyssey* are drawn out over five scenes. The director, Adrian Noble—who stepped down in 2003 as head of the Royal Shakespeare Company—cut one substantive scene for Penelope and Melanto and altered the weight of two others. These are a short solo scene for Penelope's nurse Ericlea and a spectacular gathering of the gods. When Ericlea debated whether or not to tell her mistress about the scar she has recognized while giving Ulysses his bath, Noble presented her as really anxious, rather than just befuddled and silly; the idea was evidently to make this traditional comic nurse scene truly consequential for the drama. Noble has Minerva gesticulating behind Ericlea (not the only such intervention).

In the dim lighting this little gem of a scene fails to glisten, however, and I did not get the idea behind Noble's big scene of the gods. This started just as dimly and ended unimpressively, as the carpet-sized cloud which bore Jove down from heaven eased him all the way down to a pile of cushions on the palace floor.[9] Still, *Ritorno* lives on sentiment, not comedy or spectacle, and this is the strength to which this handsome, graceful, subtle, and already well-traveled production played. Noble underlined very beautifully the parallel between the reunions which bring Acts I and II to their conclusion.[10] Well before the inevitable blissful duets at the moments of recognition, Ulysses can't check an involuntary move toward Telemachus even while still disguised as the beggar, and subtle body language from Penelope in face of the beggar betrays unacknowledged feelings that will finally burst out —and burst into song. Monteverdi points up the large dramatic rhythm by the smallest of melodies at the Act I curtain, directly after the duet between the two men. "*Vanne alle madre*," Ulysses says to the plot, as well as to Telemachus, "go to your mother": a (diatonic) scale up, a scale down, the same scale up again—almost shockingly simple, this, as a musical evocation of tenderness, hope, and dramatic anticipation. Monteverdi's little songs can move us as much as his affective recitatives.

At a time when complaints are commonplace about the dearth of adequate singers for the standard operatic repertory, it is amazing how many singers there are nowadays attuned to older opera, singers who look very well and can act and even turn an occasional somersault. William Christie led a superb cast in *Ritorno*; the seriousness, elegance, and continuity of his work—in Les Arts Florissants he has one of the few organizations devoted to the performance of old operas, many of which he has brought to BAM make him one of the great names in music today. Jane Glover, whose involvement with early opera goes

---

9. The all-purpose, quasi-Oriental *mise-en-scène*, by Anthony Ward, yields more than one elegant touch. The spare, sandy stage is spotted with a few jars of various sizes, one of them big enough for the glutton Iro to emerge from at the beginning of his suicide scene. This is funny, but when Iro squeezes back into the jar at the end, announcing that he is going to kill himself, the combination of renewed comedy and frisson, neither played broadly, catches exactly the right tone for this difficult scene, I thought. I thought of Ali Baba.

10. In this production (as in many others) Monteverdi's Acts II and III are run together as Act II.

back to a classic production of *Orfeo* in the 1970s, and who here added the Chicago Opera Theater to her Glimmerglass and New York City Opera engagements, can seldom have had the opportunity of working with so fine a singer in so large a role as the English tenor Laurence Dale. Looking back on the three operas in the BAM Monteverdi Cycle, while *Ritorno* was without question the most satisfying as a whole, as a single portrayal Dale's Orpheus was in a league of its own.

His was a truly searing performance, as impressive for its stylishness as for its passion. When Orpheus sings what Monteverdi probably thought of as an Orphic hymn to the underworld, "Possente Spirto," composed in a specially ornate musical style, one almost heard the lyre of Apollo stuccoed onto the walls of BAM's Howard Gilman Opera House, down the street, resounding in the smaller Harvey Theater. Orpheus completely dominates his opera, and by omitting intermissions and running the acts together rapidly, the director Diane Paulus achieved a near-continuous flood of emotionality such as we are rarely treated to in performances today. Glover was quoted in the program as saying that

> throughout rehearsals everybody—singers, instrumentalists, production team—will contribute. Each note or chord will have some decision made about it. Should it be short or long, loud or soft, attacked or stroked...? Above all, after making these decisions, how can we keep them alive? We must retain that very spontaneity which marked Monteverdi's response to the text....

And there can be no doubt that music of this kind—music of extreme rhythmic flexibility, responsive to every particular word or syllable—depends crucially on synergy between singer and conductor. Jane Glover's hand was wonderfully sure and sensitive.

Of course the role of Orpheus is far from continuous; there are all sorts of episodes and diversions. But these were treated so lightheartedly in this production, while Laurence Dale on the contrary sang with such serious intensity, that one left the theater reeling with the impression of stacked laments—laments when Orpheus hears of Eurydice's death, on finding himself abandoned by Hope (Speranza), when he sees his great plea to the underworld failing, as he looks back and loses Eurydice, and when he returns to the glades of Thrace and sets them echoing with his misery. These laments indeed echo over the years, in the fully developed affective recitative of Penelope and Ottavia.

Orfeo begins and ends like a masque or ritual. Orpheus' wedding is celebrated by nymphs and shepherds singing solos, duos, trios, and madrigal choruses. Paulus replaced these carefree Arcadians with a modern wedding party whose costumes (high-fashion evening dress), props (champagne flutes, animal masks), and manic routines yielded one dazzling stage picture after another. Swept away by the sheer élan of all this, I was uncharacteristically tolerant of the tuning out of Music, the opera's prologue, and the toning down of the Messenger recounting the death of Eurydice in Act II. (Monteverdi gives "gentle Silvia," as the libretto calls this nymph, a predilection for the limelight.) But in Acts III and IV, which take place in Hades, the little groups of revelers seemed more than a little lost; and in Act V, with Orpheus returned to Thrace, Paulus couldn't resist the temptation to bring them all back on again. They stood very still and they looked very sad. They intruded all the same. Orpheus (or Guarini's Silvio, or Sidney's Philisides) is never more alone, or should be, than when he is communing with his echo.

One of the animal masks worn by the revelers looked like Mickey Mouse. I began to fancy I was watching a movie with one real-life, near-tragic character surrounded by a whole lot of animated ones— two planes of being, increasingly out of sync with each other. The true Disney touch came with the entrance or apparition of Eurydice at the final curtain, in a big burst of white petals.

—2002

7

BACH: A SHORT LIFE

A SHILLING LIFE will give you all the facts, wrote Auden, and many have echoed him, but when it comes to Johann Sebastian Bach what you get for twenty-two dollars in the Cambridge Musical Lives Series is a tissue of excellent speculation. Like Shakespeare—and many have made the comparison, including the composer's latest biographer, Peter Williams[1]—Bach suffers from underdocumentation. The accumulation of every piece of paper mentioning or concerning him during his lifetime, ranging from official documents penned by himself to reviews, lists, testimonials, receipts, and mere name-drops, fits onto two hundred pages in the basic source book, updated a few years ago as *The New Bach Reader*.[2]

Underdocumentation is almost a leitmotif in Williams's *Life of Bach*, which makes as best a virtue as it can out of biographical contingency as a necessary condition for the book's existence. The sources are particularly chary of personal indications—what Bach was like, why he did what he did—and the crowd of references to him in the years after his death, which fill out the *Bach Reader*, are, for

---

1. *The Life of Bach* (Cambridge University Press, 2005).

2. *The New Bach Reader: A Life of Johann Sebastian Bach in Letters and Documents*, edited by Hans T. David and Arthur Mendel, revised and expanded by Christoph Wolff (Norton, 1998).

Williams, deeply questionable. His skepticism about one fundamental document permeates and indeed organizes his book. This is the obituary written by Bach's son Carl Philipp Emanuel. Emanuel was Europe's leading composer of his generation, a writer and intellectual ensconced at the court of Frederick the Great in Berlin, a friend of Lessing and a correspondent with Diderot. Later Emanuel became a chief informant of J. N. Forkel, author of the vastly influential biography of Bach published in 1802, and translated into English only six years later.

Emanuel had his own agenda, as Williams exhaustively shows. His obituary plants hardy seeds for the reverence that will practically choke Bach biography for 250 years and more. Although Williams wants to break out of this thicket ("perhaps a more realistic approach to his occasional weaknesses can be quite as instructive"), for all the nuances provided by his book the traditional image of Bach the Master remains essentially intact. When this biographer addresses his subject's aggrieved, contentious, sometimes almost paranoid character,[3] the main concern seems to be to soften the blows of recent iconoclasts. All Bach wanted, Williams suggests, was for people to get out of his way so he could work, so he could realize his grandiose musical visions. This is hardly a new picture of Bach.

Since contributors to the Musical Lives Series do not have a great deal of space to fill—around 80,000 words—Williams has found it possible to structure his whole book around Emanuel's ten-page obituary. He goes through it paragraph by paragraph, sentence by sentence, extracting subheads for his narrative; this allows him to draw his narrative directly from source material and simultaneously ques-

---

3. "Confrontational and insubordinate all his life," according to one leading Bach scholar, with "a pervasive sense of persecution and an attitude of spiteful defiance toward authority"; see Robert L. Marshall, "In Search of Bach," *The New York Review*, June 15, 2000, p. 45. See also Marshall's "Toward a Twenty-First-Century Bach Biography," *Musical Quarterly*, Vol. 84 (2000), pp. 497–525.

tion that material point by point ("interrogate" is the current term of choice). The result, as I have said, is a subtle tissue of speculation by a veteran Bach scholar who knows the territory as few others do, replete with terms like *perhaps*, *presumably*, *probably*, *must have*, *would have*, *may have*, and so on, with periodic strings of questions that teeter nervously between the direct and the rhetorical.

There is a lot to recommend this method, apart from its ingenuity. It makes for a choppy, niggling book but one that is continuously stimulating, once adjustment has been made for the author's incessant references to Handel, whom he sees as the implicit (sometimes explicit) benchmark against whom Bach was measured. It keeps up a guard against excessive reverence, and it encourages readers not only to reconsider ideas about the composer but also to rehear his music. The arias in Cantata 115, "Mache dich, mein Geist, bereit," for example, "are so sensuously rich as to seem well beyond the call of piety," and the long closing chorale of the Saint John Passion is "a masterpiece of uncanny music, more than a mere hymn as it moves towards its unique expression of hope." The so-called deathbed organ chorale "Vor deinem Thron," being "void of notable invention and special or inimitable hallmarks," could have been cobbled together by a competent student. It's worth noting, however, that by throwing every datum (in principle) of Bach's life into question, Williams levels the playing field to a point where ideas and opinions that he launches on his own—his passes, punts, end runs, and occasional fumbles, offsides, and unnecessary roughness, as with "Vor deinem Thron"—call for very alert referees.

And as one would expect, the device of linking the narrative to the obituary works better at some times than at others. When Bach was a student at Lüneburg "he travelled from time to time to Hamburg, to hear the then famous organist of St. Catherine's, Johann Adam Reinken," Emanuel says—a seemingly innocent report. Williams wonders why Reinken is mentioned, a venerable figure but one of less interest in the years around 1700 than Dietrich Buxtehude with his famous *Abendmusik* at Lübeck, not all that much farther away, and why another important organist in the immediate vicinity, Georg Böhm at St. John's Church in Lüneberg itself, is not.[4] Bach did indeed visit Lübeck a few years later, and stayed there longer than he was supposed to. Or was it the flourishing opera in Hamburg that attracted the young Bach? His first job was as a court musician, not an organist. "'To hear Reinken' is thus part of the self-taught picture" that Emanuel always advances. Emanuel wants us to believe that "Bach neither took lessons nor became an apprentice-assistant but made study visits, to a major figure in a major church of a major Hanseatic city."

At other times the device of referring to the obituary works less well. Interestingly, it works less well after Bach, approaching forty, has moved to his highest and most public position as cantor of St. Thomas's Church and director of music at Leipzig, in 1723. He held this position until his death in 1750. About Bach's early years as a musician at the courts of Weimar and Cöthen, and even before that, Emanuel was happy to relay facts and stories that he had from his father, or that had been otherwise sanitized by family memory. But once we come to Leipzig Emanuel says very little, if for no other reason than at Leipzig memories were still fresh. Obituaries are not supposed to ruffle feathers. It turns out that even with all the documentation available from sources beyond the obituary, we have only the shakiest understanding of the origins of or impetus behind some of Bach's most important compositions.

---

4. Years later, in a revealing letter answering questions about his father, Emanuel told Forkel that Bach "loved and studied" the works of "his teacher Böhm," among many others, but crossed the words out and substituted "the Lüneburg organist Böhm." See Davitt Moroney, *Bach: An Extraordinary Life* (ABSCM, 2000), pp. 9, 108—another recent concise biography. (That Bach was a student of Böhm was established by documents that came to light in 2006.)

On Reincken's interest for and influence on Bach, Williams takes a contrarian position; compare Christoph Wolff, *Bach: Essays on His Life and Music* (Harvard University Press, 1991), Chapter 6.

For example, why did he compose the second book of *The Well-Tempered Clavier*? The first book is dedicated to "musical youth desirous of learning" as well as "those already skilled in this study"; with this book Bach supplied himself with twenty-four preludes and fugues to serve as staple teaching material. Principled teacher that he was, it's supposed that twenty years later he wanted to supplement the first book with something more up-to-date. We are incalculably in his debt, but he could have written six new items, or twelve new items, instead of building up a matching set of twenty-four around a stockpile of older fugues that are mostly weaker than the fugues of Book I. Williams finds "the sheer thoroughness of twice collecting preludes and fugues in every major and minor key" off-putting. "So entrenched has *The Well-Tempered Clavier* become that one easily forgets how strange it is."

The sheer strangeness of the B-Minor Mass project, at the end of Bach's career, would take many paragraphs to lay out; and Williams also points to mystery at the beginning of Bach's tenure at Leipzig. Since the cantor's position entailed providing music for Leipzig's churches, he set about writing new cantatas and Passions to fill out the entire church year, also drawing on and revising cantatas he had composed before. Then he wrote more, and more, and kept writing until he had assembled *five* complete yearly cycles, if Emanuel can be believed, over a span of just a few years. Congregations must have yearned for some relief from Bach's forbidding music; simpler cantatas by other composers lay easily at hand and any other cantor would have drawn upon them heavily. It is no wonder that Bach's relations with Leipzig's church authorities soured.

In 1729 Bach took over the Collegium Musicum, one of two organizations in Leipzig that put on concerts each week, and twice weekly during the town's important fairs. This new activity is taken to mark a sharp turn from sacred, vocal music to secular, instrumental music. It looks as though Bach had something like a midlife crisis around this time. But we are reminded that hardly anything is known about the constitution, logistics, or programs of the Collegium—even whether the director was paid. The programs were of course not limited to Bach's music and it is not clear how much new music he composed for them, beyond obligatory secular cantatas for this celebration or that. Manuscripts that can be related to the Collegium contain mostly arrangements of old pieces. Increasingly Bach's main creative energies were directed to the *Clavierübung*, a comprehensive, prize collection of keyboard music that he published in four volumes, spread out over fifteen years from 1726 to 1741 or 1742. Bach, then, was now looking beyond Leipzig to the musical world at large. At the end of his life, with works like the B-Minor Mass and *The Art of Fugue*, he was looking beyond the here and now altogether.

Clavierübung translates as "Exercise of the Keyboard" or "Keyboard Studies" (I wish Bach had called it "Keyboard Art," or "The Art of the Keyboard Player"—*Die Kunst des Clavier*). Though the music was all newly composed, up to a point it fell into genres he had practiced before coming to Leipzig: thus the clavier suites (called Partitas) of Part 1 look back to the sets of English and French Suites written in Cöthen, and the Italian Concerto of Part 2 puts Bach's creative stamp on the keyboard transcriptions of Vivaldi concertos, so deeply influential on his own style, which he had labored over at Weimar. Part 3 revisits and rethinks the great repertory of organ chorales and fugues dating from the Weimar years and even earlier.[5]

Part 4 of the *Clavierübung*, however, the Goldberg Variations, comes like a bolt out of the blue. There is nothing like it anywhere else in Bach's output. The work's great phalanx of devotees will need no convincing of that, nor is this the place to spell out its novelties and

---

5. Part 3 of the *Clavierübung* also includes four Duetti which can be played on organ, harpsichord, or clavichord—recollections (admittedly, quite attenuated) of the two-part Inventions written many years earlier for the keyboard lessons of Wilhelm Friedemann, Bach's oldest son.

differences from other Bach variation works mentioned by Williams—the Passacaglia and Fugue for organ, the Chaconne for violin solo, and Cantata No. 4, "Christ lag in Todesbanden." And there is nothing even in the other parts of the *Clavierübung* that approaches the Goldberg in the demands made on the performer's virtuosity. According to a famous anecdote, it was written for a Russian diplomat, Count von Keyserlingk, who had the keyboard prodigy J. G. Goldberg play bits of it to put him to sleep; the anecdote, it has been shown, must be wrong, but the impetus behind it—to account for the Goldberg on the basis of a special commission or other circumstance —must be right. Williams thinks Bach wrote it for his beloved oldest son, Wilhelm Friedemann, who by then had made an impression as a keyboard virtuoso as well as the composer of some unusually difficult harpsichord music. Friedemann had a position in Dresden, where Keyserlingk was posted at the time, and if he really was Goldberg's teacher, as unconfirmed reports have it, that would go some way to explain the anecdote.

Williams broaches this possibility in a handbook he has written on the Goldberg Variations[6] and returns to it in *The Life of Bach*. In a cool or, if you prefer, brazen appendix to the book subtitled "A Sample Hypothesis," he first scoffs at efforts by unnamed if readily identifiable scholars to argue "from the music to the person," and then turns around and offers just such an effort of his own. The hypothesis turns on Wilhelm Friedemann. "There are many if inconclusive signs that father and son remained close for forty years," Williams begins, and soon works his way up to the notion that the son had some sort of breakdown at the death of his father, prelude to the distressing collapse of his career thereafter:

---

6. *Bach: The Goldberg Variations* (Cambridge University Press, 2001)—a useful guide to the music, though the absence of any reference to the recordings of Glenn Gould, even in a chapter on "reception," is astonishing. Another guide is Laurette Goldberg and Jonathan Rhodes Lee, *The Goldberg Variations Reader* (MusicSources, 2002).

Had he been overencouraged—outwardly or inwardly—by a driven and driving father, overburdened by living up to expectations, over-dependent on him, and over-afflicted by his death? . . . Was it a case of special love for a first son, recognition of an unusual talent, a keen desire to discern one? Anxiety to compensate for the early loss of his mother, doubt that he was robust or had the stamina or killer instinct required for great success? Inadvertent domination, making such success impossible?

Among the "many if inconclusive signs" of closeness listed in the appendix are that Bach apparently recopied a brilliant early piece of his own for his son's audition when he applied for the Dresden position (the applicant might have been expected to show off a piece of his own). Once there, "Friede" was engaged by his father in a joint canon- and fugue-writing project—not the sort of thing many twenty-three-year-olds leaving home for the first time would think of getting into right away. Later Bach transcribed one of Friedemann's concertos for two claviers, most probably for them to play together, as we know they sometimes did. The old man may have been angling for another position for his son when he took him along on his famous visit to Frederick the Great in 1747 (or did Friedemann come to Potsdam on his own accord?). On good authority Bach is said to have written his set of six organ sonatas specially for Friedemann, who eventually gained (and squandered) a reputation as the best organist in Germany.

Williams, safe under the cover of his "sample hypothesis," proposes that this was the case with the Goldberg Variations, too. As is well known, Bach belonged to a multitudinous clan of musicians, to which he had every reason to feel very closely bound. Orphaned at the age of nine, he was taken in, educated, and put on his career path by his organist brother, a family obligation he himself would accept for several less-close relatives. He found time to draw up an elaborate family tree with more than fifty biographical squibs; he took special care of manuscripts containing the work of earlier Bachs and selected a motet by one of them, his second cousin Johann Christoph (not to be confused with his brother, his uncle, or several other Johann Christophs), for use at his own funeral. The persistent efforts he made to advance his sons' careers have a dynastic aspect to them, one feels. When Bach was a boy the clan held yearly reunions, at which, after some pious preliminaries,

> they sang popular songs, some comic, some bawdy, all together and extempore, but in such a manner that the parts made harmony of a sort, though the text in every part was different. They called this kind of harmony a Quodlibet and laughed heartily at it....[7]

We have this story from Forkel, Bach's biographer, who had it from Emanuel, who had it from Sebastian, so of course Friedemann knew about it too, and so he must have gasped when he came to the end of the Goldberg Variations—to Variation 30, the Quodlibet (so labeled), with its melange of overlapping folk songs, after a great whirl of virtuosity has subsided, and before the sarabande theme puts in its almost weirdly tranquil second appearance. He understood the Quodlibet as Keyserlingk and Goldberg never could. He also must have, would have, may have understood that the Goldberg Variations had given him the greatest accolade any virtuoso might ever receive, and at the same time another instrument that bound him to the Bachs.

—2005

---

7. See *The New Bach Reader*, p. 424 (translation modified).

8

A GUIDE TO
THE WELL-TEMPERED CLAVIER

WHERE DOES A Harvard undergraduate science major who has listened to Bach's *Well-Tempered Clavier* "several thousand times" turn to find a ready ear and encouragement for his singular passion? Not, it appears, to any of the notable musicians on the Harvard faculty, but to the even more notable Stephen Jay Gould, who barely raises an eyebrow and signs Eric Altschuler on as an advisee for two whole years. Altschuler produces a senior thesis, we may suppose, consisting of short accounts of each fugue of "The Forty-eight," as the British call *The Well-Tempered*, together with numerous miscellaneous glosses. He obtains a vigorous preface from his adviser, secures underwriting from two foundations (Ford, Fannie and John Hertz), hires an agent, and sure enough: his unlikely manuscript is taken up by a major trade publisher. The outcome is *Bachanalia: The Essential Listener's Guide to Bach's "Well-Tempered Clavier."*[1]

Survival of the fittest. But *Bachanalia* is a well-meaning book, for all of its unlikely evolution: sincere, enthusiastic, hardworking, and sometimes ingenious in its effort to help people who lack musical training or practical musical experience to enjoy music. The music in question is a limited, specialized, precious repertory, examined in

---

1. Little, Brown (1994).

much more loving detail than will be found in most books of "music appreciation." To be sure, such books tend to be written by musicians, musicologists, or music teachers, not by writers who admit to and indeed insist on the same amateur status as their readers. Altschuler courts his readers in prose "peppered with fascinating lore, abounding in good humor... full of playful, clever analogies to horror movies, human nature, football games, even sex," as the jacket copy puts it. Downloaded e-mail, it feels like to me, corny in the extreme; but this should not matter much if it works for the job at hand.

What does, in fact, *Bachanalia* teach about *The Well-Tempered Clavier?* Mainly, and obsessively, it deals with the fugal subjects, the short themes that are heard at the very beginning of every fugue and many, many times thereafter. The heart of the Listener's Guides that accompany each fugue discussion is a section entitled "Form," which lists each and every appearance or entry of the subject in the composition—all thirty-seven of them, in one case.[2] Getting his readers and listeners to follow the fugal subject becomes a major concern for this author. Most of his Listening Guides include a "Listening Hint" to help with entries that are difficult to hear.

All this rests upon the conviction, stated many times, that the main thing about a fugue is its subject. The glosses referred to above turn up in the book as miniature chapters or boxes, some grouped together as an introduction and others placed strategically in among the forty-eight fugue discussions. The last of these items, forming an envoi to the book, a veritable benediction, takes off from the old story of the man who asks a great rabbi to divulge all the wisdom of the Bible, only to be told:

"Love your neighbor as yourself. The rest is commentary. Now go and learn." Similarly, we can say, "The subject is the star of a fugue. The rest is commentary. Now go and listen."

---

2. There are errors: see the Fugues in F-Sharp Major Book I and C-Sharp Minor Book II.

Listen to what: the presence of the theme, or its content and character? Even the simplest of fugues, such as the Fugue in E Major of Book 1, one of Altschuler's professed favorites, gets lost in his account. Here much of the fun or the joy stems from Bach's treatment of a special feature of the speedy subject, the way it unexpectedly hits the tonic note E on a strong beat. A built-in trip wire threatens to halt the motion at any moment. Most times Bach slithers expertly past this danger spot, but he also annexes it for purposes of sectionalization; jogs it with a fake stretto entry; blurs it with an ostentatious suspension; and then cries told-you-so with a shortened entry designed to end the little piece with a little bang.

In any case, there is another view of what is central in Bach's fugues. "It is never the theme which is of central interest in a fugue, but the way the theme is embedded in the polyphonic structure," writes Charles Rosen. The material that comes in between the subject entries of a fugue, the episodes, cannot be regarded as mere ballast or spacing. Rosen writes, "It is the episodes that largely determine the total movement of the piece, give it its rhythmic continuity, and elaborate the harmonic motion."[3] Episodes develop details of the subject as the subject itself cannot do; they control the direction of the musical ebb and flow by determining most or all the modulations; they are at least as important as the subject entries in setting up the fugue's cadence structure, which in turn determines its total shape.

As for the subject, if it appears thirty-seven times in a fugue what must be important is the varying contrapuntal web accompanying all those entries. Countersubjects, invertible counterpoint, and the vicissitudes of stretto (the introduction of two subject entries in two voices in close succession)—all come into play here, with much else. What also matters is not just where entries occur but *how*—whether they

---

3. From the introduction to his Oxford Keyboard Classics edition *Bach: The Fugue*, edited by Charles Rosen (Oxford University Press, 1975), p. 3.

are worked in surreptitiously, for example, or introduced after an expectant pause; whether they proceed into the anticipated answer or into something very different; and above all, once again, how they are coordinated with the fugue's total shape as articulated by the cadences.

That Altschuler is aware of at least some of this seems clear from a number of discussions in his book. They are rather unhelpful discussions, however. Basically, the only information he gives about episodes consists of listing (and delighting in) sequential ones. He has little to say about cadences, let alone tonality. Invertible counterpoint, always at the octave, is acknowledged on no more than three occasions. The one extended technical chapter, which is in fact a good effort, deals with real and tonal answers to—the subject.

There is a deeper problem still with Altschuler's project. While most of Bach's music was indeed written to be listened to, by congregations or by select audiences, this is not exactly true of *The Well-Tempered Clavier*, or true only in a sense that needs special definition. Book I was composed or assembled from older material, in 1722, for didactic purposes: to make a statement about the tuning of keyboard instruments, and for the instruction of the young (some of the assembled material had recently figured in the notebook of Bach's son Wilhelm Friedemann). Parallel to Book I is Book II, dating from around 1740, though we know less about it. Just a very few of the older pieces in both books appear to derive from a public performance tradition; the others clearly bespeak the private world of the studio, and in certain strictly professional circles the work achieved an underground celebrity. Thirty years after Bach's death the child Beethoven was taught out of *The Well-Tempered Clavier*. It was revered by Schumann and Chopin.

So as the traditional musical canon formed itself in the nineteenth century, perhaps only Handel's *Messiah* came to hold so solid a place in it as did *The Well-Tempered Clavier*. Yet paradoxically it has never had a place in the musical repertory, that is, in any performance tradition. There was no social setting in Bach's time for playing these fugues before an audience, nor in Beethoven's, nor Chopin's, and there still isn't today. You are unlikely to have heard anything from *The Well-Tempered Clavier* at a concert recently, or on the car radio.[4]

This music, then, was to be listened to synergically, as it were, in conjunction with being played, while also being looked at in the (hand-copied, probably by the player) sheet music. Though *Bachanalia* calls itself an "Essential Listener's Guide," the activity of listening, as today we listen to music on records, was not essential for Bach. Rosen goes so far as to say that a Bach keyboard fugue

> can be fully understood only by the one who plays it, not only heard but felt through the muscles and nerves.... Only the performer at the keyboard is in a position to appreciate the movement of the voices, their blending and their separation, their interaction and their contrasts.... Part of the essential conception of the fugue is the way in which voices that the fingers can feel to be individual and distinct are heard as part of an inseparable harmony.[5]

This is the mandarin position, and difficult to dispute...though surely the word "fully" leaves a little room for maneuver. Surely just listening, without playing, will reveal *much* if not the *full* essence of fugues (the latter ideal being unattainable even to many keyboard performers or, viewed philosophically, to any at all). Surely if one listens intently and repeatedly to music, albeit at first in a limited fashion, sooner or later one will get to hear and understand more.

So, at least, I should like to believe. And so it was with real distress that I came to understand where Altschuler has got to, after his

---

4. But today complete performances of whole books are not uncommon (2007).

5. *Bach: The Fugue*, p. 3.

thousands of sessions with *The Well-Tempered Clavier*. Another of his major concerns is with rankings, modeled on the Baseball Hall of Fame. He makes much of his choices for the Top Ten Subjects, Top Ten Episodes, and Top Ten Fugues, the latter subdivided into the Superstar Four and the Other Greats. Superstar status is granted to the Fugues in C Minor and F-Sharp Major Book I and C Major and E-Flat Major Book II—short, simple, or very simple fugues with quick, bright subjects. Four others of the same general character appear among the Other Greats. But less-quick fugues that are complex, rich, and expressive leave Altschuler unmoved. C-Sharp Minor and F-Sharp Minor in Book I, D-Sharp Minor, B-Flat Minor, and B Major in Book II: he is able to plow through the subject entries in these pieces without revealing so much as a glimmer of aesthetic engagement. A suave, spontaneous, and not so slow miracle like D Major in Book II fares no better.

How miserable to have listened so often, and to have missed so much! Only one slow piece shows up among the Top Ten, and we also hear of a Long, Slow, and Not My Favorite Club. Brevity, in this league, is the soul of fugue. One can imagine the consternation of Donald Tovey, even though he notoriously disapproved of the slow, expressive D-Sharp Minor fugue in Book I, if he had lived to hear this work described as "long, slow, boring, hateful, odious" (albeit in one of Altschuler's good-humored passages). But Tovey, in particular,[6] and other past annotators and expositors of *The Well-Tempered Clavier* could have helped an innocent enthusiast like Altschuler appreciate some of these slow, rich fugues, just as he is now offering to help others appreciate the quicker ones.

The notion that he might have something to learn, and that his project might profit from reading about *The Well-Tempered*—there

---

6. See Donald Francis Tovey, "Commentary," in *J. S. Bach: The Well-Tempered-Clavier*, edited by Richard Jones (Associated Board of the Royal Schools of Music, 1994), 2 vols., reprinted (with a few omissions) from *Forty-eight Preludes and Fugues by J. S. Bach*, edited by Donald Francis Tovey and Harold Samuel (Oxford University Press, 1924), preface.

exists a substantial bibliography of monographs, student primers, annotated editions, and the like—seems entirely foreign to this recent scion of Harvard. The one book he cites is *The Bach Reader*, a marvel of positivistic anthologizing that by giving you all the documented "facts" about Bach, unconfused by interpretation, manages also to give the strong impression that nothing else is worth reading. Nor did Altschuler ever learn about *The Well-Tempered Clavier* from his piano teacher (he never had a piano teacher). She or he would not have needed to point out the subject entries, for with the music stuck up there on the rack, young Eric would have figured them out for himself. She might have said to bring out that motif a bit more, it's so nice, lean on this cadence, it's important, play this line more legato, with more expression, look, like this, and so on. Whatever she urged, whether we approve of it or not, she would have given her pupil a sense of the feel of the music, which is quite another thing than a preliminary analytical scheme for it. She is and she has always been, surprising as the thought might be to her, the essential voice of musical tradition.

After an initial impulse, soon stifled, to extend a hand to Eric Altschuler in commiseration, I have turned instead to brooding about today's musical culture, the culture that produced him. Years ago I floated an idea about Western music history, that it might be viewed as falling into millennium-long phases: initially an oral tradition, with people performing music from memory; then a period of literacy (a term Leo Treitler was using at the time), predicated on scores and partbooks to sing and play from; and now a new model determined by sound recording and the activity (or passivity) of listening. Musicians will have a tendency, and they should fight against it, to brush *Bachanalia* aside as a case of the deaf leading the deaf. Aloof from performing music, from reading it, and even from reading about it, this book is a true, dismaying product of the new dispensation.

—1994

9

WILFRID MELLERS ON BACH

WILFRID MELLERS IS known in England as a composer, an educator of
considerable importance, and a copious writer on music. His books
run from 1946 to the new millennium, books on music in society,
François Couperin and his milieu, American music, and the Beatles,
among other topics. In his mid-sixties, he produced as a sort of
summa a two-volume study of Bach and Beethoven as religious composers. From the first, *Bach and the Dance of God*,[1] it was clear that
this composite study was not to be confined to musical works of an
overtly sacred genre. The lingering medieval mind of Bach's Lutheran
heritage, Mellers believes, equated or all but equated the sacred and
the secular spheres, so that the entire body of Bach's music is, in the
deepest sense, religious.

Mellers began as a critic writing for *Scrutiny* in the 1930s. Later he
was influenced by Marx, then even more influenced by Jung. In consequence he comes to Bach's music, and to various aspects of his
music, in a resolutely transcendental frame of mind. The cry of the
newborn child and the drumming of primitive man are what he hears
echoing ecstatically behind the earlier instrumental compositions, of

---

1. Oxford University Press, 1981. The volume on Beethoven, *Beethoven and the Voice of
God* (Oxford University Press, 1983), came out two years later.

which he discusses the Brandenburg Concertos, the cello suites, and *The Well-Tempered Clavier.*

As for Bach's later instrumental music, of which he discusses the Goldberg and *Vom Himmel hoch* variations, that reflects number as the essence of the universe. In the former work, the canonic variations at the unison, second, third, fourth, etc., are interpreted one by one according to Jung's characterization of the magical-philosophical implications of the various numbers in *Psychology and Alchemy.* This view of the centrality of canon in Bach's late music, presented also in Douglas R. Hofstadter's musically illiterate *Gödel, Escher, Bach,* is particularly silly, inasmuch as Bach did not write canons in around 73 percent of the Goldberg Variations, the Musical Offering, and the Art of Fugue, and in each work the noncanonic parts include manifestly the most powerful and beautiful music.[2]

Music is dance, dance is rite, and rite is religion. Mellers's argument grows more resonant as he gets to Bach's church music, in central chapters devoted to the Passion according to Saint John and the Mass in B Minor. Story and dogma are one, and every aspect of the music makes its contribution to the overriding Christian truth. Bach sets individual musical numbers and sections of those numbers in specific keys associated with feelings and religious states. He constantly employs musical tropes with analogous symbolic associations, such as the "sacral" sarabande rhythm, the "lamenting" chromatic bass descent, "Trinitarian" triple-time meters, four-note patterns which trace the shape of the cross on the page, and so on. All of this is discussed in great detail, and the discussion itself is embedded in a running commentary of the tautological kind that Shaw parodied in a memorable passage, the one about "Shakespear, dispensing with the

---

2. The exception among the late works, the fully Canonic Variations on *Vom Himmel hoch,* was written as a demonstration of Bach's learning on his entry into Lorenz Mizler's select Society of the Musical Sciences. *Pace* Stravinsky, few musicians and listeners consider this work to be one of Bach's great successes.

customary exordium, announces his subject at once in the infinitive, in which mood it is presently repeated after a short connecting passage in which, brief as it is, we recognize the alternative and negative forms," and so on. Here is Mellers:

> In the first section . . . the ritornello theme droops over a bass that slowly pulses, broken by rests, from tonic to dominant and back; modulates to the dominant minor; and returns to the tonic by way of a touch of relative major. The gamba melody, unlike the bass, is sustained, but moves in arches, each descent followed by an ascent—painful both because of the incidental dissonances and because of the creeping lassitude of the dotted rhythm.

Dropping in a few affective adjectives like chocolate chips does not make this sort of thing more digestible. But in fact the adjectives are what really matter to Mellers, and one is puzzled by his maddening insistence on all this mindless description, which he cannot really bother to get right, let alone make relevant. His whole cast of mind militates against careful concentration on the mere particulars before his eyes and ears. It encourages what he calls "ecstasis," the rapt contemplation of the universal emanations behind the music.

That Bach (and his contemporaries) associated keys and musical tropes with theological and other ideas is not in question. Everybody knows, too, that Bach "signed" some of his compositions with the awkward little melody B-flat, A, C, B-natural (spelling BACH in German), and others with melodies containing 14 notes (B = 2, A = 1, C = 3, H = 8), and still others with melodies containing 41. What is in question is how he regarded and valued such procedures, and how we should regard them. Many critics see them as secondary aspects, conventions, quirks, tics, the small change of Bach's craft. Mellers sees them at the heart of the aesthetic-religious-transcendental experience, as the primary manifestation of the spirit behind the art.

The history of modern thought is that of a long, stubborn war against this animistic view of the world (and of art), fought on many different fields over many centuries. The last great battles took place in Bach's lifetime, and I am frankly more interested in trying to understand his own attitudes, allegiances, and ambivalences than in mounting yet another mop-up operation against the Jungian irregulars. Bach was born in 1685, in the same decade as Montesquieu, Alexander Pope, and Christian Wolff, on the threshold of the modern world. There is no doubt that he crossed over it slowly and cautiously—but cross it he did.

As a slow developer Bach contrasts vividly with Handel and Domenico Scarlatti, two other great composers who (as every Music I student knows) were born in the same year as Bach. Scarlatti moved fastest and farthest, first with operas and then with his masterful harpsichord sonatas prefiguring the musical style of the late eighteenth century. Handel, the great cosmopolitan, studied at the University of Halle, perhaps not very seriously, but under some of the first liberal thinkers in Germany, Christian Thomasius and August Hermann Francke. After making his first great success as an opera composer in Italy, he arrived in London just in time to be attacked by the *Spectator*. Seventeen years later his lifework was challenged by that astonishingly modern piece *The Beggar's Opera*. No one insensitive to these winds of change could have made his way in mid-century London; and Handel prospered.

Bach, whose stay-at-home life in Thuringia has always met with approval from German critics, went diligently through the orthodox Lutheran gymnasium curriculum. With its overriding emphasis on theology, this course of study had changed little since the days of Luther and Melanchthon. One of the earliest of Bach's many attested disputes, during his period as organist at tiny Mülhausen, has him ranged on the orthodox side against the Pietists. In his later career at Leipzig, he lost out repeatedly in similar disputes, in which the basic issue was doctrine and liturgy as against the Christian life. The closest he got to Enlightenment thought in this city (which had expelled the Pietistic reformer Christian Thomasius in 1690) was by way of some depressingly unenlightened secular cantata texts—*vers d'occasion*—by Johann Christoph Gottsched, who came to the University of Leipzig soon after Bach assumed the cantorate there in 1723. Although Gottsched's wife, the literary Luise, admired Bach and studied with one of his students, Bach never got on well with the university and in any case would have had nothing to say to the young professor who was enthusiastically adapting Addison's *Cato* and propagandizing for the application of French neoclassical standards in German letters.

As a writer of church music, however, Bach had really surrendered to Pietism long before coming to Leipzig. His earliest cantata librettos follow the seventeenth-century orthodox model, with a strict concern for doctrine and with words drawn from the Bible and traditional German hymns. Temperamentally Bach must have felt perfectly attuned to such librettos, and the best cantatas he wrote to them—No. 106, "Gottes Zeit is die allerbeste Zeit," and No. 4, "Christ lag in Todesbanden"—have a spiritual intensity and artistic integrity that he never matched later, in my opinion.

But as court organist at Weimar, during his mid-twenties, this young German from the heartland was confronted by two powerful Italian influences—one direct and musical, that of the high Baroque concerto style of Vivaldi, and the other indirect and literary, that of the operatic cantata libretto. Bach absorbed them both into the texture of his art. And the operatic cantata libretto was frankly Pietistic in impetus. The new librettists supplemented (sometimes even supplanted) texts taken from the Bible and the hymnal with personalized effusions attesting to the kind of born-again Lutheranism that was being promulgated by Spener, Thomasius, and Francke. Occasionally allegorical figures such as Hope and Fear discuss with one another, or more often the recitatives and arias are put into the mouths of anonymous meditating Christians.

It was a bastard form, and the fact that Bach labored at it with such brilliance and tenacity should not make us forget it. To transfer dramatic action to an inner, psychological theater of the Christian soul was an interesting idea in theory that did not work well in practice. Nor should we—can we—forget the sort of language employed by the cantata librettists, a maudlin late-Baroque extravagance that makes the imagery and diction of a poet such as Crashaw seem positively Gottsched-like by comparison. The only way one can swallow these librettos at all is by concentrating on the great religious thoughts behind them and ignoring the actual words—a transcendental stance which indeed comes easily to Mellers, who manages to write eighty pages on the Saint John Passion with scarcely a mention of any actual German words that Bach set to music. Bach's two Passions follow the new operatic cantata model, with the added complication that the words of the gospel are presented as a dramatic reading. One does not have to be a close student of biblical narrative to appreciate the problems caused by this casual violation of genre, especially when the gospel in question is that of Saint John.

That Bach's first step into the modern world was taken at Weimar in his twenties has been clear since the great nineteenth-century biography by Philipp Spitta. If we now also see a second step taken in his forties, at Leipzig, we see this largely as a result of the so-called "new chronology" for Bach, one of the proudest achievements of recent German musicology (not all that much more recent, however, than our own New Criticism). The salient fact that has emerged is that Bach wrote the great majority of his hundreds of church cantatas in one superhuman spurt from 1723 to 1727, rather than spreading them out to around 1740, as had been believed previously.

The first response to this—for everybody but Mellers—was to refocus seriously (if not to junk) the traditional picture drawn by Spitta of Bach as a "Gothic" artist committed steadfastly to the

Lutheran church. The seventy-year-old Friedrich Blume issued the major revisionist statement—Blume, of all German musicologists one of the most immensely eminent and official, himself a foremost authority on *evangelische Kirchenmusik*.[3] The next response was to wonder what Bach committed himself to instead. The well-known fact that in 1729 he took over the town Collegium Musicum, a sort of chamber music society, began to assume more and more significance. In an even more sharply revisionist article, Robert L. Marshall has portrayed Bach going through a sort of midlife crisis in 1728–1730, writing little music, withdrawing from his cantorial duties, and looking with increasingly envious eyes to Dresden—Catholic Dresden, seat of the Saxon court, where he often traveled to give organ recitals.[4] Under the composer Johann Adolph Hasse and his wife, the prima donna assoluta Faustina Bordoni, Dresden was just then becoming the German center for Italian opera in its newest stage—post-Baroque, post-Handel, and post-Vivaldi.

According to Marshall, Bach now introduces many features of the modern, Italianate, operatic or opera-derived style into both his instrumental and his vocal music. The latter encompasses not only secular cantatas, of which he writes more and more, but also sacred works such as the first layer of the Mass in B Minor (written for Dresden—perhaps for Faustina?) and the favorite Cantata No. 51 for coloratura soprano and trumpet obbligato, "Jauchzet Gott in allen Landen." He adopts features from Scarlatti (in the Goldberg Variations) and other post-Baroque composers, among whom must certainly be included his own son Carl Philipp Emanuel at Potsdam, a leading modernist. In 1747 Bach impressed Frederick the Great by

---

3. Compare Blume's "Outlines of a New Picture of Bach," *Music & Letters*, Vol. 44 (1963), pp. 214–227, with his *Two Centuries of Bach* (Oxford University Press, 1950; Da Capo, 1978).

4. "Bach the Progressive: Observations on His Later Works," *Musical Quarterly*, Vol. 52 (1976), pp. 313–357.

playing on Potsdam's fifteen fortepianos, and parts of the Musical Offering he subsequently sent the King have plausibly been identified as piano music, not harpsichord music. A few years ago the piquant information came to light that Bach actually served as an agent for Germany's first piano manufacturer, Gottfried Silbermann. He had traveled quite some way, after all, from the quiet organ lofts of Arnstadt and Mülhausen.

So when Bach prepared a final version of the Saint John Passion late in life—the original version dates from 1727—the most important thing he did besides canceling some ill-considered earlier revisions was to change the words of certain of the "operatic" numbers. He wrote some of the changes himself, Philipp Emanuel wrote others. For example, in the lengthy tenor aria agonizing over the scourging of Jesus, the original invitation transcendentally to merge "His blood-stained back" into "the most beautiful rainbow, God's token of Grace" was bowdlerized into "Thy sorrowful bitter suffering... must awaken joy in me," etc. What this does to the word–music relationship (and the musical symbolism) is horrendous, as Arthur Mendel emphasized in the commentary to his *Neue Bach-Ausgabe* edition of the Passion. But evidently taste in the 1740s would no longer admit texts of the kind Bach had accommodated himself to at the beginning of the century. I remember once hearing a learned disquisition by Mendel on this subject, which ended by evoking an imaginary scene at Potsdam in which Philipp Emanuel sits his father down with the score and remonstrates with the old gentleman. "*Nein, Papa, nein,*" he is supposed to have sighed, "*das kann man heute gar* nicht *sagen!*"

What all this history implants is the strong suspicion that Bach did not place anywhere near so much stock in the transcendental qualities of his music as Mellers believes. We cannot penetrate Bach's mind, but we can infer something about how it developed. Anthologizing and ordering his life's work became the obsession of his last years, very fortunately for us; and so far from turning his back on his church music after he had given up composing any, he sorted out his best Weimar organ chorale preludes, fixed up the B-Minor Mass, and carefully revised the Saint John Passion. But let us not forget (as Mellers almost does) that the masterpiece Bach left unfinished when he died was the last of a long series of didactic works, and one whose radical scope has not always been acknowledged. The greatest numbers in the Art of Fugue are not the canons, nor are they in fact even the most conspicuously learned, artificial, and "mathematical" of the fugues. The best of Bach's late music eschews the sort of musical or numerical symbolism that can associate it even half plausibly with hypothetical religious archetypes.

I relate all this history at perhaps tedious length partly because Mellers seems almost unaware of it. Mere facts, one comes to feel, have lost their reality for him as he contemplates the dance of God. He also appears not to have seen Arthur Mendel's Saint John edition, a rather celebrated piece of musical scholarship in the grand tradition, which appeared after long preparations in 1973–1974, together with its 350-page commentary volume.[5] The true text of the work, its history, its revisions, and the various versions through which it passed over a quarter of a century—these matters do not greatly interest Mellers. Thus he labors under Spitta's misapprehension that Bach added the great opening chorus "*Herr, unser Herrscher*," the final chorale, and the lengthy "Rainbow" aria with its preliminary arioso scored for viole d'amore and lute as improvements at one of the later revivals, though we now know they all figured in the original conception. The first number, the last number, the biggest number—these are three things one should really like an author writing about the Passion to be straight about.

---

5. *Johann Sebastian Bach: Neue Ausgabe Sämtliche Werke*, 2nd series, Vol. 4, *Johannes-Passion*, edited by Arthur Mendel (Bärenreiter, 1973; Kritischer Bericht, 1974). See also the Bärenreiter Miniature Score TP 197 (1975), with its pithy bilingual preface.

And from the narrowly musical point of view, what is disturbing (and, from a composer, even somehow shocking) is the carelessness of musical description and analysis. This cannot be because Mellers does not know, but because he has lost or is losing interest in what is actually there before his eyes and ears. He says he has learned as a writer about music from Schenker, Tovey, and Réti, but one can discover precious few traces in his book of the musical thought of any of these men. None of them, discussing, say, the aria "Ach, mein Sinn," which follows Peter's denial, would have made so much of analogies with the ceremonial but also sacral sarabande, or the chromatic *lamento* bass, or the key of F-sharp minor ("for Bach often a key of transcendence through suffering"), or even the abrupt arabesque at the very end of the vocal line, which

> directly recall[s] Peter's weeping arioso and the crowing cock.... Not surprisingly Bach, whose search for the spiritual was so deeply rooted in the corporeal, creates cock-crows of singular power and achieves from this equivocal bird a resolution which is not the less positive for being painful.... Despite the music's tough complexity, the major resolution cannot be gainsaid.

When you've heard one of those chromatic basses, I say, you've heard them all. And the point Mellers is making in connection with the equivocal cock seems to involve nothing more than a *tierce de Picardie*, the resolution to a major tonic chord that occurs in the last bar of minor-mode compositions of the time almost inevitably.

Bach and the Dance of God contains many illuminating and many sensitive remarks about musical details. Wilfrid Mellers is a distinguished musician who has studied and taught Bach over a lifetime. He rightly points out that in "Ach, mein Sinn," what makes the chromatic bass special is the halting rhythm of bar 2, and he rightly lays emphasis on the "frenzy," the "melodic release" at the end of the vocal line in this extraordinarily dramatic aria. But there is much, too, that he does not say. The frenzied vocal spurt near the end owes much of its force to a sudden stop of the bass on a pedal note a moment earlier, a rhythmic effect that resolves the halting rhythm of bar 2 and its many repetitions—they have begun to sound almost desperate—as well as anticipating another bass stop on a pedal in the final orchestral bars, after the voice has come to its close. The cadential music over this final pedal repeats *in* the tonic some music that had appeared before, parenthetically, *on* the dominant; what makes this major-mode resolution special is a harmonic effect of some subtlety.

Consideration should also be given to the aria's overall structure. Save for six bars taken up with this cadential music and four other bars, the whole piece consists of half a dozen repetitions or transpositions of the opening sixteen-bar orchestral passage (the *ritornello*) or of the first eleven bars of it—all this while new words keep tumbling out. As a constructive feat this seems no less fascinating intrinsically, and no less significant aesthetically, than the canonic schemes of the Goldberg and *Vom Himmel hoch* variations.

The above technical pronouncements may be found just as indigestible as Mellers's descriptions, but I claim they are at least potentially more nourishing. Strictly technical analysis is much overused and often misused in today's serious music criticism, but in reference to Bach's music—Beethoven's is another story—we could actually use more of it. I do not believe one can get to the heart of Bach's music without paying close attention to particulars as well as universals, and I also cannot believe that Bach, consummate technician and great teacher that he was, thought otherwise.

—1981

IO

MOZART: FOUR BIOGRAPHIES

PETER GAY'S *MOZART* in the concise Penguin Lives series tells the composer's story with grace and organizes it with dexterity.[1] It is not pitched at a very high level, and the author has not found anything very distinctive to say about his subject. Gay is a distinguished historian of the Enlightenment, but his remarks on social or intellectual forces that might illuminate the life and works of Mozart are familiar and strike no sparks.

Thus Gay calls the third of Mozart's operas with Lorenzo da Ponte, *Così fan tutte*, "a belated valentine to the Old Regime." Appearing as it did in 1790, only a few months after the storming of the Bastille, "there was still time for audiences to be frivolous, especially when frivolity was being served up by a genius." The English historian John Rosselli, in his equally concise *The Life of Mozart*,[2] says it better:

> Mozart's most perfect dramatic work enshrines a society where men and women need concern themselves only with delectable follies, and where reconciliation mends all in the name of sense. Music of ideal beauty lifts the ironies of the tale onto a plane of

---

1. Viking/Lipper, 1999.
2. Cambridge University Press, 1998.

grace—but that grace...is "an illusory realm forever beyond the pale of mundane reality yet somehow still true."...*Così fan tutte* is the fine flower of the old regime at its point of dissolution. Mozart's life as much as his art shows him on the cusp of change from the old world to the new.

Well, yes, one thinks: a simple, obvious point. Then again, on second thought, not so simple. For Mozart did not enshrine the ancien régime in *Così fan tutte* until after he and da Ponte had subverted it—in two much more radical operas. *The Marriage of Figaro*, a clear provocation in spite of music's soothing touch, was first performed in 1786. A year later came that least soothing of all eighteenth-century art works, *Don Giovanni*. Why the relapse?

The term "relapse," of course, is open to objection: the composer had limited control over the order in which librettos reached him; his "most perfect dramatic work" represents, if not an advance over *Don Giovanni*, levitation to a new aesthetic level. But the fact is that in the period of just a few years between those two operas, something serious happened to Mozart and his music—both to the quantity of that music (that is, his output) and also, more ambivalently, to its quality. This needs to be faced up to in any Mozart biography, and indeed there is a book, *The Mozart Myths* by William Stafford, in which biographers are assessed and categorized according to their treatment of this very matter.[3]

David Schroeder will have none of it; his *Mozart in Revolt*[4] "is not a biography of Mozart; if anything, it will make a biography more difficult to write" (even though "rebellion," as it happens, if not "revolt," is one of Stafford's categories). Revolt is a secondary topic

---

3. *The Mozart Myths: A Critical Reassessment* (Stanford University Press, 1991).

4. *Mozart in Revolt: Strategies of Resistance, Mischief and Deception* (Yale University Press, 1999).

of this book, less original and cogent than its central thesis, which is a relatively narrow one about the Mozart family letters and how they should be read.

Mozart biography has to lean heavily on his correspondence and that of his family, including especially that of his father, Leopold—those three fat volumes that have fascinated so many readers: Mozart now as effervescent as a piano concerto finale, now as caustic as *A Musical Joke*, now as pathetic as a soprano aria in G minor. This last mood appears only in a much-discussed set of begging letters written in 1788–1791 to Michael Puchberg, a wealthy cloth merchant, friend, and Masonic brother. These letters furnish the chief source of information about Mozart's severe financial straits at this time, and also the most vivid testimony to his state of mind. Abject and desperate, barely clinging to his self-respect, Mozart "opens his heart" to Puchberg in a distressing show of groveling and self-flagellation:

> O God!—I can hardly bring myself to despatch this letter—and yet I must! If this illness had not befallen me, I should not have been obliged to beg so shamelessly from my only friend. Yet I hope for your forgiveness. . . . Adieu. For God's sake forgive me, only forgive me!—and—Adieu![5]

Can we, must we abide this? Letter writing for Mozart was not the spontaneous expression of one's real feelings, Schroeder maintains. It was a calculated literary exercise with an end in view. He notes the special passion for carnival on the part of both Mozart and his father, and he sees Wolfgang as Harlequin, slipping on one new mask after another for his different encounters. The son learned about writing letters from the father, who as an author of some note (Leopold's

---

5. *The Letters of Mozart and His Family*, translated and edited by Emily Anderson (Macmillan, 1938), Vol. 3, pp. 1383–1385. For the remark "Open my heart," see p. 1361.

treatise on violin playing gained him considerable cachet) absorbed the literary culture of his time—an epistolatory literary culture exemplified by Richardson, Montesquieu, and Voltaire. Baron Melchior Grimm and Mme d'Epinay, the Parisian friends and supporters of the Mozarts, were both great letter writers; he was responsible for that major instrument of the *philosophes*, the *Correspondance littéraire*, and she for several epistolatory texts, one entitled *Letters to My Son*.

Leopold Mozart resolved to publish a biography of his "miraculous" son—he announced this in print: it would have been an epistolatory biography, no doubt, inspired by the epistolatory essay *Lessons from a Father to a Son* by Christian Fürchtegott Gellert, a midcentury poet, fabulist, and moralist much admired by German readers who thought of themselves as up-to-date and respectably enlightened. Leopold had corresponded with Gellert. His beautifully turned out bulletins to his family and to others in Salzburg describing the European triumph of his two child prodigies, circulated, copied, and carefully preserved, would have filled the opening chapters. Gellert also wrote two manuals on letter writing (Lord Chesterfield wrote one too): he enjoined parents to leaven moral advice with wit and pleasing anecdote. Leopold covers every grain of advice offered by Gellert's father and provides an irresistible narrative to sugar the pill.

Once taught the art and artifice of letter writing by his father, Wolfgang used it against him in the long, coruscating epistolatory war of independence. This began in 1777, when at the age of twenty-one he embarked on a long job-hunting tour to various points in Germany and then Paris, accompanied by his mother—"one of the most famous disasters in musical biography," as one observer has put it[6]— and continued well past 1781, when he quit Salzburg for Vienna and the freelance life. Veracity was a casualty in this war, as Leopold soon

---

6. Ruth Halliwell, *The Mozart Family: Four Lives in a Social Context* (Clarendon Press, 1998), p. 231.

understood (and as Wolfgang once even admitted). All Mozart's statements of fact must be scrutinized as possible disinformation, all his declarations of piety and virtue as possible camouflage.

Mozart applied what he had learned to his other correspondents—his wife, friends, creditors. He grew adept at telling them what they wanted to hear. Discovering in Puchberg a susceptibility to the discourse of ego collapse, he spun out tales with what Schroeder calls "The Virtuosity of Deceit":

> For Puchberg, Mozart acted a role he played for no one else, becoming for him a real-life sentimental *épistolier*, a familiar character emerging from the pages of a recognizable literary genre to touch his subject's heart (and, in this case, purse).

Wolfgang Hildesheimer, too, in his provoking biographical study of 1982—the study that will not go away—evoked an eighteenth-century artistic genre to interpret the abject letter to Puchberg from which I have quoted. He read it as accompanied recitative:

> It begins with the exclamation "*Gott!*," much like the "*Deh!*" of *opera seria*. According to the musical grammar of the Neapolitan school, this would be a G minor chord. It is the heroine innocently plunged into distress. The pain is genuine, but the effect upon the recipient is a calculated one. A few lines later, with confused interjections, the declamatory tone dissolves and gives way to unrhetorical lament, a theme with abundant variations.[7]

Even John Rosselli, who never misses an opportunity—who indeed creates opportunities—to reject unsupported speculation about the

---

7. *Mozart*, translated by Marion Faber (Farrar, Straus and Giroux, 1982), p. 24.

composer, credits Hildesheimer's interpretation here, and one can see why. We would rather have Mozart devious than miserable.

He *was* miserable, however, all the same. The letter to Puchberg says he is too ill and miserable to compose—a threat, Schroeder might say, that he will not be able to start working again, so as to be able to work off his debts, without another loan. In fact he really was composing next to nothing when he wrote the letter and this was driving him crazy, or at least into a state that made people stop and stare.

Mozart's fallow periods are glossed over in many biographies, yet the statistics are plain enough. In good times the record he maintained of all his work—his *Verzeichnüss aller meiner Werke* —expanded as prodigiously as Leporello's catalog in *Don Giovanni*, tallying in one year, 1786, four concertos, a symphony, three trios, a string quartet, a piano quartet, a sonata for piano four hands, *The Marriage of Figaro*, and a dozen smaller pieces. In 1787, however—coincidentally or not, the year of Leopold Mozart's death— Wolfgang's output began to slow. After *Così fan tutte*, premièred in January 1790, he produced nothing of any scope for at least four months, and in midyear only a spasm of "oppressive labor" (*mühsame Arbeit*) led to the completion of two string quartets that were already half written (K. 589, 590). Then he remained inactive for another five months. The turnaround came in December, when he completed three very substantial works: a string quintet, an adagio and allegro for mechanical organ, and a piano concerto (K. 593, 594, 595).

Explanations for this dip in productivity have often been brought forward. War broke out between Austria and Turkey, distracting and dispersing the patrons Mozart relied on for commissions and subscriptions to his concerts. Emperor Joseph II died soon after the opening of *Così fan tutte* and the theaters closed. His successor showed Mozart less favor. Rosselli adds that in 1788 Joseph authorized opera to be performed during Lent, an action that drew audiences away from concerts, the staple of a freelance career. All in all, he seems satisfied with these explanations.

However, Mozart's difficulties with composition did not begin in 1790. They go back at least to his trip to Paris with his mother in 1777–1778. En route, friends at Mannheim helped get him a substantial commission for several flute concertos and flute quartets, but only a few of them were done when it came time to go on to Paris. So he collected less than half of the promised two hundred gulden, which was no small matter. Short of money, the travelers were receiving missives from home full of dire financial warnings, for they had repeatedly cited this commission as their best prospect. Wolfgang had been too busy to finish, he wrote Leopold. "Moreover, you know that I become quite powerless whenever I am obliged to write for an instrument which I cannot bear."[8] Really? How deeply can one hate the flute? To judge from those flute pieces that he does seem to have completed, it couldn't have taken him long to churn out some more. Although Wolfgang was indeed busy, now that he was out of Leopold's oversight for the first time in his life, he could write what interested him, not what Leopold demanded of him. He was writing a mass that he hoped would impress the Elector Karl Theodor, not dull chamber music that he knew would get him paid.

One can take Wolfgang's letter as a veiled way of telling Leopold this. Or perhaps he was reporting on an actual writer's block. Perhaps we have here the first sign of a syndrome that can be deduced for the rest of his life. Peter Gay attributes Mozart's problems in his late years to his lifelong contest with his father, a construction drawn from Maynard Solomon's important biography of 1995, where it is developed at length.[9] Leopold, according to Gay,

---

8. *The Letters of Mozart and His Family*, Vol. 2, p. 711.

9. *Mozart: A Life* (HarperCollins, 1995). Gay includes a tribute to this book in his Bibliographical Note.

implanted in his son irreparable feelings of guilt and an awareness of emotional and financial obligations left unfulfilled, obligations that would continue to plague Mozart as long as he
lived.... Leopold Mozart had taught Mozart that to fail to repay
loans promptly was to lose one's credit, and to lose one's credit
was to lose one's honor. The father, even more powerful in death
than he had been in life, had, it seems, won the duel after all.

Gay's focus here is on Mozart "The Beggar"—his chapter title—
rather than Mozart the composer. If we balance submission to parental
demands on one level with resistance to them on another, the picture
may become clearer. Distaste (or lack of enthusiasm) for the flute trig-
gered his first episode of aggressive writer's block. Later in life, there
were more such episodes, and by this time it looks as though in general he did not function at his best except under unusual stimulus, a
sort of musical shock therapy.

Not only did the quantity of his music shrink, something happened
to its quality. A change in its mood, hard to analyze, has evoked adjectives from commentators and other listeners such as simple, spare,
disengaged, resigned, veiled, death-chilled, melancholy, or merely
sad. "Every stirring of energy is rejected or suppressed," said one of
them.[10] Mozart's music of the later 1780s has lost the verve and the
immediacy of the earlier music. It does not communicate as unself-
consciously as it once did, as though the composer, less involved, is
beginning to lose interest in his audience.

The change comes through most clearly in those beloved music-
theater pieces where Mozart, at the piano, puts on a dazzling show
for his admirers, those of them in the orchestra as well as those in
the audience. Passionate piano concertos in the minor mode work the

---

10. Alfred Einstein, *Mozart: His Character, His Work*, translated by Arthur Mendel and
Nathan Broder (Oxford University Press, 1945), p. 314.

crowd as ably as scintillating ones in the major—no fewer than fifteen piano concertos between 1782 and 1786. In contrast to these extroverted scores, Piano Concerto No. 27 in B Flat, K. 595, of 1788–1791 has become "a touchstone of Mozart's 'late style,'" in Rosselli's words. One passage "has about it an infinite yet detached mercy," another "work[s] through a pallid to an uncanny and, last, to a universal sadness, yet the music never raises a cry, never goes beyond self-communion." When the piano first enters in this concerto, far from trumping the orchestra's theme it offers a subtly submissive variant, and when the orchestra responds to the piano, the response almost fades away. Solo and orchestra have become slightly wary collaborators here. Something new (and certainly something very beautiful) has replaced the vivacious and stimulating friction in the old solo/orchestra relationship.

Rosselli responds to the special beauty of works from what he calls "The Last Phase" and also to their reserve. In the Clarinet Concerto of Mozart's last months, passion seems withdrawn:

> A conductor can nudge it towards wanness, but even that goes no further than the transparency of a life self-consumed; Mahler's "farewell" last movements in *Das Lied von der Erde* and the Ninth Symphony are, by comparison, memory-laden.... The astonishing modulations, the varied wind harmony of the "royal" piano concertos and the late symphonies give way to accompaniments so finely calibrated as to make a sound at once enchanting and diaphanous. We might call this the draining of Eros from Mozart's creative personality.

For a palpable sense of the sheer joy of creation, it is hard to match Mozart's earliest opera for Vienna, *The Abduction from the Seraglio*, dating from just before the earliest of the Viennese concertos. This is a composer exuberantly at the top of his form, showering the singers with everything they needed to impress and more, luxuriating in the orchestra, and turning out such unheard-of inventions as Pedrillo's serenade and Osmin's famous breakdown in the closing vaudeville. For the first time he found a marvelous musical outlet for his notoriously well-developed sense of fun, in the comic numbers and also in the so-called Turkish music that crashes ludicrously into the score at unexpected moments. (Not much of this drum-thumping, triangle-rattling, and piccolo-squealing survives the decorum of today's productions, such as the one in New York in 1999. In spite of the New York City Opera's capacity for amplification, only "early music" performances and recordings give us a charivari, Mozart with his carnival noisemakers.)

Also palpable, in the operas of the mid-1780s, is his more mature elation at the new dramatic virtuosity he could achieve in *The Marriage of Figaro*. With *Don Giovanni*, the virtuosity turns hectic, tragic, obscene. *Così fan tutte*, on the other hand, "an opera about opera," is exquisite, literary, and super-sophisticated; low humor is now out of the question, and the wit is tinged with melancholy. One year later, in 1791, came *La clemenza di Tito*—"a distinguished work," Rosselli remarks, yet

> how much of it lives in the minds of the audience after curtain fall? ... We seem to hear the composer turning out music to a high standard but deliberately rather than spontaneously engaged.

Increasingly, I think, this composer needed the stimulus of novel challenges. *The Abduction*, needless to say, had provided such a challenge—his first opera for Vienna. So had *Figaro*: he had been starved of the theater for four years, and collaboration with da Ponte made it all the more exhilarating; he had never before sat down with a librettist on terms of intellectual equality. With *Don Giovanni* the stimulus was the subject, not the poet. I have never felt that Mozart was happy with the libretto of *Così fan tutte*.

The troubled genesis of the quartets for King Wilhelm Friedrich of Prussia seems indicative. On the return journey from his visit to the Prussian court in 1789, Mozart got to work at once, drafted three quartets almost simultaneously, and brought one to completion; yet he let a year go by before finishing the others. He had risen to a self-imposed challenge: since the King was a cellist, the texture of the scores would be heavily biased toward the cello parts. Then after finishing one piece he lost interest or impetus. He always found the medium of the string quartet difficult, and in the last movements of the "Prussian" Quartets the cello returns to its normal role.[11]

With the three last symphonies of 1788 we may infer an unspoken challenge from Joseph Haydn. Like Mozart's earlier set of six string quartets, these symphonies laid claim to a genre that Haydn had made his own, and that Mozart would now enhance. The two earlier symphonies from the Vienna years (the "Linz" and the "Prague") had not achieved the individuation of character that he now provided for the "Jupiter" Symphony and its companions in E flat and G minor. There is no lack of verve or engagement in these great works.

But an entirely unsubstantiated anecdote tells about another case of writer's block. For the première of *La clemenza di Tito* in 1791, the maestro is in Prague with the singer Josepha Duschek, a friend of many years. But where is the overture? Messenger after messenger arrives to call for it:

---

11. This was a particularly elegant discovery by Alan Tyson, in *Mozart: Studies of the Autograph Scores* (Harvard University Press, 1987), pp. 36–47 (see Chapter 11). Tyson was also the first to doubt statements in Mozart's letters of 1789 to the effect that six quartets (and six piano sonatas that were never written) had in fact been commissioned from Berlin, doubts taken up by Maynard Solomon in his revisionist reading of all the letters from Mozart's enigmatic trip to that city (*Mozart*, Chapter 28). Like many such readings by Solomon, this one is resisted by Rosselli and Gutman. Schroeder as usual does not mention skepticism about letters registered by other scholars, and not many will prefer his idea about the present batch (Mozart was considering an epistolary autobiography) over Solomon's (Mozart was having an affair).

Mozart calmly answered the reiterated injunction with "Not a single idea will come." [Josepha] shouted at him, "Then for heaven's sake begin it with the cavalry march!" He flew to the spinet and after the first two bars of the cavalry march, with which the overture really does begin, the melodies tumbled into place, the overture was finished, was quickly orchestrated, and the messengers hurried off with the sheets, still wet.[12]

While the messengers hurrying in and out with their inky papers sounds like a clip from *Amadeus,* the idea of Mozart dragooned into action by a musical joke sounds right.

Two great projects came his way in his last year to raise his spirits, *The Magic Flute* and the Requiem. He would have found much about the opera project stimulating: the novelty of it, the Masonic aspect, the solemnity and the silliness, perhaps the invitation to reinvent the flute, as well as the incentive, not always considered salutary, of Schikaneder's companionship. Emanuel Schikaneder was the easy-living actor-manager who wrote the libretto, with Mozart looking over his shoulder. Robert W. Gutman also believes that the project realized a long-standing ambition to create a major German opera.[13] Although he may take Mozart's statements to this effect too seriously, since other statements record his enthusiasm for Italian opera, something must account for *Zaide,* the *Singspiel* he composed in 1779–1780 almost to the end—an hour and half of music—without any commission. German opera had launched Mozart's career in Vienna; Gutman thinks that he got Schikaneder to model the plot of *The Magic Flute* on *The Abduction,* which remained Mozart's greatest success.[14] In

---

12. Otto Erich Deutsch, *Mozart: A Documentary Biography,* translated by Eric Blom et al. (Stanford University Press, 1965), pp. 571–572.

13. *Mozart: A Cultural Biography* (Harcourt Brace, 1999), p. 735.

14. It was enormously popular. By 1790 it had been staged ninety times all over Europe, as far as Amsterdam (without, of course, earning any royalties).

both operas a noble young man with a humble companion sets out to rescue his beloved from a tyrant who turns out to be benign, and in both the lovers prepare to meet death together just before the end.

As for the Requiem: before this commission began to haunt Mozart he must have welcomed it. He had just gained the promise of a good position at St. Stephen's Cathedral, where the Kapellmeister seemed near death, so he would now be devoting himself to church composition for the first time in years. He seems to have had his eye on this position for some time, and had begun making sketches with sacred texts. It is a tragedy that the Requiem was left unfinished at Mozart's death and had to be completed by his student Franz Xaver Süssmayr; a performance is always a trial because one cannot shut one's ears (or walk out) when Süssmayr's portions are sounding. Gutman solemnly exonerates Süssmayr: "If, at moments, solecisms mar its instrumentation or musical grammar, the burden sustained by a mediocre talent attempting to intuit the processes of genius provides pardon." More to the point, Rosselli remarks sourly that parts of "this hybrid work...are merely decorous—and they are not all Süssmayr's."

Perhaps. But both this unfinished and certainly uneven work and *The Magic Flute* mark a return, I think, from the mood of *Tito* and the late concertos. Mozart was newly engaged. If he had lived, he would likely have written his best (perhaps his only) music to meet further unprecedented trials—challenges, breaks, dares that would have come his way or that he would have gone out of his way to find. Like Tamino and Pamina he would have emerged, as W. H. Auden wrote, "out into sunlight."

Clearly a labor of love, *Mozart: A Cultural Biography* by Robert W. Gutman is the fullest biography available, the most colorful and crowded, and the most oracular in tone. The author announces at once his loving admiration for this affectionate and generous man, an austere moralist of vital force, incisiveness, and strength of purpose who, though—like all—bearing the blame of faults and lapses, yet played his role in the human comedy with honor, engaging with grace the frustrations of his complicated existence: his goodness of heart, unaffected charm, winning ways, and self-humor run like gorgeous threads through its web.

Hence Gutman's devotion to all the minutiae of Mozart's career, his determination to fill in every detail of fact and implication to be squeezed out of the letters, whatever the cost in compacted sentences and breathless footnotes. Virtually every personage visited, every opera attended, every music lesson, every hostelry gets its mention. Also included are sections or whole chapters on the Enlightenment, the War of the Austrian Succession, Freemasonry—where is the storming of the Bastille?—and annotated lists of music throughout.

The contingency of biography is barely acknowledged in this book. If there are gray areas in Mozart biography, or other writers with divergent things to say about it, the reader will never know. The only documentation given is for the two thousand or so quotations, mostly from the Mozart family letters. Gutman has read the necessary literature, though he does not cite or credit it, and as he says, the reader "will discover more than one unaccustomed interpretation of familiar documents and incidents" in his text, though he does not say where. In those that I have detected, speculation is sometimes pushed hard. I have learned from some and disagree with others.

What I also detect is a resolve to put the best possible construction on everything Mozart said, felt, and did—another outcome of this biographer's attested admiration for his subject. In eight hundred pages Gutman includes only one or two sentences on the begging letters to Puchberg and none at all on Mozart's reported strange behavior in the late years[15]—his depression, his involuntary hand movements, his inappropriate horseplay. Even his students receive the benefit of the doubt, as the sentence about Süssmayr demonstrates. High on detail, low on focus, *Mozart: A Cultural Biography* is biased inexorably by love.

—2000

---

15. On the favorite mystery of Mozart biography, where did the money go, Gutman does not see this as a problem. Rosselli thinks that the pattern of loans suggests gambling losses, a theory also voiced by others. But Rosselli has no good answer to the standard objection, which is that gambling does not figure at all in the inordinate mass of posthumous rumor and gossip.

II

MOZART'S LAST YEAR

THAT PETER SHAFFER'S *Amadeus*, play and movie, left in its wake widespread curiosity, even anxiety, about its eponymous antihero is probably true. At parties musicologists are still being asked what Mozart was "really" like, what "really" did him in. What went wrong in his last years? At the more bookish of such parties, people remember the disturbing *Mozart* by Wolfgang Hildesheimer, Shaffer's inspiration, which appeared in translation in 1982.[1] So I am not at all surprised to learn from the music historian H. C. Robbins Landon that he was pressed to write *1791: Mozart's Last Year*, on Mozart's "decline and fall"—his own term, and his own quotes: a book that, on the basis of "authentic and contemporary documents," would set the record straight.[2]

Landon both was and wasn't the obvious choice for such a job. Probably no other scholar has looked at so many documents pertaining to eighteenth-century music and musical life. Well known as an indefatigable Haydn researcher, editor, biographer, and booster, he is the author of a five-volume *Haydn: Chronicle and Works* that consists of upward of three thousand pages of documentary material,

---

1. Translated by Marion Faber (Farrar, Straus and Giroux).

2. Schirmer, 1988.

along with unbuttoned commentary on his music. But Landon has not shown himself to be a particularly subtle or, it must said, always a careful reader of those documents. What he enjoys is recycling great sheaves of eighteenth-century data in an enthusiastic, alfresco style that certainly resembles no other current musicological discourse. And so he has produced an amiable little mine of miscellaneous information about Mozart's last year, 1791, some of which is old, some quite new, and some entirely original. All of it will be of interest to Mozart buffs. A series of short chapters go into considerable detail about Viennese concert life, Mozart's "second career" as a composer of dance music and his prospects as a church composer, his concert trips, major projects such as *The Magic Flute*, his final illness and death, the later history of the man who commissioned the Requiem, "Constanze [Mozart]: A Vindication," and so on.

Landon also has his say about the picture drawn by Hildesheimer and Shaffer of Mozart's personality. The trouble here is that Landon is not much of a psychologist; his perceptions about the motives, attitudes, and feelings of historical subjects tend to be one-dimensional. And while he knows very well, of course, how to read documents skeptically, he reads them for their facts, not for their nuances. Reading for implicit references and meanings is just where Hildesheimer excels—though also where he is most irresponsible. The trick to picking apart Hildesheimer's devious web of argument, speculation, presupposition, and innuendo is to discover which threads are genuine. Or, in Shaffer's case, which will play.

To all this Landon seems impervious. He casually mentions the well-known memoir by Caroline Pichler:

> Mozart hummed the melody with me [she was at the piano playing "Non più andrai" from *Figaro*], and beat time on my shoulders; suddenly, however, he pulled up a chair and began to improvise variations so beautifully that everyone present held

his breath.... But all at once he had had enough; he jumped up and, as he often did in his foolish moods, began to leap over tables and chairs, miaowing like a cat, and turning somersaults like an unruly boy.

(When she was young, Pichler's father, a well-to-do amateur, held quartet parties which provided Mozart with some support. Later she became something of a literary light in Vienna, and was the author of several Schubert song texts.) In fact, Landon does not fail to mention all of the things we would like explained—Mozart's erratic, disoriented behavior, the mystery of his disappearing assets, the rumors of his profligacy, the evidence of his declining status. But Landon dismisses such matters with a commonsensical shrug; maddeningly, he often tucks away more substantial bits of counterevidence in short endnotes, where they are not pursued.[3] For him, Mozart was a good man, a solid professional, and a loving husband, a model of normalcy and probity. This strikes Landon as so obvious that he doesn't even bother to engage with Hildesheimer (or even Shaffer) on their own psychological ground.

Landon may be right about Mozart's psyche, but those who have stayed curious or anxious about it for all these years are not likely to be convinced by his soft arguments. Ultimately the polemic that was supposed to give the book its rationale remains detached from all the discursive historical material. The historical data he presents also remain detached from any sense of the actual music, the pieces Mozart wrote in 1791—the Requiem, the two late operas, the last

---

3. An example is Landon's treatment of the old rumor that the son born to the Mozarts in 1791 was illegitimate. It would appear that this is effectively scotched by a report that the child inherited a special ear-form ("Mozart Ear") from his father. Yet Landon does not mention the report except in an endnote, and even there he does not trouble to establish its credentials. He does, on the other hand, scold Alan Tyson for bringing up the rumor—rather unfairly, since Tyson was commenting upon Hildesheimer's heavily embroidered version of it (*The New York Review*, November 18, 1982).

string quintets and concertos (or at least parts of them), and a number of smaller works. For in a departure from his usual practice, Landon forgoes any attempt to engage with the music by means of critical discussion or commentary. That was his choice, of course; but I think the book will seem thin to many readers as a result.

Much that is of value in Landon's book consists of summaries of recent research—by a medical historian, Peter J. Davies, on Mozart's illnesses; by Else Radant on his apartment and wardrobe (with many illustrations); and by Landon himself on his Masonic brothers. (To Davies Mozart's personality is no mystery; he categorizes it as obsessional, infantile, and prone to paranoia "associated with a possessive jealousy and emotional lability"—a description that leaves Landon unruffled.) The information Landon presents about the most hectic episode of Mozart's last year—the composition of *La clemenza di Tito* for the coronation of Emperor Leopold II, at Prague—is summarized from an essay by Alan Tyson reprinted in *Mozart: Studies of the Autograph Scores*.[4] This is a collection of studies begun in 1975 that have appreciably changed the accepted chronology of Mozart's music. The book's synoptic essay, "Redating Mozart: Some Stylistic and Biographical Implications," indicates the scope of this body of research precisely. Its method, the details of which Tyson sets forth again and again with the greatest of elegance and expertise, rests on the physical analysis of the paper of Mozart's autographs.

The autograph score of *La clemenza di Tito*, to take that as our example, proves upon close examination to include five different types of paper, seemingly shuffled at random. The papers can be sorted according to their quality, watermark, and the way the music staffs are ruled. They can also be chronologically ordered, if not always dated exactly. When information obtained in this way is put together with other historical evidence, we see that when Landon

---

4. Harvard University Press, 1989.

calls the composition of this opera "a rather hair-raising operation" he is indulging, if anything, in understatement. As has long been known, the planning of *Tito* was botched. The work was needed for an imperial wedding in Prague on September 6, 1791, but only on July 8 was an impresario sent off to Vienna to commission it. No subject, composer, or librettist was specified, though Salieri seems to have had first refusal. Even after signing up Mozart and the librettist, Mazzoli, the impresario still had to dash off to Italy and engage the singers.

There must have been some kind of marathon all-night story session. We can imagine Mazzoli throwing up his hands; all he could do on this schedule was adapt a classic text by Metastasio. Mozart for his part found a way to save a little time by incorporating a big concert aria he had already composed, on what Tyson labels Paper Type IV (though in the event, the piece required rewriting at a later stage— see Types III and V). Then he reached for some ternions of a later paper, Type I, and began composing not the opera's solo and ensemble numbers in the sequence of the actual libretto, but, rather, selected ensembles—because in those, evidently, it would be less damaging not to take into account the vocal idiosyncrasies of singers who had yet to be engaged.

According to tradition, the opera was composed in eighteen days, which by Landon's calculation is about right for the time Mozart would have had available to compose the main arias (on Type III) after learning about the singers. Then, after coming to Prague on August 28, he used local paper (Type V) for the overture and some loose ends, and also for some extra numbers for Titus, a role that apparently ballooned at the last moment. The various batches of paper were of course interleaved so as to produce a sequential score. Unshuffle them, and we learn something about how the opera was composed.

Tyson tells this story at some length (Landon retells it). It is certainly an interesting one. Its "biographical implications," as Tyson would say, are clear. Mozart wrote very fast but not as fast as legend demands; he paced his work shrewdly to meet practical conditions; and even so, he had to stop and rewrite in ways that can be specified quite closely. Looking at the whole book, the biographical implications of Tyson's various discoveries are wide, in fact. Back in 1778, on Mozart's trip to Paris, he produced a good deal less music than one would gather from letters to his father, Leopold. His *Musical Joke* was not written right after Leopold's death in 1787, much less in jeering response to it, as was claimed by Hildesheimer; most of the piece was written earlier. In spite of this composer's reputation for great facility, he had chronic difficulty with one genre, at least: the string quartet.

Less clear are the "stylistic implications" of a study such as that of *La clemenza di Tito*. One would like to know more, for example, about the ensembles that Mozart composed in a less "characteristic" vocal style than the arias. Once alerted to this disparity, will we notice it when listening to the opera? How will we respond to an opera in which characters speak in a more nuanced, personal musical language in moments of meditation than they do in episodes of interaction? Tyson never pursues such questions. Mozart, as he gracefully remarks, is "the man whose genius is the only excuse for inquiries such as the present one"; but Tyson has chosen as his subject Mozart's manuscripts, Landon Mozart's last year, and neither scholar takes it upon himself to trace the impact of such studies on our understanding of Mozart's genius, on an interpretation of the music which is the residue of that genius.

Given the popularity of this composer's concertos in our time—in 1988 the Schwann CD Catalog listed twenty CDs of the D-Minor Piano Concerto, K. 466, including the Bilson and Lubin fortepiano performances which have elicited so much comment and reaction— the disclosure that as many as six of these works were begun (on one paper type) several years before they were completed (on another) is perhaps the most interesting and suggestive of all the discoveries that have come out of paper studies. Tyson seems to acknowledge this, though he does not pursue it.[5] Two of the works whose autographs he has studied, Piano Concerto No. 27 in B Flat, K. 595, and the Clarinet Concerto, have long held a special place among the denizens of that "hauntingly beautiful autumnal world of music written in 1791," as Landon puts it, "where the sun's rays are slanting sharply and are soon to turn into sunset and twilight." Tyson shows that the two concertos were both begun before Labor Day, as it were, during the high summer of the "Jupiter" Symphony. He places the beginning stage for the opening movements of K. 595 in 1788, and of the Clarinet Concerto "possibly even as early as 1787."

Received opinion about the style of this music would certainly seem to be due for some strenuous revision, as Tyson suggests:

> Any sharp picture of stylistic development must acknowledge that some works were started, and in certain cases a good part of the first movement outlined, long before their completion date.... The implications of this for style-study are obvious, and I need not dwell on them.

Dwell he does not, and it is ungracious to ask a scholar of Tyson's eminence to exceed the boundaries of a carefully delimited project. Still, the sharp focus on musicological method here leaves musical implications hazy.

—1988

---

5. To be sure, the book is not set up for extended treatment of the concertos; none of Tyson's individual studies concentrates on a piano concerto autograph. There is an illuminating essay about the unfinished horn concerto that Mozart resumed in 1791 but did not finish, the D Major, K. 412. The other works in question are the piano concertos in E Flat, K. 449; A, K. 488; and C, K. 503.

12

PLAYING MOZART:
THE PIANO CONCERTOS

SEVERAL COMPLETE OR nearly complete recordings of Mozart's piano concertos are listed as available—though whether you will be able to find them at your local record store, or even order them, is another question.[1] What you are more likely to find are CD reissues of famous old Mozart performances: performances by Artur Schnabel, Robert Casadesus, Dinu Lipatti, Arturo Benedetti Michelangeli, Myra Hess, Clifford Curzon, and others, none of them much improved by digital remastering. The first to issue a complete Mozart set was Alfred Brendel, whose ten CDs span the transition from the analog to the digital eras (1970–1984). He was followed by Murray Perahia, Vladimir Ashkenazy, and, most recently, Malcolm Bilson, playing the "Mozart piano," the fortepiano.[2] There will be many more.

Bilson's series has stimulated occasional gusts of interest ever since the first disc, containing Piano Concerto No. 9 in E-Flat, K. 271 ("Jeune-homme"), was issued in 1983. As a Mozart player Bilson stands up very well, I believe, not only to his more renowned contemporaries,

---

1. Or even, today, find your local record store (2007).

2. The complete Bilson performances are available today on Archiv, as a boxed set (2007). By 1989 Brendel and Perahia had recorded all twenty-seven concertos for one or more pianos and orchestra, Perahia adding Mozart's early concertos arranged from works of other composers. Ashkenazy had recorded sixteen, and Bilson reached twenty when his final disc containing the piano concertos in C Minor, K. 491, and B Flat, K. 595, was issued later in 1989.

but also to the venerable remastered masters. His achievement has a good deal to tell us about the current scene in musical performance, as I shall try to suggest later.

Most of Mozart's thirty-odd piano concertos and concerto rondos were written in the 1780s, the last decade of his life, after he had broken away from his traditional position as provincial court servant and set himself up as a freelance composer and performer in Josephine Vienna. Brilliant successes were matched by depressing failures; his final success—*The Magic Flute*—came just too late and he died young, of course, in straitened circumstances. Among his earlier successes were a run of *Akademien,* or subscription concerts, which he was able to set up, most of them featuring concertos.

With these concertos, Mozart attempted to make the scene in music's capital city. On one level, the inner drama of concerto relationships invites a metaphorical reading as one person's effort to gain acceptance from the group. On another level, the concerto is the genre that more than any other (even opera) was fine-tuned by its composer to dazzle and delight his contemporaries. That the Mostly Mozart audiences of today are pleased by exactly what the composer wrote to please his own paying public must count as a mysterious circumstance, possibly even an ominous one. Our special empathy for these works is much less easy to understand than the lack of interest in them during the nineteenth century. Only one concerto survived in the repertory for very long after Mozart's death, the turbulent Concerto No. 20 in D Minor, K. 466, and it had to pay a price for its solitariness. "The D minor Concerto is almost as much myth as work of art," Charles Rosen has observed; "when listening to it, as to Beethoven's Fifth Symphony, it is difficult at times to say whether we are hearing the work or its reputation, our collective image of it."[3]

---

3. *The Classical Style: Haydn, Mozart, Beethoven* (Norton, 1972), p. 228. I cite the original edition; while details of the revised edition of 1988 are important for anyone following Rosen's work, the body of the old text remains with the same pagination (2007).

The canonization of Mozart's other concertos can be attributed primarily to the activity of two great pianists, Artur Schnabel and Edwin Fischer, in the 1930s and 1940s. Connoisseurs have been known to prefer the interpretations of Fischer, who specialized in Bach and Mozart—Schnabel favored Beethoven and Schubert—and who actually founded his own chamber orchestra to present the concertos in a "historical" fashion. But Schnabel was the more important international figure, and his recordings have never been allowed to remain out of circulation for very long. A recent CD series, *Mozart and Schnabel*, transmits six of his concerto recordings, along with his famous performance of the Rondo in A Minor, K. 511, and several sonatas.

A CD changer with repeat function makes it a simple matter to compare Schnabel and Bilson in, let us say, the solos that introduce the piano in the opening and closing movements of the D-Minor Concerto. (This kind of comparison doesn't speak to the nature or quality of their interpretations as a whole, of course, but at least it speaks with some specificity.) In the first movement, the piano enters some time after the orchestra, as always happens in classical concertos; here—and this happens rather rarely—the piano enters with a completely new theme that is notably expressive. Schnabel does a number

From Piano Concerto No. 20 in D Minor, K. 466

of little things with tempo and dynamics in order to make this entry theme into something assertive and particularly characteristic.[4] There are six tiny phrases—two plus two plus two—in the entry theme (see the score on page 125).

Schnabel is renowned for his impeccable molding of melodic lines; by speeding up the tempo a little at the start, he tints the line with urgency and disquiet. Playing phrases 1–3 more and more intensely and freely, with increasing volume and rubato, results in a precipitous emotional climax at the end of phrase 3. But then Schnabel is more or less forced to play phrase 4, the highest so far, more quietly, and it trails away.

The solo persona projected by Bilson seems to be thinking less about the presence it is going to establish than about the theme it has just heard in the orchestra (as well it might: it is an astonishingly tormented theme). Slowing the tempo slightly, Bilson plays phrases 1–2 and 3–4 in a straightforward soft/loud (*piano/mezzo forte*) pattern. Besides reflecting the inherent paired structure of the phrases, and their register, which is low/high in each case, this brings the music out at a *mezzo forte* so that phrases 5–6, which are the highest of all, can soar beautifully. Notice how Bilson glides through the grace note in the last measure. Certainly he underplays phrase 3—and gains a quiet pinch of pathos without having to work for it. Distinguish this from Schnabel's underplaying of phrase 4, which has to be called sentimental.

All the phrases are linked by repetitions of a single four-note figure in the left hand. Bilson (like most other pianists) plays these calmly and consistently—a reasonable reading, since the very neutrality of the figure serves to anchor the wide-ranging, emotional span of the

---

4. *Mozart and Schnabel*, Vol. II: Mozart, Piano Concertos No. 20 and No. 21 and Sonata No. 12 in F, K. 332, Artur Schnabel with the Philharmonia Orchestra, conducted by Walter Susskind, and the London Symphony Orchestra, conducted by Malcolm Sargent (Arabesque).

right-hand melody. By accenting the figure in various different ways, Schnabel destroys this anchor; his concept of this entire entry passage as basically disruptive is easier to accept than the arbitrary measures he takes to achieve the effect.

But if Schnabel is more idiosyncratic and Bilson more restrained in the first-movement theme, attitudes are reversed in the finale. Within the rondo theme a number of little fragments repeat themselves, and Schnabel makes no effort to distinguish these one from another. However stormy, his playing seems bland compared to Bilson's, where the entire theme mounts in intensity, fragment by fragment, driving from a percussive trajectory at the beginning to a furious climax at the very end.

On paper, this may seem like a very "unclassical" strategy for a Mozart theme. But it sounds thrilling, and it suits both the angry, impacted theme itself and also the deeply unclassical movement which that theme launches. Usually, once a rondo theme has been played by the soloist, the orchestra repeats it and so appropriates it; not so in the D-Minor Concerto. After the piano's first offer of the aberrant theme, the orchestra can't get even the music right for more than three measures, and when it attempts to develop the theme rather than repeat it, the orchestra simply gets lost. The piano's second offer of the theme, some time later, throws the other players into a virtual panic. After the last offer, which now begins to sound like a challenge, the orchestra declines to deal with the theme at all—it literally changes the subject. Bilson's explosive interpretation helps to rationalize the orchestra's failure to cope, both technically and emotionally.

Patient analyses of this kind can be carried out with other discs slipped into the changer; and the comparison is not always so clearly to Bilson's advantage. The pendant to the D-Minor Concerto, the Piano Concerto No. 21 in C, K. 467 is a vehicle for some of Schnabel's finest playing. Bilson's performance may be preferable as a whole—it is certainly less erratic—but he does not quite capture the verve with which Schnabel projects the opening piano entry in the first movement, for example, or the piano entry after the main theme in the finale, or many of the bravura passages. Also in the finale Schnabel finds just the right combination of wariness and charm for the delightful passage of mock uncertainty that starts the development section. Phrases in the slow movement are molded with a pensive grace that is almost unbelievable, especially in view of the slow tempo (more than half again as slow as Bilson).

Bilson does, however, have an in-built advantage in playing Mozart concertos on an eighteenth-century instrument—the so-called "Mozart piano," or fortepiano—together with an orchestra of period or period-style instruments. The fortepiano he uses is a reproduction by the American maker Philip Belt, and the orchestra is conducted, very well indeed, by John Eliot Gardiner. The Bilson-Gardiner enterprise represents, in fact, another major foray by the early music movement into the later reaches of the canonic concert repertory: first Bach and Handel, now Mozart and Beethoven. Moreover, Roger Norrington has already conducted period-instrument *concerts monstres* of music by Berlioz, and Bilson is said to be eyeing the Schumann Piano Concerto on a piano of 1838. Small wonder that the old dispute among musicians about so-called "historically authentic" performance has flared up once again.

The action may be viewed at a safe distance in an anthology called *Authenticity in Early Music*, edited by Nicholas Kenyon.[5] Not much of intellectual substance remains to the idea of "authentic" performance after Richard Taruskin, in a withering essay, has challenged its historical plausibility, denied its desirability, and mocked the pretensions implicit in the loaded term itself. His own term, "authentistic,"

---

5. Oxford University Press, 1988. Taruskin's essay, "The Pastness of the Present and the Presence of the Past," appears on pp. 137–210.

is handily backloaded, "authentistic being to authentic as Hellenistic was to Hellenic." At times Taruskin writes as though the whole early music movement were a scam in aid of the recording companies, similar to the hoax that Joseph Horowitz claimed was perpetrated by the mass culture industry around "authentic" versions of symphonic classics by Toscanini.[6] This is less convincing than Taruskin's argument that the true ideological basis of "authentistic" performance is not really historical reconstruction at all.

Is not—or was not. For some time after World War I, it is certainly true that both historical performance and "traditional" performance tended toward the impersonal, the objective, and what T. E. Hulme called the "geometrical," as opposed to the "vitalistic" in nineteenth-century art. The original impetus behind the early-music movement was the revulsion against romantic emotionality endemic to early-twentieth-century modernism, the modernism of Pound, Eliot, Hulme (who admired "the dry hardness which you get in the classics"), Ortega, and Stravinsky. Historicism became important only later. Stravinsky is a key figure, with his astringent music of the neoclassical period, his influential polemics against musical expression in the Harvard lectures *The Poetics of Music,* and his likewise influential piano performances (as in an almost unbelievably mechanical Mozart recording of 1938).

A common ideal animated both historical and traditional performers, or at any rate many traditional performers, not to speak of poets and composers. The ideal was to find poetry in geometry. And while it is not entirely clear where musical performance is supposed to be right now, fifty years after Stravinsky's days as a pianist, and about thirty after Eliot's as a culture hero, an authentically modern style appears to have surfaced: "authenticism" without cant and stripped of geometry. Taruskin mentions a late recording by Gustav Leonhardt with approval:

---

6. *Understanding Toscanini* (Knopf, 1987).

What a lilt due attention to meter can impart!... Leonhardt's recording also demonstrates the joyful results of thoroughly passionate and committed experiment with old instruments. His players have truly understood what I see as the inestimable and indispensable heuristic value of the old instruments in freeing minds and hands to experience old music newly.[7]

What, then, does experiment with old instruments free us to experience newly in the Mozart concertos? Mainly, and most simply, we hear new proportions. The use of old instruments tips the balance between soloist and orchestra that grounds Mozart's concerto aesthetic, and thus sharpens up the inherent contrast between them. Paradoxically, although the fortepiano is quieter than the modern piano, it comes out ahead in the relationship between solo and orchestra.

The relationship depends less than one might think on volume of sound and more on sound quality. In spite of its thin tone and low volume, the fortepiano "speaks" more clearly than a modern piano because of its characteristic attack—a sharper attack than a modern Steinway, not to speak of a Bösendorfer or a Baldwin. Early orchestral instruments, on the other hand, attack more softly than modern ones (the timpani excepted). Donald Tovey, whose pioneering accolade to the Mozart concertos is still well worth reading, made much of the way the soloist's agility and expressiveness is pitted against the orchestra's sheer mass and range of instrumental color. With old instruments, distinctness of voice is added to the soloist's side of this calculus.

The orchestra used by John Eliot Gardiner in the Bilson recordings is much smaller than a modern symphony orchestra, even a reduced modern orchestra. (In some performances of Mozart's time the orchestral strings were cut down to one on a part when the piano was playing. This might not have been necessary at performances in

---

7. Taruskin, "The Pastness of the Present and the Presence of the Past," p. 203.

theaters, where the piano was presumably onstage and the orchestra in the pit.[8]) Even so, there are places in nearly every concerto where the piano writing is so thin one has to strain to hear the soloist. On the other hand, where the piano writing is full the fortepiano becomes a real contender. It does this most vividly in the fairly long bravura passages, such as those at the end of the exposition and recapitulation sections of the first movements. The fortepiano goes all out in these passages; the fragile instrument fairly rattles with exertion. Scales, octaves, and such in the low register cut through with special vigor. A Mozart concerto is and should be played as a virtuoso vehicle, not just as an elegant dialogue, and in a fortepiano performance the sweat is all but palpable, up to and including that notorious concerto trademark, the trill at the end of the cadenza. On a modern piano, this long trill can sound blank and merely formal, a gratuitous pirouette appended to fast runs which the soloist has negotiated with suspicious ease. On the fortepiano the trill sounds like the last triumphant gasp of an athlete completing a particularly exhilarating turn. When the orchestra roars its approval—a loud orchestral ritornello follows the trill—we can only endorse the applause. The soloist has earned it.

One should certainly acknowledge the skill with which modern pianists have learned to fake these bravura passages—to somehow give the impression that they are achieving the same kind of prodigies with the passagework of Mozart's concertos as with that of the Liszt Totentanz, Chaikovsky, Prokofiev, and the Ravel Concerto in G. I have already mentioned Schnabel in this connection. But the exercise must be a rather dispiriting one, and pianists are sometimes tempted to try something more creative. Murray Perahia's recording of the "Coronation" Concerto, No. 26 in D, K. 537, is an interesting case in point.[9]

---

8. These are the conclusions reached by Richard Maunder in *Early Music*, Vol. 17 (1989), p. 139.

9. Mozart, Piano Concerto No. 26 in D, K. 537, and Rondos K. 382 and 386, Murray Perahia with the English Chamber Orchestra (CBS Masterworks).

Perahia shades the first-movement bravura sections with *forte* and *mezzo forte* articulations (undreamed of by Mozart, by the way)—a subtle and delicate reading, but one which I am afraid confirms the current reputation of this work as rather slight and mannered. Bilson's extra-strenuous performance of the piece gives it a fighting chance.

What has been said about the bravura passages applies a fortiori to the cadenzas. Bilson plays excellent cadenzas, but I would not be ready to say that they are better than other pianists' or that he plays them better. I can only say that played on a fortepiano they convince in a way they never have before as supreme demonstrations of improvisational *virtù*, outdoing even the bravura passages and shaming the orchestra into what is, with Mozart, always a somewhat subdued roar in the final ritornello.

True, the cadenza is not a feature of the concerto that has fared well with critics. The cadenza cuts a spontaneous, incorrigible swath through formalist critical constructions, like a runaway power mower in a formal garden. "A bad cadenza is the very appendicitis of concerto form," grumbled Tovey, and Charles Rosen wrote an entire chapter on the Mozart concertos in *The Classical Style* barely mentioning the cadenza at all. With Bilson's fortepiano performances in our ears, perhaps we can begin to appreciate freshly the sawdust-ring atmosphere that is essential to Mozart's as to all other good concertos.

The fact that pianists have had to hold back when they play Mozart on a modern instrument has surely contributed to the image of the composer as a contained, even muted spirit—witty rather than intense, precise rather than exuberant. To be sure, this image is not unique to the piano concertos. Mozart's installation in the canonic musical repertory starting in the 1920s was another outcome of the same anti-Romantic movement that led to "geometrical" performance styles, and to the music of Stravinsky, Hindemith, Poulenc, and early Copland. The times demanded a brisk, clear, restrained Mozart, and that is what Edwin Fischer with his chamber orchestra (not Schnabel!) provided.

From Piano Concerto No. 23 in A, K. 488

It is not what is demanded today. Listen to Bilson's use of rubato, the expressive stretching of music's steady beat always associated with Romantic interpretation, in the adagio middle movement of Piano Concerto No. 23 in A, K. 488 (see above). Most pianists—Brendel is an exception—shade the rhythmic values at least a little bit in bar 7 of the theme, where the fast-note figures can be made to seem more emotional than ornamental. Bilson leans so hard on the first note in each of the figures that bar 7 becomes a passionate parenthesis within the overriding muted lament. In addition, he takes an astounding *Luftpause* before bar 2 (without, however, a Schnabelesque reduction of volume) and another after bar 4, playing the next half-measure in each case slightly slower. As a result bar 2 hovers in a kind of strained distress, which cedes to resignation at the half-cadence in bar 4. The full cadence at the end of the theme is treated analogously.

Bilson may have risked this highly inflected reading because the theme looms so large within the slow movement as a whole: most of its other material closely resembles the theme, and the austere form of the movement highlights the theme in its two solo presentations. Though these presentations are identical in the score, they should not be played identically, especially in so distinctive an interpretation. Bilson adds (improvises?) small but telling ornaments at the repetition, in bars 2–3. On the whole he tends to err on the side of caution when it comes to the embellishment of Mozart's slow melodies—perhaps in conscious reaction (overreaction, in my view) to some rather frilly efforts that have been turning up on recent records. It so happens that this Adagio is the one Mozart concerto movement to survive in a fully ornamented contemporary copy.[10] The atrocious chromatic runs in this source should give pause to even the most hardened historical reconstructor.

Nearly all other players count as geometricians compared to Bilson when they come to this Adagio theme. It would be otiose to go into detail about recordings by Brendel, Malcolm Frager, Richard Goode, Steven Lubin, Perahia, Christian Zacharias, and more. (Make what you like of certain similarities of detail between Bilson and Horowitz, in his extraordinary recording of 1987; Horowitz is something, as they say, else again—something calculated and eccentric.) Ashkenazy is a special case.[11] Although he applies only the most discreet rubato, he makes emphatic use of his own proper resource— the modern piano, with its rich and subtle range of tone quality far exceeding that of any eighteenth-century instrument. He molds the theme almost entirely out of sonority, rather than rubato, dynamics, or articulation. Thus while the high A at the beginning of bar 2 comes on time (with Bilson it comes very late), it has in Ashkenazy's recording a quiet ringing quality that seems to well up out of the previous bar and that makes the melodic climax radiant. The specially sonorous B in bar 2 flows like liquid to the cadence, and so on. Ashkenazy lingers a little on some of the single ornamental sixteenth-notes (in the dotted-eighth/sixteenth motif) so as to make them sing. The result may seem more limpid than distressful, but it is certainly very beautiful indeed.

---

10. A copy that has actually been traced to the composer's estate: see *Neue Mozart Ausgabe, kritische Bericht, Konzerte, bd. 7* (Cassel: Bärenreiter, 1964), pp. 8–17 (and has since been attributed to his pupil Barbara Ployer, dedicatee of the Piano Concerto No. 14 in E-Flat, K. 449).

11. *Favourite Mozart*, Piano Concertos No. 23 in A Major, K. 488, and No. 27 in B-Flat Major, K. 595, Vladimir Ashkenazy with the Philharmonia Orchestra (London).

Bilson cannot even try for this effect because the fortepiano lacks the necessary range of sonority; this was a resource that was developed by piano makers only in the nineteenth century. I spoke confidently above about Bilson's advantages in playing an eighteenth-century instrument. Ashkenazy reminds us (in this concerto and others) of the advantages of the modern piano—advantages that pianists traditionally leave aside when they play Mozart.

What comes very naturally to the fortepiano are sentimental, delicate effects, which Mozart indulged in the slow movements of several of his earlier Viennese concertos, such as No. 11 in F, K. 413; No. 13 in C, K. 415; and No. 18 in B flat, K. 456. (Gardiner too does very well by these, with his deep-sighing low-vibrato strings.) Browsing through the complete set of Bilson recordings, one can only admire his responsiveness to the shades of expression called for in this amazing and amazingly diverse repertory. Charm, serenity, *Empfindsamkeit*, melancholy, pathos, majesty, power, high comedy, low humor—he is always there. Bilson and Gardner can also project impressive long-range effects, as for example in their performance of Piano Concerto No. 25 in C, K. 503. This slightly forbidding work depends to a large extent on the manipulation of large rhythmic proportions. Though the finale starts lightly, as usual, it develops unusual grandeur; the balance achieved with the weighty first movement is projected here as in no other recording I know.

What would you rather hear—a great performance on modern instruments, or a fair-to-middling performance on historical instruments? People in the "traditional" camp would always trot out this mindless question as an argument-stopper when the pros and cons of historical performance were debated. The question was not only mindless but rather offensive. Nobody ever asked whether you would rather hear a great performance on the wrong instrument or a great performance on the right one. The answer to *that* question, of course, is "both."

Still, after one has had some experience with the fortepiano, the use of a Steinway for a Mozart concerto can begin to feel like overkill, like using your twelve-cylinder BMW 750 to tool around in the back streets of Salzburg. (Even in the bravura sections, Mozart's Autobahn, the thing only seems to be going at about eighty kilometers per hour.) Listening to Murray Perahia or Peter Serkin, one senses a certain reserve in their performances that has nothing to do with their feelings about Mozart, only with the consciousness that they are underplaying their instrument. Malcolm Bilson, a player of comparable stature, deploys the resources of his instrument to the full, resources that he has discovered in a process of passionate, committed experiment over many years. He has to be the exemplary Mozart pianist for our time.

—1989

13

THE MAGIC FLUTE

IT IS HARD to experience or even think about Mozart's *The Magic Flute* without a sense of wonder at how much it differs from all his other operas, ranging from *Così fan tutte*, the opera of choice today, *Don Giovanni*, and *The Marriage of Figaro*, to less frequently performed works such as *Idomeneo*, *The Abduction from the Seraglio*, and *La clemenza di Tito*. Kierkegaard saw the "magic marriage" between Mozart's genius and his subject matter in *Don Giovanni*; but I argue that Mozart's supreme dramatic work is to be found not in that fire-and-brimstone morality play but in the Masonic fable of his final year, 1791. As I wrote in *Opera as Drama*,

> Everything we know or feel about Mozart should assure us that the inflexible view of sin and death set forth in the [Don Juan] legend must have been distasteful to him. Mozart never saw man's will as inevitably opposed by the will of God. He conceived an essential harmony expressed by human feelings; his terms were brotherhood and sympathy and humility, not damnation and defiance. The magic marriage is *The Magic Flute*.[1]

---

1. Revised edition (University of California Press, 1988), p. 104.

Anyone interested in the opera has probably learned that *The Magic Flute* was not the outcome of some visionary initiative by the composer or the librettist. It emerged more or less naturally from the opera scene, so vital and so various, of Mozart's time. Several different genres of Italian, French, and German opera had their day in late-eighteenth-century Vienna, among them a type of *Singspiel*, or German operetta with spoken dialogue, that inclined toward magic, spectacle, and fairy tale. In 1782 Vienna flocked to Ignaz Umlauf's setting of *Das Irrlicht* (The Will o' the Wisp), "one of the most popular fairy-tale singspiel texts of the late eighteenth century," including "an elaborate trial scene with maidens at the temple with a prophetic fire on the altar."[2] Mozart didn't think much of this piece, which played the Hoftheater just before his own *Abduction from the Seraglio*.

All the same, *Das Irrlicht* was to be one of *The Magic Flute*'s more immediate models. A few years later magic opera became all the rage when Emanuel Schikaneder took over one of the city's suburban popular theaters, the Theater an den Wien. Schikaneder's first efforts along these lines—many more came later—were *Oberon*, by Paul Wranitzky, a Masonic lodge brother of Mozart's, which held the stage from 1789 to 1847, and two pieces composed by committee, a team including Mozart and several of his close associates: *The Benevolent Dervish* and *The Philosopher's Stone, or the Magic Island*.[3] Another theater countered with *Kasper the Bassoonist, or the Magic Zither*. These works have many dramatic and musical features that played directly into Mozart's masterpiece. Schikaneder opened *The Magic Flute* in September 1791, three months before the composer died.

2. David J. Buch, "*Die Zauberflöte*, Masonic Opera, and Other Fairy Tales," *Acta Musicologica*, Vol. 76, No. 2 (2004). For more on the background and much else about the opera, see Peter Branscombe, *W. A. Mozart: Die Zauberflöte* (Cambridge Opera Guide, Cambridge University Press, 1991).

3. Both operas have been recorded, very handsomely, by the Boston Baroque, conducted by Martin Pearlman: *Der wohltätge Derwitsch* (rec. 2001) and *Der Stein der Weisen* (rec. 1998) on Telarc.

Schikaneder was an important theater director, a librettist, a some-time Shakespearean actor, and a star comedian. He was also a composer. He had known Mozart and his father in Salzburg about ten years earlier when Mozart had written an aria for one of his plays. A dozen years later he had the wit to conceive an opera project that might appeal to Beethoven, which Beethoven worked on and then abandoned. He was thoroughly experienced as a writer of plays and librettos, and there are some brilliant things in his conception of *The Magic Flute* and in his working out of the drama (as well as some less than brilliant things). Best of all was his placement of the action in the barely disguised context of Freemasonry. Some of the numbers paraphrase Masonic texts. The setting draws freely on Masonic iconography. The initiation process that consumes the opera's second act meshes not exactly, of course, but plausibly and powerfully with the Masons' secret rites.

The Viennese magic operas regularly featured quests and trials, with temple scenes of some solemnity, priests, and pageantry. In a stroke Schikaneder raised all of this to a new level of seriousness, contemporaneity, and, to a degree, mystery and even scandal. Since Mozart was evidently an enthusiastic Mason, and Schickaneder had been ejected from the order for his low morals, some commentators believe that Mozart himself proposed to draw on Freemasonry. In any case, Mozart was the man to capitalize on it.

Schikaneder deserves all the praise he has received for the libretto —in particular, perhaps, for the climactic passages he devised for the finales at the end of each of the opera's two acts. The two passages are roughly parallel, each bringing the lovers Tamino and Pamina together after an entire act of separation. In Act I, the separation is literal. The two have been searching for each other aimlessly until well into the finale, when Tamino is led across the stage to meet Pamina for the first time, in the presence of Sarastro—the much-talked-about and feared High Priest of Isis and Osiris, now at last before us, an imposing figure in a chariot drawn by lions through adoring crowds. Tamino has been stalking Sarastro, and Pamina has been pleading with him, but for all the attention they pay him now he might as well have been dusting the Masonic paraphernalia rather than holding court. It is extraordinary how fifteen seconds of rapturous greeting music of the simplest kind can cement the bond between these fairy-tale lovers, a bond reaffirmed hardly less simply at the parallel place in the Act II finale.

Though in Act II the lovers have not been literally separated, their meetings have been fraught with anxiety and grief. After surviving two of the trials set for him by Sarastro, Tamino steps up to the last and most profound one:

> *No fear of death shall daunt or bate me*
> *The gates of hell already wait me,*
> *I hear their dreadful hinges groan*
> *My feet must dare the path alone!*[4]

I think Tamino should indeed step up—up a little twisting path, I would recommend, leading to the gates of Fire and Water, which should have started opening by the time he turns, on hearing Pamina cry "Tamino, I must see you!" from offstage. He should have approached the gates before Pamina enters to greet him—now with the greatest of tenderness—and accompany him through the ultimate trial. As in the Act I finale, the voices merge, the personalities dissolve.

So concludes the progress of the hero and heroine, a special feature of this opera. For Edward J. Dent, whose pioneering book on Mozart's

---

4. From the version of *The Magic Flute* prepared for NBC television fifty years ago, at the bicentennial of Mozart's birth, by W. H. Auden and Chester Kallman, reprinted in *W. H. Auden and Chester Kallman: Libretti and Other Dramatic Writings by W. H. Auden, 1939–1973*, edited by Edward Mendelson (Princeton University Press, 1993), p. 177. I draw on the same translation below.

operas from 1913 is still well worth reading today, the sense of growth and development made *The Magic Flute*

> comparable only to the operas of Wagner. In all his operas, Mozart is remarkable for his characterization; but in none of them before this, except to a slight extent in *Idomeneo*, did he make a single character show a gradual maturing such as we see in Tamino and Pamina. It was indeed almost impossible to do so within the limits of conventional drama. But *Die Zauberflöte*, although it starts as a conventional opera, very soon departs from all precedent.[5]

The work starts with conventional fairy-tale figures. Tamino is a prince without a history. At the opening curtain, as he stumbles onstage with his empty quiver, he doesn't even know where he is; he has shot his last arrow, and when he passes out, about to succumb to a serpent that advances toward him, he succumbs to womanhood instead, in the form of Three Ladies who arrive to save him. It is taking some time for our hero's heroism—indeed, his masculinity—to establish itself. Mozart sees this, and writes vulnerability into Tamino's falling-in-love song to the girl whose portrait the Three Ladies press upon him, and whose rescue the Queen of the Night so thunderously orders him to undertake—vulnerability, as well as ardor to spare.

After the Ladies slay the serpent, they want Tamino for their pleasure, but can't agree on which of them gets the prize. Instead they take charge of his affairs, outfitting him with magic tools, a companion, and a virtual road map for his quest. Tamino's dependence on women in Act I makes the first of his trials in Act II, where he must show that he can resist women, a more serious matter than might otherwise seem.

When we first see Tamino he is alone and afraid. When we first see

---

5. *Mozart's Operas*, second edition (London: Oxford University Press, 1949), p. 262.

Pamina a little later, threatened by Monastatos, "a Moor in the service of Sarastro," she is less afraid than alarmed and very irritated. In this situation she starts explaining herself almost as a reflex, and her brief exchange with Monastatos (she sings for less than half a minute) is the first of many which relate or enact her various relationships—with him, with her mother, later with Papageno, Sarastro, and Tamino, and finally, to fill out history, her father. Her character grows richer and richer, and we end up knowing as much about her as about any of Mozart's other *grandes dames*—Constanze in *Abduction*, Ilia and Electra in *Idomeneo*, the Countess Almaviva, Donna Anna, Donna Elvira, Fiordiligi, Vitellia—even though Pamina has only one aria, "Ach, ich fühl's," and they all have two or three.

I have a friend who has sung Tamino in various *Magic Flute* productions—one of them set in the New York subway—and he has little affection for the role. For the male lead never catches up with Pamina, emotionally or intellectually. His famous scene comes halfway through Act I, as he arrives at Sarastro's temple and attempts to confront the evil abductor, as he thinks, of his lady love. In an exceptionally long accompanied recitative he disputes with a strange Speaker he meets at the temple door, a priest of Sarastro's order. It is the first serious musical moment in an opera which will introduce more and more of such moments over its course. As Tamino blurts out one question and answer after another, we hear the generic prince growing into a person. He seems like a little boy: enthusiastic, impetuous, tactless, insecure, uncertain how to respond, quick to despair.

But a tenor can do only so much with a recitative of this kind, however excellent it is. While he can hardly fail to get it across adequately, he has somehow to avoid being overshadowed by the baritone, a deeper role in every respect. (A little later Tamino will find himself upstaged by forest animals.) Paternal, sometimes severe and sometimes sympathetic, the Speaker is in no position to enlighten Tamino, only to try to make him think. This is a wonderful small role for the right singer—Willard White, for one, in an old video of David Hockney's first *Magic Flute* at Glyndebourne.[6]

Ingmar Bergman's much-loved version of *The Magic Flute*, from 1973, makes expert use of the small stage of the restored eighteenth-century Swedish Court Theater at Drottningholm.[7] In the temple scene, however, Tamino moves through the onstage temple door out of stage space into a half-lit room with a low fire in the grate, where he stands like a schoolboy in front of the bespectacled Speaker, seated at a desk. After much talking at cross purposes the Speaker makes his final pronouncement and gets up to go, leaving Tamino by himself, to think for himself. "O everlasting night, when will you end?" he says. The Speaker has blown out his lamp. Reading Mozart in his own way, Bergman has turned this moment into one of revelation. In fact, all Tamino can really think of at this point is his continuing commitment to Pamina, and in fact, it's all he needs.

(In an early and persistent variant text of *The Magic Flute*, Tamino says "*o dunkle Nacht*," rather than "*o ew'ge Nacht*"—darkened night, rather than everlasting night. I wonder if Bergman knew this. It looks as if someone were tinkering with the libretto, to make it less redundant (for the Speaker has used the word *ewig* in his previous pronouncement), more elegant (*dunkle* rather than *dunkel*), and perhaps also a little more sensible (if night is everlasting, why ask immediately when it will end?). This variant text has been known about for almost as long as the opera has existed, but it remains a puzzle.[8] While

---

6. With Felicity Lott, conducted by Bernard Haitink (Video Arts International).

7. Criterion Collection DVD (2000).

8. See Michael Freyhan, "Toward the Original Text of Mozart's *Die Zauberflöte*," *Journal of the American Musicological Society*, Vol. 39, No. 2 (1986), pp. 355–380, and "Rediscovery of the 18th Century Score and Parts of 'Die Zauberflöte'...," *Mozart-Jahrbuch 1977*, pp. 109–148. C. A. Vulpius, a Weimar man of letters, prepared a more thorough overhaul of the original text for the local première in 1794, to the irritation of Schikaneder, but it never gained currency. Vulpius was the brother of Goethe's mistress Christiane Vulpius; Goethe's unfinished sequel to *The Magic Flute* dates from around the same time.

sometimes it seems to improve the libretto, at other times it produces little more than elegant variation, and at others it makes an uncanny fit with the music—a better fit than is the case with the regular text.[9] Consider this not unimportant place in the Act I finale, just before the lovers come together before Sarastro. Pamina apologizes for her attempted escape from his realm. She explains that Monastatos tried to take advantage of her. Sarastro answers—his first words in the opera—

> Arise, take courage, my loved one! For without having to draw it out of you, I know more about your heart. You love another deeply.

Here the music takes a brief but striking melancholy turn, as Sarastro repeats the words for emphasis:

> You love another deeply. I will not force you to love [*Ich will dir nicht zur Liebe zwingen*], yet I will not allow you to leave.

The variant text gives Sarastro a personal stake in the action that is only hinted at in the canonic text:

> ...I know more about your heart. It harbors no love for me, no love for me [*es ist für mich von Liebe leer*: accent on *mich*]. I will not force you to love, yet I will not allow you to leave.

With these words and Mozart's melancholy music, Sarastro becomes a less hieratic, more human figure as soon as he opens his mouth—and also one with a clearer message. Although you do not return my love any more than you return the love of Monastatos, he says, I will

---

9. Michael Freyhan believes these places show that the variant text must be the one actually set by Mozart—especially since he can make the case that it originated in Vienna in the year of *The Magic Flute*, 1791. But he cannot explain how, if Mozart set the variant text, the canonic text appears in both his autograph score and the libretto printed in 1791.

not force myself on you as he has—just as in Act II he will tell Pamina that although the Queen of the Night has sworn revenge on him and ordered Pamina to kill him, he will not reciprocate. Revenge has no place within *diesen heil'gen Hallen*, any more than rape.)

Returning to Tamino, and how he fails to catch up with Pamina: the scene with the Speaker at the temple door is followed by one of the libretto's less happy inventions. Lacking any obvious course of action, Tamino recollects the magic flute he has been given by the Three Ladies and plays, hoping to summon Pamina. Instead his music attracts the Peaceable Kingdom animals beloved by stage directors and audiences alike—to speak only of the Metropolitan Opera, Marc Chagall's airborne shtetl beasts, the cute critters of David Hockney, or the great spirit bears kited across the proscenium in Julie Taymor's current production at the Met.

Again, give Schikaneder credit for seeing the need to demonstrate the flute's power in Act I as a prelude to its more epochal demonstration in Act II. Like Orpheus' lyre, the flute first charms wild beasts and later brings man past death and back again (as shown in the opera's trial of Fire and Water). Important as all this may have been to Masons, I think the reason it leaves me unimpressed goes beyond a general feeling that *The Magic Flute* suffers from a surfeit of symbolism. For one thing, in Act II Tamino and Pamina surely owe their success at the trials to their own virtue, especially Pamina's, rather than to magic. Another thing is the fitful action of the flute-playing scene itself in Act I. Tamino grows sad when the flute fails to attract Pamina (Bergman's fluffy animals gather around and hug him). Then he becomes somewhat hopeful again. It was clever to have his flute answered by Papageno's panpipe, and charming, but the music is not Mozart's best.

The role of Tamino wilts further in Act II. For until the climactic moment at the gates of Fire and Water, once he submits to initiation into Sarastro's order he spends his time enduring trials to which Schikaneder allows him no musical response. Not only does the libretto deny him arias or even recitatives, for much of the time Tamino is sworn to silence, and for an operatic character there is no state more conducive to emasculation. Tamino is forbidden to communicate with Pamina; after her famous lament, "Ach, ich fühl's" (Hearts may break), he has nothing to say or do except listen to Papageno mocking the action. One of the places I most cherish in the Bergman film—another is the intermission, of course, with the dragon (Mozart's serpent) trotting around backstage—comes at the end of "Ach, ich fühl's." When the singing is over, the orchestra has a few bars of doleful music echoing her cry "See, Tamino, Tamino, Tamino, Tamino, Tamino." The camera pans away from her to Tamino, who is covering his face and silently weeping.

Meanwhile, while Tamino appears stuck throughout Act II, whether musically or in the libretto, Sarastro and the order are portrayed more and more fully and beautifully, as is also the personality of Pamina. Since Pamina cannot submit to the official trials, which exist for men only, Schikaneder contrived less formal tribulations for her that are parallel and much more intense. She too must reject the wiles of women—a major motif in this opera, like it or not. One may be tempted to cut the little misogynist duet sung by the Two Priests—

> Be on your guard for Woman's humors:
> That is the rule we follow here.
> For often Man believes her rumors,
> She tricks him, and it costs him dear.
> She promises she'll never hurt him,
> But mocks his heart, that's true and brave;
> At last she'll spurn him and deceive him:
> Death and despair was all she gave.

—but it has a function in the music drama, confirming by music what has been spoken in the dialogue many times. The Queen of the Night's berserk demand that her daughter kill Sarastro shocks

Pamina into disillusion and drives her to attempt suicide. Then in her suicide scene, observed by the Three Boys—a scene that is half comic, half excruciating, and astonishingly original—she faces death alone, in a moment of protracted grief.[10] Compare Tamino's manly if mindless reaction at the gates of Fire and Water.

Pamina does not undergo the official quasi-Masonic trials—at least, not before the last of them. Her initiation is central to the drama, surely, but since the initiation of women was a sensitive matter, Schikaneder probably had good reason to soft-pedal it. "Am I allowed to speak to her?" Tamino asks, when he hears Pamina calling offstage as he approaches the final trial. Yes, say the guardians of the gates, the two Armed Men:

> *A woman who fears neither Night nor Death*
> *Is worthy and will be initiated.*[11]

By this time Pamina has already survived her own trial of death, so she is prepared to lead Tamino now. The voices merge and the souls, as I have said, dissolve into one another. Woman leads, yet man plays the flute, and it is shards of music from the first scene in the opera—his scene—that haunt the unearthly flute music as they pass through the Fire and Water.

So Pamina takes her place with Tamino among the elect. There was a debate at the time about the initiation of women as Masons, and some say Schikaneder and Mozart can be seen as taking sides in favor

---

10. It was a winning idea, incidentally, to introduce the Three Boys as rather cold figures uttering maxims, and then turn them into caring spirits who act. They rescue Pamina and later Papageno.

11. "*Ein Weib, das Nacht und Tod nicht scheut,/Ist wurdig und wird eingeweiht.*" It has always seemed odd to me that Tamino and Pamina should appeal to the Armed Men, heraldic figures. An early illustration for this scene includes two priests, who would be more natural interlocutors (shown in Branscombe, *W. A. Mozart: Die Zauberflöte*, p. 188, see fn. 2; one priest carries what looks like an initiation hood for Pamina).

of women in that debate. Look at it this way: magic fairy-tale operas often had scenes of trials and initiation and moral uplift, as has already been noted. By underpinning *The Magic Flute* with Masonic lore and reference, its authors transcended this sort of generic idealism so as to present what was for them the best contemporary vision of a humane order. But Pamina brought with her imperatives of her own, and by the time they were through, they had developed a humane vision that transcended that of eighteenth-century Freemasonry.

Dr. Johnson's indelible definition of opera as an exotic and irrational entertainment predated the significant operas of Gluck, let alone those of Mozart. For Gluck, in theory as in practice, opera was art, not entertainment, dramatic even when it was exotic (as in his *Iphigénie en Tauride*), and as rational as can be possible for an art that lives on music. Mozart admired Gluck, and stylistic and technical characteristics of his music drama certainly found their way into *Idomeneo* and *Don Giovanni*, if not *The Magic Flute*. But Gluck is a frame of mind, someone has said, rather than a congeries of musical forms and styles, and Gluck's spirit hovers over all the "serious" numbers in *The Magic Flute*, however different their styles: Tamino's recitative with the Speaker, the choruses and marches of the priests, Sarastro's aria, the chorale fugue sung by the Armed Men, and the march for the trial of Fire and Water. Mozart was pleased when Salieri came to a performance and loved it, insisting that the piece was no low-class amusement but an *operone*, a grand opera. Salieri was a pupil of Gluck.

Still, Dr. Johnson's view has prevailed, for *The Magic Flute* in particular, if not for opera in general. Almost everyone is happy to think of *The Magic Flute* as a combination of sublime music and irrational plot. One can see why. For all its strengths, the libretto takes full advantage of the license it enjoys as a fairy tale, the license to blur continuity, consistency, coherence. The role of Papageno, written for the great comic ad-libber who was running the show—Schikaneder—

wears thin today, especially since the singers who tend to be cast in it are not really very funny. The role can be cut down a good deal without diminishing its function in the drama; Bergman showed that. Nor is the case for rationality helped by setting the opera on the Broadway–7th Avenue Line or in the new terrain of the Lion King, up on ground level. Or in a sanatorium, with Sarastro as the head psychiatrist, the concept behind a recent Paris production.

I prefer activist productions that combine sublime music with the plot smoothed and coaxed to make it less irrational, as in the Bergman film, and also in the translated version that W. H. Auden and Chester Kallman made in 1956. Such efforts require some violence to the original text —too much violence in the Auden version, which unfortunately is now almost forgotten. Not so the film, which recently came out on DVD: a continuing challenge to purists. True, it is not well sung, but connoisseurs must remember that the original Papageno was not a singer of the caliber of Wolfgang Brendel or Bryan Terfel. Tinkering with the libretto in order to clarify the action is a small matter that should raise no hackles; many directors do it. Years ago, Auden complained mildly about

> *Director Y who with ingenious wit*
> *Places the wretched singers in the pit*
> *While dancers mime their roles, Z the Designer,*
> *Who sets the whole thing on an ocean liner,*
> *The girls in shorts, the men in yachting caps...*

But he did not neglect to add:

> *Yet genius triumphs over all mishaps.*[12]

—2006

---

12. *W. H. Auden and Chester Kallman: Libretti*, p. 155.

14

SONATA FORMS

WHAT CHARLES ROSEN does to the concept of sonata form in his near-eponymous book is not so much deconstruction—though there is some of that, as we will see—but rather reconstruction.[1] The old textbook definition of sonata form has been hammered away at on many occasions; Rosen himself did a pretty thorough job of pulverization in *The Classical Style* of 1971. Now he builds a whole new book out of the dust. It is a paradoxical and brilliant performance. Inasmuch as the first and often the other movements of nearly every sonata, trio, quartet, quintet, and symphony by Haydn, Mozart, and Beethoven are "in sonata form," the meaning, status, and implications of the term are obviously important to anyone interested in this music.

Important in different ways, however, to listeners and critics today and to the music theorists of the early nineteenth century. The eighteenth century knew neither the term nor the definition, and Rosen traces with exemplary clarity the reasons why sonata form, when it finally got defined, got defined so poorly. The nineteenth century needed a prescriptive, didactic formula that would enable composers to emulate the classics—in particular, to emulate Beethoven. And since composers of the time cared above all about melodies, themes,

---

1. *Sonata Forms* (Norton, 1980).

and motives, the basic tension or conflict that generates sonata form was interpreted as a conflict of themes. A pre-sonata piece by Bach— a fugue, typically—has but one theme; a sonata piece by Beethoven has two, sharply contrasted. People liked to speak of the "first theme" as masculine, the "second subject" as feminine. The fact that these adjectives were attributed (fraudulently, as has recently been shown) to Beethoven himself reflects clearly enough the classicizing, authoritarian impetus behind the original formulation of sonata form.

Any modern impetus must be historical or critical. We no longer need a pattern such as sonata form for composing in the high style; we need simply an aid to understanding Haydn and Mozart (and Beethoven). Nineteenth-century theory was never intended to provide this and so was soon found wanting, and was hammered at; later critics typically began to look below the surface level, the level inhabited by themes. In his famous "Sonata Forms" article in the eleventh edition of the *Encyclopaedia Britannica*, Donald Tovey dealt brusquely with the thematic question by printing the first half of the Gigue from Bach's C-Major Cello Suite, which contains at least four distinct themes, next to the first-movement exposition of Haydn's Quartet in D Minor, op. 42, which contains only one. (Compare Rosen's use of Bach's B-Flat Partita and Haydn's Symphony No. 44 in E Minor, the "Trauersymphonie.") Sonata style does indeed depend on conflict and resolution, said Tovey, but it is not conflict of themes but a deeper-level conflict of tonality. What is fundamental is the process of modulation—Haydn's change from the key of D minor to F major, and especially the "dramatic" way in which he makes this change perceptible.

In short, revisionists early in this century substituted keys for themes as the basic structural determinant of sonata form. This, by the way, allowed sonata-form analysis to be extended from sonatas and symphonies to concertos, opera ensembles, and even pieces of church music. Rosen goes further and emphasizes the function rather than the pattern of music elements, drawing on a central principle of "symmetrical resolution" which applies to tonality, themes, rhythm, texture, and nuance. Sonata form, he insists, depends on the wonderfully flexible new classical style developed by Haydn in the 1770s, a style so sensitive that almost any musical gesture that draws attention to itself asks to be confirmed, to be accounted for, and ultimately to be resolved symmetrically—which I take to mean that gesture and resolution can be clearly perceived to be in some sort of temporal balance. Admirers of *The Classical Style* will find another masterly exposition of this central insight in the chapter entitled "Motif and Function," with its full-scale analysis of the first movement of Mozart's "Prague" Symphony.

This author is not one to overemphasize tonality, then, in the way that old writers overemphasized themes, but he does not slight it either. Some of his best writing deals with modulation. And it is probably true that this matter more than any other eludes modern listeners as they try to deepen their appreciation of classical music. Themes, rhythm, texture, and nuance are all easier to hear than keys; perhaps as a result of the atrophy of classical tonality recounted in the book's final chapter, on "Sonata Form after Beethoven," people seem to be less sensitive to niceties of relative key quality and modulation today than they presumably were in the late eighteenth century. That is why Tovey spent so much time trying to "explain" tonality ("The curtain of hail is lifted away into blue sky, and we find ourselves in the very key in which the development started," "Schubert in the slow movement of the Quintet produces a mysterious brightness by going from E to F sharp," etc.). If most of the time he must have failed in this, at least he never missed a chance to assure his nonprofessional readers that the structural tonal elements of the sonata style existed within the sphere of their own perception and experience. Tovey strove to sophisticate his "naïve listener" by repeatedly drawing attention to aesthetic effects achieved by means of tonality.

Rosen does not feel the need to offer such assurances or make such explanations. He writes for readers who either share his ear for tonality or more often, I expect, take him willingly at his word. Yet in many ways he resembles Tovey (both pianists, prodigies, classicists in music, formalists in criticism, anti-academic academics, stylists of different sorts (!), connoisseurs, legendary conversationalists); and the fact that he writes down to his readers less than Tovey did does not mean he believes any less that keys derive their aesthetic character from musical processes which can be followed over a span of time, such as modulations, preparations, or juxtapositions with other keys. Writers such as Rosen and Tovey adhere to what has been called the "gignetic" view of tonality, as opposed to the "ontic" view—tonality as a static system, abstracted from time. (These may not be the best terms, but they are ones that have recently been brought to the controversy by Siegmund Levarie.[2]) The quality of a key is defined contextually, by how it is approached. Thus in the first movement of Beethoven's "Eroica" Symphony, the F-major horn passage in the recapitulation section does not sound like an enhanced dominant of E flat but (Rosen almost says) an enhanced subdominant, because of the way Beethoven leads into it. And this carries his discourse forward:

> The contradiction of the normal significance of [the enhanced dominant, F major], its transformation into its opposite, makes this moment one in which all genuine harmonic motion appears to stop: the dynamics, *piano* and *dolce,* reflect the cessation of harmonic energy. The main theme is poised over these harmonies for a few bars. This is a crucial passage: the main theme is essentially a horn call in its character, but the horn has yet to play it solo. It tried to, a few bars before, in E flat, but was cut off brutally in mid-theme by the full orchestra. It plays the

---

2. *19th-Century Music,* Vol. 3 (1979), pp. 88–89.

theme at last, but with a different sonority—not the natural E flat sonority of the instrument but F. The swift move to D flat major, and the delicacy of the flute solo confirm the exoticism of this section.

This is criticism building on what we actually hear in music, even on what we feel about what we hear (though to my taste there is too little here about that).

The distinctiveness of this kind of criticism, criticism based on experience and effect, becomes clear if Charles Rosen is compared to a typical academic writer, or even with one who is more perceptive and flexible than most. David Epstein, for example, discusses the "Eroica" recapitulation in his recent analytical study,[3] but all he wants to point out is how the bass traces the interval of a descending third, which as E flat–C (an extension of the interval E flat–C sharp at the beginning of the piece), leads into the F-major horn entry, and then as D flat–B flat also leads out of the D-flat flute entry. A "basic shape," in Schoenberg's term, generates all parts of the composition in all musical "domains" and on all levels. Of the strange quality of F major in this context, the cessation of harmonic energy, the delicacy and exoticism, Epstein sees or says nothing.

Concern for musical experience and effect also helps to explain the paradoxical fact that this author has written this book, a book on this particular subject. Sonata style, sonata principle—these have been the preferred terms in recent years, and *The Classical Style* included a strong attack on the canonical concept of sonata form, as has already been mentioned. But the way this music is appreciated, Rosen claims, is still through the experience of form: not any single, simplistic sonata *form* but multiple sonata *forms*, as different from one another as snowflakes all inspired by the same guiding principle. This

---

3. *Beyond Orpheus: Studies in Musical Structure* (MIT Press, 1979).

reconstruction of sonata forms will probably cause as much raising of eyebrows (and clenching of fists) in music-theoretical circles as Rosen's late entry into the field of mid-eighteenth-century music history will in musicological ones. Compare Epstein, once again—who in his discussion of the "Eroica" does not exactly ignore sonata form: in fact he points out (quite in Rosen's spirit) how the descending-third bass figure articulates the major sonata-form divisions. Yet his overriding, "ontic" concern is with how basic shapes control every gesture in the movement, large or small—irrespective of its location in the form. No follower of Arnold Schoenberg or Heinrich Schenker would ever dream of undertaking the dizzy taxonomy of multiple sonata forms that occupies the center of the present study.

There is much to learn and much to quibble about in this taxonomy. Rosen proposes First Movement Sonata Form, Slow Movement (or Aria) Sonata Form, Minuet Sonata Form, and Finale Sonata Form, and then goes into subtypes, three (or more) mid-century "stereotypes," a miscellaneous series of eleven expository devices, and so on. Readers who have the musical training and the enthusiasm to follow all this will certainly be convinced of the wonderful multiplicity of formal solutions achieved by the classic masters within the guiding principles of sonata form; though perhaps it should also be added that such readers will probably not need much convincing. Not only does Rosen give us this snowstorm of sonata forms, he also rearranges the basic crystal structure. Often the tonic establishes itself firmly long before the recapitulation. Usually a Second Development comes directly after the recapitulation of the first theme. In Minuet Sonata Form the first half can close in the tonic and the fundamental contrast of key and/or material occur in the second. All this will excite debate; it will also enhance perception.

Rosen's growing involvement with history can be followed in his articles and reviews for *The New York Review of Books* over the past ten years. The strong historical bent of *Sonata Forms* may still surprise those who remember the anti-historical or at least anti-musicological polemics of 1971. His strategy now is to trace the evolution of many different early-eighteenth-century forms and genres in order to show how all contribute something to the classical synthesis. Since there is no single sonata form, there can be no single or simple history of it. In *The Classical Style* we were given a magnificent view of three great mountain peaks looming up out of an ahistorical fog. It is both a pleasure and a relief to find in *Sonata Forms* that some lesser promontories such as Carl Heinrich Graun, Niccolò Jomelli, and the Bach sons, and even some valleys such as G. B. Sammartini, are now exposed and illuminated.

The book is less useful, I fear, about the nineteenth century. The introduction gives clear warning to those who pick up his book in the hope of learning the history of sonata form—its origin, development, and fate:

> These questions seem reasonable enough, on the face of it; but as they are generally put, they are doomed to remain unanswered because they make untenable assumptions.... They assume that a form has a history—in other words, that it is subject to change: but if a form "changes," it is not clear when it would be useful to consider it the same form, although changed, and when we must think of it as a new form altogether.

Rosen himself has changed enough since *The Classical Style* to see in the prehistory of sonata forms a fascinating record of individual stylistic elements grasped here and there and sometimes combined, sometimes not, in ways that anticipate the classic solution. But for Rosen sonata form depends on the classical style; he does not see how the form can be squared with the evolving style or styles of musical Romanticism. One by one Schubert, Schumann (in a lengthy discussion of the Sonata in F-sharp Minor), Chopin, Mendelssohn, Brahms, and Bruckner bear melancholy witness to the decline. Bartók's Fifth Quartet "is not so much a new version of sonata form as a brilliant twentieth-century metaphor for sonata form."

And Beethoven? The nineteenth-century prescriptive stereotype of a single sonata form based on themes was imposed by theorists closely connected with this composer. Reicha, Czerny, and A. B. Marx molded their stereotype to fit certain Beethoven works, the stifling prestige of which tempted nineteenth-century composers into endless ill-considered bouts of imitation. According to Rosen's little deconstruction Beethoven himself must be seen leading the decline, however unwittingly and indirectly, and he returns icily to this fact in a late chapter entitled "Beethoven and Schubert." There is much material about Beethoven in this book, all of it illuminating, but not much in this chapter, in which Rosen reminds his readers that he has "treated Beethoven throughout as if he were a late eighteenth-century composer" and seems mainly concerned to restore the composer to a state of pre-Marxist purity:

> Above all, Beethoven retains the classical sense of the resolution of large-scale dissonance by the reestablishment of a symmetrical equilibrium.... The emotional climate of his music, of course, is that of the Napoleonic and post-Napoleonic eras, and so is its ideological content. Jens Peter Larsen insists that a stylistic cut must be made between Beethoven and his predecessors because Beethoven's music is so much louder than theirs.

This is droll but possibly unfair to Larsen. In the "Eroica," once again, we hear of the large-scale dissonance produced by the E-minor development theme, and on its resolution in the coda, where this theme

> is heard first in F minor, the relative minor of the subdominant, and then in the tonic minor (E flat) as an introduction to an

incredibly long passage that does nothing but repeat a V–I cadence over and over again in E flat major.

Something appears to have gone wrong with symmetrical equilibrium here. What is so "incredible" about this musical passage, so unlike Haydn or Mozart? Not just the loudness, surely, nor the length. Rosen makes a rare and rather revealing slip when he says the passage does nothing but repeat a cadence; it does nothing less than resolve the main theme, played at last by the E-flat horns. It also provides an emotional resolution or rather an apotheosis, in which Beethoven for the first time, perhaps, expresses his response to Schiller's "Ode to Joy"—

Laufet, Brüder, eure Bahn,   *Run your course, brethren,*
Freudig, wie ein Held zum Siegen!   *Joyfully, like a hero to*
                                   victory!

—a poem that is known to have attracted him long before he set it in the Ninth Symphony. In the Third Symphony as in the Ninth, the ideological content skews the form, makes it incredible. In a symphony entitled "heroic" the emotional climate cannot, I believe, be separated off from form and style as clearly as Rosen would like.[4]

Shortly after the "Eroica" Beethoven wrote another incredible passage in the "Appassionata" Sonata, the new *presto* theme in the coda of the last movement. Whether symmetrical or not, the resolution it provides can only be conceived in terms of the total work—whose three movements Beethoven has indeed linked and related in an

---

4. The "Eroica" has, in fact, appalled many listeners. The dissonant horn-call at the end of the development section was bowdlerized by early conductors, even as late as Hans von Bülow. Schoenberg frowned on the beginning of the development section, which he said aims for "greater contrasts than structural considerations require" (Epstein draws attention to this in *Beyond Orpheus*, p. 137). Schenker could not get himself to consider the coda, which also eludes Epstein's search for "triadicity."

unusually close way, as is well known. Probably the most serious lacuna in *Sonata Forms* is any consideration of the nineteenth century's extension of sonata principles over total works, not just movements. One can share Rosen's distaste for the end product of this tendency in the so-called cyclic form of Mahler and Tchaikovsky, but still admire it in Beethoven. To judge from the way Rosen plays Beethoven, so does he. He has written about it, too, very well, in the big analysis of the "Hammerklavier" Sonata in his earlier book.

Another lacuna—almost bizarre in a seemingly methodical book of 350 pages on sonata forms—is any sustained discussion of the sonata-form coda. Only one short routine paragraph is to be found on this necessary topic. It is of course in his codas that Beethoven makes his musical apotheoses, so different in spirit and form from the symmetrical resolutions of Haydn and Mozart.[5]

But if Rosen gives us a picture of Beethoven seen through a filter, and a Brahms sadly underexposed, his Haydn and Mozart are wonderfully textured. Nobody writes better about the music of these composers. Nobody writes better about music. One may think at first that he is just extremely ingenious with examples, finding exactly the right Haydn symphony of the 1770s or Mozart aria from *Zaide* to make his points brilliantly. Then comes the "Prague" Symphony and the "Harmoniemesse" and the "Emperor" Concerto, and one realizes that to familiar and unfamiliar music alike this critic brings not only an uncommonly refined ear and sensibility but also, again and again, unerring insight into just the features that make the music special and fine. That is why his writing can be so economical. He is helped by a plenitude of music examples that is without precedent in book publishing, as far as I know; more than half of this book consists of music.

—1980

---

5. But see the revised edition of *Sonata Forms* (Norton, 1988) (2007).

15

BEETHOVEN: WORKS AND LIFE

LEWIS LOCKWOOD IS a leading musical scholar of the postwar generation, and one of the leading American authorities on Beethoven. He has published influential articles on the composer, some collected previously in *Beethoven: Studies in the Creative Process* (1992), but no full-length book until 2003. He has chosen to make his first major statement in the form of a life-and-works study. *Beethoven: The Music and the Life* is expressly not a work with a thesis, but a magisterial work of consolidation, aligning the author's own contributions with the broader tradition that has constructed the master musician of the Western canon.[1]

Such studies are typically, if not perhaps altogether inevitably, conservative, a term with—inevitably—both positive and negative connotations. While the book is said to be aimed at lay readers, the academy is certainly another target. W. W. Norton publishes major studies in music as well as both high- and low-level music textbooks, and this Beethoven will fill a gap in their distinguished, though aging, list.

Trade book or textbook, Lockwood has produced a more balanced account of Beethoven—balanced between life and works— than any other study I know of. Although his priorities come through

---

1. Norton, 2003.

clearly enough in his slightly bumpy title, Lockwood has sought to treat the music and the life with equal responsibility and indeed to make his peace with the inherent problems of artistic biography. As an introduction to these problems, a prologue chapter begins with three letters from Beethoven's early, middle, and late years (mirroring the familiar division of his output into three periods). At sixteen, writing from Bonn, Beethoven twists a letter of apology into a cry of pain: he is ill, heartsick at the loss of his mother, and overwhelmed by his obligations in a rudderless family. At forty-one, he writes a humble and almost fatherly letter from Vienna to a girl in Hamburg who sent him a fan letter and the gift of an embroidered wallet. At fifty-six, he answers (a year late) a childhood friend from Bonn, Franz Wegeler, who has written to him out of the blue: how fondly, Beethoven writes, I remember those old days, and our friendship, how differently our careers have progressed. He barely mentions any present troubles; in fact he is deeply ill and will die four months later.

Lockwood is a very astute and perceptive reader. The thread he teases out of these moving letters is the extraordinary sense of artistic mission that this composer developed when he was, as far as anyone knew, no more than a talented teenager, and that drove and sustained him ever after. He must get out of Bonn to pursue the great career he foresees—this he intimates almost parenthetically, more to himself than to his correspondent Joseph von Schaden. "Miss Emilie M." is urged to ponder the meaning of music, not just study piano technique. Art has no limits, he tells the little girl, and the true artist has always to acknowledge how much further he has to go. And in 1826 Beethoven is still hoping to create "a few large-scale works" before retiring among old friends, "like an old child"—a child driven in much the same way as the one Wegeler had known in Bonn.

If there is one theme stressed above any other in the present book, it is this sense of artistic mission. It allows Beethoven to float above every tragedy and misfortune. Life shrinks into career; everything else becomes epiphenomenal. This is, of course, hardly a new way of looking at things—Donald Tovey, self-appointed conservator of "the main stream of music," planned a comprehensive book on the composer that would say virtually nothing about the life, as did Theodor Adorno, to judge from the two-hundred-odd pages of his notes and prolegomena, recently published.[2] Lockwood brings in support for his view from Schopenhauer ("In the composer, more than in any other artist, the man is entirely separate and distinct from the artist") and Rilke:

> [Beethoven's] artistic involvement was so intense that it tended to reduce the rest of his life to a struggle for equilibrium in which the pressure of the work could cause the life almost to wither away, "like some organ they no longer require," as Rilke said of Tolstoy and Rodin.

On the other hand, it is acknowledged somewhat gingerly that "certain features of [Beethoven's] life, such as his persistent illnesses and his depression, are apparently mirrored to some extent" in the movement entitled "La Malinconia" from the opus 18 quartets and the "Hymn of Thanks to God from a Convalescent" from opus 132. Indeed,

> The theory of an absolute separation is self-defeating and will not hold. Works...are created...by individuals carrying out specific imaginative purposes; they are not made by abstract processes or algorithms. Accordingly, we can acknowledge that deeply rooted elements in the creative person's personality, angle of vision, speech habits, interactions with people, and

---

2. Donald Francis Tovey, *Beethoven* (Oxford University Press, 1945); Theodor W. Adorno, *Beethoven, The Philosophy of Music: Fragments and Texts*, edited by Rolf Tiedemann and translated by Edmund Jephcott (Stanford University Press, 1998).

ways of dealing with the world find resonance in many of the artist's works.

Still, as Beethoven's life and Beethoven's works roll past us in Lockwood's leisurely motorcade, they tend, we notice, to keep each other at a safe distance.

As I have said, this is a magisterial study without being overbearing. It is often beautifully written and it is supported by a lifetime of wide reading. Formidable musicological authority lurks mostly in the endnotes, though specialists will feel it on every page. (The notes are also lightly sprinkled with Ivy League insider references and scholarly irritations.) Frequent clear headings on comfortably spaced pages make it a simple matter to locate material on the individual compositions discussed—about eighty in all—as well as incisive mini-essays over and above the chronological survey: "Life and Works," "Entering the Publishing World," "Deafness," "Napoleon and Self-Made Greatness," "Improvising and Composing at the Piano," and "Relations with Women." Consolidation entails saying some well-known things: Lockwood says them in his own voice and with his own, often subtle nuance.

The composition he discusses at greatest length, nearly thirty pages, is the Symphony No. 9, the "Choral" Symphony. No doubt the Ninth has to count, if count we must, as Beethoven's key work. "There are actually two 'Ninth Symphonies,'" Lockwood points out—the so-called Joy Theme of the finale and its choral anthem, which has inspired millions, and a highly intricate four-movement cycle culminating in the finale built on that theme...and on a second theme, one that almost usurps the first before the finale is over. Topics he discusses include the current mythic status of the Ninth, its political and ideological background, its genesis in sketches and other sources, the work's reception, and finally its character, movement by movement and section by section.

Lewis Lockwood's major research has been concentrated on the genesis of Beethoven's compositions, and he gives us more information than we need about preliminary drafts, altered or abandoned early plans, and the like, some of which tell us more about the music than others. With the Ninth, a chance letter of 1793 reports that the young man on whom Bonn pins such high hopes intends to tackle Schiller's "An die Freude" ("Ode to Joy"), still recent at that time and already a theme song for the idealistic and the radical. Indeed in a curious composite song written in 1794–1795, "Seufzer eines Ungeliebten und Gegenliebe" (The Sigh of One Unloved and Requited Love), the Joy Theme begins to form itself. The theme is almost there in the Choral Fantasy for Piano, Orchestra, and Chorus of 1808, and in basic outline so is the aberrant and much-debated form of the symphony finale. Sketches and notations for the symphony date from 1812, 1816, and 1818, long before serious work on it began in 1821. Genetically as well as in nearly every other way, this is *the* exceptional work by Beethoven.

As for the work's reception, Lockwood wishes principally to oppose Adorno's charge that the Ninth was written in bad faith:

> Some reject... its forthright, naive, powerful assertions of ethical and political ideals... [because of] current disillusionment in the face of modern history and a twentieth century in which monumental crimes against humanity were committed, above all the Holocaust.... But if we look at the Ninth as the product of an attempted revival of these ideals, written at a time when political tyranny had returned to the European world after 1815, a symphony that originated as an effort to reinstall some hope into a world even then desperate for assurances of the survival of such ideals—then we can see that modern skepticism unwittingly tends to replicate the political despondency of the time in which it came into being.... By using Schiller's "Ode" to

directly address humanity at large, Beethoven conveys the struggle of both the individual and of the millions to work their way through experience from tragedy to idealism and to preserve the image of human brotherhood as a defense against the darkness.

This eloquent, even lofty peroration looks back to a section in the book on "The Character of the Ninth," the author's credo on the matter of interpretation, placed near the end of the book as though to parallel the one on artistic biography at the beginning. Little sympathy is expressed here for the notion that the artwork can accommodate many different interpretations, that it transcends its maker's mortality to engage changing subjectivities in successive generations of readers and listeners, indeed that its meaning may consist of a congeries of interpretations. (The Ninth Symphony, Maynard Solomon has said, "encompasses larger relevancies and manifold meanings that have given it unassailable status as a model of human transformation." Lockwood gets uncharacteristically angry with what he calls today's ideological criticism, focused as it is on art's supposed political and social content:

> With great éclat, a feminist critic has denounced the first movement as an example of "horrifyingly violent" masculine rage, and a feminist poet reviled the entire work as a "sexual message" written by a man "in terror of impotence or infertility, not knowing the difference."

What is so very awful about these interpretations? They draw attention—violently, to be sure, and so what?—to a cardinal feature of the first movement's recapitulatory passage: its unique combination of violence and frustration. The timpani blast away as never before in classical music and literally disorient the harmonies screeching and grasping at them. Tovey calls the passage "catastrophic" and "very terrible," Leo Treitler calls it "the high point of dramatic conflict and tension" rather than the "moment of arrival and resolution" expected in sonata form, and Lockwood, to his credit, quotes them both. The only other "political" interpretation he discusses that is at all recent, from an unpublished dissertation, gains a measure of respect if not approval.[3] Critics who refuse to give in to ideology may find they can do so

> only by recommitting themselves to [musical] analysis, which concerns itself exclusively with the structural, or recommitting to history, that is, to understanding the Ninth not as a disembodied art product out of time and space, but as the work of an artist living in a particular period and context.... Our job would then be not only to try to understand the work in the context of its origins but to make that understanding, as nearly as possible and with minimal distortion and loss of content, meaningful in the present.

The thinking of Hans-Georg Gadamer seems to be acknowledged here, but not that of Roland Barthes or Hans Robert Jauss or Hans Heinrich Eggebrecht, an *éminence grise* of musicology, whose eye-opening *Zur Geschichte der Beethoven-Rezeption* does not figure in Lockwood's bibliography of works cited. Back in the Beethoven bicentennial year, 1970, Eggebrecht was already urging us not to "separate—absolve—Beethoven's music from its reception," finding the source of its greatness and beauty in "the music itself.'"

I am sorry that *Beethoven: The Music and the Life* does not include another sustained reflection, perhaps even a credo, in addition to the

---

3. Stephen (not "Edward") Rumph. Rumph's *Beethoven After Napoleon* was published by the University of California Press in 2004.

ones on biography and interpretation, referred to above. The subject I miss is how to write about music, the actual sounding notes and patterns of music, and after that how to write about it in a book of this kind. Readers will find much to learn here about particular Beethoven pieces, much that extends beyond received wisdom.[4] Again one senses the distillation of long experience with the music, derived this time from performance as well as learning. Lockwood is a cellist, and some of his most valuable observations concern music for cello and other string instruments (the Violin Concerto, the Quartet in E Flat, op. 127).

But for me, and I think this will be true for many of Lockwood's intended readers, the musical coverage of this book as a whole—the sum of what he calls his "short critical accounts" of Beethoven's compositions—succeeds less well than the grand historical narrative in which he embeds it or, for that matter, less well than the biography. Too often, those well-known things about canonical works that need saying in a comprehensive study of this kind don't get said. In the thirty-page discussion of the Ninth Symphony, for example, the bizarre *Alla Marcia* for solo tenor, male chorus, and "Turkish" instruments in the finale receives no mention at all. With the Fifth Symphony, Lockwood's account of the first movement consists of a novel (to me) point about the underlying key scheme and little else. There is no reference to the crucial alternating string and woodwind chords prior to the recapitulation—"orchestral gasps," for Berlioz, "coming and going while gradually growing weaker like the painful breathing of a dying man"—or to the time-stopping oboe cadenza, or the out-

---

4. To mention just one of many points that struck this reader: while one or two other Bach fugues are regularly cited as influential on the great opening fugue of the Quartet in C-Sharp Minor, op. 131, Lockwood points also to the Fugue in B Minor from *The Well-Tempered Clavier*, Book I, of which a little-known copy exists in Beethoven's hand. A simple sequence from this fugue is copied in opus 131 almost literally; yet what was a cliché for Bach becomes luminous in Beethoven.

sized coda, or the quite unanticipated intervention of a new strong melody in that coda. With Piano Concerto No. 3 in C Minor, we hear, once again, about the underlying long-range key relations (twice) and scarcely anything about the musical surface.

Of course one can't say everything one might want to say about every piece in any book, let alone a book planned to be "of moderate length,"[5] but then shouldn't one choose the most salient things? The strategy here seems better suited to fairly advanced students than to lay readers. Lockwood's fluent prose runs dry when he addresses the character and characteristics of the compositions. No dying gasps for him. This is a work of consolidation, an objective book, one that no doubt aims to be a standard text for years. Lockwood relies on technical language or language that can be reduced to the technical, seldom reaching for subjective, imaginative, or metaphorical terms to characterize music's affect. Imaginative flashes such as "a celestial exercise piece" for the finale of the "Tempest" Sonata, op. 31 no. 2, appear less often than bromides like "arabesque" for the solo-violin passage that tears through the beginning of the Quartet in A Minor, op. 132. The highly exceptional *fortissimo* ostinato passage in the scherzo of the Quartet in F, op. 135, is merely an "odd" element, an example of "mordant humor."[6] That the passage in opus 135 is odd (that is, highly exceptional both in itself and in its context) can be established by technical analysis of a reasonably objective sort. But serious listeners have also experienced this and the many other such passages in Beethoven as uncanny, sinister, transgressive, horrifyingly violent, and so on, feelings that are muted by the language in this

---

5. Many pages are saved by relegating most music examples to Norton's Web site—an innovation in music-book publishing. A book of this kind deserves better illustrations; the cramped autograph facsimiles are unhelpful, and the fine, unvarnished Waldmüller portrait of 1823 used for the dust cover appears in the text in a ham-fisted idealized version.

6. If I may borrow E. T. A. Hoffmann's dry remark about a place in the Fifth Symphony: "Many find the passage humorous, but it stirred sinister feelings in this reviewer."

book, and also by Lockwood's choices of what to emphasize. Famous —notorious—Beethoven moves are not reported. In the Ninth Symphony, the contrabassoon greets the cherub who "stands before God" with what is sometimes called an unmentionable noise. In the Fifth Symphony, C-major chords in the final cadence replicate themselves hyperbolically. There's the unforgettable moment of piano–orchestra confrontation in Piano Concerto No. 5 ("Emperor"), and the uncanny first-movement coda in No. 3. A sudden fireball lights up the end of the "Appassionata" Sonata. There are many such events.

The unruly in Beethoven startled and dismayed most of his contemporaries. It took a Romantic like Berlioz to love it, and this aspect of his work still engages a generation that takes Adorno for granted and cares about discontinuity and physical presence in music as well as transcendence and organic form, a generation that will be teaching Beethoven courses (assuming they—the courses, the teachers—survive) in the twenty-first century. On one particularly distracted day in his last years, the composer was pulled in by the police as a peeping Tom, but they let him go in embarrassment once they realized who he was—Lockwood looks the other way, too, when he sees the great man tooling down the Autobahn toward postmodernity.

The section on "Relations with Women" begins with the observation that these have become "the stuff of endless speculation, some of it poignant and some of it prurient," and it's clear this author wants to distance himself from this strand of Beethoven biography and also, perhaps, from the tell-all fashion that seems to prevail in lives of the great as so frequently depicted today. But his account of the love affair with Antonie Brentano, the Viennese matron who with her husband entered into the composer's circle in the years 1809–1812, when he was around forty, seems laconic, even heartless. The affair brought to a close Beethoven's involvements with high-born women, often his students, from whom he seems typically to have withdrawn if he was not rejected outright, as Lockwood says. He does not quite say that this relationship was of a different order, nor does he quote from the letter to a famously unnamed "Immortal Beloved," written in 1812, in which Beethoven spills out his passions, though other letters are quoted to very good effect—Josephine Deym turning aside his overtures for "sensual love," and Antonie Brentano describing Beethoven as "greater as a human being than as an artist." Who else besides Brentano, as Lockwood remarks, would have felt that?

The focus, though, is not really on her feelings and how they affected her lover, but on her identification with the letter's recipient: for there are still Antonie deniers out there—less poignant or prurient, I think, than appalled at the thought of their hero involved with a married woman who was pregnant when the affair ended.[7] In any case, Beethoven was shattered, finding himself reacting in his usual way—withdrawal—in relation to a woman whom he loved and who for the first time fully accepted him. Not long afterward he went into a severe depression and a creative slump that resulted in no new compositions of any consequence in the year 1813. Luckily for him the Congress of Vienna convened in 1814–1815, making him the musician of the hour. He went into a whirlwind of composition, producing quantities of mindless and distasteful patriotic music which was played repeatedly (it is never played today) and brought him more fame and money than ever before. There was a revival of his opera *Leonore* in a new version, *Fidelio*, somewhat tailored to the mood of the congress. It cost him more labor, he said, than a new piece started from scratch.

---

7. The identification was clinched twenty-five years ago, by Maynard Solomon, and in the current Master Musicians volume the identity of the Immortal Beloved is said to be "now as well established as many of the other 'facts' in Beethoven's life" (*Beethoven*, Oxford University Press, 2000, pp. 210–211). As to the likelihood that Beethoven was the father of Antonie's child, argued with some force by Susan Lund in her annotated novel *Raptus* (Melstamps, Cambs., UK, 1995), Cooper dismisses it with a bad joke and Lockwood doesn't mention the pregnancy at all. Solomon and David Wyn Jones, in *The Life of Beethoven* (Cambridge University Press, 1998), leave the question open.

Distracting labor, one would guess. From 1815 to 1818 he wrote no more than four large compositions. A piano trio and a piano concerto were half-composed and aborted. Beethoven's slumps are not like other people's, and the few substantial compositions of the period between 1813 and 1818 include some of his most marvelous. Life and career: two of these pieces seem to me directly and profoundly affected by events of the life in 1812, whether or not Beethoven understood that his career had reached a "critical turning point," a "crossroad," as Lockwood proposes. "Women could be part of his life but not part of his career.... In his relationship to women, there could now be only renunciation and stoic acceptance." The song cycle *An die ferne Geliebte* of 1816 shows the poet-composer-lover putting the crisis behind him, figuring a past love as a distant love, affirming that only songs—a new commitment to his artistic mission—can cover the pain. And I am certainly not the first to sense an utterly unprecedented tenderness in the opening theme and the whole first movement of the Piano Sonata in A Major, op. 101, of the same year. This is the music of caress, like Debussy's "La Fille aux cheveux de lin," only purer. Not by accident is it recalled, like a poignant memory, between later movements of the sonata which turn away to a kind of forced energy or gaiety, forced innovation.

This type of thematic recall—it also occurs in the song cycle and in the Cello Sonata in C, op. 102 no. 1, of 1815—Charles Rosen has seen as an "essay in, or at least a movement towards, the open forms of the Romantic period."[8] Romantic indeed; there was more being recalled here than a theme, than music.

—2003

---

8. *The Classical Style* (Norton, 1972), p. 403.

16

BEETHOVEN HERO

IN 1969 ALAN TYSON, the leading British authority on Beethoven, who was also a psychoanalyst, published a short, quiet, and by now rather well-known article called "Beethoven's Heroic Phase."[1] Its subject is the young musician's psychological state (bad) in the years when he first began to experience deafness, from around 1799 to 1802. Beethoven says again and again, in letters sent and unsent, that he must accept his affliction with resignation. Yet resignation was obviously hard to attain, for he also keeps mentioning alternatives: death as a release, a woman's love that may rescue him, and especially immersion in his art. "The goal which I feel but cannot describe" was to create a future music of transcendent greatness. Tyson observed that three compositions written or commenced in the year 1803, the oratorio *Christ on the Mount of Olives*, the opera *Leonore* (later *Fidelio*), and Symphony No. 3, the pathbreaking *Sinfonia Eroica*, virtually act out each of the three alternatives.

One might expect "Beethoven's Heroic Phase" to figure somewhere in a book about the great composer and heroism that concentrates on the "Eroica" Symphony. But in Scott Burnham's *Beethoven Hero*[2] Tyson's article does not even figure in the substantial bibliography.

---

1. *The Musical Times*, Vol. 110 (1969), pp. 139–141.

2. Princeton University Press, 1996.

Strategic economy is a very striking feature of this book, as striking as its breathtaking ambition. Its ultimate goal is to demonstrate how the master figure of Western music affects the way we understand all music; it concentrates, that is, on the reception of music, not the composition of music, and the reader is warned at the outset not to look for such traditional historical topics as the development of musical style, biography, or even the influence of the biographical Beethoven myth. Yet with all these exclusions, situating the composer historically may be the book's outstanding success, as we shall see.

Burnham begins with a survey of what he calls "programmatic" accounts of Beethoven compositions, stories invented by commentators as a way of explaining or comprehending their aesthetic force. One remembers fondly, perhaps, the infestation of goblins visited on the Fifth Symphony by Helen Schlegel in *Howards End*. Describing Berlioz's program for the "Eroica" Symphony, Burnham writes that Berlioz "hit upon the happy expedient of hearing the scherzo as a musical transcription of ancient Greek funeral games." Some very good points are made about this kind of criticism. First of all, the stories are about the music; whatever the critics may say or imply, the music is not about the stories. Second, this kind of writing was developed in the early nineteenth century to cope with a new kind of listening experience expressive of human values, or so it was felt, beyond the reach of the rhetorical or rationalistic interpretative methods of previous generations. The composer was no longer viewed as an artisan but as a creative genius. His music had to be approached not as exercise or representation but as organism or myth.

Burnham and a number of other musicologists were attempting to reclaim programmatic criticism, which had been largely discredited and derided, or at least to make the case for its value alongside the technical analysis that has largely replaced it.[3] Such programs or tales

---

3. One of Burnham's most important witnesses is Wagner, whose Beethoven criticism receives careful scrutiny from Thomas S. Grey, *Wagner's Musical Prose: Texts and Contexts* (Cambridge University Press, 1995). Grey's emphasis is of course on the storyteller rather than the story.

about the music, Burnham argues, serve to identify a new theme, for instance, as an important turning point in a psychological or dramatic process, where current analytic methods might merely trace the presence of a web of thematic relationships. His own criticism has its unashamed programmatic moments, as when he writes that the famous hushed half-note chords in the first movement of the Fifth Symphony suggest "the suddenly audible respirations of a nervous soldier."

A very few compositions, Burnham points out—he tallies no more than two symphonies, two piano sonatas, several overtures, and one piano concerto—control our impression of Beethoven and have had enormous historical impact. Among these works in the "heroic style" the "Eroica" Symphony has pride of place. The stories that have been told about it over the years differ; the protagonist is now Napoleon ("the default choice"), now Hector, Beethoven himself, or a quasi-Hegelian Idea. Burnham's contention is that they all come down to the same basic myth, the quest plot or the hero's journey:

> Something (someone) not fully formed but full of potential ventures out into complexity and ramification (adversity), reaches a ne plus ultra (a crisis), and then returns renewed and completed (triumphant).

The myth can also be traced by analyzing details of melody, rhythm, harmony, and so on in the score. Formalist musical analysis as currently taught in the schools, then, tells an old story in a different way; an essentially ethical narrative is presented in a seemingly abstract form, even though the analysts would deny that it is really a story at all. (Another difference is also worth bearing in mind, especially in view of the final swerve of the argument of *Beethoven Hero*: formalist criticism can be comprehended only by specialists, while programmatic criticism is available to all.)

One movement of the Third Symphony and two movements of the Fifth—the opening and closing movements standing for the whole, with the middle movements of the sequence elided—suffice for a dazzling demonstration of music's articulation of the heroic journey. While Burnham's structuralist analysis of the stories he has encountered works better with some of them than with others, his analysis of the music is always on target, in fact marvelous. It is analysis of the "phenomenological" kind, correlating musical phenomena systematically with listener response, analysis "taking note of our reactions to the music and finding out how the music makes such reactions possible." Amazingly, one finds oneself learning much that is new and right about these very familiar works. To give just one example, I have never heard the first-movement recapitulation in the Fifth Symphony (after those hushed chords) characterized so acutely:

> After the intense drama of the end of the development and the arrival of the motto, the opening of the recapitulation seems to pull back from the action. This is felt not as stability but rather as a kind of breather: the important arrival of the home key and first theme is made retroactively to feel like the goal of a struggle whose intensity has made such a reprieve necessary and highly deserved.

There is hardly time to note the absence in this book of the Ninth Symphony—or of any attention to its arguably "heroic" status, past a quiet footnote—before the author is pressing on. Listeners *engage* with Beethoven's heroic music and its masterplot in a way they do not with any earlier music (or, it is strongly implied, with any later music). "The music of Mozart remains, always, at a remove"; this composer grabs listeners by the lapels, draws them along with it, sweeps them away. In contrast to the eighteenth century's "artful play with convention and representation," his compositional processes "seem undisguised and experiential." Indeed, a comparison between Haydn's experiments in symphonic form and the similar techniques in Beethoven merely throws into relief what is

> truly unprecedented in Beethoven: the sense of an earnest and fundamental presence burdened with some great weight yet coursing forth ineluctably, moving the listener along as does the earth itself.

Later on, in one of the book's more eloquent passages, the music seems "to animate and empower its listeners.... One becomes literally enthused, flushed with the interiorized presence of the sublime."

Though it is not exactly news that Beethoven's heroic music engages the listener in a special way, I doubt that this quality has ever been explored so deeply as in the chapter "Musical Values." The very fact that the symphonies stimulated heroic stories made it easier for listeners to relate to them man to man (always man, I think). The music projects the passage of time in a new way that can be specified, once again, by means of analysis of rhythm, harmony, upbeat-downbeat cycles, and the like. Wagner's remark that in the "Eroica" "everything becomes melody" means that by analogy to a simple melody, every element of the symphonic web counts, and therefore can engage us on the same primal level as when we find ourselves absorbed by the progress of a song from note to note and word to word. While all this may not add up to an explanation of the "presence" Burnham feels so strongly in the heroic music—he probably never expected it to—it illuminates much about this primary feature of musical experience.

A chapter entitled "Cultural Values" treats the resonance of "the premier story of Western mythology"—the story of the struggle of the hero for freedom—in the composer's own time. For Burnham, the Beethovenian version of this myth projects the values of selfhood that evolved in the *Goethezeit*, at the hands of Kant, Goethe, Schiller, and

Hegel. The argument here becomes complex and can only be sketched summarily. It starts with Kantian self-consciousness. Becoming, striving is the essence of Goethe's idea of the self; the ability of a distinctly identifiable self or subject to create itself and its own world is the essence of Hegel's. One concept is open, the other closed, and Beethoven's heroic style captures both concepts. Thanks to his unique way of developing themes, the music seems to arrive at destinations in ever-new consequential ways, and these arrivals have the feeling of decisions freely made, of musical events based on, but not determined by, what has preceded them. The action-reaction, downbeat-upbeat pattern of Beethoven's commanding macrorhythm mirrors the polar forces of deed and reflection that we find in the heroes of classical German drama—Goethe's Egmont, Schiller's Marquis of Posa, and William Tell.

The developing themes also give the illusion of demanding or creating their own unique musical forms. Yet at the same time sonata form can be seen as a universal principle, and the coda in sonata form—the final section—works a closure that is suggestive, to Burnham, of the Hegelian merger of the individual with a higher world. We now hear of a "telling presence"; this means to say that the music both enacts mythic events and also narrates them, producing a pervading sense of irony.[4] In sum,

> A perspective simultaneously objective and subjective allows the heroic style its particular presence as a modeling of ironic self-consciousness, while the narrated projection of an end-

---

4. Thus, for example, the codas of heroic works are often marked by a great deal of loud banging away at the final cadence—much more than is required to make the listener feel the piece has come to rest. The excess cadencing is more than an enactment of closure, it is also an announcement or narration of closure by some agent or agency that is conscious (self-conscious) of the enactment.

On the universality of musical forms: it should be said that sonata form in Beethoven's heroic works rubs shoulders with sui generis forms, as in the finale of the "Eroica" Symphony or the scherzo (the goblin movement) of the Fifth.

oriented process...expresses the ethos of the self as hero—whether as an individual realizing a personal destiny or as the cosmos coming to know itself. The great and defining experiment of the age of both Goethe and Hegel was to model human consciousness in this way. Beethoven simply does it best.

Indeed, Beethoven's music for *Egmont* realizes Goethe's vision of heroism better than the play itself. A well-known difficulty with the culmination of Goethe's drama is Egmont's sudden transformation, in a single final scene, from an agreeable but apolitical being into a heroic symbol of freedom. As he goes to the scaffold, Goethe calls for a "Symphony of Victory"—which Schiller dismissed as a "somersault" into opera; but when in 1811 Beethoven composed music of almost hysterical rejoicing for this final curtain, he also planted much the same music as the coda that caps the play's overture, before the curtain ever rises. Burnham points out that

> because the music of the drama's apotheosis acts in the overture also as the harmonic closure of the preceding music, what is only a political afterthought in the drama appears to become the whole story in the overture. In Goethe's play there is no comparable sense of something within the play generating its own closure; indeed, its end arrives *ex machina*, and there are too many other issues (like the fates of Ferdinand and Brackenburg) that find no ultimate resolution.

Only the medium of music—Beethoven's music—could accomplish this consummation:

> Depending on one's point of view, either Goethe's bad faith about his ending prompted him to appropriate the overdetermined closure of music, or his supreme faith in the sense of his ending

called for the only medium felt to be equal to such consummate finality.

(In either case we must admire Goethe's prescience, since when he wrote *Egmont* in the 1770s Beethoven was still in diapers.)

Equally persuasive is the demonstration of the heroic style's endurance, its stubborn persistence. A powerful, if technical chapter entitled "Institutional [i.e., academic] Values" studies its impact on theorists of music, and the use they have made of it in developing methods of technical analysis. For Beethoven has figured overwhelmingly in the thinking of music theorists since his day. Burnham shows how the characteristic features of the heroic style—development, culmination, closure, teleology: in a word, process—have in effect become the basis of the musical-analytic systems of four influential theorists, from A. B. Marx in the 1850s to Rudolph Réti in the 1950s. (The others, in between, are the even more formidable Hugo Riemann and Heinrich Schenker.[5]) In a brilliant deconstructive exercise that will doubtless rattle the cages of music theory, they are each shown to have articulated the repressed ethical values of the heroic style in technical terms. The terms are different, the covert values always the same. The institutional image of music is, quite simply, that of the Beethovenian heroic style.

Musical values, cultural values, institutional values: all receive original and profound treatment in this study.[6] "My goal is to engage

---

5. These theorists are all Germans or Austrians of a past era, or past eras; the youngest of them, Réti, was born (in Serbia) in 1885. He published his work at an advanced age and enjoyed a brief run, as Burnham says, in the 1950s and 1960s, especially in England. In many ways Réti, with his special Beethoven obsession, works well for Burnham, but his place in the theorists' pantheon really belongs to an even earlier figure, Arnold Schoenberg, as a somewhat uncomfortable footnote makes clear.

6. I cannot resist noting the occurrence of the word "value" in three out of the five chapter titles of this book—almost a little manifesto of the so-called "new musicology" characterized by (among others) Charles Rosen in "Music à la Mode," *The New York Review*, June 23,

as directly as I can the fundamental importance of this music," says Burnham, and engage he does. It is a pity things get out of focus in the final chapter, where Beethoven Hero, his almost coercive immediacy undimmed, is seen as throwing a paradoxical shadow across today's aesthetic landscape.

This is because of our "urge to make teleological process the *exclusive* and *defining* agenda of music" (my italics). The heroic style unconsciously "controls our thinking to the extent that it dictates the shape of alterity (i.e., perceptions of other music); it is the daylight by which everything else must be night"—so that non-heroic compositions such as the "Pastoral" Symphony have been pushed to the margins, and figures like Schubert are found wanting in the Beethovenian balance.[7] Thanks to *Beethoven Hero*, a discredited Romantic model of selfhood is being kept alive. Obsession with Beethovenian closure has closed the canon of music and closed music history. There may be a remedy, but only if we can learn new ways of listening to music for presence, not for process.

This seems overheated and probably exaggerated even as a polemic directed narrowly toward music theory. More serious is a confusion between music theory and Music, academic musical discourse and musical experience at large. One may accept that academics remain manacled to the heroic myth without supposing that this says very much about the attitudes of off-campus listeners. One may also allow for the handing down (not always so smoothly) of theorists' lore to their students, and its trickling down to others by way of program notes, music appreciation courses, TV intermission

---

1994, pp. 55–62. Even ten years earlier, when positivistic music scholarship began to be questioned, such headings in a musicological study would have been inconceivable.

7. Tell it not at the Y! When Beethoven's reputation was first being established in Germany, in the 1830s, the "Pastoral" was his most popular symphony; see Sanna Pederson, "A. B. Marx, Berlin Concert Life, and German National Identity," in *19th-Century Music*, Vol. 18 (1994), pp. 871–107.

features, and the like, without indulging in the fantasy that theory permeates the essential experience of the classical music audience. If Burnham means to imply that most people—men and women—listen to Bach, Mozart, Debussy, Stravinsky, and all other composers with Beethovenian ears, I frankly don't believe it. And if all this other music "remains, always, at a remove" as compared to music in the heroic style, non-Beethovenian intense engagements can also be cited: with Gregorian chant, with Terry Riley's *In C*, with *Andrea Chénier*.

The totalizing, all-embracing thrust of Burnham's polemic makes so little sense that perhaps nobody will be confused by it after all. But there are cases of slippage in the prose:

> A particularly compelling concept of self was animated by Beethoven's music and through it seems ever renewable. The experience of this music has been primarily an ethical experience. How else could it have assumed pride of place in the musical-theoretic thought of the next two centuries? How else could it have come to stand for Music itself?

Here Music with a capital letter conflates with musical-theoretic thought. In another characteristic sequence, when "our current musical discourse" in one sentence is followed by "the unhappy results of our collective repression of this ethical dimension" in the next, while no actual slippage occurs, the referent of "us" seems unobtrusively to expand from those who reflect upon music professionally to a larger, universal collective. By the time we are being told to mend our ways and listen differently, the rhetoric is attuned to far more than a modest band of academics.

As already noted, there is nothing in this book about the biographical circumstances discussed in Tyson's article, circumstances that support the familiar and no doubt naive view that the presence in Beethoven's music is that of a miserable young musician who was going deaf and who was actually picturing himself as a tragic hero. Nor is much said about other composers (save for the paragraph on Schubert, and brief formal comparisons with Mozart and Haydn). Though it may seem unfair to tax the author with this particular economy, I come back to the issue because an inevitable question arises: If the overwhelming response to one composer's music depends on its projection of a model of self-consciousness that means so much to us, what explains the response to other music that means just as much to us (or many of us), or more? Bach, Mozart, Wagner, Mahler, Debussy, Stravinsky—are they all locked into the same secondary status that Burnham ascribes to Schubert? The naive view that all composers of genius engender their own individual, indeed personal engagements at least allows us relatively uncomplicated traffic with multiple musical presences, other selves.

It is perhaps just as well not to bring such arguments too heavily to bear on Burnham's book, for his densely (and elegantly) reasoned study has no need of extra complications. Following its essential direction is easy enough—and stimulating, or so I found—but a full grasp of the underlying structure supporting its argument will require readers with a stomach for both musical analysis and Idealist philosophy. Those with intestinal fortitude will find much to ponder, admire, and digest in *Beethoven Hero*.

—1996

17

TEXT AND ACT:
BEETHOVEN'S CONCERTOS[1]

IN 1791 A LISTING was made of the several dozen musicians in the employ of the episcopal court of Bonn. "Herr Ludwig van Bethoven plays clavier concertos" is the extent of the entry on the young man who was to become Bonn's and perhaps Germany's most celebrated citizen. At the age of twenty his output included three concertos for piano (one arranged from a violin concerto, as was not uncommon at the time), as well as a concerto for piano with two other instruments, and possibly a lost fourth piano concerto, if some extant early sketches were ever completed. A young pianist-virtuoso-composer needed concertos to make his way—indeed, the encounter between the concerto's solo instrument and the orchestra can stand as a metaphor for the freelance musician and his support system of audience and patrons. Before Beethoven found himself as a symphonist, the concerto was the public genre that marked the stages of his march to success and, as the nineteenth century saw it, greatness.

Around 1801, when he published the first of his five canonical piano concertos, Beethoven knew he was becoming deaf, and by 1809, when he composed the last of them, the so-called "Emperor,"

---

1. My title is homage to Richard Taruskin, *Text and Act: Essays on Music and Performance* (Oxford University Press, 1995).

he could no longer play in public. So in the eighteen years remaining to him he no longer wrote concertos. The story of Beethoven's concertos is a story of the obligatory and no doubt painful relinquishment of a favorite genre. (In later years he began work on more than one concerto, only to leave them unfinished. The Eighth Symphony was first sketched as a concerto.) Yet in this arrested development Leon Plantinga can trace a grand panorama of change in the very concept of Western music and in the model of a composer.[2] It is a transition from music as activity to music as text, from the performer-composer known to the eighteenth century to the genius-creator postulated by the nineteenth. In the sphere of the concerto, deafness was both cause and symbol of this transition.

This historical process has been the subject of much discussion (as well as complaint) in recent years. It is bound up with the issue of "absolute" music, music thought to be autonomous irrespective of verbal texts, social contexts, and even performance considerations. It is the subject of an entire book by the late, much translated musicologist Carl Dahlhaus, and the subject of a full half of a book on the ontology of music by the philosopher Lydia Goehr.[3] When did European music change over from a fluid performance activity, passed on from master to student over the ages, as it was and is in other cultures, and become a written, read, and (eventually) digitally recorded artifact to be contemplated as well as—as much as, one sometimes feels—heard?

Over a period of roughly a thousand years, according to music historians of the *longue durée*. Somewhat abruptly around the year 1800, according to Goehr. It is easy for Plantinga in one of his argumentative footnotes to show her case to be "overdrawn." Yet it

---

2. *Beethoven's Concertos: History, Style, Performance* (Norton, 1999).

3. Carl Dahlhaus, *The Idea of Absolute Music*, translated by Roger Lustig (University of Chicago Press, 1989); Lydia Goehr, *The Imaginary Museum of Musical Works* (Clarendon Press/Oxford University Press, 1992).

contains "a kernel of truth"; no one doubts that the process accelerated decisively in Beethoven's lifetime. It accelerated as a response to
his extraordinary music but also as a response to Romantic musical
speculation.

I am reminded here of another recent study, also overdrawn, by a
sociologist who attributes Beethoven's early success in Vienna—
exactly in the years he was making his way with concertos—to a need
felt by his essential patrons for a new elevated musical ideal in the
face of social change.[4] If the Viennese aristocracy had a historic need
for a new master musician, the philosophers of Jena needed him even
more. Though Vienna was certainly no hotbed of Romanticism,
Maynard Solomon, for one, whose classic biography of Beethoven
now appears in a revised edition, has always patiently searched out
Romantic traits and resonances in the composer's thought and in his
music.[5] And there was only one composer who could have steered the
conception of music from Kant's "pleasurable stimulation" to E. T. A.
Hoffmann's revelation of the "spirit realm." The Romantics from
Tieck and Schlegel all the way up to Adorno saw the musical master-
work as an autonomous product of the free "subject." Beethoven's
metaphysical freedom with the musical tradition he inherited from
Haydn and Mozart was as evident as the secular freedoms he
assumed in his daily life, already the subject of myth in his own day.

A great strength of Plantinga's book is the light he throws on this
topic from the perhaps unexpected special standpoint of the concerto.
He draws on an enviable control of the historical record and from

---

4. Tia DeNora, *Beethoven and the Construction of Genius: Musical Politics in Vienna, 1792–1803* (University of California Press, 1995). See the review by Charles Rosen, *The New York Review*, November 14, 1996, pp. 57–63.

5. Maynard Solomon, *Beethoven* (second, revised edition, Schirmer, 1998); and "Some Romantic Images in Beethoven," in *Haydn, Mozart, and Beethoven: Studies in the Music of the Classical Period: Essays in Honour of Alan Tyson*, edited by Sieghard Brandenburg (Clarendon Press/Oxford University Press, 1998), pp. 253–282.

detailed analysis of the music itself. His scrutiny of the sources of the music—the complicated, overwritten autograph scores and the even more complicated musical sketches—is especially thorough. Here is a case where the musicologist's typical preoccupation with sources results in broad historical understanding.

The earliest of the well-known concertos, the irregularly numbered Piano Concerto No. 2 in B Flat, exemplifies very well the fluidity of the concept "concerto" when Beethoven took it up. This concerto was his first warhorse, and every time he was called on to play it, it seems he rewrote or rejected parts of the score and substituted others. The *partition du jour* served as a basis for improvising or half-improvising the piano part.

Of four different versions that can be identified, dating from Bonn in the late 1780s to Vienna in the late 1790s, the earliest survives in two fragments: a single loose page from the score—just enough to show that the first movement as we know it was present in some form—and a draft of a melody in a discarded finale (which survived and was published posthumously as the Rondo in B Flat for Piano and Orchestra). On the basis of sketches that can be dated for revisions, musicologists have distinguished two further versions in the mid-1790s; these can be matched up with concerts by the composer for which we have notices and dates but no programs. Only for a fourth version in 1798 does a full score exist—and even here the piano part Beethoven "entered only in fits and starts, leaving much to his celebrated powers of improvisation," as Plantinga puts it.

Those powers were exercised most spectacularly, of course, in cadenzas, the concerto's moments of sanctioned carnival. Extended formal cadenzas come near the ends of many movements, while numerous other short ones, "run-ins" (*Eingänge*), and fermatas, or pauses, inviting on-the-spot ornamentation, appear often enough. In addition, improvisation of a different kind continued throughout the score, improvisation against a background of harmony, phrasing, and so on laid down by the orchestra, with the surface spun out extempore by the solo. Indeed the young Beethoven never wrote out—never really "composed"—concerto piano parts until he had to because publication was in the offing. When the B-Flat Concerto reached the printer as opus 19 in 1801, the orchestra part, too, was still in flux, subject to the composer's last-minute tinkering.

At this point the long-bubbling soup of the B-Flat Concerto became a text and the composer could put it behind him. Concertos were performing vehicles; they would not be published until they were no longer needed, when they had worn out their welcome with the public and a new one was ready. The manuscript of Piano Concerto No. 3 in C Minor, op. 37, of 1803, about which Plantinga tells us more than we probably want to know, also started life as a "performance autograph." That is, it contained the orchestral music with, at many places, no more than piano cues to guide Beethoven's improvisation. The piano part was only fixed conclusively when it had to be, in this case for a performance in the next year by another pianist.

The evolution of Beethoven's compositions can be traced in astonishing detail from his many sketchbooks and loose work sheets, none of which he seems ever to have thrown away. Just as sketchy piano parts served him as the basis for improvisation in the body of his concertos, so did actual sketches serve as *aides-mémoires* for his improvised cadenzas. That Beethovenian free fantasy did not leave overly much to chance is clear from the rather extensive notations for cadenza ideas preserved among his papers.

Indeed, cadenza sketches provide some of the evidence for the various versions of the early concertos. The earliest sketch we have for Concerto No. 3, an isolated jotting from around 1796, is not for the body of the piece but marked for the cadenza. Its importance can be gauged from the fact that when Beethoven wrote out cadenzas for all his earlier concertos in 1809, he returned to this very idea.

It was at just around this time that he saw he would have to give up performing; he also, as he composed his last concerto, the "Emperor," saw to it that all the constituent cadenzas were written out in full. By assuming control of the main sites of spontaneity the composer sharply attenuated the role of the performer—as composers have continued to do ever since. By also writing out cadenzas for the earlier concertos, was Beethoven proposing to give a full text for works that he would never himself control again? Or was he trying to pump some performative life back into frozen texts which he had not, after all, finally put behind him?

He did not publish those cadenzas—for lack of a market, no doubt, rather than for any qualms about such a project; in 1810–1811 he did publish the originally improvised Fantasy for Piano, op. 77, and another extended improvisation at the beginning of opus 80, the Choral Fantasy for Piano, Orchestra, and Chorus. (We do not know, of course, how closely the printed versions correspond to what he originally played; we do know that the music was worked over in sketchbooks before publication.) In any case, history's decision about the cadenzas was never in doubt. They have now been safely absorbed into the primary texts. After they were first published in 1864 they at once found their way into performance scores; and few pianists ever since have played anything else. Some musicologists have analyzed these cadenzas, too, and claim to find in them an organic relation with the body of their hosts.

One who does not play the master's own cadenzas is Robert Levin, the fortepianist and musicologist who has developed an impressive gift for improvisation in the styles of Mozart and Beethoven. His recent series of Beethoven concerto recordings with John Eliot Gardiner gives us a sense—sometimes a vivid sense—of what the concerto was like in its pretextual stage when it was dependent on personal performance.[6]

---

6. Robert Levin, fortepiano, with the Orchestre Révolutionnaire et Romantique and the Monteverdi Choir directed by John Eliot Gardiner, *Beethoven: The Piano Concertos and Choral Fantasy* (Archiv, 1999).

Flamboyant, powerful, and—the first time you hear them, at least—admirably unpredictable, Levin's cadenzas make these recordings distinctive, indeed unique.

Of course all improvisation is part prestidigitation. The musician has his formulas, as the conjuror has his tricks; if a virtuoso is like an athlete in some ways, he is like an illusionist in other ways. Levin creates the magical illusion of a pocket of music history innocent of and prior to scores—though not of course innocent of cues and *aides-mémoires*. His art is built on internalizing historical documents like the opus 77 and opus 80 fantasies, which capture spontaneity and preserve it like a pinned butterfly. In his case preservation is accomplished through recording, and his recorded cadenzas and ornaments bring us closer to the actual experience of improvisation than any scores can. (The ontology of written-down and recorded improvisations would make a good project for a musical philosopher like Lydia Goehr. If Levin spliced his recording takes—he does not—edited recorded improvisations would be something further for her to mull over.)

It takes nothing away from Robert Levin's art to observe that what he does depends on the fortepiano. Virtuosos play at their instruments' limits, and limits which Mozart and Beethoven tested when they improvised come nowhere near the limits of a modern piano. In modern-piano performances Mozart's written-out cadenzas sound tame and should be retired in favor of modern versions, such as one that Benjamin Britten wrote for Sviatoslav Richter, which can be heard in some recordings of the Piano Concerto No. 22 in E Flat, K. 482. Virtuosity matters more to concertos than stylistic consistency. This is certainly what Beethoven appears to have thought when he wrote those cadenzas for the early concertos, at a time when piano technology was deveoping rapidly. Their unrestrained bravura makes the rest of the music sound very meek indeed. (Though on the other hand, maybe he assumed that any competent performer would upgrade the early piano parts extempore to match the new cadenzas.)

In the main body of the concertos, to be sure, Levin departs little from the scores, less than he often does with scores by Mozart.[7] In works like the "Emperor" even this programmatic improviser is somewhat daunted, it seems, by the prestige of Beethovenian textuality.

Piano Concerto No. 4 in G, op. 58, was the first that Beethoven published before playing it in public. Plantinga takes this precipitate publication, in 1808, as the first symptom of a new concept of the concerto. Beethoven was starting to conceive of a concerto as a "work," like a symphony or a string quartet. Publication fixed the text and with that action canonized it.

Certainly today no Beethoven concerto is more willingly granted masterpiece status than the Fourth. One doesn't need a fastidious nose to catch a whiff of a vehicle for virtuosity in the Violin Concerto or the "Emperor"; not so the Fourth. Its unusual, pensive opening movement, its even more unusual Andante for piano and strings alone, heavy with intimations of tragedy, its ebullient finale, witty, raucous, brilliant, lush, crisp, and expansive in turn—did Beethoven ever write a more scintillating finale?—all this, plus the intimate, subtle sense of dialogue in all the movements have made the Fourth a favorite with critics and commentators. In his discussion of the music itself, as opposed to the sources, Plantinga devotes more space to this work than to any of the others.

Yet two source documents for the concerto—the only two manuscript sources, in fact—each put this text in limbo. We may have a "text" here, but hardly an authentic text. One source is a set of instrumental parts for an arrangement of the piece for piano and string quintet. Concertos were often played as chamber music, in

---

7. In his Mozart concerto series with Christopher Hogwood and the Academy of Ancient Music, Levin goes all out in the slow movements of the piano concertos No. 17 in G, K. 453, and No. 23 in A, K. 488 (Oiseau-Lyre, rec. 1995–1996). There are places in Beethoven where one might enjoy something more boisterous.

domestic settings; the only concertos Mozart was able to publish (his opus 4, containing K. 413, 414, and 415; this was in 1784) were issued with optional wind parts to allow for such performances. Arrangements were a natural feature of the polymorphous performance culture, one that survived the change from music as act to music as text when it was discovered that publication could lead to commodification as well as canonization. Contemporary with Beethoven, Schopenhauer pondered the metaphysics of music to the accompaniment of Rossini operas arranged for two flutes.

The other source for the Fourth is a copyist's score that served as printers' copy (and also as the basis for the quintet version). What is interesting about this score is that Beethoven has entered a wealth of cues and indications for extravagant virtuosity in the piano part. He was now writing for a piano with a higher range than sufficed for the published edition; as the piano underwent rapid technological development in the 1800s (as rapid as the development of techniques of reconstructing old instruments in the 1980s), piano sonatas as well as concertos show the composer racing to keep up. But over and above this, he was making the work at hand a good deal less pensive, intimate, and subtle.

Plantinga argues that the drastic autograph notations for Concerto No. 4 must relate to its first public performance in 1808, which he suspects was also the première:

> To whatever degree Beethoven had begun to dissociate the idea of the concerto from his own performances, in its creator's hands the Fourth Concerto continued to be less the presentation of a "work" than a live activity, a unique event subject to whim, its nature flowing partly from the mood of the moment. The piece seemed to exist for Beethoven on two levels. One was for publication, probably in most cases for performance with reduced forces or even with piano alone in private; the intricacies of

balance between solo and tutti, and a certain intimate and sub-dued quality in the piano remind us of chamber music. But Beethoven also had his public conception of this music, in which the solo part (at least at points) commands, dazzling and astonishing a rapt audience in a large hall.

The paradox is reflected in the program of that 1808 concert, a notorious marathon at which the heating system broke down, and so did the orchestra, to Beethoven's fury. Among the array of new works premièred on that occasion was the Fifth Symphony, which, ever since the influential essay by E. T. A. Hoffmann from 1810, has become the very model of autonomy and musical textuality. But the concert also included two improvisations by Beethoven, in works already mentioned, the Piano Fantasy and the Choral Fantasy, improvisations that Beethoven soon fixed in print.

The Choral Fantasy participates in the evolution of musical textu-ality in its own peculiar way, through its utter metamorphosis into another great canonic text, the Ninth Symphony. In the fantasy, the capricious to and fro of an opening piano cadenza is settled by an ensuing melody, much repeated. In the symphony, fifteen years later, melody (a very similar melody) answers the distressed questions of an orchestral recitative. On the Levin-Gardiner discs, which include the Choral Fantasy, Levin plays the fantasy's opening cadenza (mar-velously well) and adds not one but two alternative improvisations of his own on separate CD tracks, allowing for three versions of this music. Like Beethoven, Levin does not flaunt "freedom"; both of his efforts pay homage to the composer's own text before spinning off into the uncharted and the fantastic. The first of them goes to the flat side and develops a lyric fragment with some passion, whereas the second goes sharp, turns pathetic, and forecasts a certain masterpiece from his third period.

Neither is quite as wild as the Beethoven. "Beethoven the architect turns into a genius running amok," Alfred Brendel has written. "No composer has ever hazarded cadenzas of such provoking madness."[8]

Composed in 1809, the "Emperor" Concerto in E Flat, op. 73, carries the process of textualization to a terminus. Not only was this concerto published before it was ever played, there is no evidence that Beethoven had any occasion in mind for its performance. (In the event it was not premièred until 1811, and then in Leipzig, presumably at the instigation of the publishers, Breitkopf & Härtel of that city.) That he never expected to play it himself is suggested by the fact that this work—and the concerto now really counts as a "work"— was written out completely from the start. The piece is famously virtuosic; it even begins with mini-cadenzas for the piano, in between grandiose single chords in the orchestra. They are written out note for note both at the beginning and also when the passage returns, most unexpectedly, later in the movement.

Moreover Beethoven took unusual trouble with the published score. He added simplified versions for difficult passages. He filled in the piano part dutifully during the orchestral tuttis, thus contributing to a long-lasting controversy on performance practices that Plantinga discusses at length. The entire project reeked of paradox:

> With this concerto Beethoven and Breitkopf & Härtel confronted a central conundrum of the nineteenth-century virtuoso's address to the public. Glittering virtuosity in concert performance was counted on by publishers to spur sales of printed music to an admiring public; but the technical wizardry that had most excited audiences in the first place was the element least reproducible at the living-room piano.

---

8. Liner notes to *Beethoven: The Five Piano Concertos*, Alfred Brendel with James Levine and the Chicago Symphony Orchestra (Philips, rec. 1983), pp. 7–8.

Plantinga has little to say about the prehistory of the Fifth Concerto—he does not discuss the sketches—and I wonder about the impetus for it, and for the Fourth Concerto also, for that matter. By 1807 Beethoven's fame had grown and he was publishing more and more. Would Plantinga go so far as to say that the Fourth was projected as a relatively intimate concerto for piano and a reduced orchestra with an eye to a market of amateurs, for informal performances outside the concert hall? In any case, I think that by this time Beethoven must have felt there was something missing in his output, a concerto in his characteristic "heroic" style, the style he had launched with the "Eroica" Symphony of 1803. He might well have felt impelled to write such a piece, entirely apart from questions of performance and publication.

For Plantinga, the concept of the heroic

> is a very poor designation for Beethoven's middle period as a whole.... There is no ignoring that this was also the period of the "Pastoral" Symphony, the Violin Concerto, the String Quartet Op. 59, No. 1,

and so on. Still, there is a kernel of truth to it, much more than a kernel, and Michael Steinberg, in his adroit new book about concertos, says just what needs to be said when he characterizes the "Emperor" as both the summit and the termination of Beethoven's "heroic decade."[9] What we have here in the first movement is a grandiose opening, an episode of crisis in the middle (or development) section, and a transcendent coda at the end—heroic markers that occur in none of the other concertos. Past Piano Concerto No. 2, indeed, all of them actually start *piano* or even *pianissimo*: a rather remarkable circumstance.

---

9. *The Concerto: A Listener's Guide* (Oxford University Press, 1998).

In symphonies like the "Eroica" and the Fifth, the central crisis typically stages some kind of breakdown, from which the music heroically recoups. In concertos, where a likely hero is actually present, namely the solo instrument, heroism is projected differently. In the "Emperor" a dramatic confrontation confirms the soloist's domination. The orchestra starts a big surge driven by a martial motif, the solo breaks in tumultuously with the same motif, they battle back and forth, and the solo emerges as winner. The effect is electrifying, not only because the fortepiano bangs out eight- and ten-finger chords at maximum volume, but also because it plays a martial motif that up to now, in the concerto's first ten minutes, has been played only by the orchestra. Having seized the initiative (along with the motif), the piano now turns the gesture into a Byronic outcry which the orchestra can only mimic lamely. Next the hero veers unhesitatingly toward the sublime, appropriating another of the orchestra's themes that it had never sampled previously.

The "Emperor" is also the first concerto whose first movement receives (or, rather, requires) a typical coda, a transcendent resolution added to the traditional sonata-form model of dynamic statement, uncertainty, and stable restatement. A grand passage of orchestra–piano dialogue carries the main theme up and up in triumph—a familiar effect in all heroic genres except, until now, the concerto. (The passage was echoed by Brahms in his Piano Concerto No. 2.) After this the piano takes charge of the discourse by once again playing an orchestral theme it had not played before.

Although the Fourth Concerto has something similar—near the end of the first movement the piano picks up a hitherto exclusively orchestral theme—the difference is beautifully characteristic. In the Fourth the piano steps up quietly, almost abashed to find itself more eloquent than the band whose place it has taken. In the Fifth the piano plays not the whole of the theme but waits and seizes just the end of it dramatically, loudly, heroically.

In addition to the historical and the source study outlined above, *Beethoven's Concertos* includes more than a hundred pages of analytical and critical matter, "close readings" of the major concertos, the Violin Concerto, the Triple Concerto for Violin, Cello, and Piano, and the lesser works. Musical analysis is more or less doomed to bristle with technicalities, and its application at this length does not make for easy reading. The student rather than the general reader seems the target here, and while he or she is spared the tortures of the higher analysis, the emphasis on considerations of musical form, in particular, becomes wearying. Musicologists like to talk about form because it is one thing that texts appear to make manifest, but the plain fact is that despite the many innovations Beethoven introduced into concerto form, overall he was *less* innovative about form in this genre than in most others. Nor is emphasis on musical form the only academic feature of Plantinga's discussions.

Yet his prose is alive and graceful, and the musicality it communicates is individual and true. Besides a good deal of what the critic Hans Keller once called "eminently professional tautology," there is also much sensitive observation and insight on display here. At the same time, there are some baffling omissions. Among these are the two "heroic" episodes of the "Emperor" Concerto noted above, the confrontational passage in the development section of the first movement and the emphatic coda. To read a leisurely book on Beethoven's concertos that glides past these salient episodes is strange indeed.

But Plantinga's exhaustive study is full of good things, the result of much careful deliberation and very wide-ranging research. He observes that the entry about "Bethoven" in the 1791 court listing lacks the asterisk provided for all the important musicians under survey, and draws the conclusion that the young musician's sphere of activity was less the court of Bonn than Bonn high society—a forecast of his later experience in Vienna. He has discovered a newspaper report from 1820 of something called "To Psyche: a Melodramatic

Essay after the Andante of Beethoven's Concerto, Op. 58," in which a poem said to be related to Goethe's "Kennst du das Land?" was "spoken rhythmically to the music." (What is Psyche doing on Orpheus' turf, never mind Mignon?) In another vein, Plantinga contrasts piano concertos No. 2 and No. 1 very effectively to pinpoint Beethoven's growing maturity of style in the mid-1790s; No. 1 in C, op. 15, was composed later than No. 2 but published first—Beethoven said it was the better work and probably deemed it more saleable. Plantinga's reading of certain movements is especially original and illuminating: the finale of Piano Concerto No. 4 and the first movement of No. 1 (though the development section is again skimped). He convincingly associates the Triple Concerto with Beethoven's tropism toward France and things French, and writes toughly and justly about the music.

He also reports that Hans von Bülow—pianist, conductor, Wagnerian, and an influential nineteenth-century editor of Beethoven—boasted that he could always count on applause for his playing of the opening mini-cadenzas in the "Emperor" Concerto. Did people applaud during the orchestral music that follows directly? Did Bülow stop the orchestra? Can he really have stimulated applause by playing the notes as written in the score, which his audiences knew as well as we do, or did he improvise something even more magnificent? Beethoven and Robert Levin to the contrary notwithstanding, Bülow would have been well within his rights to do so.

—1999

18

THREE RIFFS ON THE NINTH

I

THOSE CONCERNED ABOUT the kind of democracy that will be coming to Iraq, and about the kind of democracy that our own may be becoming, might like to think about the kind of utopian community recommended by Beethoven's Ninth Symphony under the aegis of *Freude*, Joy.

"All men become brothers," Schiller declared in his "Ode to Joy," not long after others had proclaimed "All men are created equal." Both ideals have proven porous. Beethoven on his part made use of only a few verses (not necessarily in order) from Schiller's ode—stanza 1, of course, and among a few others the four-line refrain ("Chor") to stanza 4, "*Froh, wie seine Sonnen fliegen*," which happens to becomes stanza 4 of the symphony text. This is heard in the jaunty section with "Turkish" instruments that serves as a sort of scherzo within the work's multipartite finale.

"Heroic tone conceals a celebration of thraldom," writes Maynard Solomon in his book *Late Beethoven: Music, Thought, Imagination*. "The brothers rejoice to be part of the clockwork of God's universe ('*Wie seine Sonnen fliegen*'),

> *Gladly, as the suns fly*
> *Across heaven's mighty path,*
> *Hasten, brothers, on your way,*
> *Joyfully, like a hero on to victory—*

their orbits are fixed, their task is to glorify and obey the Father."[1] Certainly Beethoven makes their "way" (*laufen*) into a military march, and has them march in lockstep. A proto-Wagnerian tenor cheers them on. Citing stanza 2 (in both Schiller and Beethoven), "*Wem der grosse Wurf gelungen*," Solomon continues:

Dissenters and deviants, however, are not welcome in this compliant community:

> *He who has had the great fortune*
> *To be a friend to a friend*
> *He who has won a gracious wife.*
> *Let him mingle his jubilation with ours!*
> *Yes, and he who has one kindred soul*
> *On this globe to call his own!*
> *But he who has never known these, let him*
> *Steal away, weeping, from this band.*

"All men become brothers" has imperceptibly slipped into the subjunctive, even the imperative—"All men must become brothers!" Fraternity is intolerant of difference. Ecstatic brotherhood is bound by fear—of the Creator, of lovelessness, of isolation, of expulsion. That is why—for us, if not for Schiller and Beethoven —the hidden hero of the Ode to Joy may be precisely that weeping heretic who rejects joyful conformity and accepts exile ("*der*

---

1. University of California Press, 2003 , p. 225.

stehle weinend sich"). Those who choose Elysium yield up their individuality to the group, receiving, in return, promises of eternal youth and love (*"ein holdes Weib"*). But these may be empty promises, conditional on blind obedience.... It is a Faustian bargain without a Faust.[2]

"*Freude!*," the baritone sings out, like a drill sergeant, and the (male) chorus chants "*Freude!*" at the lower octave: voices of instant assent, willing submission.

2

For millions around the world the Ninth Symphony and especially the Joy Theme spells freedom, democracy, joy. In performances with political resonance—most famously Leonard Bernstein's celebration of the fall of the Berlin Wall—the word *Freude* can be replaced by *Freiheit* (freedom), though both the poet and the composer meant more than freedom, also the rapture of union with Him who dwells beyond the Milky Way. Each of Schiller's eight stanzas ends with a four-line chorus enraptured by the Creator beyond the stars, the "suns of heaven," the *Sternenrichter*, the loving Father, the Unknown, God Himself; Beethoven took a particularly stirring pair of these choruses (besides "*Froh, wie seine Sonnen fliegen*") for the devotional second theme of his finale, which almost swamps the Joy Theme itself.

I wonder how many of those millions could sing the Joy Theme

---

2. This goes back to Theodor W. Adorno, *Beethoven, The Philosophy of Music: Fragments and Texts*, fragment No. 81, footnoted by Solomon, p. 297. See also No. 193, which reads in its entirety "Hitler and the Ninth Symphony: Be encircled, all ye Millions"; the translator, Edmund Jephcott, quietly skirts the traditional rendering of *Umschlungen* as embraced; in older dictionaries the only equivalents given are enclosed, encompassed, and surrounded. Writing in 2003, I was also swayed by ideas of Stephen Rumph, soon to be disseminated in *Beethoven After Napoleon* (University of California Press, 2004).

accurately. While the tune is famously elemental and "universal," it contains sophisticated features seldom mentioned in the vast literature on this work. There is an altogether unusual syncopation after the melody dips down in the second half of the tune, with an equally unusual *crescendo* leading to it, and after the dip, the syncopated high note that recoups it brings a rapid return to *piano*.

The effect is uncanny in a context defined by Joy. Uncanny? Listen to it three times when the great tune is first introduced by the orchestra and then repeated in two orchestral variations. As a strictly instrumental effect, however, it succumbs to the voices when after the return of the opening racket (the so-called *Schreckensfanfare*) and the entrance of the baritone, they body out the tune with words, the words of stanza 1, "*Freude, schöne Götterfunken.*" The *crescendo–subito piano* disappears, and the tune's syncopated high note now carries the accented syllable *Al-* in the word *Alle*: All men will, should, must become brothers. Beethoven dwells on the most problematic moment in the text he carved out from Schiller.

3

The bassoon in the first two orchestral variations: debonair, skeptical, amazing. She picks up on, exactly, the uncanny syncopation.

—2003

19

THE ROMANTIC GENERATION

CHARLES ROSEN IS admired both as a concert pianist and as the author of *The Classical Style: Haydn, Mozart, Beethoven* (1971) and many other writings. His new book, long awaited, is *The Romantic Generation*.[1] The dust jacket reproduces a familiar Romantic painting showing a pianist (he is Liszt) playing for a group of rapt listeners, while he himself gazes upon an outsized classical portrait bust of Beethoven which seems to levitate outside his window, in an otherwise Romantic landscape. The listeners are leading intellectuals and musicians of the time; Rossini, Paganini, Hugo, Dumas père, and George Sand have all fallen under the pianist's spell.[2]

It is not hard to decode this image, especially if you know that the young Rosen was a student of a student of Liszt. The most obvious message is that *The Romantic Generation* will not lack for self-confidence. Rosen's criticism never has. Assured, dogmatic, Tory, sometimes even imperious, he is the sort of critic who knows what the canon is and wherein lies its greatness. It is right there in the notes,

---

1. Harvard University Press, 1995. A compact disc comes with the book, containing piano music played by the author to illustrate the discussion.

2. There is an amusing analysis of this painting—Josef Danhauser's *Liszt at the Piano*, which has in fact become a staple of music-book illustration—by Alessandra Comini in *The Changing Image of Beethoven* (Rizzoli, 1987), pp. 207–215.

which sing past centuries of footlights for an endlessly applauding ideal audience. Outside of the notes, political and ideological considerations, composer biography, and the programs of program music do not carry much weight with this essentially formalist criticism. Rosen delights in connoisseurship—he will leaf through two dozen Chopin mazurkas to show you the bits he likes best—and he writes as though he were playing opera fantasies by Liszt. The style is high, the manner ex cathedra.[3] One can't play Liszt, of course, without plenty of self-confidence.

When Charles Rosen's criticism first burst onto the scene in 1971, its effect was dazzling, and it still is. The National Book Award jury of 1972 was sufficiently dazzled to give *The Classical Style* a prize, even though one of its members complained publicly that the book was so technical he could not read it. Still, it has sold many, many more copies than any other trade book directed solely or primarily to music professionals, and it is still in print. One must gather that many nonprofessional readers have been able to negotiate these technicalities, or at least negotiate around them.

They have been able to do so, I think, because although this criticism is rooted in musical detail—in technical commentary on hundreds of moments and passages of music and of many complete compositions—this *Ursatz* (as music analysts would say) generates a foreground that is a consistently brilliant compound of interpretation, opinion, enthusiasm, potted musicology, homily and polemic, wit, wisdom, and learning. It sometimes seems that each musical analysis, however brief, and some are not brief at all, leads to a confident interpretative aphorism confirming the mastery of one master-composer or another. (I am exaggerating a little, and of course there

---

3. Rosen is not, obviously, a critic for the postmodern age—as he knows, having himself chronicled recent trends in music criticism perceptively, and not without sympathy. See "Music à la Mode," *The New York Review*, June 23, 1994, pp. 55–62, and Rosen's reply to subsequent letters, September 22, 1994, pp. 74–76.

are some counterexamples, even one about Chopin.) Rosen is possessed of a formidable fund of general knowledge—he writes about art and literature as well as music—and he draws upon this to great effect as he weaves his rhetorical fabric.

But for all the bravura, I think the real power of his criticism rests on his immediate musical insight. He has a fantastic ear for musical detail, and also for what I would call the details of musical form—for those elements in a long string of events that make the whole, as he might say, radiant. His analytical talent extends to both music and language, so that again and again he finds just the right words to describe a musical effect simply, clearly, and to perfection.

Granted, the line is not always easy to draw between the beautifully clear, the aphoristic, and the cathedral. Those who have followed Charles Rosen's work from the 1970s (and even earlier) will feel that it has mellowed. The tone seems less imperious than before, and less disputatious. It has broadened out significantly from its earlier classicistic, formalistic core. In *The Romantic Generation*, as we shall see, Liszt-Rosen is sometimes to be found staring at a ghostly gargoyle that has taken up a position next to the bust of Beethoven, or he eyes a distant ruin in the landscape beyond.

The first thing a reader probably wants to know is what a book called *The Romantic Generation* is actually about. It consists, in fact, of three two-hundred-page books in one. The first is a study of song cycles by Schubert and Schumann and of Schumann's cycles of piano pieces, such as *Carnaval* and *Davidsbündlertänze*, in the light of certain Romantic themes. The second book is devoted to Chopin. The third deals with other early Romantic music: Liszt, Berlioz, Mendelssohn, French and Italian opera; and a final chapter returns with a quiet sense of purpose to Schumann.

The organization and style of the three books are quite different, so much so that the whole has the feel of one of those open-form novels by Jean Paul and E. T. A. Hoffmann that Schumann so much admired. The first book is the most original and imaginative. It explores three routes to Romantic music, one of them internal to music, the other two external. These are sonority, especially piano sonority, the Romantic fragment, and landscape and memory.

A beautiful opening chapter, "Music and Sound," makes the most important technical point that has to be made about Romantic music:

> [Before the Romantic generation,] tone color was applied like a veneer to form, but did not create or shape it.... The Romantics cannot be said to have enlarged musical experience except insofar as all original composers have done so, but they altered the relationship between the delight in sound and the delight in structure.

We notice that nothing is said in this chapter about the orchestra; sound here is piano sound, and among the topics treated are pedaling, piano transcription as developed by Liszt, and the nature of keyboard polyphony, starting with Bach (a major presence from first to last). We are never allowed to forget that this is a pianist's book, almost all about music for or with piano, music comprehended through the fingers as well as through the ear and in the mind. There will be many asides about piano performance—about fingering, rubato, and so on —and even one heartfelt page on the physical pain of piano virtuosity.

Everybody who writes about nineteenth-century music takes account of the Bach revival at the time, and Rosen links it emphatically to sonority. Schumann and Chopin were both devoted to *The Well-Tempered Clavier*; the characteristic homogeneous texture of Bach's preludes, so different from any classical texture, provided a model for the texture of the small Romantic piano piece. Chopin saluted Bach's most famous prelude (the C Major) in his first etude and in his first prelude. The influence of the fugues in *The Well-Tempered* was just as important. Bach's polyphony—Rosen has made this point before—was never intended to make you hear all the voices of a fugue at once. Its purpose was to create a sonorous unity out of those voices which become "intermittently audible," sometimes when the composer makes them stand out and sometimes when the player does—or when the player simply considers or feels them. Bach's "private art" mediates between the audible and the inaudible. Rosen is at his most dazzling when he shows how it was the inaudible in Bach that fascinated Schumann.

Chopin, on the other hand, was interested only in the audible. (Schumann was a failed pianist, of course, Chopin a very successful one.) Chopin's counterpoint is eminently public:

> The voices reach full independence only when the listener need be aware of them: elsewhere they remain buried in an apparently homophonic texture. When only latent, they may be hidden but they can always be uncovered—which has given so many pianists the delicious possibility to bring out apparently irrelevant and insignificant inner voices....

A powerful disquisition on Liszt's invention of a new piano sound comes in due course; Chopin's exquisite sonorities are predicated on the classic art of counterpoint.

Schumann was the outstanding man of letters in a Romantic generation of composers that was exceptionally rich in literary talent. Among other things, he published aphorisms in belated tribute to the *Athenaeum* fragments of Friedrich Schlegel, and the impact of the idea of the Romantic fragment on music has been the subject of some attention recently.[4] For Rosen the fragment becomes a highly suggestive

---

4. See John Daverio, *Nineteenth-Century Music and the German Romantic Ideology* (Schirmer, 1993), for acute analysis of Schlegel's criticism as it impinged on Schumann, and Richard Kramer, *Distant Cycles: Schubert and the Conceiving of Song* (University of Chicago Press, 1994), for song fragments by Schubert actually set to Schlegel's poetry.

Utterly casual, in his imperious way, about citations, Rosen does not mention these books; he doesn't even mention his own *Romanticism and Realism*, co-authored with Henri Zerner (Viking, 1984), with its highly pertinent chapter on the Romantic vignette.

critical tool of notable breadth and richness. A song like Schumann's "Im wunderschönen Monat Mai" exhibits multiple tensions of fragmentariness, of which its lack of a conclusive final cadence is only the simplest. (How many Romantic pieces end, and how differently, up in the air!) In addition, the voice part and the piano part are each incomplete, making sense only as fused together by Schumann, as also happens in many less familiar songs (and in the slow movement of the Piano Concerto). In addition, of course, the song appears at the beginning and forms a fragment of a complex totality, the song cycle *Dichterliebe*.

Rosen is endlessly subtle and responsive in teasing sense or, rather, sentiment out of these cycles of fragments. It must be done gently. There is no *rote Faden* such as Goethe detected in classical works of art; Romantic fragments adhere through multiple elastic threads of shifting hues. The last song of *Dichterliebe* shares the same key as the first song, but that key was ambiguous in the first place. Its poem issues a long string of hyperbole about a huge coffin: Why so big?— the last couplet explains why, but the music qualifies the explanation. The piano postlude quotes a melody from an earlier song, so the earlier words return inaudibly, clarifying nothing, suggesting much. Schumann cut four songs out of *Dichterliebe*, Romantic remnants (they receive handsome eulogies here) from a multifragmented whole.

A quotation is one kind of fragment, and Schumann was addicted to musical quotations. He quoted himself, his fiancée Clara Wieck, Beethoven, "La Marseillaise, "Caro mio ben" (a sentimental wedding song), and more. In a critical tour de force, Rosen uses "Florestan," one of Schumann's pair of self-portraits in *Carnaval*, which quotes from his own *Papillons*, to read the great Phantasie, op. 17, which quotes from Beethoven's song cycle *An die ferne Geliebte*. His emphasis with both works—one tiny, the other very substantial—is on the art by which the quotation is made to suffuse the larger entity. The whole first movement of the Phantasie seems retrospectively to emerge out of the Beethoven quotation at the end. The quotation is both absorbed by its host and maintains its integrity at the same time.

As contrasted to the song and piano cycles, which are congeries of fragments, the Phantasie "reveals the aesthetic of the single Fragment magnified, with a sweep and energy that occurs nowhere else." Schumann creates what maybe counts as his most successful large form out of a fragment, a procedure so idiosyncratic, says Rosen, that it could never be repeated.[5] He is here expounding a Romantic aesthetic of instability, very different from the aesthetic of resolution that he has upheld as the great glory of the classical style.

The CD that comes with *The Romantic Generation* includes Schumann's "Florestan," "Eusebius" (his other self-portrait), the entire first movement of the Phantasie and the original ending of the third movement, which the composer excised—"if an editor had made this change, we would call him a vandal"—and which waited till 1979 for rediscovery and restoration.

Landscape, like the fragment, also turns up regularly in discussions of Romanticism. Simon Schama has published a large book called *Landscape and Memory*, a title that also appears as a section subtitle in *The Romantic Generation*. But music does not appear in Schama's index, and I do not know of any other treatment of landscape and memory in connection with Romantic music.

For the Romantics, landscape painting and landscape poetry meant freedom from the traditional subject matter of the arts. The model for that freedom, they came to see, was music, because of the very lack of subject matter that had worked against music in the aesthetics of the Enlightenment. "Insofar as landscape painting or landscape poetry works musically, it is a representation of the power of feeling, and

---

5. It is interesting to compare this account of the Phantasie with its adumbration in the epilogue of *The Classical Style*. Echoes of the earlier book are often heard in *The Romantic Generation*, which even begins without missing a beat where *The Classical Style* left off (prior to its epilogue).

consequently an imitation of human nature," wrote Schiller. Romantic travel literature—sampled here at possibly excessive length—depicts landscape suffused with multilayered memories. Music, the art of time, becomes the art of memory:

> It is above all through landscape that music joins Romantic art and literature.... The creation of the song cycle is a parallel to the replacement of epic poetry by landscape poetry and the elevation of landscape painting to the commanding position previously held by historical and religious painting—more than a parallel, indeed, as these achievements supported each other, and were all part of one cohesive development.

Beethoven's *An die ferne Geliebte*, the first of the great song cycles, features both landscape, evoked in all six of the poems, and memory —on many levels. Song no. 1 is remembered (recapitulated) as no. 6; no. 2 includes simulated horn calls, the musical topos for memory, absence, and regret; and no. 5 recalls no. 1 imprecisely, as though through a mist described by Wordsworth or painted by Turner. Distance in space merges with distance in time. The composition of *An die ferne Geliebte* in 1816 was a half-conscious effort, we think, to purge the "Immortal Beloved" affair that had devastated Beethoven four years earlier.

Schubert's song cycles encompass future time as well as present time and time remembered. Both *Die Schöne Müllerin* and *Winterreise* lead to death, which begins to be presaged halfway through each cycle: with the songs "Tränenregen" (*"Wir sassen so traulich beisammen"*) and "Der Lindenbaum" (*"Am Brunnen, vor dem Thore"*) respectively. Each receives particularly trenchant readings.[6] The former song is manifestly a fragment, since its way of acknowledging

---

6. Rosen has a particular affinity for Schubert. A discussion of a handful of Schubert songs forms the high point of his *The Frontiers of Meaning: Three Informal Lectures on Music* (Hill and Wang, 1994).

the future is by ending unresolved in the minor mode. But the latter song is a fragment, too:

> Within the context of the cycle, "The Lime Tree" is the first intimation that death is a grave consolation after despair: as a separate song, it is merely sentimental and even pretty. The Schubert song cycle embodies a paradox: each song is a completely independent form, well rounded and finished, which nevertheless makes imperfect sense on its own.

Schubert's landscape-soaked song cycles lead to Schumann's, where the immediate experience of landscape can and often does disappear, leaving only "the complex sense of time in which past, present, and future coexist and interpenetrate each other." It comes as no surprise when the next stage of abstraction brings us counter-chronologically back to Schumann's "song cycles without words" of the 1830s. With the *Davidsbündlertänze*, however, the leap from keys, rhythm, and form to time and memory is precarious. Too much, I think, is made to hinge on the recapitulated slow piece in B minor (no. 2: for some reason called a *Ländler*). Some account should also be taken of memories of the "Wie aus der ferne" number (no. 17) in the final waltz— even if these two pieces are not in the same key.

The Chopin chapters of *The Romantic Generation* are preceded by a "Formal Interlude" addressing technical matters (tonality and phraseology)—a signal that extramusical themes like fragments and landscape will now be retired in favor of internal musical analysis. As the least literary of Romantic composers, Chopin invites this treatment, and Rosen rises to the occasion. Two principles govern the analysis, Chopin's mastery of form and Chopin's mastery of counterpoint.

We are on familiar formalist ground here, and the exposition is fairly straightforward, with particularly solid sections dealing with major repertories, the mazurkas—an astonishing, original, and heart-warming survey—the ballades, and the etudes. Much other music is covered en route; two nocturnes are also covered by very beautiful performances by the author on the accompanying CD. Schumann, reviewing Chopin's Sonata in B-Flat Minor, threw up his hands at the finale, a masterpiece of the Romantic grotesque: "From this musical line without melody and without joy, there breathes a strange, horrible spirit which annihilates with its heavy fist anything that resists it, and we listen with fascination and without protesting until the end—but without, nevertheless, being able to praise: for this is not music." Rosen turns this criticism on its head: "We might add in passing that to have been told that one had exceeded the bounds of music while holding listeners fascinated to the end may not have been an unwelcome criticism to a young and ambitious composer." Schumann acknowledges that Chopin's forms are intuitively satisfying even when he is at his most rebarbative. The music fascinates or at least interests throughout. It never loses its sense of direction, it never bores. The forms are not classical, but Rosen, starting with that finale, demonstrates again and again how they can be construed and illuminated in classical terms. Chopin "is most original in his use of the most fundamental and traditional technique."

The discussion is not entirely about structure; we learn, for example, that Chopin sometimes played his mazurkas with so heavy a rubato that listeners had to count them in four-four rather than three-four time. And in a section entitled "Morbid Intensity," the question of expression is addressed head-on. Chopin evaded the sentimentality of the salon style "by magnifying it and exaggerating it, by forcing it to the point of morbidity"; the overloading of intense detail is demonstrated in several pieces, including one truly ripe camembert of a nocturne, Op. 55, No. 2 in E flat. Chopin made false sentiment real by intensifying it, says Rosen, and of course he dilates upon the technical means of this intensification. One might add that the technical high finish also militates against sentimentality by establishing authorial distance. The silky counterpoint and the elegant forms make it impossible to forget the agent who is manipulating sentiment, false or real, from the outside.

A reading of the Berceuse addresses the question of technical display in Chopin. Virtuosity is transmuted into tone color:

> The work is pure tone color. Structure—conceived as harmony and melody—is close to minimal, but then structure in this piece has largely become texture. The harmony is painfully simple.... Over this monotonous underpinning the right hand delicately plays a series of minuscule etudes, two- and four-bar structures in each of which a simple but tricky figuration rises or falls sequentially over the keyboard almost independently of the basic harmony. The apparent indifference of the right hand to the left, of the figuration to the underlying harmony, creates a web of delicate dissonances, a grill of sonority like the mixtures on a Baroque organ that never disturbs the insistently repeating harmonic structure but seems to have a life of its own.

If I say less here about book 2 of *The Romantic Generation*, as I am calling it, than about the other books, that is not for any lack of appreciation or admiration but because it offers fewer surprises to admirers of Rosen's work. Book 2 is the most cohesive, lucid, and comprehensive of the three. These are classical virtues, and this book-within-a-book is an extraordinary tribute to the flexibility of classical criticism—in the hands of the right critic. It will change the way we think about Chopin, and it should change the way we play him.

Book 3 raises, as it were, the historical ante. It is the most various of the three books, covering Liszt, Berlioz, Mendelssohn, and opera, and probably the liveliest. Sometimes it is also haphazard, virtuosic, or jokey (I think). Works and topics that are manifestly central turn up here—the Liszt Sonata and his Transcendental Etudes, the "Scène d'amour" from Berlioz's *Roméo et Juliette*, Bellinian melody—together with some engaging peripheral subjects. Liszt's "Die Lorelei," a song that begins a little like *Tristan und Isolde*, provides occasion for some thoughts on artistic influence and a professional joke about the famous "Love-Death" harmonies. Hard by this comes what can only be called a small seminar paper, fortified with tables, comparing five different versions from 1838 to 1861 of the Sonetto di Petrarca No. 104. Liszt's *Réminiscences de Don Juan*, a fantasy on themes (and more) from *Don Giovanni*, testifies to virtuosity in another sense. Rosen reads it as Liszt's self-portrait as Don Juan. It is the first track on the CD accompanying the book.

One might expect the chapter venomously entitled "Mendelssohn and the Invention of Religious Kitsch" to treat the oratorio *St. Paul* and "O for the wings of a dove," but no, it unpacks an early concert fugue for piano, in E Minor, Op. 35, No. 1, in which Bach-like meditative counterpoint is interrupted by an inspirational chorale. This music "substitutes for religion itself the emotional shell of religion," "it does not comfort, but only makes us comfortable," and it is said to initiate the whole strain of nineteenth-century pseudo-religious music extending to the César Franck Organ Chorales and *Parsifal*. The aphorisms take on an uneasy cast if we know that eighteen-year-old Mendelssohn composed the E-Minor Fugue while sitting up all night with a dying friend.

There is a certain amount of musicological boilerplate in book 3, splendidly polished up, of course, but still somewhat vacant—about Liszt and his vulgarity, Berlioz and his solecisms, opera and politics, and so on. The ex cathedra manner becomes more noticeable. The *chef d'oeuvre* of the Berlioz chapter, an analysis of tonality in the "Scène d'amour," contains many fine insights. Rosen helps us hear this music; but he does not help us fathom the particular fervor that attaches to the love theme when it comes in the dominant key, just twenty-three bars before the final cadence, by telling us only that Berlioz's plan is unclassical. This is criticism in need of a new paradigm. In the bad-tempered opera chapter, the pages on Bellini seem less illuminating than usual, though they display some ravishing unfamiliar melodies, and while Meyerbeer puts in a cameo appearance, Carl Maria von Weber is not so much as mentioned (we meet him elsewhere as a composer of piano music that interested Chopin, like Hummel and John Field, never as the father of German Romantic opera). Presumably this is a joke, or else it is exceedingly absentminded.

After Liszt the falloff is pronounced, and the disturbing thought presents itself that a magnificent study of the best early Romantic music for and with piano is turning itself into an ill-conceived history of early Romantic music. But Rosen is not writing history, of course, and certainly he does not make any such claim. What he is doing is presenting us with some very striking personal snapshots, not all of them in the best possible focus, to go along with his richly textured portraits of Schumann and Chopin. That does not add up to a historical panorama; and it needs to be criticized, and appreciated, in its own terms.

In a final chapter Rosen circles back to Schumann because he feels that he is the most representative figure of the Romantic generation, a position he occupies as much for his limitations and failures as for his genius and his triumphs. Schumann's decline in his late years becomes emblematic.

This is a debatable historical judgment; others would say the generation's representative figure was Wagner. (There may have been a reason after all for the silencing of German Romantic opera.) But Rosen feels what he feels, and unless I am mistaken this final chapter was not written without some twinges of distress. Unhappy biographical considerations come quietly to the fore: Schumann's

madness, his systematic bowdlerization in later years of his radical
early music, and his helpless ambition to produce a German music
worthy of Beethoven. From adolescence on Schumann was fascinated
and terrified by insanity, like many Romantic artists, and in a series of
powerful analyses we are shown how he incorporated "elements of
madness" into his work. We are also told that life and art are separate,
and that those elements are "stylistic rather than autobiographical";
but can't they be both? The maddest Schumann piece of all is "Florestan," his depiction of his own violence—I think that when Clara
Schumann played *Carnaval* in concert, leaving out the family portraits
"Eusebius," "Florestan," and "Chiarina," she particularly did not wish
to play "Florestan."

The decline can probably be laid partly to burnout or mental deterioration and partly to self-imposed objectives that were unrealistic as
well as overweening and chauvinistic. Shame fueled those ambitions:

> By comparison with the monumental output of Beethoven, his
> own works and those of his colleagues seemed to him trivial.
> There were, he wrote, too many composers of nocturnes, baga-
> telles, dances, characteristic pieces; what was needed was sym-
> phonies, sonatas, quartets—the sublime, in short. No one, least
> of all Schumann, was able at the time to acknowledge that the
> fundamental task and achievement of his age was to attain the
> sublime through the trivial.

Least of all Schumann—because the "need" he was postulating and
publicizing was for a specifically German music. The route through
triviality was ideologically blocked.

Some other feeling—puritanism, fear of appearing mad—caused
Schumann to tone down audacities in his early work when he returned
to it later. He purged his work of eccentricities to prepare himself for
the high style. According to Rosen, his symphonies, oratorios, and so

on suffer first and foremost from his inability to vary the pulse, to move persuasively and powerfully from one kind of motion to another—an art that died out with Beethoven. In large forms (and even in some shorter ones) the rhythm becomes obsessional and ultimately inert.

Still, limitations can have their virtues, and *The Romantic Generation* ends with a marvelous outburst of enthusiasm for (and by) the little-known Novelette in A Major, Op. 21, No. 6, in which Schumann dashes incomprehensibly from theme to theme and key to key in a continuous acceleration, with the tempo ratcheted up by successive metronome marks, up to a brave little joke at the final cadence. It is a pity room was not found on the CD for this piece of inspired madness.

Charles Rosen's Schumann stands out as his most original and haunting portrait (here or elsewhere), both because of his character— as Rosen presents him—and because of the author's patent involvement with his subject. He is gripped by Schumann the poet of the fragment, the radical, the obsessional, the joker flirting with chaos and the irrational—with Florestan, in other words. There are other Schumanns; there is the "jolly, old German, beer-drinking college student" mentioned in a depressing aside, the waltz-composer *manqué* doggedly churning out the undanceable, and mawkish Eusebius, who never learns to stay at a proper distance from his work. More importantly, there is the symphonist and the writer of large-scale works.

One understands after reading this book why no true classicist can contemplate Schumann's large forms with sympathy. Chopin, with his instinctive understanding of classical formal principles, could produce strong Romantic forms; Schumann, lacking that understanding, produced what seem distended pseudo-classical ones. This music will require another critic or critics, bringing new critical apparatus, like the nexus of ideas that Rosen draws together under the rubric of the

Romantic fragment to embrace and illuminate the unclassical, anti-classical Florestan. I think we can predict that the Schumann of the piano cycles and the song cycles will now be Rosen's, for some time. Together with his Chopin, another extraordinary portrait, this will be the lasting contribution of this important book.

—1995

20

SCHUBERT'S SONGS

BECAUSE THEY ARE there: that must be one reason why the huge corpus of Schubert songs proved to be irresistible to a singer like Dietrich Fischer-Dieskau. No major performer of today or perhaps any other era has been so fascinated by the sheer extent of the musical repertory available to him. It is claimed that Fischer-Dieskau is the most recorded musician in the classical catalog, and his most celebrated effort, released in 1970 by DGG, is a monumental collection of more than 450 Schubert songs on twenty-eight LP discs.[1] This amounts to about 75 percent of the total number and 85 percent of those suitable for male voice. He has also written a book about Schubert's songs, now published in English, the sort of book that works through the entire corpus and finds at least a few words to say about nearly every member of it.[2] This book seems to have been impelled largely by Fischer-Dieskau's enthusiasm for the *manche schöne Perlen,* as Heine might have put it, which rest in the depths of the Schubert complete edition.

---

1. Schubert, *Lieder*, Volumes 1–3, Dietrich Fischer-Dieskau, baritone, and Gerald Moore, piano (Deutsche Grammophon). Still available, transferred to CD, though of course since the 1970s recordings and studies of Schubert songs have multiplied vastly (2007).

2. *Schubert's Songs: A Biographical Study*, translated by Kenneth S. Whitten (Knopf, 1977).

But conquest, or salvage, cannot be the only reason. Clearly for Fischer-Dieskau, as for many other musicians, the Schubert songs occupy a unique place in the aesthetic firmament. This composer stands apart decisively from the others who followed him to form the great nineteenth-century Lied tradition, in a way that is hard to explain on the basis of compositional technique, the Zeitgeist, or even individual talent. The fact that there are slack moments in certain Schubert songs—in many Schubert songs, if we assume Fischer-Dieskau's perspective—seems to make no difference to enthusiasts. Every song and every gesture within the songs has a special resonance which separates them from those of other composers. There is a special mystery about this music, a mystery too about the devotion it inspires.

Fischer-Dieskau, who is a very distinguished singer but not a very distinguished critic, contributes little to its elucidation. What raises Schubert so far above other composers, he writes, is that he is (in italics) *"authentic"*: which is no more helpful than the traditional rhetoric as relayed by, for example, his friend and collaborator Gerald Moore, the great piano accompanist:

> This book was written under compulsion, the compulsion of my love for Franz Peter Schubert. I cannot leave him alone and find myself in the evening of my life turning more and more to the master whom Artur Schnabel described as the composer nearest to God. No one ever expressed himself with such utter lack of artificiality; so spontaneous is his song that the process of transplantation from mind to manuscript without loss of freshness or bloom is miraculous. His heart was full of music which in its unerring directness, unsurprising naturalness and sublime eloquence uplifts the soul.[3]

---

3. *The Schubert Song Cycles* (London: Hamish Hamilton, 1975), p. ix.

But one must not throw stones in the glass house of Schubert criticism. Academic critics, such as they are, seem equally at a loss when dealing with Schubert's strengths or his weaknesses—in the instrumental music as well as in the songs, but especially in the latter. The strictly technical criticism ("analysis") that is so popular in this country is in any case better suited to large works than to small ones. The difficulties of implicitly equating complexity with character and value can be manageable when the critic considers the whole span of a symphony and has room to maneuver; they become troublesome within the limited compass of a song and positively nasty with a simple song. Why is a simple Schubert song better than a Beatles song? students used to ask in the 1960s; they still ask it about Schubert and Hugo Wolf.

Some recent highly refined textual-musical analyses of Schubert songs have also run into trouble. The one that has been most discussed is Professor T. G. Georgiades's effort to plunge down into the *Schlichten* and show how Schubert works not with the *dichterisch* surface of German poetry but with the *sprachlich* essence beneath.[4] In a famous close analysis of Schubert's setting of Goethe's "Wanderers Nachtlied ('Über allen Gipfeln ist Ruh')"—and in a notorious invidious comparison with the later setting of this poem by Schumann—Georgiades developed his thesis further: Schubert dissolves a poem in order to re-create its utterance as "natural" musical form, whereas later composers preserve the poem and seek merely to express the moods it releases, without touching on its speech-substance.

This latter idea, predictably, has met with stiff resistance, the more so when the meticulous and often brilliant detail of Georgiades's

---

4. *Schubert, Musik und Lyrik* (Göttingen: Vandenhoeck und Ruprecht, 1967); for contemporary controversy, see *Die Musikforschung*, Vol. 24 (1971), p. 135f, 229f. A selection of Georgiades's work appeared in English in 1986: "Lyric as Musical Structure: Schubert's *Wandrers Nachtlied* ("Über allen Gipfeln"–D. 768)," translated by Marie Louise Göllner, in *Schubert: Critical and Analytical Essays*, edited by Walter Frisch (University of Nebraska Press, 1986) (2007).

technical writing gives way to cloudy historical theorizing. But even apart from such special pleading, close analysis, of whatever school, has to face a basic problem of decorum with material of this kind. Simple songs do not so much disintegrate under a formidable critical apparatus as float right through it; what seems appropriate to a song from Schoenberg's *Das Buch der hängenden Gärten* seems absurd when applied to "Das Wandern," "Die liebe Farbe," and other of the more transparent members of *Die schöne Müllerin*. These are songs that disarm, or should disarm, "analysis."

To say this amounts to saying that our love for Schubert is an article of faith, and perhaps this in turn is a reflection of his own faith in his poets. Other song composers may have loved their poets more and read them more closely, but none gives the appearance of having believed in them as implicitly as Schubert. Several biographical circumstances help to explain this, no doubt. He started writing songs at the age of twelve, and by the time he reached the age when he might have attended university—might have, but did not—his attitudes toward poetry were well fixed. Friendships meant everything to Schubert, and more of his friends were poets or amateur poets than musicians. He actually roomed with a poet for a period of years, the Censorship Bureau official Johann Mayrhofer, who wrote many texts especially for him. Was it, too, that his own phenomenal spontaneity as a creative artist predisposed him to take the work of other artists as absolutely natural and true? Schubert believed poems about the early violet who wilts while awaiting her bridegroom, poems about God's trombones in the hurricane, about the limits of the human condition, about Ossian and Ganymede, green ribbons and red sunsets, carefree butterflies and ominous ravens. Only this boundless capacity for belief, obviously, enabled him to write songs in such numbers and of such variety. He was not only the most prolific of songwriters but also by far the most various.

Schubert cannot make us believe all this poetry, but the power of his own belief is at the heart of his power as an artist. He can set down German sixth chords and parallel-major sonorities as innocently as his poet friends write of *Blumenherzen* and *Liebestränen*. In its freedom and simplicity, his career as a songwriter contrasts with those of later figures such as Hugo Wolf, who never set the work of living poets and came to prefer foreign verse in translation, or Schumann, who after trying his hand at song composition as a boy shrank from it self-consciously for more than a decade, only to embrace it just as self-consciously in the year of his marriage. The elaborated piano parts of Schumann's songs act as a barrier against directness; a new persona has been added to the song which often comments beautifully but from the outside and with the benefit of hindsight. According to Georgiades, the song no longer takes over the substance of the poem but becomes a "vehicle" for the poetic substance. As for Wolf, the nature of his accomplishment is well indicated by the praise he received in 1890 from the Goethe Society of Vienna for his explication (*explizieren*) of their hero. The late nineteenth century wanted very much to believe in Goethe, but this was no longer easy to do without some pretty strenuous interpretation.

Schubert's own belief can shine brightly when one of his songs is heard along with a later setting of the same poem. The later composer has always chosen his own ground, of course, and Schubert is generally made to look like a complete innocent. On one occasion Brahms went so far as to publish a song that is little more than a heavily blue-penciled version of a Schubert original. The poem, Goethe's "Trost in Tränen" (Consolation in Tears), consists of four pairs of artless question-and-answer stanzas according to this pattern:

> "*Wie kommt's, dass du so traurig bist,*
> *Da alles froh erscheint?*
> *Man sieht dirs an den Augen an,*
> *Gewiss, du hast geweint.*"

> *"Und hab ich einsam auch geweint,*
> *So ists mein eigner Schmerz,*
> *Und Tränen fliessen gar so süss,*
> *Erleichtern mir das Herz."* [5]

Composed at the age of seventeen, on a day which also produced two other settings of Goethe poems, Schubert's fragile little song seems hardly able to survive the comparison. The transitions and the declamation are Brahms's most obvious improvements, as well as (one thinks at first) the modulatory scheme. How intelligent to save the main modulatory gestures of the piece for the stanzas spoken by the rather brash questioner, leaving the answerer's music depressingly rooted in its single minor-mode tonality.

Yet in cases of this kind Schubert's faith leads again and again to greater awareness. Brahms's sophisticated descending chromatic sequence at line seven provides a climax of mournful intensity—for when the answerer says that tears lighten his sorrow Brahms does not, of course, believe him. Goethe must mean those lines ironically! Schubert does not know about irony. Though a little incredulous, he would not presume to disbelieve the poet, and this leads him to a condensed threefold setting—the first emotional, affirmative, and a little vainglorious (relative major); the second more depressed (tonic minor); the third calmer and more genuinely consolatory, but also tinged in a way that forecasts the characteristic effects of

---

5. "How comes it you're so sad
  When all are glad?
  One can see from your eyes,
  To be sure, you've been weeping."

  "If I have wept in solitude,
  It is my own distress,
  And tears so very sweetly flow
  Lightening my heart."

pathos in his later work (parallel major). At the end of the fourth stanza-pair—

> *"Verweinen lasst die Nächte mich,*
> *Solang ich weinen mag."*[6]

—while the initial parallel-major articulation may fall on the word *weinen*, the threefold setting does not subside on weeping, rather on the ambiguity of weeping. Taking Goethe's title seriously, Schubert responds to his sentiment more directly and also more richly than does the later composer.

In Schubert the questioner and answerer really address each other; in Brahms they seem to be taking part in some discreet public debate (this is owing largely to Brahms's replacement of Schubert's awkward fermatas at the ends of the two stanzas by perfectly tooled transitions). Schumann sings to Clara, Wolf sings to the Goethe-Verein, but Schubert sings mainly to himself, asking for no audience and making no effort to get people to share his beliefs. A consequence of this is that with Schubert one is never made to feel guilty of a rejection, as so often with Brahms—only embarrassed, sometimes, by one's own *auditeurism.*

There is a sense in which Fischer-Dieskau's comprehensive recording project serves to underline this quality. When the set was issued in 1970 it greatly impressed but also repelled many people. Critics did not know what to make of the "text" that was presented to them; typically a record or record set simulates an actual performance in the concert hall or opera house, but this set seemed to aspire to the condition of a definitive complete scholarly edition in the library. Several hundred unknown Schubert pearls proved to be something of a

---

6. "Let me weep the nights away
As long as I may weep."

choker, and there was talk to the effect that Fischer-Dieskau might well have spent less time diving and more time polishing, even so serious a critic as David Hamilton complaining of "performances untested by the experience of confrontation with an audience" and of the set's "bulk and format resisting the kind of informal presentation and listening that should surround this literature."[7] In not many drawing rooms of today, however, is singing German songs at the piano treated as a more informal activity than turning on the hi-fi.

We always remark on the difference between the milieu for which these songs were conceived—the drawing room—and the modern concert hall, without really sensing the difference; and we still do not understand the characteristic musical milieu of our own time, the hi-fi den, and what it has done to our music. Fischer-Dieskau and Moore knew perfectly well that their record set would not and could not be played through to produce a surrogate song recital. Like Schubert, they seek no confrontation with an audience, and the very removal of their monumental project from the concert setting gives it a tranquillity that is curiously Schubertian.

To be sure, one hates to think of the songs being removed to the complete tranquillity of the library shelf. Perhaps Fischer-Dieskau's book *Schubert's Songs* is to be regarded as a kind of library resource, an information-retrieval tool to be used in conjunction with the recordings. It can be recommended to those who feel the need for a guide to the Schubert song repertory that is less flowery and "sensitive" than Richard Capell's *Schubert's Songs*, which was first published in England as long ago as 1928 (and republished in 1957 and 1973). Fischer-Dieskau opens no new windows on Schubert studies, and if there is a slightly disconnected, even distracted quality about the thought sequence at some points, that may be explained by a remark in the introduction to his book *Wagner and Nietzsche*,

---

7. "Lieder by the Litre," *The New Yorker*, May 29, 1974, p. 125f.

in which he thanks various people "who made it possible for me to work on this book between concerts."[8] But his fundamental control of the material is certainly very impressive indeed. The book contains much interesting and sensitive comment on individual songs, and a mass of information on poetry, personalia, and musicological matters.

As for *The Fischer-Dieskau Book of Lieder*,[7] that may be described as a library item par excellence, a collection of over seven hundred German song poems with translations—more than twice as many as in older anthologies such as Philip Miller's *The Ring of Words* or S. S. Prawer's *The Penguin Book of Lieder*. There are nearly two hundred songs each by Schubert and Wolf, and about a hundred by Brahms and Schumann. There are also more than a hundred by German and German-speaking song composers of a conservative cast who are seldom indeed to be heard in this country: Fortner, Knab, Marx, Pepping, Pfitzner, Reger, Reutter, Schoeck, Zillig, and others. The translations (one is cited above) are of varying quality, none poorer than that given to the author's fifteen-page introductory essay on "German Song."

—1977

---

8. Seabury Press, 1976.

9. Translated by George Bird and Richard Stokes (Knopf, 1977).

21

BERLIOZ: A LIFE

"MY WHOLE LIFE has been one long, ardent pursuit of an ideal which I created myself," Berlioz wrote to Pauline Viardot in 1859. "Love or music—which power can uplift man to the sublimest heights?" he also wrote, in a much-quoted passage from his *Memoirs*. "Love cannot give an idea of music: music can give an idea of love. But why separate them? They are the two wings of the soul." His ideals in both love and music were formed as a child, and what strikes one after traversing David Cairns's impressive and beautiful new biography,[1] or what strikes one with new force, is the way Berlioz attained those ideals: not by adjusting them to the requirements of mature experience, but by returning to them self-consciously, late in life, in their childhood innocence.

On one wing, the wing of music, the ideal was Gluck, which should not come as a surprise, given the recent history of French music when Berlioz came to it around 1810. What is more surprising is that the ideal developed without this child ever knowing more than a few pages of Gluck's music. But at seventeen Berlioz's first musical revelation after arriving in Paris was the composer's *Iphigénie en Tauride*,

---

1. *Berlioz*, Vol. 1, *The Making of an Artist 1803–1832* (1998; second edition, University of California Press, 2000); Vol. 2, *Servitude and Greatness 1832–1869* (University of California Press, 2000).

and in between copying out Gluck scores at the library of the Paris Conservatoire, he laid the groundwork for his formidable career as a critic with polemical squibs rhapsodizing about Gluck and his student Spontini and attacking the *dilettanti*—canary fanciers, we used to call them—attendant on Rossini, now in his ascendancy at the Paris Opéra.

Les Troyens, his homage to the older master, came at the end of his career, in 1863, after many digressions: successful symphonies and large-scale sacred works, and a series of dismal operatic failures (one opera completed, mounted, and hissed, and several others aborted). Charles Rosen compares *Les Troyens* to the *pompier* paintings of the time, but others see it as a luminous, almost miraculous re-creation of Gluck's neoclassical vision in the twilight of Romanticism. A subject taken from myth, noble poetry nobly declaimed, songs of intense, simple expressivity, an orchestra of the greatest eloquence—these were the very qualities, Cairns tells us, for which Gluck was praised in the *Biographie universelle* of 1811 that was young Hector's introduction to Gluck and his music. Where Gluck turned to Euripides, Berlioz turned to Virgil, even picking up the episode from the *Aeneid* that drew tears when the boy construed it at his father's knee.

By a turn of fate, in 1861 the Opéra engaged the composer in the role of dramaturg to supervise revivals of Gluck's *Orphée* and *Alceste*, as vehicles for the incomparable Viardot. Another ideal! He started to fall in love again, to the considerable distress of that sympathetic and worldly lady.

Attaining the ideal in love also took place late in life, again after many digressions—digressions much more serious than that of Pauline Viardot. Berlioz makes sure that we hear the story from him, in his *Memoirs*. In the main draft of this famous and marvelous work, we hear about the older girl he fell in love with, hopelessly, as a twelve-year-old boy growing up in the Dauphiné, near the French Alps. *Stella montis*, he calls her, for Estelle Duboeuf was as firmly fused in his mind with Romantic landscape as his first wife, the actress Harriet Smithson—she of the "Fantastic" Symphony—was with Shakespeare. He will never forget the rock in the neighboring mountain village where Estelle stood gazing out over the valley.

A subsequent, altogether lyrical update to the *Memoirs* has the author returning to his childhood home and climbing the mountain path to Estelle's rock, thrilling or trembling at every old landmark that is or isn't there. He learns that she still lives in the region, recently widowed. In a final update, probably sixteen years later, he retraces his steps up the mountain path and this time presents himself to a very surprised Estelle—this is in 1864; she is now sixty-seven—attends on her with caution, ultimately proposes to her, is turned down, and settles for an epistolatory relationship that casts a glint of light over his depressed, pain-wracked last years.

So while the book originally ended with a vintage Berlioz rant at his enemies—

> As for you, maniacs, mastiffs and stupid oxen, as for my Guildersterns and my Rosencranzes, my Iagos, my petty Osrics, insects and snakes of every species: farewell, my...friends! I despise you, and my cordial hope is not to die before having forgotten you

—(all carefully footnoted to *Hamlet*), the final text prints some of the relevant letters and ends on a different note: "Let us try to think no more of art. Stella! I can die now without anger or bitterness."

Add the scintillating prose to the strong story line, and you will require no convincing that the *Memoirs* is the work of a very fine and a very experienced writer. Loaded with literary artifice, it does its work as a chronicle, a rhetorical exercise, and a spin center for a quintessential Romantic self-image all at the same time. "What an incredible novel my life is," Berlioz exclaims at the age of thirty, and on another occasion: "My life is a novel that interests me deeply." He presented the updated *Memoirs* to Estelle before putting the question.

The book is also, of course, a primary source for the biographer, and long before completing what is bound to be regarded as the standard biography, David Cairns prepared a much-admired edition and translation of the *Memoirs* in 1969.[2] Two high-quality publishers have let it go out of print. The extended apparatus, a major contribution, sorted out errors and also adjudicated cases of possible misrepresentation, of which many had been alleged. Berlioz almost always came out ahead; the effort was to make this text transparent, with predictable consequences for the biography. For while Cairns knows and says that the *Memoirs* has to be understood as a literary construction, the book's fictive quality never seems to dent for him its "largely and essentially true record of fact." It is the French editor of the *Mémoires*, Pierre Citron, who has no problem seeing Berlioz pushing at facts, giving himself *le beau rôle*, even succumbing to paranoia and the like, without giving up an inch to his opposite number in admiration and love for his subject.

The strength of Cairns's biography lies in its thoroughness of research, amplitude, authority, and the author's remarkable sensitivity and sympathy for Berlioz—and indeed for all those around him. It is a life, not a life-and-works, as he makes clear at the outset, though each of Berlioz's major works receives an unhurried appreciation, in nontechnical language, on a level of warmth and insight that music critics seldom achieve. Cairns's limpid prose glows in these sections, but it is also extraordinarily successful in imparting quotidian detail while still holding the reader's attention. Nor is this biography a psychobiography, he says,

> not so much from unwillingness as from lack of competence. Maybe in falling in love at the age of twelve with a goddess-like

---

2. *The Memoirs of Hector Berlioz*, translated and edited by David Cairns (Knopf, 1969).

young woman years older than himself Berlioz was projecting an image of the good mother he had not found in infancy.... But I have left such promising inquiries to others who have the skill.

What are some of the gray areas in this biography—mysteries that Cairns has not been able to illuminate, and that psychobiography maybe could?

Of course the love ideal that the boy formed in Estelle Duboeuf on her rock, transferred to Harriet Smithson on the stage, and sought out again in Estelle, has to do with his not finding a "good mother" in infancy. Not much mystery here. "*Méchante mère!*" he exclaims in the *Memoirs*, after describing a trick she played on him in connection with this very Estelle. Joséphine Berlioz is one of several people who are edited out of the *Memoirs*, or treated very selectively. She appears only one more time, in a terrible scene in which she furiously implores twenty-one-year-old Hector to abandon a career in music, kneels at his feet, and after cursing and disowning him, refuses to stay in the same house with her son or receive his farewells when he leaves for Paris. Music and Estelle, two wings of the soul: Did these two ideals develop in some way from the same vexed source? What remains a mystery, after all, is how a boy brought up by parents who were only mildly musical in a tiny country town almost devoid of music, who never traveled, never heard a symphony, let alone an opera, should have developed the incredibly fierce passion for music that he did.

Another person edited out of the *Memoirs* is Marie Recio, for whom Berlioz left Harriet and whom he later married. "I married again ...*I was obliged to*...after eight years of this second marriage I lost my wife," he writes (his ellipses, his italics); she is buried, exhumed, reburied, and neither named nor spoken of further. The exhumation scene draws from *Hamlet* and *La Dame aux camélias*. This unpleasant woman, an indifferent singer ("she sings like a cat"), prone to bad behavior in public, casts a mysterious dark shadow over Berlioz's biography. In the letters, too, two hundred of them, she remains a complete cipher. We get only a few new details to touch up the picture: her will stipulates that if her portrait is not kept, rather than being sold it should be given to a friend; in a letter Berlioz hints at fantasies of murdering her. His distressed friends said the composer was "wantonly ruined" by the relationship, "subjugated," "like the powerless King Lear himself"—that was Robert Schumann's impression—and Cairns documents several occasions when he tried to extricate himself from it.

I doubt that he meant it. Marie gave him something he had to have—sex, support, stability, perhaps something more. He was lonely without her and distraught when she died. That this exacting composer allowed her to sing at his concerts "argues a degree of weakness which on his own terms was criminal," says Cairns, for once really vexed, and I certainly think this argument could be extended to the relationship as a whole, if by "weakness" here we mean failing to live up to or betraying one's ideals. Berlioz's terms were Berlioz's ideals. And whereas Marie quit singing quite soon, the "criminal" betrayal of ideal love extended over a period of twenty years, twelve years as lovers and eight as man and wife.

What dominated Berlioz "beyond reason," wrote his close friend the pianist Ferdinand Hiller,

> was the constant contemplation of himself, of his own passionate feelings, his behavior, everything he did. He was one of those people for whom it is necessary always to appear interesting to themselves, who need to attribute an exalted significance to everything they do, feel, suffer, the good and the bad.[3]

There was no exalted significance in his relationship with Marie, as there was with Harriet and Estelle. There was just the bad. The worst

---

3. From Hiller's *Kunstlerleben*, 1880, cited by Cairns, *Berlioz*, Vol. 1, p. 306.

of all was that so far from living ardently for his ideals, as per the letter to Viardot, he was living with a daily reproach to his self-image. What bitterness this must have caused him, bottled up because he could not express it in the expansive language and behavior that vented his other passionate feelings. It may have externalized itself and spilled over into his cosmic bitterness about persons and institutions that blocked his way in Paris.

Berlioz's love–hate relationship with Paris runs through the *Memoirs* like an *idée fixe*. He felt about Paris the way Dr. Johnson felt about London, and without Paris his career would be inconceivable; Paris enabled his career. But Paris also crushed him. As a flamboyant and aggressive antiestablishment crusader he attracted enemies in the profession and in the government bureaucracy only too naturally. The official opera and concert institutions shut him out; he had to put on most of his concerts entirely on his own and they cost him blood. The bottom line was that Paris never yielded him a job as conductor, professor, music administrator, anything above his minor sinecure at the library of the Conservatoire. He supported himself as a critic, work that he loathed, that left him no time for composition, and (of course) made him more enemies.

Les Troyens forms an ambiguous climax to this sorry story. Although the score may have realized a childhood ideal, the première in 1863 precipitated a lifetime of bitterness. In brief, as the outcome of lengthy intrigues and lobbying the work was first accepted at the Paris Opéra, the one venue that might theoretically have done it justice. It was set aside in favor of the notorious 1861 production of Wagner's *Tannhäuser*, then transferred to an inferior theater where only half of it could be mounted, for the opera is very long; meanwhile things dragged on for five years, tight money required the production to be scaled down, also the size of the orchestra, and drastic cuts were taken both before and after the opening.

In spite of all this, the truncated half, renamed *Les Troyens à Carthage*, was rather successful, if not on the *Cats*-like scale that Berlioz envied in Meyerbeer and Halévy. It was acclaimed in the press and made so much money that Berlioz could at last afford to retire from journalism. He fired off a whole series of letters describing his success as terrific, stunning, splendid, and magnificent, and on returning to the theater after some weeks of illness, and discovering that new cuts had been taken, he still wrote to Humbert Ferrand, his best friend, that the performance was superb. Meyerbeer came twelve times.

It was only some months later, in a new "Postface" for the *Memoirs*, that *Les Troyens* became a calamity, expounded in some of the most acrid and despairing pages in the whole book. The published score seems to have tormented him particularly:

> To see a work of this kind laid out for sale with the publisher's cuts and arrangements—oh, can there be greater torture! A dismembered score in the window of a music shop, like the carcase of a calf in a butcher's stall, with pieces cut off and sold as little treats to titillate the concierge's cat!

Although the impresario, Carvalho, mooted a production of the opera's other half, *La Prise de Troie*, and there were inquiries from London and Germany, Berlioz squelched all initiatives. He canceled a concert performance of the fourth act when the issue of cuts came up. (Of course it was outrageous to demand cuts from someone in Berlioz's position. Still, what did he have to lose?)

It may be too strong to characterize Berlioz's overreaction here as a mystery, but it does seem to call for an explanation, and I would look for it in the context of the momentous step he had been mulling over for some years. Defeated by Paris, he had decided to give up composition, and now was the time. He made public announcement of his renunciation in the Postface to the *Memoirs*—the same Postface in which his despair over *Les Troyens* is so vividly recorded and, I think we may suspect, consciously or unconsciously exaggerated. *Les Troyens* is treated as the last straw. What I called the *idée fixe* of the *Memoirs* receives its final and fatal transformation, even as the two wings of the soul, it seems, are separated after all.

David Cairns, taking the Berlioz persona of the *Memoirs* at his word, sees neither exaggeration nor novelistic license. After the initial euphoria, he says, it was inevitable that reality would crowd in. Berlioz will not, cannot compose because he is deeply, bitterly, and justifiably discouraged and depressed, and he is in constant pain.

There must have been something else, too. It is fearful to read in his letters about the pain, month after month, year after year—from four in the morning to four in the afternoon continuously, he says, during one spell. Yet the phenomenal resiliency of his youth was not entirely dulled. There was some kind of love relationship in 1863, and more Gluck coaching at the Opéra. We hear of many operas that he took in—eight *Don Giovanni*s in July of 1866—ebullient promenades down the boulevards, some splendid dinners, even high jinks with Stephen Heller. He had renounced composing, but not conducting; on the podium the pain tended to dissipate. He traveled to Weimar, Strasbourg (audience of six thousand), Vienna, Cologne, and in the winter of 1867–1868, a year before his death, dragged himself to Russia for no fewer than eight concerts, conducting his own music, half a dozen Beethoven symphonies and concertos, and more.

Berlioz was never one to miss an ironic twist. "To *Les Troyens* at least," he writes in his dispirited Postface, "the unhappy feuilletonist owes his deliverance." A much more distressing irony is that after complaining all his life that criticism left him no time to compose, when he retired as a critic he stopped composing. There would seem to be rich material for psychobiography here—an artist who had to fight for fifteen years to gain parental approval of his calling abandoning it at the height of his powers.

As well as illness, age, and depression, a compositional crisis must also have affected the decision, for it is evident that Berlioz was going through an extended period of uncertainty about his artistic direction, which in turn intensified his depression and set up a vicious circle. His output had slowed significantly in his late years, and it used to be said that his inspiration had simply dried up. Nobody is likely to credit this who knows *Les Troyens* and the opera *Béatrice et Bénédict*, his last work, written for the opening of a new theater in Baden-Baden (one of Berlioz's rare commissions) in the period between the composition and the première of *Les Troyens*. Read Cairns on these two pieces—read Cairns after listening to the music.

The crisis, I should think, devolved not on composition itself but on composition in the grand, innovative, sensational, often grandiose genre that he had made into his signature and that sustained his self-image. The last composition prior to *Les Troyens*, the oratorio *L'Enfance du Christ*, had excited comment for its mildness. *Les Troyens* exorcized heroic ghosts from long ago. *Béatrice et Bénédict* is light-hearted, delectable, playful, lightly orchestrated—understated Berlioz, Berlioz lite—and its genesis seems symbolic. Asked for a three-act Gothic melodrama, he offered instead a one-act *opéra comique* after *Much Ado About Nothing* emptied of the role of Claudio.

We could view these works as ideologically wrong for Berlioz, wrong at least for the young Berlioz. A French critic has written dryly of his "insatiable appetite for glory," and for this composer *la gloire* meant presenting revolutionary works to thunderous acclaim, preferably in Paris. (It sometimes seems as though the acclaim mattered more to him than the music.) This had been difficult enough in the 1830s and 1840s, when Berlioz represented the musical avant-garde virtually alone. Now he was no longer the man of the hour, as he knew from his unhappy experience with Wagner, Wagner's music, and Wagnerianism in 1860–1861. Dinner with his dear, true friend Liszt was not possible unless they agreed not to discuss music. He was facing a challenge that most artists face at some point in their careers—at a later point, in fact, than most others. For Berlioz, this challenge appears to have been complicated by another, arrived at equally late, the challenge of maturity.

—2000

22

READING OPERA

ROMANTIC OPERA AND LITERARY FORM, by Peter Conrad, is the most provocative (and provoking) book on opera to appear in a long time.[1] One is first struck by its brilliance and then astonished that such a sophisticated critical structure can rest on such simplistic foundations. The polemical thesis which runs through the chapters is that opera is not a form of drama, as Wagner and others have maintained, but a form of the novel:

> Drama is limited to the exterior life of action, and romanticism increasingly deprecates both the tedious willfulness of action and the limits of the form which transcribes it. The novel, in contrast, can explore the interior life of motive and desire and is naturally musical because mental. It traces the motions of thought, of which music is an image. Opera is more musical novel than musical drama [because] music can probe states of mind but not advance action.

Conrad traces this view of the novel to unimpeachable Romantic sources, Schopenhauer and Hofmannsthal, and his view of music also

---

1. University of California Press, 1977.

stems if not from Schopenhauer then at least from the pervasive nineteenth-century philosophy of music for which Schopenhauer was a principal spokesman.

In fact music can do a good deal more in opera than probe states of mind. This became clear particularly in the nineteenth century, when the expansion of music's power went hand in hand with the development of Romantic opera. Music, with its special unifying capacities, can assert a unique mood over an entire train of action, can as it were define a field in which a certain range of action and cognate feeling, and only that range, is possible. Verdi strove to achieve a special *tinta* or *colorito* in every one of his works. Each of the Mozart operas— even each of the Italian comedies done with Lorenzo da Ponte—has its own quite distinct atmosphere determined by the music; the psychology and agency of Susanna or Zerlina are not possibilities in the world of *Così fan tutte*. Works like *Tristan und Isolde, Carmen, Pelléas et Mélisande,* and *Die Dreigroschenoper* exist in private worlds created by their music as a whole, apart from anyone's state of mind at any particular moment.

And music can indeed "advance an action" in the sense of interpreting action or conveying the characters' apprehension of it. Otello's fit and Iago's ascendancy at the end of Act III of *Otello,* Wotan's renunciation in the scene with Erda in *Siegfried,* Wozzeck stabbing Marie, the *Abramo Lincoln* steaming into Nagasaki harbor—the quality of these actions is unforgettably portrayed by music. As Romantic composers became more and more skillful in probing states of mind, defining unique settings for action, thought, and feeling in general, and portraying the quality of actions in particular, music grew into a more and more effective medium for drama.

But drama, too, is conceived by Conrad in a very narrow sense. Disingenuously, perhaps, he does not formulate as sharp a concept of drama as of music or the novel, and he does not rely so heavily on any particular critic (though again Hofmannsthal is in the background).

He finds his concept of drama implicit in the Romantic attitude toward Shakespeare, which is expressed as much in various Romantic recyclings of the plays and characters as in criticism:

> The plays are treated either as lyrical monologues, in which case the corresponding [musical] form is the symphonic poem, or else as frustrated novels.... Hamlet longs to escape from the busy routine of revenge drama into the inactive privacy of the dramatic monologue; Macbeth is traduced by the drama, which presents him as a murderous fiend, whereas in the solitude of his lyrical meditations he reveals a lucid, entranced detachment from the crimes the drama alleges he commits. The symphonic poem satisfies the yearning of these characters to exchange the compromises of dramatic action for solitary pensiveness.

The suggestion that Hamlet and Macbeth find their true rest in the symphonic poem—"a species of musical novel, since in its submergence of plot in atmosphere it snubs the drama and prefers to record, like the novel, the meditative life of motive and self-examination"—is bizarre indeed. But not more so than the implication that drama is solely a matter of plots, routines, events, and actions. Drama has always dealt with actions and "meditations," in order to get at the relation between them, the relation between doing and feeling. Otherwise drama would never have formed an alliance with poetry, let alone music.

Conrad may perhaps be laboring under a genuine misapprehension about music, but this really cannot be the case with drama. Some way into *Romantic Opera and Literary Form* one begins to understand that his critical strategy is very deliberate. He forges a tool for dealing with Romantic art by pushing Romantic theory to its most provocative, dogmatic, paradoxical extreme. The result is a brittle instrument that will shatter at the first critical pressure, whether from within the book or without; but it does throw up some good sparks when held up against the grindstone of modern literary criticism. Sparks rather than hard flames or slow fires come to mind as one considers Conrad's criticism. His work proceeds by repetition, by the multiplication of epigrams in a process of evolving variation, rather than by the logical development of argument.

In fact Conrad says some of his most illuminating things when he is not talking about drama or music at all. In the chapter "Operatic Shakespeare," for example, he discusses elegantly how a famous passage from *The Merchant of Venice*—the "duet" of Lorenzo and Jessica—is used in *Les Troyens*. He observes justly that Berlioz takes Shakespeare as a sentimental artist in Schiller's sense, while Verdi takes him as a naive one:

> For Berlioz, Shakespeare is the kind of artist Schiller called sentimental: ironic, self-interrogating, delighting in irregular forms and quizzical, conceited verbal wit.... For Verdi, Shakespeare is the kind of artist Schiller called naive: self-effacing, a force of calm and natural order rather than disruptive, self-exhibiting intelligence. Whereas Berlioz becomes impatient with Shakespeare's characters and, as in *Béatrice et Bénédict*, dismisses them in order to write musical journalism against his enemies, Verdi, like Shakespeare himself, rests in astonished contemplation of characters whose mysterious objectivity he respects.

On the other hand, the suggestion that the political motif running through so many Verdi operas should be viewed in light of the Shakespeare history-play cycles is made no more and no less convincing by the comparison of these operas to a historical novel. The same could be said of the chapter "Operatic Epic and Romance," with its powerful and powerfully elaborated juxtaposition of *Les Troyens* and *The Ring*, "epics of the two contrasted kingdoms of romantic imagination, the lyricism and lucidity of the Mediterranean and the visionary dreariness of the dark, fearful North." One of Conrad's feats is to interpret *The Ring* as a backward demonstration of the history of literary genres from epic (*Götterdämmerung*) to romance (*Siegfried*) to novel (*Die Walküre*) to thesis-play of the Ibsen-Shaw variety (*Das Rheingold*). This splendid lit-crit tour de force would lose none of its élan if *Götterdämmerung* were categorized as an "epic drama," *Walküre* as a "psychological drama," etc. Moreover it is an argument quite independent of any philosophy of music, or indeed any substantial reference to music.

"In Shakespeare, Hofmannsthal says, the music alone matters." So should not the critic concentrate on the music—which is to say, the poetry? That would mean close reading of the text, and this critic is simply not interested in close reading, whether literary or musical, even apart from the question of his musical competence. Unexpectedly, his most detailed bits of criticism are applied to some pictures of Salome by Beardsley, Klimt, and Munch in his final chapter. What he does concentrate on is character, abstracted—he would say liberated—from the action, which he regards as a mere embarrassment to opera. It makes little difference whether a character is in Act I or Act III, or for that matter whether he is in this play or that. In Romantic criticism characters had an imaginary life of their own outside the drama. For Conrad they have a life outside the text in other texts.

His characters are constantly in motion. Hamlet longs to escape from revenge tragedy into inactive privacy, Salome unfurls into an array of images, Papageno is rescued or released by allegory. Works of art and criticism are also on the move: those that get star billing in one chapter of his book inevitably put in spot appearances in others. Like Ingmar Bergman's Sarastro, who studies his *Parsifal* score during the intermission, Conrad's Falstaff wanders from chapter to chapter and from genre to genre, equally present at Eastcheap, in the Hostess's report, in Verdi's orchestra, and in a letter from Eleanora Duse.

In the discussion of Verdi's *Falstaff*, then, Conrad makes much of the importation of speeches from *Henry IV* into a libretto based on *The Merry Wives of Windsor*. But he deals only with Sir John himself, never Nannetta or Fenton—creatures of no character whatsoever, to be sure, who nonetheless constitute the essential counterforce in Verdi's total dramatic action. Conrad is so oblivious of this and of them that he attributes to Falstaff music's "own form of heroism, which consists in setting a solitary individual to sing against and dominate the mass of an ensemble," forgetting that in the Act II finale it is not Falstaff who does this—he is in the laundry basket—but Nannetta and Fenton, singing in octaves.

Conrad's chapter "The Operatic Novel" begins arrestingly:

> When the Rostovs visit the opera in *War and Peace*, Natasha coldly notes the grotesque unreality of the scene, ashamed at the imposture but sardonic as well at the expense of the shabby artifice of cardboard and glue, the semaphoric arm-waving, the attitudinizing and courting of applause.... The supposed lovers ignore one another to bow to the public, the distracted maiden has the self-possession to manage several changes of costume, a devil sings and gesticulates until suddenly a trap-door opens and he plunges beneath the stage. Drama has become an image of cynical deception and bad faith, and it is exposed as such by the small alarms of novelistic spontaneity which crowd the "entr'actes"—the appearance of Pierre, sad but stouter, Kuragin's gaze, Natasha's blush, and Anatole's pressure on her arm. Drama is shamed by these starts of unpremeditated feeling, which are the prerogative of the novel.

At best, however, this is only a tangential way of getting at the theme of opera's escape from drama to the novel, and the chapter turns instead to an account of the decay of the operatic idea in *Ariadne auf*

Naxos and *Capriccio*. The fact is, of course, that while novels are often turned into operas, operas that turn into novels are exceedingly rare. The single interesting case is *Die Frau ohne Schatten*, written by Hofmannsthal in two versions around the same time: an opera libretto for Richard Strauss and a 150-page *Erzählung*, or "novel." It would be whimsical to say that the novel is a more authentic work of art than the opera, though perhaps even more whimsical to fuss very much about the issue one way or the other. Things are clearer with the transformation of *La Dame aux Camélias* into *La Traviata*. Proust said that Verdi's opera raised Dumas's novel to the level of true art and most people would agree with him.

And by the way, Hamlet never really escaped to Chaikovsky's dreadful symphonic poem, but remains in Shakespeare's play, where his meditative, inactive tendencies were dealt with altogether adequately by that author. Most people have been quite happy to leave him there—even most people in the nineteenth century.

For all his ingenious play with genres Conrad sees opera as a typically open-ended Romantic continuum, in which chords and characters, ideas and sentiments, works of art and of criticism are blurred and blended together. Into the blend he introduces (with some justifiable satisfaction, it seems) what he gratingly describes as "para-operatic" works, texts in a twilight zone between art and criticism. He certainly makes them all seem very interesting. A chapter on "Operatic Allegory" treats Mozart's *Magic Flute* and its sequels in Goethe's fragment *Der Zauberflöte zweiter Theil*, the two versions of *Die Frau ohne Schatten*, and the translation (or rather version) of the Mozart opera by W. H. Auden and Chester Kallman—with a bow to Auden's *The Sea and the Mirror*, which is both a poem and a critique of *The Tempest*. Conrad's book itself crosses from criticism to art as it gradually changes from an analysis of Romantic opera employing literary categories to a rumination on "the larger romantic disquiet about form, to which opera, being a problematic union of the arts, is central." The subject matter escapes from literature as it follows Salome into the arts of painting and the dance. Conrad's writing escapes from critical discourse—albeit highly charged discourse—to a kind of enthusiastic prose poem. The book is at once a disquisition on artistic form and an example, a new posthumous text to add to the Romantic continuum.

The deflection of an essay on opera which starts with the Romantic philosophy of music to other purposes, and particularly to literary purposes, is characteristic enough. For literature was also the main beneficiary of that philosophy, which valued music above language because of its direct communion with the basic, ineffable springs of life and feeling. Poets and philosophers from Novalis to Mallarmé nurtured the philosophy for their own ends—mainly, it seems, as a stick to beat language with. But musicians had no quarrel with language. In music itself Romantic philosophy such as Schopenhauer's stood at best in a dialectical relation to the practice of nineteenth-century composers, who from the first displayed a regrettably unphilosophical tendency to represent the ineffable. "Words and music are united by antagonism," exclaims Conrad, voicing a persistent complaint of Romantic aesthetics. But his favorite composer, Richard Strauss, turned away from "absolute music" and symphonic poems to lieder and operas, linking his music first with programs and then with lyric poems, libretti, and even, in *Salome*, with a preexisting stage play.

The deflection is also rather cold-blooded, for one's final impression is of a self-indulgent criticism absorbed by its own constructions and its own brilliance at the expense of the works addressed. It is a bad sign when a critic ascribes equal values to works of art and to criticism—as though Goethe's fragment and Auden's version have the same independent status as Mozart's *Magic Flute*. None of Conrad's texts, I believe, is confronted in its integrity; he picks and chooses from them what he can use and turns it to his own ends. To take what is perhaps the least important case, his partial treatment diminishes Auden's *Magic Flute*. Fascinated as always by character, Conrad considers only the light poems which are appended to the translation proper, poems which comment amusingly on the dramatis personae in a contemporary milieu. Nothing is said of the explicit criticism of the opera in Auden's preface or of the major modifications he made in the plot and dialogue—even though these extend to the insertion of a speech parodied from Prospero in *The Tempest*, a work very much to the author's purpose. The case is unimportant in itself but indicative, in that it concerns a text for which Peter Conrad seems to show genuine affection.

Affection is not a quality lacking in Gary Schmidgall's *Literature as Opera*.[2] Unlike Conrad this critic sets out to "do" works of art in their fullness: he treats twelve operas in nine chapters, covering the history of opera from Handel to Benjamin Britten. While Conrad's operatic Valhalla is inhabited by Strauss, Wagner, and such long-standing honorary Aryans as Berlioz and late Verdi, Schmidgall's is not: the only representatives of the dark, fearful North are *Salome* and *Wozzeck*. Mozart, too, is seen from his Mediterranean side in *The Marriage of Figaro*. The complete absence of Wagner and the presence of Berlioz's *Benvenuto Cellini* rather than *Les Troyens*, *Macbeth* rather than *Don Carlos*, and *Eugene Onegin* rather than *Boris Godunov* suggest that Schmidgall is not inclined to tackle the most monumental operas in the canon.

Schmidgall brings forward a number of arguments for his choice of operas. They do not persuade, but it does not matter much, for while the book has a method it has no theme or thesis. The method is to select operas derived from works of literature—from epic, autobiography, drama, and the novel—and discuss them in conjunction with their sources. It is never clear what sort of insight the juxtaposition is supposed to provide. In fact it is not clear that Schmidgall

---

2. Oxford University Press, 1977.

claims to be providing any fresh insight at all, so diffident is his critical position, so dutiful his rehearsal of literary clichés, so literally self-effacing his compulsion to quote from opera pundits and writers of every other kind. The general conclusion seems to be that Mozart found much in common with Beaumarchais, Berlioz with Cellini, Berg with Büchner, and so on.

None of this is exactly news—good news seldom is—and Schmidgall does not seem to know what to do with a real scandal when he stumbles onto one. A case in point is the notorious misreading of Pushkin in Chaikovsky's *Eugene Onegin*. "As a faithful translation of literature it is a catastrophe, but it is nevertheless an *operatic* success"—because the opera adheres to the composer's own aesthetic of simple emotional immediacy, is imbued with brilliant Russian color, and recalls Chaikovsky the symphonist at his best. "If this does not convince as a kind of apologia for *Eugene Onegin*, little more can be said." Saying this, however, will scarcely satisfy those who feel that the opera's insufficiencies lie in the limitations of Chaikovsky's music. And it will not satisfy Chaikovsky's admirers either, at least those among them who are looking for something more than the confirmation of their own tastes.

It is a pity Schmidgall cannot find a better approach to convey his affection for *Onegin* and the other operas he has chosen. He really likes the operas (which is why he chose them, of course, rather than others) and he could try telling us why and how. This might seem like an unfashionable thing to do, but hardly more so than assembling conscientious literary "backgrounds" for operas which are not really analyzed in their own terms. His chapter on *Salome* covers some of the same ground as Conrad's, using a good many of the same secondary texts—and while Conrad makes them all sparkle, Schmidgall somehow manages to do the reverse. But it is Schmidgall who gets closer to the opera's actual texture. A sense of commitment is his best suit as a critic, and he might just as well try to capitalize on it.

Irving Singer's *Mozart and Beethoven* consists merely of a fifty-page essay on *Don Giovanni* and a thirty-four-page essay on *Fidelio*, preceded by a general essay on the nature of opera and linked by a relatively swift run-through of the other famous Mozart pieces.[3] In an earlier book Singer, who is a professor of philosophy, developed a theory of the erotic imagination, which he distinguishes into "sensuous" and "passionate" sides. He now views the operas in question from the standpoint of the theory. Naturally *Don Giovanni* is the linchpin of this particular system.

The results are predictable of writing where the critic's thesis obscures the work itself. The *Don Giovanni* chapter contains hardly anything on the opera's first and last scenes—though it would seem obvious that in any drama the first and last scenes in which a major character plays a major part cannot help having a major impact and hence a major influence on the total dramatic trajectory. The first scene shows Don Giovanni struggling to break free of a strong-minded woman whom he may or may not have tricked or assaulted but who is now battling him and slanging him on even terms. It shows his dry, unthinking assent to the duel with the Commendatore and his extraordinary response in music to the outcome of that action. The last scene shows how he faces a frightening death. Show me a critic who writes convincingly about these scenes, and you can have any number of others who go on about the life force, daemonic sexuality, and the like.

There is much talk in Singer's opening chapter about opera being a mixed art form that cannot be understood by musical analysis or musical response alone. This is true, and in addressing opera enthusiasts of a certain type the point may be important to make. But here the important point to make is this: from Singer's proposition it does

---

3. *Mozart and Beethoven: The Concept of Love in Their Operas* (Johns Hopkins University Press, 1977).

not follow that opera can be understood by *neglecting* music. Can anyone doubt which of the arts in opera is the decisive one? Singer's fifty pages on *Don Giovanni* include scarcely enough lines of comment on the music to fill a single page, even including pap like "he and the music are always on the go," "before long the entire orchestra is rollicking with laughter," "there is something female about the beauty of sensuous music," "Don Ottavio sings with all the sweetness of a troubadour," and so on. Peter Conrad, too, who makes the priceless observation at one point that for Hofmannsthal music was "more literary paradox than sonic actuality," says not much that can be squared with sonic actuality in his book, rich as it may be in references to music as a paradoxical idea. Alone among the three critics discussed here, Schmidgall at least tries to achieve some sort of balance between his literary and musical perceptions.

Discussing Mozart without considering tonality, rhythm, phraseology, and form is a little like discussing Bergman without considering the camera, or Shakespeare without considering verse. "Given a few / Incomplete objects and a nice warm day / What a lot a little music can do," the sarcastic Antonio says of Sarastro's arrangements in *The Sea and the Mirror*. An opera critic who cannot get past that level is going to produce very limited work. Whether he or she has technical training in music is not important, so long as he is able to pay continuous, sensitive attention to what the composer is doing. He ought to be in a position to respond with more than average susceptibility to the many shades of music's articulation of mood, character, and action. Music criticism is, in fact, a real skill, like typesetting, coloratura singing, philosophy, and literary criticism, not learned overnight, not even learned over many enjoyable evenings at the opera.

—1978

23

VERDI: A LIFE

CONSIDER, COMPARE, AND CONTRAST the opera composers Giuseppe Verdi and Richard Wagner. Born in the same year, 1813, and both granted long, fulfilled lives, they dominated opera in their respective spheres and, each in his own astonishing way, reinvigorated the genre as a political instrument of the greatest power. Both were notorious characters, quite literally legends in their own lifetimes. Both made lasting, sustaining second marriages with remarkable women. A significant amount of what they reported about their early lives was calculated to mislead biographers.

Both men were rebels, consumed with rage at the theatrical conditions of their time and place. This cannot be overestimated as a driving force behind their art as well as their day-to-day existence. Wagner's way of dealing with his rage was to generalize it into active rejection of bourgeois culture *tout court*, with fateful results spread out in ten volumes of *Gesammelte Schriften*. When praxis was called for, Wagner took part in Dresden's 1849 rebellion and got himself banished from effective concourse with the opera world he hated. Not very practical in the short term, it must have seemed, but over the long haul of history, brilliantly so.

Verdi's rage at the theater was less public than Wagner's, though he never hesitated to write to newspapers when it suited his purpose. He vented his rage in letters of almost unbearable ferocity and despair and dealt with it time and time again by fighting the opera establishment in the trenches. Impossible to skip, in Mary Jane Phillips-Matz's lengthy new biography,[1] is the dense, searing documentation of Verdi's struggle in dozens of scores and hundreds of premières and revivals: a struggle with impresarios who tried to bend contracts, publishers who cheated him, intermediaries who lied to him, librettists who slowed him down, singers who got sick on him, or said they did, conductors who cut his operas and inserted numbers from *Norma*, audiences less than instantly enthusiastic about his admittedly novel scores, official censors doing their thing, critics doing theirs, and even (at least in Paris) insolent pit musicians. Lured to Naples in 1858 for the première of *Un Ballo in maschera* by assurances that the censors had passed an already heavily compromised version of the libretto, Verdi withdrew the opera when he found that they had not. His passport was lifted—this was at the height of his fame—and he had to sit around for weeks penning a ninety-page brief for breach of contract.

Both men waited, though only Wagner, not Verdi, sensed that he was biding his time. Banished from the theater, he created in his head a new, ideal kind of opera entirely on his own terms: music drama. For fifteen years, broken only by the revised (and rejected) *Tannhäuser* for Paris, Wagner had no new work produced.

In that same period—between *Lohengrin* (1850) and *Tristan und Isolde* (1865)—Verdi oversaw ten premières. The list runs from *Stiffelio*, which did not reach the Metropolitan Opera until 1993, through the unstoppable trio *Rigoletto*, *Il Trovatore*, and *La Traviata*, to *La Forza del destino* in its original version for St. Petersburg. Verdi fought for his operas time and time again; yet from the very start he acted out his love-hate relation with the theater by gestures of withdrawal. That is the meaning of the famous fairy tale he told about giving up

---

1. *Verdi: A Biography*, with a foreword by Andrew Porter (Oxford University Press, 1993).

after the fiasco of his second opera, *Un Giorno di regno*, only to be drawn back by a near-magical coincidence (with the impresario Merelli playing the unlikely role of good fairy). After the success of his next opera, *Nabucco*, the composer promised himself he would work like a galley slave for ten years, then retire.

His model must have been Rossini. But when the ten years were up, even though the retirement nest was purchased, the promise seems to have evaporated. Seven years later, however, after *Un Ballo in maschera*, he produced no music for four years. And after the triumph of *Aida* in 1871, another dozen years later, he really did quit. He was in his late fifties. Verdi outlived Wagner by eighteen years. Finally history in the persons of publisher Giulio Ricordi and poet Arrigo Boito came to him and begged, connived, and cajoled him to write opera entirely on his own terms. *Otello* (1887) and *Falstaff* (1893) were his first new operas since *Aida*.

Both men built: Verdi with his own money, Wagner with other people's. Bayreuth, of course, remains one of the most extraordinary phenomena in the history of the arts; a recent description of it as a "customized theater for Wagner's works," while amusing, is far short of the mark. Verdi built a hospital in a village near his home and a retirement home for indigent musicians, the Casa di Riposo, in Milan. Like Bayreuth, they are still in operation though very seldom in the news.

Verdi also built in another, more primal way. His ancestors had owned land at Sant'Agata, a tiny village near Busseto, like his birthplace Roncole, and before he was forty he bought a fine farm there for his retirement, which he threatened to commence at any time, as we have already seen. When he was able to plunge into work on the farm, between his many trips to supervise opera productions, the stomach pains that had plagued his galley-slave years would disappear. Soon the new landowner launched into an unnerving twenty-year remodeling program that transformed the farmhouse, the farmlands, the garden, the irrigation system, indeed the entire watershed. Atheist Verdi even added a chapel. He supervised every detail obsessively, often spending from 5 AM to 10 PM on the estate, except for meals and a one-hour nap. On his next visit to Villa Sant'Agata Angelo Mariani, the leading Italian conductor of the day, is instructed to bring a marble statue, a hunting rifle, and a dozen magnolia grandiflora plants between one meter and one and a half meters in height, wrapped in straw; the next letter changes that to fourteen. More here to contrast with Wagner, certainly, than compare.

Mary Jane Phillips-Matz has written the most thorough and authoritative biography of Verdi available in English or any other language. It is nearly 750 pages long, plus ample back matter; in the front, some two hundred individuals and institutions are thanked for assisting the author in the dogged, loving enterprise that she began in the 1950s. The book is jammed with newly discovered material from public (if, in many cases, highly obscure) archives, private libraries, and on-the-ground research. It makes slow but fascinating reading.

Fascinating but also rather sad. Verdi was a chronic depressive, and the devoted Giuseppina Strepponi grew more and more despondent over the fifty years she lived with him as mistress and wife. Verdi was enormously successful, both as composer and farmer; he became enormously rich and universally honored; he was the recipient of extravagant love and devotion from a great variety of people, ranging from his wife, his father-in-law, and his faithful student and factotum Emanuele Muzio to a rich circle of friends, as many of them outside the music profession as in it. Yet the tenor of his letters is almost universally bleak. It is the failures—fewer and fewer, as the years go on—that gnaw at him, the betrayals, the decline of art, the corruption of morals.

It is especially sad to read about Verdi's life after reading about Wagner's in, say, the 1983 biography by Martin Gregor-Dallin, let alone in the composer's own *My Life* or in the fat volumes of Cosima Wagner's diaries. Whatever else they were, the Wagners were glad for themselves.

We judge Verdi from his letters, and no doubt he was more likely to take pen in hand when he was angry or disgusted (when he was feeling good he would rather plant magnolias or shoot quail). Yet most of the letters had to be written anyway, and the dour tone that surfaces in them was more than a pose, more than a crusty epistolary image cultivated by the "Bear of Busseto." It has been known for some time that the bear could behave like a boor or a brute toward his wife, servants, and friends like Mariani who he felt had betrayed him. Relations with Busseto were so bad that Verdi's neighbors occasionally killed his cats, and the much-traveled composer would take long detours to avoid the little town's coach stop. Small-town spite goes a long way; yet it is also clear that for years Verdi never took even the smallest step toward reconciliation.

What outraged the Bussettini was that their favorite (but very unappreciative) son was living among them with the soprano Giuseppina Strepponi, living seclusively without so much as saying whether they were married. Strepponi and Verdi went back together a long way. A woman of the greatest intelligence and spirit, launching a highly promising career, she had helped the young composer when he needed help most—with his very first opera, *Oberto*, in 1839. (*Oberto* was what Italians call a *successo discreto*; it did reasonably well.) In 1842 she created the role of Abigaille in *Nabucco*, Verdi's first *successo di fanatismo*. By then she had already ruined her voice by singing onstage almost continuously for eight years, through several pregnancies, which Phillips-Matz has over the years researched thoroughly. Later Verdi and Strepponi fell in love. Marriage would have exposed Verdi to claims from the three children Strepponi had abandoned at orphanages, and was now supporting. He brought her to Busseto, where she was very far from welcome, and in effect parked her there, since it was awkward to have her around when he was traveling.

The knot was finally tied in 1859 (the year her firstborn and only male child, Camillo, reached his majority). But the marriage was a troubled one, and in bad times Giuseppina would start a rueful little diary, abandoned a few days later. It was for her eyes alone, of course —as contrasted to Cosima Wagner's diary, better described as an admiring chronicle of Life with R. and definitely destined for posterity. Still, Giuseppina's abortive diaries were not destroyed—not all of them, at any rate. They tell of her growing isolation and depression, which reached a peak during the elderly composer's four-year affair with Teresa Stolz, the star of *Aida* and his Requiem Mass.

Unlike some of Verdi's earlier biographers, Phillips-Matz clearly doesn't believe that Giuseppina may have had nothing to worry about. But it is not her way to offer dramatic revelations, or even novel interpretations. Her way is rather to pile up details of new circumstantial evidence. In a previously unpublished letter, Verdi makes hotel arrangements so that he, Giuseppina, and Stolz can take meals together in the Verdis' room. The hotel where Stolz stayed in Cremona (near Sant'Agata) is on a street that has since been renamed via Verdi. Reprinted in full are the astoundingly scurrilous newspaper articles which appeared about the affair. One has to sympathize with all of the principals; but on the evidence of the paper trail it is the two women who gain our respect, not Verdi. Things must have reached a showdown in 1876. There are rumors of wrenching scenes, and Stolz retreated to St. Petersburg, where she accepted a long engagement.

Giuseppina continued to love Verdi, as did so many others around him. Probably it came too late. We know little about his relations as a child with his parents, and what we do know suggests not love but conflict. His father, Carlo Verdi, was a vestry official for the local parish, conspicuous in his old age for piety. Never so the son: at age seven, serving as altar boy at Mass, he cursed the priest out loud when he was cuffed for inattention. ("May you be struck by lightning!"; this anecdote, one of very few about the young Verdi, doubtless owes its survival to the lightning that actually struck this same priest eight years later.) At some time between ages ten and fifteen, the precocious boy musician was taken under the wing of the merchant Antonio Barezzi, Busseto's premier melomane. Barezzi paid for his education in Milan, masterminded his early career, and when the time came actually gave him his daughter in marriage. Dozens of letters over years attest to the mutual bond between Verdi and the man who is always spoken of as his "second father." What the senior Verdis thought about all this is not recorded, though there are intimations of friction between Carlo Verdi and Barezzi. Later Verdi was involved with his father in property transactions, not a good omen; and in view of the importance that Villa Sant'Agata came to assume for Verdi, it was disastrous for him to have purchased it on behalf of his parents. He then turned them out when he determined to move in himself, two years later.

This was in 1851: a very bad year. Chapter 17 of this book, imperturbably entitled "November 1850–Spring 1851," proves to be a humdinger. In *Rigoletto* Verdi knew he had his best libretto to date, but also the most radical, and the battle with the censors in Venice almost drove him to distraction. Giuseppina was in great distress for reasons of her own. Verdi drew up papers for legal separation from his parents, who were sick at the time, and soon after he rousted them from Sant'Agata his mother died. It is hard to know what appalled Busseto more, Verdi's flaunting of his relationship with Strepponi or his unfeeling behavior toward his parents.

Also, Phillips-Matz has discovered another child abandoned by Strepponi (at the orphanage in Cremona) in April 1851. Conceivably it was her sister's, or a servant's (fathered by Verdi?); but if it was hers, as is most likely, that would go a long way toward explaining the passions displayed by all the actors in this unhappy drama. It is not clear whether Verdi was reconciled with his father, who died in 1867, the same year as Barezzi. Verdi was not at his deathbed.

Interestingly, the very few things we hear about Verdi as a boy and an adolescent confirm what we know about the man. He was very talented, and very shy (i.e., depressed?); he worked very hard, and he wore a beard (i.e., he was a rebel, in both personal and political terms, for a beard proclaimed one's allegiance to Mazzini—at a time when all "serious" men in Milan, it is said, shaved from nose to throat). Rebellion expressed itself in his adherence to the anticlerical party in Busseto; indeed, this composer became (and was manipulated as) a symbol of local anticlericalism long before he became famous as the symbol of national liberation. Also rebellious was that fierce independence that made him insist, for example, that it was nobody's business if he chose to install himself in one of Busseto's finest *palazzi* with a loose woman.

Most profoundly, I think, Verdi's defiance played itself out in what I have called his love–hate relationship with the theater. Constraints on his self-defined image of opera, whether political, institutional, or merely the result of someone's personal weakness or venality, drove him into fury or depression. At age seventy-one he is still writing of "that prison that other people call the theater" and raging about audiences past and present:

> I wore armor, and, ready to be shot, cried: "Let's fight!" And they were truly battles always! Battles that never left me satisfied, even when I won!! Sad! Sad![2]

Clearly his alternating revulsion and attraction to the theater, his withdrawals and returns, were for Verdi an allegory of life and death. When he reminisced about *Un Giorno di regno*, his memory played him false by conflating that early fiasco with the death of his first wife and his two children. Locked into this grim syndrome, Verdi none-

---

2. Letter to Clara Maffei, January 29, 1884; cited by Phillips-Matz on p. 674.

theless found the resource to create for himself an alternative life *in* death, namely life at Sant'Agata.

What unlocked the syndrome for Verdi was not Sant'Agata, however. It was composing opera entirely on his own terms—and on his own time. Approached (on tiptoe) to compose *Otello* in 1879, he pondered, dawdled, and positively courted distractions until 1887 before completing it. The eight-year period was interrupted only by the far from inconsiderable task of revising *Simon Boccanegra*, which he polished off in six weeks! *Otello*, as is well known, marks an extraordinary advance over Verdi's previous work in dramatic profundity and musical sophistication. One of many very vivid marks of this is how Verdi had learned to cultivate understatement—in, say, Iago's narration of Cassio's dream in Act I. Starting like a diatonic barcarolle ("honest Iago") touched by a single sleepy chromaticism, this piece turns into a pornographic nightmare as chromatics seep deeper and deeper into an evil parody of aria form. Balancing phrases begin their orderly modulations, only to drop disconcertingly back to the tonic key; the opening vocal music returns harmonically denatured in the orchestra, accompanying Iago's obscene mumbling. The orchestra sums up the growing chromaticism in a sequence so sensuous it is positively sickly.

Whenever Iago quotes Cassio talking in his sleep he quotes a weirdly transformed recollection of the music for Monterone's curse in *Rigoletto*. Certainly this evoked dream, this phantasmagoria that enchants and drugs Otello is utterly un-Wagnerian. It's equally certain that only one composer of the time could have done anything as rich and subtle, and as powerful—the recently deceased composer of *Parsifal*.

And *Falstaff* is a quantum leap past *Otello*. Musicologists have long yearned to see the composer's musical sketches for these works, if they have been preserved. A few select scholars have had access to unknown Verdi letters and other script materials at Sant'Agata, and recently the Verdi heirs have been working with the Verdi Institute, at Parma, to release his musical documents.

What did composing "on his own terms" mean to Verdi (this is, of course, my formulation, not his)? It did not mean the development of a new kind of opera, a new theater, like music drama at Bayreuth. It meant negotiation with the theater world as it existed—but negotiation on Verdi's own terms. To take a simple (perhaps oversimple) example, in *Falstaff* Verdi nearly completed his campaign against that most venerable symbol of opera's formality and artificiality, the aria. The title character is given no aria, only a diminutive canzonetta (which has, however, proved susceptible to encores!). Master Ford gets a dramatic monologue, Mistress Quickly a brief, free solo number, and Nannetta in her disguise as the Queen of Fairies a song with chorus. Only Fenton, the tenor, gets an actual aria—a gift-offering to the opera audience, and also a wry acknowledgment that his voice then as now is the one irrevocably marked "operatic." As to artifice, Fenton's aria is set to a sonnet that quotes Boccaccio. And lest these little jokes, among so many in *Falstaff*, seem too esoteric, Fenton is made to lose the end of his aria to Nannetta, and when he tries to recoup by singing along with her, the two of them are unceremoniously cut short by Alice, the operatic (or, rather, anti-operatic) Mistress Ford.

Even Quickly's brief, free solo number (the delightful "Giunta all' Albergo della Giarrettiera" in Act II, scene ii) was not part of Verdi's original conception.[3] The mezzosoprano who created the role, Giuseppina Pasqua, is pictured in one of the rare photos accompanying this new biography. When she auditioned with Verdi and he explained to her that she would have no solos, she assured him she didn't mind, she was so honored to have been chosen by the Maestro for the *Falstaff* première. However, Verdi wrote afterward, he could tell that *in petto* she was disappointed—and he added the solo. Was this because he was impressed by Pasqua's high G, or because he sensed that

---

3. First pointed out by James A. Hepokoski in "Verdi, Giuseppina Pasqua, and the Composition of *Falstaff*," *19th-Century Music*, Vol. 3 (1980), pp. 239–250; see also his book *Giuseppe Verdi: Falstaff* (Cambridge University Press, 1984).

a happy mezzo would make the role go better than an honored but slightly unhappy one? Verdi's earlier love–hate relationship with the theater is distilled into an ironic, fruitful ambivalence.

In any case, *Otello* and *Falstaff* seem finally to have calmed Verdi's demons. He has never been happier nor, it seems, more vigorous. He busies himself with the estate and his building projects and shuttles back and forth between Sant'Agata, his winter home in Genoa, and Milan. Giuseppina accompanies him even though she now has trouble getting around and is frequently ill. Teresa Stolz, who never married, is back in the picture; doubtless the relationship is very different from what it was in the 1870s, but Giuseppina may well have felt that after winning the battle she had lost the war. Phillips-Matz may think that, too—she does not quite say—for as her narrative winds to its conclusion, Verdi's wife plays less and less of a role in it. She died in 1897. Phillips-Matz prints warm, affectionate letters written by Verdi to Stolz after that time. Stolz assisted at Verdi's deathbed vigil in 1901; she died a year later.

As I have already indicated, Mary Jane Phillips-Matz is conservative when it comes to interpreting her sources, more conservative than I think she needs to be, though in today's climate of biography, many readers may want to stand up and cheer her for erring on the right side. Writing what will certainly become the standard biography, she earns our gratitude for an acute sense of responsibility in the matter of coverage and objectivity. Her central chronicle of Verdi's personal and professional life is richly supported by accounts of his lineage, the impact of the various Italian wars on the Po valley, his parliamentary career (he started out attending every session of the Senate for two months), staff lists and pay scales at Sant'Agata, his prodigious charities, his impossibly tangled business dealings with Paris, and much else, including a full inventory of Carlo and Giuseppe Verdi's land holdings. Something of a specialty for this biographer is the ferreting out of vital statistics for all the minor players in her epic story.

This said, it should also be said that hers is not a book that gets into the deeper reaches of Verdi's personality. His politics are discussed at due length, but with little nuance, and his intellectual development is scarcely addressed: the process by which his artistic ideals were formed and projected first into his libretti, then into his scores. Anyone who might be interested in possible resonances between Verdi's biography and the themes treated repeatedly in his operas— jealousy, anticlericalism, fathers and daughters, fathers and sons— will have to look for them elsewhere. Indeed, the content of the operas is reported only sporadically. We are not told, for example, of the topsy-turvy reversal of values between the original St. Petersburg version of La Forza del destino in 1800 and its revision for Milan in 1869. The version we know ends with Don Alvaro's conversion in a pious haze of high strings that would have gladdened the heart of Carlo Verdi. In the original version, Alvaro jumps off a cliff declaiming of death, the devil, and the end of the world.

The great strength of this biography is the author's comprehensive sweep, her firsthand knowledge of Verdi's world, and her control of a vast store of documentary evidence, much of it new. She provides us with a new solid basis for addressing the numerous questions that still remain regarding the life and works of Giuseppe Verdi.

—1993

24

VERDI: THE LATE OPERAS

THE THIRD VOLUME of Julian Budden's monumental work will present no surprises to those who, knowing the earlier installments, have already recognized *The Operas of Verdi* as the major scholarly and critical study written to date on this composer.[1] The operas covered in the latest book "offer no special problems of treatment which have not already been touched upon in the Preface to Volume 2." What this means is that the basic organization of the first volume—chapters on each of the operas in chronological order discussing their genesis and early stage history, their musical and dramatic content scene by scene and number by number, and (more briefly) their reception by critics and public—has been kept and expanded to reflect the much more copious documentation available for the later works and, of course, their much greater artistic density. Volume 1 covers the seventeen earliest Verdi operas, devoting an average of twenty-five pages to each. Volume 2 gets through only seven operas, requiring an average of seventy pages for the six important ones from *Il Trovatore* to *La Forza del destino*. Volume 3 contains four essays of from 100 to 150 pages long, on *Don Carlos, Aida, Otello,* and *Falstaff.*

---

1. *The Operas of Verdi*, Vol. 3, *From Don Carlos to Falstaff* (Oxford University Press, 1981). The earlier volumes were published in 1973 and 1978.

Some reviewers have criticized this format as too closely beholden to a genre much favored by British writers on music, the amateurs' vade mecum exemplified most venerably by George Grove's hundred-year-old *Beethoven's Nine Symphonies*, Ernest Newman's *The Wagner Operas*, and such Verdi books of the late 1960s as Charles Osborne's *The Complete Operas of Verdi* and Spike Hughes's *Famous Verdi Operas*. The criticism has some substance, particularly, perhaps, with reference to this very volume. By presenting a major scholarly study as though it were a much-expanded "analytical guide for the opera-goer and armchair listener," in the words of Spike Hughes, Budden confuses us and sometimes confuses himself about the audience he thinks he is addressing.

It is hard to know, however, what other format he could have used for such a comprehensive work—and especially what other format he could have used without distracting and even alienating many readers. You can call the organization that Budden decided on (or settled for) many things—safe, traditional, unimaginative. But there is room for a serious study of this traditional kind dealing with the Verdi operas, I believe: not because it will or should ever be regarded as "standard," but because it provides a solid, broadly accepted frame for the works of amplification and revision that will follow.

What has always stunned people about Julian Budden is how much he knows not only about Verdi's operas but also about those of his contemporaries, from Donizetti, Meyerbeer, and Ponchielli on down to Mercadante and Pacini, the Riccis, Cagnoni, Marchetti, and a host of even lesser maestri. There are two sources for this seemingly inexhaustible fund of information. First, in his career at the BBC, especially when he was chief producer of opera from 1970 to 1976, he put on dozens of little-known operas and must have read carefully through dozens more. The BBC also broadcast Verdi operas such as *Macbeth* and *Simon Boccanegra* in their earlier, unrevised versions. In Britain it may be that people's sense of opera owes as much to him as to the directorship of Covent Garden or the English National Opera; even in this country, pirate discs spread his anonymous influence. The man is the model of a modern practical musicologist, in fact—a calling that is not all that common but not so rare as is commonly thought, either.

Second, as far as Verdi is concerned, Budden has been able to draw on a body of research that has been growing as prodigiously, in its own way, as has the prestige and presence of Verdi's operas themselves in the international repertory. Verdi scholarship—itself notably international in range—is something of a phenomenon in contemporary musicology. Much though not all of it has been channeled through the Institute of Verdi Studies founded at Parma (the capital of Verdi's home province) in 1959, joined after 1976 by an American institute at New York University. There have been Verdi congresses and congress reports, reconstructions of historical Verdi performances, newsletters, *bolletini*, Ph.D. dissertations, even an incipient Verdi variorum edition.[2]

Budden himself has written some Verdi articles that are now required reading, and has tucked away much unobtrusive original research within the covers of his three volumes. Equally impressive is his control over the sprawling, uneven Verdi literature of the last twenty years and his ability to distill the best out of it. With his third volume he was triply fortunate, for major bodies of directly relevant source material have become available just recently: correspondence between Verdi and his librettists for *Don Carlos*; an enormous collection of documents of various kinds concerning *Aida*; and, most important of all, the Carteggio Verdi–Boito, the complete correspondence between the composer and the librettist of *Otello* and *Falstaff*.[3]

---

2. A critical edition of *The Works of Giuseppe Verdi*, launched in 1983 by the University of Chicago Press in collaboration with Casa Ricordi, Philip Gossett, General Editor, is scheduled for completion in 2015 (2007).

3. Articles on *Don Carlos* by Ursula Günther and Andrew Porter; Verdi's *Aida: The History of an Opera in Letters and Documents*, collected and translated by Hans Busch (University of Minnesota Press, 1978); *Carteggio Verdi–Boito*, edited by Mario Medici and Marcello Conati (Istituto di Studi Verdiani, 1978). An English version was duly published by the University of Chicago Press in 1984, translated by William Weaver (2007).

Consequently Budden's account of the genesis and stage history of the late operas is especially fine. The composite story he tells of the way Verdi and his poets hammered out plotlines, situations, verse structures, and actual details of wording—and then came back to revise and refine after the rehearsals or the première—will make luminous reading for anyone interested in the stage. I know of nothing to match it as a record of practical dramaturgy in the musical theater except the Strauss–Hofmannsthal correspondence and, in a more antic vein, the post-Catskill section of Moss Hart's classic *Act One*, with its unforgettable odor of limp ham sandwiches consumed with George S. Kaufman in New Haven and other dreary tryout locations. Verdi's tremendous dramatic intelligence is everywhere in evidence; what changes is his relationship with the librettists, his dominant role in the collaborations with Camille du Locle and Antonio Ghislanzoni giving way to the heartwarming intellectual (and personal) symbiosis with Boito. We should have the whole *Carteggio Verdi–Boito* in English.

Special interest attached to the earlier volumes of *The Operas of Verdi* because of the fresh interpretations and appraisals offered for many of the operas treated. Such was not to be expected from the present volume, dealing as it does with established works that have been thoroughly hashed over by critics. When Budden says that *Don Carlos* "is now considered by many as Verdi's masterpiece" he surely exaggerates (how many is many?), but he speaks the cold sober truth when he says that "no other work of his explores such a variety of human relationships" and that "each of the principals has a rounded individuality, that is nowhere surpassed in the Verdian canon." (Even in *Otello*, for example, it might be said that Desdemona is too repressed and Iago too satanical to have a "rounded individuality," and Otello's introspective soliloquy "Dio! mi potevi scagliar," though Budden likes it well enough, is not the score's strongest number.) In this country the prestige of *Don Carlos* has been growing steadily since Rudolf Bing's debut production of it at the Metropolitan Opera in 1950, staged by Margaret Webster and sung most memorably (in my memory) by Giorgio Tozzi as Philip. The Verdi specialists have added to the opera's panache by their enthusiastic dissemination of the very many discarded bits left over from Verdi's cutting and revising in 1866, 1867, 1872, 1884, and 1886. Budden threading his way through all these different versions does not make for an easy read—the *Don Carlos* chapter is his longest—but those who persevere and follow him may come to feel they are almost inside the mind of Verdi the dramatist.

On the various notorious problems posed by *Don Carlos*, our author is judicious, not to say generous, not to say bland. The four-act version (used by Bing) makes a good, taut design, but if there is enough time the five-act version "will doubtless be preferred" despite its longueurs. He allows as how the splendid opening pages cut out by Verdi during the original Paris dress rehearsals might well be reinstated (as they are by James Levine in the current Metropolitan version); in a footnote he even grants some merit to the opening of another cut, the great threnody sung by Philippe and Carlos over the dead Rodrigue whose tune became the "Lacrimosa" of the Verdi Requiem. (Claudio Abbado opens it at La Scala.) Yes, the music fits the original French words much better than the Italian we nearly always hear—but Verdi never expected the piece to be sung outside Paris in any language other than Italian. Anyway Italian singers seldom do well by French. The unsatisfactory ending *coup de théâtre*—unsatisfactory in all versions—we must just live with, though "it may be felt...that the quiet ending of 1867 has more to recommend it than that of 1884 with its pealing brass...."

By contrast with *Don Carlos*, *Aida* has indeed turned "just a little sour." For the taste of our time, everything about *Aida* seems depressingly straightforward: the definitive text of the opera, the poster-color *tinte* of most of the principals, and (as Budden points out) their unquestioning attitude toward state authority as formulated by the warrior priests of Ptah. (*Aida* has been issued in Italy as a comic book. In this eye-catching redaction, the two women do not seem to be distinguished in *tinta*, but Aida's breasts are always rounded, Amneris's pointed.) To some listeners, it may be added, a good deal of the chromatic writing in this opera seems less problematic in an interesting way than uncontrolled. Nor does the curiously mechanistic system of recurring motives associated with Aida, the priestly hierarchy, and Amneris please.

Otello and *Falstaff*, the two late Shakespeare operas, have long been admired almost universally down to the last *acciaccatura*, even by those who do not otherwise warm to Verdi. In fact Budden's chapters on these great works call forth so many superlatives as to tax even his considerable skill as a writer. His one reservation corresponds to Verdi's own, expressed in both words and deeds, concerning the big Act III ensembles in each work—in *Otello*, the scene of the Venetian embassy leading to Otello's fit, and the laundry-basket scene in *Falstaff*. The music of the latter scene, Verdi wrote to Ricordi after the Milan première, "is too long and is too obviously a *pezzo concertato*," and he cut ten bars out of it for the definitive score he had Ricordi publish. The former he shortened even more at *Otello*'s Paris première, seven years after La Scala. Budden, wondering why this cut was not formalized as in the case of *Falstaff*, would clearly like to stage the Paris version and see how well it works in a practical performance situation.

Verdi's remark leads us to the heart of the critical methodology in the previous volumes of *The Operas of Verdi*. The *pezzo concertato* or concerted piece is just one of a whole catalog of musico-dramatic formulas or *convenienze* that the young Verdi inherited from Rossini, Donizetti, and Mercadante in the 1840s. Our difficulty with his early work is understanding and accepting these *convenienze*. In key historical chapters, Budden explains them with great authority, and in his actual run-throughs of the operas the best thing he does is show again and again how Verdi is turning standard conventions to his own dramatic ends. This is the musicologists' standard way of tracing this composer's artistic development, and it is a good way. Step by step Verdi, staying just close enough to the *convenienze* in order to keep his audience, evolved an entirely individual operatic style by blurring and ultimately exploding their edges.

Don Carlos and *Aida* mark the end of this process. Since he was less at home with the traditions of the Parisian grand opera of Meyerbeer than with those of Italian melodramma, Verdi had more trouble with *Don Carlos* in this regard. In too many spots Meyerbeer has not been sufficiently exploded. With *Aida*, on the other hand, he achieved what Budden calls a "classical" solution. As such, *Aida* was not and could not be a forward-looking work:

> Though the drama is continuous the structure is basically that of formal numbers embedded within a continuous texture; and though for a decade at least composers such as Ponchielli and Gomes would continue along this path..., future progress was to be towards a freer, more orchestrally based continuity....

But mention artistic progress to Verdi and he was sure to go into a tirade running down the whole notion, meanwhile proclaiming the sanctity of Italian musical traditions. After *Aida* in 1871 he simply decided to give up composing operas.

So Budden's book falls into two halves. When Verdi returned—*Otello* was mooted in 1879 but not staged until 1887—the "progress" had been miraculously accomplished, as though it had been incubating all the while under his continual growls and grumbles about the decline of Italian opera. In *Otello* operatic conventions are transformed and in *Falstaff* transcended. Neither work has anything much to do with anyone else's operas. Hence the rationale is really lost for the interchapter on Italian opera from 1870 to 1890, in which the political, economic, and artistic background for that decline is sketched with a masterly hand. With a nod to the *veristi* of the 1890s, Budden pinpoints the failure of Ponchielli, Gomes, and Catalani to resolve "A Problem of Identity." And lost along with it is the strategy used so powerfully in the previous parts of this study to place Verdi in high relief against the background of contemporary opera.

It is mainly by reason of this loss, I believe, that the analytical-descriptive sections on *Otello* and *Falstaff* are ultimately less illuminating than those on earlier, lesser operas. This may seem a paradoxical, even a mean judgment, for the author has clearly lavished more space, love, and ingenuity on these works than on any others. But he really has no guiding critical methodology for dealing with them. All he has left is a rather airy style of musical analysis coupled with a sharp sense of local dramatic effect and an overflow of subjective response.

With the two late masterpieces any writer is at a disadvantage because we all bring our own extensive, truculent preconceptions with us. We have so much less to learn here, we feel, than from *Nabucco* and *I Due Foscari, Attila,* and *Il Corsaro* (to mention some early works not entirely at random). Budden allows himself a good deal of space for the *Otello* and *Falstaff* run-throughs, as has already been observed: but still not enough, given his "analytical guide for the operagoer and armchair listener" method. Does it seem ungrateful (or ludicrous) to complain that 18,000 words are inadequate for a serious analysis of *Otello*? Not, I think, when the author commits himself to telling the story in relentless detail and working his way systematically through the music of every single number in the score. This is like trying to tell it all about Shakespeare's *Othello*—a work of comparable richness and complexity, certainly—scene by scene, speech by speech, line by line, in a like compass.

Inevitably with such a method, the greatest proportion of illuminating points are of a local kind that can be made briefly: points about orchestration, for example, or the effect of Italian verse meters on Verdi's musical phraseology. Budden is especially sensitive to musico-dramatic nuance—to the way musical details convey psychological states, tones of voice, or dramatic beats—and inventive in the prose that characterizes it:

> Desdemona is more child-like and impulsive; and her twelve bars of melody (*"Mio superbo guerrier!"*) wander more freely [than Otello's previous melody]. Her subdominant cadence at the words *"soavi abbracciamenti"* suggests a happiness almost too great to be believed. Inconsequentially she wanders off on a pattern of sixths....

> As sung by Desdemona [the Act III duet melody] is all innocence and charm; when taken over by Otello (*"Grazie, madonna..."*) and edged by the oboe it assumes a bitter sarcasm that sets the listener's teeth on edge.

> Desdemona [being murdered] screams over a diminished seventh outburst *"con tutta forza,"* in which the sense of shock is immeasurably increased by the sudden switch into triplet motion.

On the other hand, a passage that is as important (at least to sopranos) as Desdemona's dying speech is hurried past in half a sentence. Other prominent passages are unaccountably skimped in the run-through.

On a technical level, too, Julian Budden the musician promises more than he delivers—more than he could possibly deliver in 18,000 words, too many of which are telling the story ("'A sail, a sail!' they cry..."). There is so much talk about keys, motives, harmony, and thematic connections that one is constantly challenged to check one's own image of the music against Budden's often maddeningly (if necessarily) elliptical descriptions. Why does the Act I Love Duet veer off to D-flat after all that F major and E major beforehand, and sound so good when it does so? Why is the main vocal theme of Iago's "Credo" not mentioned while its orchestral themes are illustrated in two of the book's 350-odd music examples? Why does Budden never respond to Verdi's always sensational passages involving parallel fifths and octaves? Why does he not associate the doom-laden ostinato of hollow chalumeau chords in the Act IV Introduction with the filled-out chords preceding "*Emilia, addio*" and "*Niun mi tema*," later?

It is not likely that this general line of objection to Volume 3 will come as any great shock to its author. He must have seen it coming only too clearly back when he started work on the earliest operas for Volume 1. Unless I am mistaken, there is a sense of dutiful slog about many passages in his present round of run-throughs—along with many passages of high enthusiasm and insight. An author, too, who spends fewer pages on Act IV of *Otello* than on the additions to and subtractions from Act III in the Paris version is making his priorities plain. It is for its authoritative account of the genesis, stage history, and revision of the late operas that Volume 3 of *The Operas of Verdi* will be most gratefully read.

Finally there is the whole question of the broader view. Always alert to local dramatic effects in individual scenes and numbers, Budden is less interested in the global issues that some critics see raised by Verdi's operas when they are considered as total artistic structures. Do these works not deal with great themes of human action and feeling, and if so what are they; why are they shaded, interpreted, and balanced as they are; and how are Verdi's values projected by dramatic form on the highest level? Budden does not have much to say about any of this. He devotes only one or two pages on each opera to the work as a totality, in general terms, and in these pages that peculiarly British underground stream of bluff, no-nonsense, know-nothing-beyond-what's-in-front-of-my-nose criticism bubbles aggressively to the surface. Budden is at his most traditional or, rather, conventional —and unhelpful—in these pages. He is not above ex cathedra put-downs of ideas he has not fully digested, not even above an occasional platitude. What little he says in broad terms about the operas does not always stand up to scrutiny.

Thus in defense of the unsatisfactory "happy" ending of *Don Carlos*, we are told that the original Schiller play is "a myth; and in myths the deus ex machina is perfectly acceptable whether he be a dead Emperor or a Voice from Heaven." The novel on which Schiller based his play "has the making of an archetypal myth.... Freudians might see in it the classic Oedipal situation." Indeed they might. But seeing this in *Don Carlos*, or in *Hamlet*, does not shunt these works into some sort of special genre that doesn't have to behave like a drama. No one has ever recommended that the Ghost might return at the end of *Hamlet* and pick everybody up off the floor. The *lieto fine* is in fact less a characteristic of myths than of classical serious operas (as John Gay's Beggar observed). If Budden is right and the contrived happy ending was still alive or at least workable in French grand operas of Verdi's time, then that was another of the *convenienze* the composer failed to master fully for his own dramatic purposes in *Don Carlos*.

With *The Merry Wives of Windsor*, on the other hand, perceptions of its mythic content have proliferated ever since the fat knight was dubbed a "fertility spirit" in the 1950s by Northrop Frye. Verdi's *Falstaff* has its own strong mythic elements: the exquisitely modulated transition in the last two scenes from the grubby corporeality of the Garter to the fairyland of Windsor Forest; the quiet climactic wedding music which reminds Budden of Arne or Boyce but reminds me of the dignified and commodious sacrament on a summer midnight in "East Coker," "dauncinge, signifying matrimonie"; and especially the treatment of the young lovers.

For the first time Verdi was looking at life from a feminine perspective, through the eyes of Mistresses Ford and Page and Quickly. Honor, lust, fury, and old age are brushed aside for the essential business of coupling the young with the young. For practically the first time he gives us a pair of lovers who are not doomed, a tenor and a soprano who instead of being thwarted by a baritone are rescued, master-minded, and mothered by a battery of sopranos and mezzos. Though only at a price: Nannetta and Fenton live in a world apart, symbol-ized by physical barriers—the potted trees, the screen, the disguises—and especially by their music, so constant and so distinct from that of the other characters. Gradually they are disembodied into spirits, the true nighttime denizens of the magic forest. Young love can succeed, but only by removal from or transcendence of the Garter world of ugliness, appetite, and intrigue.[4] For Nannetta and Fenton are also Verdi's least passionate lovers—if, in a sense, his most physical. Fore-play is their thing, not consummation. Surprisingly, Budden finds all of their music to be "instinct with the 'lacrymae rerum,' that underly-ing melancholy that Keats associated with 'beauty that must die...'"

One could go on, especially about the general discussion of *Otello*, which acknowledges no Shakespeare criticism beyond Coleridge, Shaw, and the rather obscure M. T. (*sic*: it should be M. R.) Ridley, though in fact his talk about "rounded individuality" sounds suspi-ciously like A. C. Bradley. Bradley was a contemporary of Boito, to be sure, but that only means that Bradleian criticism might serve as a beginning, not the end, of a serious examination of Verdian drama. Dramatic criticism today, like musical analysis today, has to go beyond nineteenth-century criteria.

But to complain even further about Julian Budden's book along these lines would be, if not altogether unfair, altogether ungrateful. Global dramatic criticism was never a part of his scheme and is

---

4. This was beautifully put in a classic article by Edward T. Cone, "The Old Man's Toys: Verdi's Last Operas" (1954), reprinted in: *Music: A View from Delft*, edited by Robert P. Morgan (University of Chicago Press, 1989), especially pp. 172–175 (2007).

evidently not to his liking. As it is, he has produced what will long remain the definitive history of the twenty-eight Verdi operas, together with an analytical-descriptive account of them all which is certainly the most detailed, sophisticated, and acute that is available, by a large margin, in any language. A great achievement.

—1982

25

WAGNER AND WAGNERISM

BOOKS CONSIDERED IN THIS ESSAY

The New Grove Wagner by John Deathridge and Carl Dahlhaus (Norton, 1984).

Opera Quarterly, Commemorative Wagner Issue, Vol. 1, No. 3 (1983).

I Saw the World End: A Study of Wagner's Ring by Deryck Cooke (Oxford University Press, 1979).

My Life by Richard Wagner, translated by Andrew Gray, edited by Mary Whittall (Cambridge University Press, 1983).

Richard Wagner: His Life, His Work, His Century by Martin Gregor-Dellin, translated by J. Maxwell Brownjohn (Harcourt Brace Jovanovich, 1983).

Richard Wagner: Three Wagner Essays, translated by Robert L. Jacobs (Da Capo, 1983).

Richard Wagner: Dichtungen und Schriften, Jubiläumsausgabe edited by Dieter Borchmeyer (Frankfurt: Insel Verlag, 1983).

Tétralogies—Wagner, Boulez, Chéreau: Essai sur l'infidélité by Jean-Jacques Nattiez (Paris: Bourgois, 1983).

The Fertilizing Seed: Wagner's Concept of the Poetic Intent by Frank W. Glass (UMI Research Press, 1983).

Wagner and Aeschylus: The Ring and the Oresteia by Michael Ewans (Cambridge University Press, 1983).

Kingdom on the Rhine: History, Myth and Legend in Wagner's Ring by Nancy Benvenga (Harwich, England: Anton Press, 1983).

Staging Wagnerian Drama by Adolphe Appia, translated and with an introduction by Peter Loeffler (Birkhäuser, 1982).

Wagner Rehearsing the "Ring": An Eye-Witness Account of the Stage Rehearsals of the First Bayreuth Festival by Heinrich Porges, translated by Robert L. Jacobs (Cambridge University Press, 1983).

Wagner's Siegfried: Its Drama, History, and Music by Patrick McCreless (UMI Research Press, 1982).

In Search of Wagner [*Versuch über Wagner*], by Theodor W. Adorno, translated by Rodney Livingstone (Schocken, 1981).

RICHARD WAGNER DIED in 1883. Readers who feel in need of a quick Wagner fix in this centennial year, but who may be put off by the multitude of recent literature (as is the present writer), will do well to await *The New Grove Wagner*, an offshoot of *The New Grove Dictionary of Music and Musicians*, first published in 1980. It contains a concise, merciless account of Wagner's life by John Deathridge and, at somewhat greater length, a treatment of Wagner's music, aesthetics, and individual operas and music dramas by Carl Dahlhaus, a tour de force in its short space. In addition, there is a valuable up-to-date work list based on the comprehensive catalog of Wagner's music that is about to be issued in Germany—the first "Köchel" for the composer.[1]

Perhaps this *New Grove Wagner* is not quite the little book for neophytes that its format seems to promise. Deathridge writes with some asperity against the background of previous Wagner biography,

---

1. *The New Grove Wagner* came out in 1984. The *Wagner Werk-Verzichnis*, edited by John Deathidge, Martin Geck, and Egon Voss appeared in 1986 (Schott) (2007).

and Dahlhaus takes musical literacy in his readers for granted. He also assumes familiarity with nineteenth-century German philosophical and political thought in another trenchant but (as Dahlhaus himself might say) more "dubious" chapter on Wagner's "Theoretical Writings." "Theoretical writings" they are; they are also the prolix and powerful writ of the ideology of Wagnerism. Indeed, the central issue with Wagner must be seen as the complicity in his work between art and ideology, between art and Wagnerism. In the summary to his chapter, Dahlhaus, who is the foremost Wagner scholar of our time, restates his position on this question squarely. The writings, he says, should be seen as

> statements in which a composer who was also an intellectual formed in the "Vormärz" period summoned almost the entire intellectual inheritance of his age and forced it into service to justify his conceptions of musical drama. This process involved some drastic *reinterpretation* of the philosophies upon which it drew; yet the conceptions they were supposed to serve stood in no need of justification.... Wagner varied the philosophical, aesthetic and political theories he proclaimed in his writings entirely for the sake of his musical dramas, which in the last analysis were the only thing that truly possessed him. The works are the key to the writings, not vice versa.

That is, the operas and music dramas must be understood first in their own, internal terms, and only second as reflections of ideology. Back of this conviction lies another, articulated elsewhere by Dahlhaus—that the *music* in these works must be understood before they can be understood as operas or music dramas.

This may seem obvious enough. But it is a long-standing complaint among musicians that the staggering Wagner literature contains so few studies of the music *qua* music. There is no generally accepted model for the way the mature music "works," as there is for Bach, Beethoven, Schoenberg, and even Palestrina. An aura of mystification about the technical basis of his music was promoted by Nietzsche's "Cagliostro of modernism" himself. "Silence was hard for Wagner," Dahlhaus remarks, but he also reminds us that this polymath who wrote about everything else scarcely ever wrote about his music in its practical (as opposed to its metaphysical) aspects. "It is as though he fought shy of utterances about the thing on which, in the last analysis, all else depended."

Of the dozen or more recent Wagner books mentioned in this article, only two deal centrally with the music—both of them Ph.D. theses published in a sheltered dissertation series. Few of the others devote much attention to music at all. The Wagner issue of a new journal, *Opera Quarterly*, which runs to more than three hundred pages of material by nearly seventy writers, has not a single illustrative example in music notation. A symbolic omission: Can one imagine a similar pile of writing about Manet without a single illustration?

The widely noticed book on *Der Ring des Nibelungen* by Deryck Cooke, *I Saw the World End*, is a different case. In the introductory chapters Cooke announces that his comprehensive study will culminate in a definitive musical analysis. However, the book was a posthumously published fragment, and at his death in 1976 Cooke had only got halfway through a preliminary discussion of the librettos. In view of the fact that he began his study in 1963, it has been suggested unkindly that even if he had lived he might never have got around to the music. It has also been suggested that maybe it is just as well that he didn't, for enough is said in Cooke's introduction, and enough is known from his other books, to make it clear that his way of dealing with the music would have been through an intricate analysis of the semantics of Wagner's leitmotifs. What interests most Wagner scholars today is not this aspect of the music dramas, but larger questions of form and process. They are interested in the principles of structure, principles involving leitmotifs as functional rather than semiotic elements, and involving rhetorical modeling, narrative strategies, ambiguities of tonality and phraseology, and much else. A valuable bibliography of current work along these lines—much of it produced by Dahlhaus and his circle—is appended to a recent article by Anthony Newcomb, whose work counts as the best in English on this subject.[2]

Musicologists have their work cut out for them. Some of them are now talking about Wagner studies as a major growth industry. There is still a lot to find out about the way Wagner's mature music works, and this in turn has a lot to tell us about later music, whereas it is hard to believe that anything remains unsaid about Wagner's ideology. But musicology, of course, can be a way of defusing ideology. The statement by Dahlhaus cited above can be read as an invitation to accept Wagner's works as dramatic structures, or even merely as scores, drained of their ideological content.

It can also be read as a tacit invitation to accept Wagner literally on his own high-minded terms. There is philosophy of a sort in Wagner's "theoretical writings," but there is also a strong element of hype—the same hype that suffused his day-to-day conduct and that also penetrates right into his works of art themselves. If Wagner "summoned up the entire intellectual inheritance of his age" in his writings, as Dahlhaus says, he wrote not only to justify his conceptions of musical drama, but also to promote those dramas; even saying that his art was "the only thing that possessed him" seems inadequate, for it was not only the art but its promotion that possessed Wagner. More is involved here than an artist's appropriate or inappropriate egotism. That Wagner was the greatest egotist in the history of the arts is perhaps debatable, but there can be no doubt that the world has never seen his equal as an artistic booster.

---

2. "The Birth of Music out of the Spirit of Drama," *19th-Century Music*, Vol. 5 (1981), pp. 38–66; see also his "Those Images That Yet Fresh Images Beget," *Journal of Musicology*, Vol. 2 (1983), pp. 227–245.

Amazing as Wagner's music dramas are in strictly artistic terms, equally amazing is the way he merged art with promotion and promotion with ideology. This is why, on the one hand, the complicity of art and ideology is the central issue with Wagner, and why he has always been suspected of somehow caring less about art than about Wagnerism. And this is why, on the other hand, he began issuing his *Gesammelte Schriften* in ten volumes when still in his fifties, and why he labored to create a myth out of his own life that even today, after a hundred years of often skeptical scrutiny, seems to defy demythicization.

According to this myth, Wagner was destined to redeem human society, which had been slipping badly since the days of Aeschylus, and which had arrived at a particularly poor state in Germany of the Vormärz period, the becalmed political time between the Congress of Vienna and the revolution of 1848. This he would do by seizing the torch of German art from Beethoven and creating a series of novel art works. Dramas fashioned from the newly powerful and prestigious art of music would function in the regenerated world in the way that Aeschylean tragedy did in ancient Athens. As Martin Gregor-Dellin puts it in his new biography, long before Wagner openly wrote *Religion and Art* in 1880, "a religion in disguise" was already the real substance of the writings of 1849–1851, whose ostensible subjects are revolution, autobiography, and operatic theory. Eschatological fanaticism, paranoia, and "mental elephantiasis" overcome Wagner from this period on.

Even before being forced into exile in 1849, Wagner while in his thirties had planned out the series of novel artworks he would require: *Der Ring des Nibelungen*, *Die Meistersinger*, and *Parsifal* (*Tristan und Isolde* was a later inspiration). The *Ring* story was outlined in most of its details in 1848, though only its ending, *Siegfrieds Tod*—what is now *Götterdämmerung*—was originally meant to be set, as is well known. Less well known, though hardly the secret Gregor-Dellin makes them out to be, are the musical sketches that the composer rejected in 1850. They made him see that the poem had to be expanded; and around this time he also formed the idea of a special shrine for his new religion. This he would ultimately bring into existence in 1876 at Bayreuth; the temple, the priesthood, the ritual, and the aura all remain more or less intact to this day. In the 1930s, too, a vision of a new society embracing the ideology of Wagnerism was for a few years realized, with Wagner performed Aeschylus-fashion on the new annual holy days. With no other artist does the *Rezeptionsgeschichte* of his work take on such grisly importance.

After having orchestrated his career by this amazing plan of work, Wagner set about similarly orchestrating the image of that career. He was already altering facts to fit the myth in his essay *A Communication to My Friends* of 1851, and he did this systematically—indeed, with an epic sweep—in his famous and fascinating autobiography. *My Life (Mein Leben)* goes up to 1864, the first year of his providential support by Ludwig II of Bavaria and of his involvement with Cosima von Bülow, née Liszt. Nothing that has to do with Wagner is uneventful; even the history of this book makes an intricate and instructive tale. Suffice it to say that when in 1963 a scholarly edition was finally made from Cosima's manuscripts—Wagner dictated the book to her—it turned out that while previous editions were riddled with tiny errors and omissions, they had not been subjected to the sinister major expurgation that had been suspected.

This, however, says nothing about what the editor of the authoritative edition characterizes rather hastily as "the inexactitudes, the bland artifices" that make the narrative so dangerous as a source for an objective biography. In *The New Grove Wagner* John Deathridge describes *My Life* as "tendentious dramaturgy" and makes a special point of exposing as many of its lies (or selective slips of memory) as possible. That Wagner thought nothing of distorting the nature of personal relationships has been understood more clearly than his readiness to rewrite musical history. Thus he falsified two of his alleged musical epiphanies that linked him to Beethoven—his hearing of Wilhelmine Schröder-Devrient as Leonore in *Fidelio* (which did *not* happen in 1829) and his attendance at Paris rehearsals of the Ninth Symphony (ditto in 1839). And Wagner repeatedly fudged dates and circumstances concerning his own works so as to heighten their aura with colorful and positive autobiographical images.

The authoritative edition of *My Life* (as reedited in 1976) has now been issued in a much-needed new translation with notes identifying personalia, etc. Still needed is an edition with annotations, which would have to be extensive, checking Wagner's account of the facts point by point with what can be learned about them objectively. In the absence of such correctives, *caveat lector*—who should also be warned about the diaries Cosima kept from 1869 to 1883.[3] Their publication as two huge volumes a few years ago attracted much interest. Viewed by some as a testament to a great love story, or at least as the basis of a promising seven-and-a-half-hour television miniseries, the diaries can also be viewed as a continuation, under joint auspices, of the polishing of her husband's image that he himself had begun years earlier. Redemption Through Love is only one of the leitmotifs sounded, as it seems artlessly, in the Gospel according to Cosima.

Martin Gregor-Dellin is a novelist, man of letters, and a specialist in the work of Thomas Mann, which seems to have drawn him to Wagner. As editor of the definitive *My Life* and also of Cosima's diaries, he has been able to draw on much that is new for *Richard Wagner: His Life, His Work, His Century*. His is an elegant and entertaining book that wears its learning lightly. As has now become the rule in this genre, there is a certain amount of psychologizing: the

---

3. *Cosima Wagner's Diaries*, edited by Martin Gregor-Dellin and Dietrich Mack, translated by Goffrey Skelton, Vol. 1, 1869–1877 (Harcourt Brace Jovanovich, 1978), Vol. 2, 1878–1883 (1980). A paperback abridgement containing a mere 536 pages was issued by Yale University Press in 1999 (2007).

infant Wagner's peripatetic existence in war-torn Saxony, and the death of his father during his first year, are seen as contributing to a "mother complex" which affected both his later relations with women (no virgins) and his fetishistic attachment to silks. Deathridge for his part speaks of an "identity crisis" in response to the dead father and the live stepfather, the actor Ludwig Geyer, who may well have been Richard's natural father. (In *Siegfried*, of course, the hero kills a false father who is named Mime.) But basically Gregor-Dellin's is an old-fashioned biography—a richly woven, no doubt slightly embroidered ground cloth fit for the greatest actors in the history of nineteenth-century Europe to strut their hour upon. There are virtuoso splashes of atmosphere, pages of diverting narrative, and not a few interjections by the author. He has a particularly sharp eye for the absurd scenes that Wagner's hectic and ruthlessly tactless social life seems to have precipitated again and again.

Gregor-Dellin assumes an authorial tone of ironic detachment toward all his subjects, which is indeed sometimes reminiscent of Thomas Mann. In such a mood, he can react to one situation in a highly censorious way, and merely wryly to another which may perhaps appall the reader just as much. He preserves no illusions about Wagner's devious, malicious, monomaniacal ways: "monstrous," he calls them. At the same time, he does not conceal his admiration for the resilience, imaginativeness, self-assurance, and *élan vital*—Bernard Shaw's life force—which Wagner also possesed to such an extraordinary degree. "A scoundrel and charmer he must have been such as one rarely meets," Virgil Thomson once remarked, adding that while in effect he could take or leave Wagner's music, what he "would like most of all is to have known the superb and fantastic Wagner himself."[4] Gregor-Dellin shares—and conveys—something of the same feeling.

---

4. *The Musical Scene* (Knopf, 1946), p. 87.

Several of his most provocative chapters must be understood in connection with other recent Wagner biographies, in particular the main postwar item published in German. This was by Curt von Westernhagen, a nondescript scholar who started writing on Wagner during the 1930s. This ambience shows up clearly enough in his postwar writings, which are shamelessly soft on Wagner; the 1979 English edition of his biography was, to put it gently, a miscalculation, especially since anyone in publishing should have known that Gregor-Dellin's was due out (in Germany) in 1980. Gregor-Dellin seems to have set out to put the record straight on Wagner's role in the 1849 Dresden uprising, and on his ideology as expressed in writings of 1849–1851 and 1878–1883. How far has he been successful in this?

Let us take, inevitably, the subject of Wagner's anti-Semitism. *Judaism in Music* of 1850 is described as an eruption of irrational rage at the current musical scene, fed by envy of Mendelssohn and Meyerbeer, which turned into an alarmingly explicit but otherwise typical chauvinistic product of Young Hegelian and Young German radicalism. The Jew as banker: in the current Wagner literature one reads almost as much about Karl Marx's anti-Semitism in the Vormärz period as about Wagner's. Gregor-Dellin says the reason Wagner needed the Jews to vilify was that they alone could help him denounce contemporary music.

But while *Judaism in Music* was already ominous enough, there was much worse to come. In *Know Yourself, Heroism and Christianity*, and other writings of 1879–1883, the themes of the 1850 tract —the Jews' repugnant appearance, speech, and song; their inexpressiveness, lovelessness, and alienation from German culture—all crystallized around a doctrine of racial purity that before was only implicit. Gregor-Dellin can write about Wagner's redemptive "religion in disguise" without seeing, or saying, that Wagner needed the Jews because they alone came to represent that from which society had to be redeemed. Art alone, it seems, would never do it; purification of the blood was a prerequisite to regeneration of the spirit (that was one reason for the incest in the *Ring* and for Klingsor's self-castration in *Parsifal*). Miscegenation, above all, had to be rooted out; it was the Jews' racial status that counted, not their financial power—let alone their musical one. Wagner knew he had won the musical battle. But modern German society disappointed him more and more, notably by its refusal to embrace Wagnerism. As he grew more and more consumed by his role as its redeemer, racial purity became his obsession.

This is of course not an issue that can be defused by taking note of the composer's association with Jews almost to the day of his death—his pitiless manipulation of the conductor Hermann Levi, for example, which is mordantly discussed by Adorno, or even what seems to have been a certain affection for the pianist Carl Tausig. Wagnerism attracted Jews—Elaine Brody provides an astonishing list in one of the *Opera Quarterly* articles—like flypaper. Nor will it be defused by Wagner's coolness to the official political anti-Semitic movement of the 1870s that was promulgated by Bernhard Förster and others. The historian Paul Lawrence Rose has argued convincingly, I think, that Wagner was bound to distrust Förster's initiative because it was narrowly linked with Prussian statehood, with conservatism and bourgeois philistinism. Political anti-Semitism seemed to him a debasement of the true utopian anti-Semitism that he had nurtured since his overtly revolutionary days, and that he was glad to meet with again in recent racist literature by aging Young Hegelians such as Bruno Bauer and Wilhelm Marr. One who had been prepared to co-opt the 1848 revolution for his own ends was not going to see what Rose calls his "noble anti-Semitism" co-opted by the mere politicians of an unredeemed Germany. That Germany had very nearly betrayed Bayreuth.[5]

---

5. See Rose's review-article of the Westernhagen biography and of Richard and Cosima's diaries in *Historical Journal*, Vol. 25 (1982), pp. 751–763.

Even Deathridge, I find, handles all this somewhat elliptically, though his biography in *The New Grove Wagner* is written from a standpoint that is safely to the left of center. Deathridge too is writing contra Westernhagen, for if you look at the actual original *New Grove Dictionary*, you will find under "Wagner" in Volume 20 another biographical whitewash by that much-translated author. Deathridge's biography in *The New Grove Wagner* is a substitution. It is also, I have to say, a pretty chilly piece of work. Mann wrote about the "Sufferings and Greatness of Richard Wagner," but one would not guess much about either from this essay. I noticed only one unambiguously favorable adjective (*Parsifal* is "sublime"), and Deathridge spends his next paragraph taking it back.

Shades of Ernest Newman. It is quite a change to read an English Wagner specialist who takes a hard, cold line with the Master.

What does one *do* with Wagner's racist and other obnoxious writings? One can attempt to reclaim them, as was done not so many years ago by the English philosopher Bryan Magee and an American professor of medicine, L. J. Rather.[6] Or one can bury them. In a welcome new translation of *Three Wagner Essays* ("Music of the Future," "On Performing Beethoven's Ninth Symphony," and "On Conducting"), Robert L. Jacobs simply cuts out what he calls the unpleasant, unbalanced bits of the latter. (A veteran Wagnerian, he knows better than to start an argument by calling them extraneous.) "On Conducting" appears with its unpleasantness intact in the attractive pocket *Jubiläumsausgabe* of Wagner's poetry and prose issued by Insel Verlag—an edition that includes some hard-to-find early opera drafts; but *Judaism in Music* and *A Capitulation* are excluded because the editor says he is not doing a complete edition and other writings are more important. There is no rule that a ten-volume edition has to

---

6. Bryan Magee, *Aspects of Wagner* (Stein and Day, 1969); L. J. Rather, *The Dream of Self-Destruction: Wagner's Ring and the Modern World* (Louisiana State University Press, 1979).

be a representative edition, I suppose. Questionable on other grounds is the (unacknowledged) cutting of about 75,000 words of the original book by Gregor-Dellin at Harcourt Brace Jovanovich, though this was reportedly done with the author's agreement.

Everyone accepts that the *Ring* does not succeed as a total work of art—both the adherents who see it as a profound and fascinating "problem" work (like *Hamlet* and *Faust*, according to Deryck Cooke), and the rest of us who will tolerate it only in evening-, act-, or scene-length segments. Everyone also accepts it as Wagner's *Hauptstück*, and this for many reasons beyond its sheer scope and ambition. The book that Bernard Shaw ironically entitled *The Perfect Wagnerite* is a book about the *Ring*.

"The forging of the *Ring*," as Westernhagen called it, has been traced many times, most recently in Jean-Jacques Nattiez's *Tétralogies—Wagner, Boulez, Chéreau*. Nattiez is a Canadian music theorist who has attracted attention for his attempts to develop a semiology of music; but there is not much semiology in the present book, and its semantic undertaking is hardly subtle. By means of a close analysis of the internal development of the drama over its twenty-six-year gestation period, Nattiez seeks to show that the final result is at best confused, at worst meaningless. All the more reason, therefore, for the stage director of a modern production—he is thinking of Patrice Chéreau—to supply meanings of his own.

Yet even Nattiez fails to take account of external factors that led to the ultimate confusion. They were Wagnerian factors. There was a great pause in the *Ring* project: after six years of mulling over the story and the poem, and after four more years of intense, enormously fruitful work on the music, the composer abandoned it in the middle of the third opera, *Siegfried*. This was in 1857. Why? Whole books have been written about the *Ring* and even about *Siegfried* without suggesting what I am sure was the deepest reason: misgivings about the outcome that

Wagner dared not admit. For he could not abandon Wagnerism, and his great "Festival Drama in Three Days with a Preliminary Evening" was central to Wagnerism. Someone who had written *Lohengrin* just before having to flee Germany and did not get to hear it all until 1861 had learned the hard way to wait. In the late 1860s he schemed and lied with at least some success to prevent his impatient patron King Ludwig from producing the early *Ring* operas singly at Munich; he wanted them presented as a whole in their own special shrine or not at all. Only when that shrine became a real prospect did he resume composition of the *Ring*, completing it in time for the opening celebration.

The reason the tetralogy was completed was that Bayreuth had become a reality—and its completion was less a testimony to Wagner's artistic conscience than to his commitment to Wagnerism. Wagnerians such as Cooke always try to dismiss *The Perfect Wagnerite* as a one-sided political reading of the *Ring*, but Shaw did more than characterize the end of the work as—inevitably, in the historical situation—a political or ideological impasse. He also characterized it as an artistic sellout, which he saw as less than inevitable, in that the composer retreated to musical and dramatic ideals he had campaigned against for years and long since abandoned in his own work.

Not inevitable, but certainly understandable. Wagner was facing musical and dramatic material that he had outgrown by twenty years and more. Between 1857 and 1869 he had written *Tristan und Isolde* and *Die Meistersinger* and his style had of course matured very significantly; but he was stuck with his old leitmotifs. One must indeed admire the skill with which he managed to transform some of them to suit his astonishingly sleek new developmental style—that "art of transition," as he called it, which in *Götterdämmerung* sometimes sounds like ripe Richard Strauss. But the discrepancy between the musical process and the crudeness of some of the themes—the Ride of the Valkyries theme, for example, goes all the way back to those 1850 sketches—has always been glaringly obvious. And Wagner could make use of that same skill to transform a merely stupid theme (Siegfried's Horn Call) into a portentously vulgar one (Siegfried the Hero).

Meanwhile dramatic unity presented him with insuperable problems both of form and content. What was strange but innovative about the *Siegfrieds Tod* poem of 1848 was the way the basic action was intercalated with scenes referring to the gods who never appear (the Norns scene, the embassy to Brünnhilde begging her to give up the Ring, etc.). These scenes, the seed of the work's multiplication, led ultimately to the best of the *Ring* as we now have it. Wagner wrote one of his greatest scenes after the "pause"—the opening scene in Act III of *Siegfried*, for one, the scene with Erda in which Wotan finally accepts his renunciation. But central to the tetralogy's final poem (as to the saga material from which it drew) is the unedifying tale, so hard to make edifying, of Siegfried and Brünnhilde's embroilment with the Gibichungs. In plot, tone, and form, the scenes that embody this recall not only *Lohengrin* but also the operatic style that lay behind *Lohengrin*, the hated grand-opera style of Meyerbeer. Rewriting the *Siegfrieds Tod* poem as *Götterdämmerung*, Wagner did what he could to "de-Lohengrinize" it, in Nattiez's term, but he could not do much, or anyhow would not. Thus writing the music entailed employing all those traditional operatic forms that so disgusted Shaw —love duets, trios of vengeance, choruses of vassals, and the like. Wagner's own probable self-disgust about this may have been one reason why he reissued *Judaism in Music* at just this time, causing a great and wholly unnecessary scandal.

As to dramatic content: it is puzzling that even in 1848 so experienced a theatrical craftsman should have contemplated a "grand heroic opera"—his term for *Siegfrieds Tod*—in which the hero is much of the time under the influence of a potion that makes him act unheroically. Or was this a projection of Wagner's utter confusion about the idea of heroism in the *Ring*? Mankind's redeemer must be free of the gods' guilt, fully confident of his own vitality, therefore fearless, therefore innocent, therefore vulnerable to the Gibichungs' wiles. The result is a hero who has nothing to strive against. Even at the famous place in *Siegfried* where he breaks through fire and breast-plate to Brünnhilde, he experiences no more than the briefest spasm of fear (a hero who learns fear only to forget it again, as Adorno remarks). At Siegfried's death, Wagner's music has him recapturing that great shared love with Brünnhilde which is to redeem mankind; it is Siegfried's one conscious and sympathetic, hence perhaps "heroic," moment. Against it one has to set the assault on Brünnhilde and all the other scenes showing the drugged hero as recidivist. This is impossible dramaturgy.

Also dramatically debilitating, of course, was Wagner's vacillation about the ending. The work bore the full brunt of his egregious conversion from the philosophy of Feuerbach to that of Schopenhauer, the subject of so much tedious commentary including now that of Nattiez. Brünnhilde's immolation, originally a joyous negation of the ego in the spirit of universal love, was reinterpreted so as to match the decisive shift in focus from Siegfried the redeemer of mankind to Wotan the renouncer of the Will. But Wotan does not even appear in the last opera, *Götterdämmerung*. Almost incredulously, Nattiez concludes that at this point Wagner didn't know what to do with Siegfried anymore. Indeed. Instead of having the immolated Brünnhilde transport the murdered hero to Valhalla, Wagner had her abandon both him and Valhalla, along with the Ring, to the waters of the Rhine.

"Le Ring de Wagner a-t-il un sens?" wonders Nattiez. People have been asking (and answering) this question ever since Nietzsche's "Do you understand it? You won't catch me understanding it...." Wagner was wary, also: almost at the last minute, he cut out Brünnhilde's much-altered final speech entirely, remarking airily that all would be made clear by the music alone. This from an operatic reformer who had insisted that music must be "impregnated" by words to express "poetic intent"—Frank W. Glass has written a whole book about

this, *The Fertilizing Seed*—and who always specified staging and gesture with the greatest care so that things indicated by words and by music would also be seen. ("Dr. Johnson kicking the stone to confute Berkeley is not more bent on common-sense concreteness than Wagner," as Shaw remarked.) The meaning of the music in the immolation scene is no clearer than the meaning of the so-called Redemption Through Love leitmotif with which it culminates—a notorious bone of contention among exegetes. Deathridge has found out that the composer himself once associated this leitmotif with "the glorification of Brünnhilde," thus deflecting attention from who is being redeemed and how.

Unable to bring his grand plan to a clear conclusion, Wagner simply left it open as a "problem." Despair, necessity, cynicism, cunning, self-deception—it was in any case the supreme act of hype in a lifetime devoted to the cultivation of that function (among, of course, others). Once he had built a shrine for his redemptive religion, all that the new Aeschylus could come up with was a work of which the redemptive message was thoroughly obscure. Something less ambiguous was urgently needed. While only the *Ring* could have led to the creation of Bayreuth, only *Parsifal* could have saved it.

As for the "problem": pondering the meaning of the cataclysm at the end of *Götterdämmerung* helps those so inclined to forget the meaninglessness of the middle. It has provided an inexhaustible field for explicators, both scholarly and amateur, and made the *Ring* a happy hunting ground for directors with confused ideas of their own to substitute for the composer's. Then there are the fisher kings and queens who find deep meanings for the *Ring* in the teeming waters of universal mythology and mythologized history. Lévi-Strauss has not fished them dry; more recently, L. J. Rather has come up with the Oedipus cycle, Michael Ewans with the Oresteia (*Wagner and Aeschylus*), and Nancy Benvenga with the saga of Frederick Barbarossa (*Kingdom on the Rhine*). If one includes this year's *Ring* program booklets, Nancy Crookes weighs in at Bayreuth with the Tolkien tales and Christopher Fulkerson at Seattle with dragon lore (see Joseph Fontenrose's *Python*). One awaits with sinking heart the appearance of the Jedi in the *Ring* literature. A Spielberg influence was noted by more than one observer at Bayreuth last summer.

Nattiez's *Tétralogies* is a paean to the Bayreuth *Ring* production of eight years ago, by Patrice Chéreau and Pierre Boulez. A stiff-necked little book by Uwe Faerber, *The Bayreuth Festival's Centenary Ring*,[7] mounted a systematic attack on this production, which has now been perpetuated on television. Between the two, I side with Faerber, but what I find most wonderful is the persistence of the Wagnerian hype that has propagated whole books and countless ephemera about this programmatically controversial and (as I think) basically foolish production.[8] Chéreau's direction incorporated a number of imaginative details together with a greater number of inept ones, all out of sync with the music, and what it conveyed as a whole was not the four levels of meaning that Nattiez tells us Chéreau was working for, not an "aesthetic of mélange," but a half-playful, half-portentous mishmash. Boulez's conducting often projected fascinating details of sonorous clarity, but it systematically eliminated the lushness and the "long line" that Wagner's music absolutely needs to make its points.

The whole enterprise was less significant in itself than as a turning point in the history of postwar Bayreuth, a turning away from the style of its guiding genius, Wagner's grandson Wieland. Wieland developed his own version of the extraordinary vision of Wagner staging created by Adolphe Appia, a vision that was articulated in Appia's *La Mise en scène du drame wagnérien* of 1895, and that indeed inspired the life work of this great pioneer of the modern

---

7. Translated by Stewart Spencer (Berlin: Bote & Bock, 1977).

8. Not as I think today (2007).

theater. Costumes, action, and Appia's abhorred "scene painting" were minimized, while intense effort was devoted to the actor's quiet gesture and to effects of lighting. With a minimum of distraction away from the music, Wagner was "interiorized," "essentialized" as never before. Almost all who witnessed Wieland's best productions were overwhelmed by their beauty.

This belated vindication of Appia by the Wagner establishment was ironic enough, as Peter Loeffler, the editor of the English edition of Appia's little pamphlet, reminds us. Not only had Appia received a snub from Bayreuth such as only Cosima could deliver, but when in his old age he finally got a chance to stage the *Ring*, in peaceful Switzerland, the second half had to be called off because of the audience's hostility. But Appia's style not only suited Wieland's talents, it also accomplished a process of abstraction that was clearly understood at the time as altogether necessary if Bayreuth was to survive. Anything that might be interpreted or misinterpreted as Nazi— the brutality, the amoralism, the eschatology, even the gables of Nuremberg—was filtered away into a static play of *son et lumière*. Interiorization defused unwanted ideology. By suggesting an atomic holocaust at the end of his 1951 *Ring*, Wieland even contrived to suggest a source of cataclysm far from the Rhine.

Times change, passions fade, and in the late 1960s a new style of opera production came into fashion: vigorous, glamorous, provocative, expensive, gimmicky, and *moderne*. Bayreuth, which had mounted no fewer than three *Rings* in Wieland's manner, decided that it was time to make the move. A German paperback of 1978 called *Theaterarbeit an Wagners Ring*[9] documents *Ring* productions from 1970 to 1977 by eleven different directors, among them Jean-Pierre Ponnelle, the best-known member of the new school; Wolfgang Wagner, who was responsible for the lackluster Bayreuth *Ring* of 1970; and Patrice

---

9. Edited by Dietrich Mack (Munich: R. Piper, 1978).

Chéreau, who at the age of thirty-one received the improbable invitation to make his debut as an opera director with Bayreuth as his sandbox. Reading the statements of intent by these eleven directors, and looking at the nearly three hundred postage-stamp-sized photographs of their work, helps put Chéreau (if not Boulez) into proper context. In modern Bayreuth, the artistic realpolitik of Richard, Cosima, and Wieland Wagner survives at least on the level of superior public relations; a French *Ring* would make a bow to the spirit of the EEC and might be hoped to defuse Wagner's notorious anti-Gallicism (though some of his best friends were French). It would make French intellectual waves around Wagner such as had not been seen since the days of Villiers de l'Isle-Adam and Catulle Mendès. For this, it seems, Bayreuth was prepared to put up with a *Ring* that was sometimes, as Nattiez admiringly says, not just skeptical about Wagner but actually "derisive." It would not need to run for long. The next year Bayreuth mounted an English *Ring*, with Sir Peter Hall and Sir Georg Solti, which was supposed to effect another major revolution in staging—a return to Wagner's own Romantic stage traditions.

Something went wrong, and the result was not very Romantic or, it seems, very newsworthy. Nevertheless, the idea of neo-Romantic Wagner staging is definitely in the air, as witness the Metropolitan Opera's 1980 *Tannhäuser* and another new *Ring*-in-progress at San Francisco —though that, alas, turns out to be inspired by Chéreau at least as much as by Caspar David Friedrich and Karl Friedrich Schinkel.[10] And a guidebook is ready and waiting—has just been issued—should neo-Romantically inclined directors and conductors want to make use of it. *Wagner Rehearsing the 'Ring'* is a scene-by-scene account of Wagner's own musical and scenic instructions at rehearsals of the *Ring* prior to the 1876 première, recorded by one of his close musical associates, the conductor Heinrich Porges. It is a fascinating historical

---

10. See Chapter 26 (2007).

document, though as is the case with *My Life* and Cosima's diaries, one would have to thread carefully through the Wagnerian hype to get out of it what one needs.

Nattiez argues vehemently against such "fidelity" to Wagner's staging, as indeed to any aspect of his text.[11] There is a real and not unfamiliar argument here, but Nattiez could hardly have chosen a shiftier ground for it. With Wagner's *Ring* it is only too easy to undermine authorial intention, and with Chéreau's, interpretational integrity or, indeed, competence. But of course what is so uncanny about the Chéreau-Boulez *Ring* is its suitability to the bastard medium to which the work has finally been transferred. "Chéreau's staging abhors a vacuum," writes Nattiez—"*la scène de Chéreau a horreur du vide.*" Busy, heterogeneous, anecdotal, and motley, it positively cried out for video. (Imagine sixteen hours of televised Wieland.) While this masterstroke of Wagnerian hype may well have been serendipitous, for the American market Bayreuth did not fail to press advantage and minimize derision. Reverential intermission features were added, presided over by Wagner's granddaughter Friedelind.

Adorno's *Versuch über Wagner* is an astonishing book, comparable only (as the author must surely have planned) to the late Wagner tracts by Nietzsche. It is a little like them in its conciseness, ambivalence, poetry, passion, and humor, in the violence of its attack on Wagner, and in a quality of incandescence and authority that drives the reader on whether he understands all, much, some, or very little of the argument. What makes for difficulty is not so much the Frankfurt School apparatus, which has by now become fairly familiar, at least in a general way, nor even the half-dozen musical excursuses of a technical nature. Rather it is Adorno's Nietzschean self-indulgence in the

---

11. An earlier, shorter version of his argument was translated for *October*, Vol. 14 (1980), pp. 71–100.

matter of aphorisms, his well-known haughty assumption that his readers all know as much as he does, and his virtuoso development of what one might call, paraphrasing Wagner, the art of non sequitur.

Unlike Nietzsche, Adorno claims to stay strictly outside his book. Thus while his critique of Wagner (relieved, to be sure, by more than a few "twists of the dialectic") is much more extensive than Nietzsche's, it is ostensibly impersonal and indeed pales beside Adorno's critique of the culture which produced the composer, and of which Adorno wants to see him as the embodiment. This critique is less extensively presented; it is simply assumed. For Adorno, the complicity of art and ideology is certainly the central issue with Wagner, but the ideology in question is not Wagnerism—it is a Frankfurt School reading of the ideology of the postrevolutionary bourgeoisie at mid-century. So epic is his view of the historical process that even in the years between 1937 and 1939, when he wrote the book, he found little to say except in passing—though that little is said pungently enough —about Wagnerism and Nazism. Nazism too seems to have paled for him into a mere episode in the decline of bourgeois capitalism.

In Adorno's deterministic music history, the nineteenth century falls between an era in which art and society are perfectly attuned and an era in which they are—or should be—wholly alienated. Suspended in history between Beethoven and Schoenberg, the barely submerged pylons of Adorno's construction, Wagner is a profoundly conflicted, ambivalent, and hence inauthentic figure. This is equally true of his personality—his "social character," as Adorno calls it in a masterly opening chapter—and of his art. Adorno sees the pessimism expressed there as the philosophy of the apostate rebel, the bourgeois revolutionary who nonetheless desperately identifies with the class he has betrayed. "In Wagner, the bourgeoisie dreams of its own destruction, conceiving it as its only road to salvation even though all it ever sees of the salvation is the destruction." And later:

The category of redemption is stripped of its theological meaning, but endowed with the function of giving solace, without however acquiring any precise context. It is a homecoming without a home, eternal rest without Eternity, the mirage of peace without the underlying reality of a human being to enjoy it. The reification of life extends its domain even over death, since it ascribes to the dead the happiness it withholds from the living.

On the way to this cosmic rejection of the Wagnerian enterprise, Adorno has much to say about Wagner's musical processes in specifically technical terms. Technical and sociological analyses merge brilliantly and recklessly. He writes most richly and admiringly about factors of sonority, harmony, and orchestration, categories that seem to him definitely to be progressive—on the way to Schoenberg's "emancipation of dissonance"—rather than regressive; though to turn the page in Adorno is always to run the risk of being upended by another of those dialectical twists. It is essentially by means of sonority that Wagner creates his "phantasmagoria," most easily recognized in those famous passages where time seems to stand still in a mystical "mirage of eternity," but extending ultimately to the whole of his music dramas. Like the commodity for Marx, music drama for Adorno is flawed by its very nearly successful attempt to hide the elaborate technique and division of labor involved in its production. This is Adorno's way of articulating a problem many feel with the late Wagner works and their exceedingly high finish. Even Dahlhaus seems to be made a little uncomfortable by *Die Meistersinger*, perhaps the most prominent case in point.

In more general terms, the combination of words and music in music drama is (for Adorno) another case in point. Certainly he has little use for the ideas behind the words. On the status of Wagner as a major thinker, confidently upheld by certain of the contributors to

Opera Quarterly—there are one or two in every crowd—Adorno is predictably silent. He is caustic about Wagner's turn to myth, which he sees as a way of expelling history and actuality. One who felt Adorno's influence was Wieland Wagner.

About the whole system of leitmotifs Adorno is quirky, claiming with some vehemence that since they are basically "gestural" in quality they cannot also be "expressive." Recognizable here is that pervasive antitheatrical prejudice, recently pinpointed by Jonas Barish,[12] which is also an obvious factor in Nietzsche. But whether or not this claim is discounted, Adorno's resistance to the whole leitmotif system is still useful as a counterweight to writers like Cooke on the one hand ("The leitmotivs are miniature pictures," Adorno insists, "and their supposed psychological variations involve only a change in lighting") and Dahlhaus on the other ("instead of unfolding in a genuinely free and unconstrained manner, [Wagner's musical continuity] has recourse to small-scale models and by stringing those together provides a substitute for true development"). I say this even though Adorno's polemic, based on the rigid Lorenzian interpretation of Wagner's large forms, is now badly dated, thanks largely to Dahlhaus (another who has been influenced by Adorno).

Following Adorno, one can see a typical ambivalence in the way leitmotifs work on characterization, too. The characters gain their psychological depth largely (though not entirely) from the subtle application of leitmotifs. At the same time, the density of leitmotif use gives the fatal impression that the dramatis personae are being completely manipulated by the dramatist, in much the same way that real-life persons of considerable psychological complexity were manipulated by the man. The one figure Wagner found he could not manipulate was Tristan in love, and this may be why for Adorno and many others *Tristan und Isolde* is the truest of the music dramas:

---

12. *The Antitheatrical Prejudice* (University of California Press, 1981).

The feverish passages in Act III of *Tristan* contain that black, abrupt, jagged music which instead of underlining the vision [i.e., the phantasmagoria] unmasks it. Music, the most magical of all the arts, learns how to break the spell it casts over the characters. When *Tristan* curses love, this is more than the impotent sacrifice offered up by rapture to asceticism. It is the rebellion— futile though it may be—of the music against the iron laws that rule it.... By voicing the fears of helpless people, it could signal help for the helpless, however feebly and distortedly. In doing so it would renew the promise contained in the age-old protest of music: the promise of a life without fear.

Adorno's *Versuch* is essential reading for anyone seriously involved with the composer, and now we can read it, thanks to a superior translation of a notoriously difficult author by Rodney Livingstone (who acknowledges help on musical questions from Eric Graebner, and who cannot be responsible for the foolish mistranslation of the original title). It is rather off-putting to meditate on the multitude of expendable words about Wagner that have rolled off English and American presses between the first appearance of Adorno's 145 pages in German, in 1952, and this still little-noticed translation of three years ago.

—1983

26

A *RING* FOR SAN FRANCISCO

Accursed Hagen,
alas! alas!
for you counselled me on the venom
which bewitched him from his wife!
Ah sorrow!
Suddenly I understand—
Brünnhilde was the true love
whom through the drink he forgot!

GUTRUNE, BEFORE SHE sings these lines near the end of the *Ring*, has
waited in trepidation for Siegfried's return. She screamed and swooned
when Hagen brought in Siegfried's corpse, and lamented while Gunther tried to comfort her. She confronts Brünnhilde, only to learn that
the husband she is lamenting was a bigamist. Now, in her final words,
Gutrune blames Hagen, Gunther's brother, and she also blames herself. If she had only taken a little more time, understood a little more,
she would take responsibility not only for the "venom"—the magic
love potion—that caused Siegfried to fall in love with her and forget
Brünnhilde, but also for his murder.

What makes us read so much into these few lines? This is the first
time when Gutrune is singing that the orchestra plays that weirdest of

all *Ring* leitmotifs, the alternating chords of *Das Rheingold*'s Magic Helm, which are transformed in *Götterdämmerung* so as to indicate the Magic Deception engendered by that love potion. (I am using the classic labels by the French musicologist Albert Lavignac.) Then Gutrune's own weak, pretty motif is painfully bent, forced together with the Magic Deception chords, and finally liquidated into the motif of Destiny. It is a perfect little example of Wagner's virtuosity at manipulating leitmotifs in the service of the precise and moving depiction of human feeling.

And this speech of Gutrune's was set in place with the greatest craft. The next speaker, Brünnhilde, also suddenly understands—and in ways that count to Wagner, she understands a great deal more than Gutrune. "*Alles, alles, alles weiss ich,*" Brünnhilde sings in one of her greatest (and lowest) lines of the entire drama. On the basis of this higher understanding, Wagner contrasts her superhuman, urhuman, or inhuman response to the death of Siegfried with the human, all-too-human response of Gutrune. From the start of Brünnhilde's Immolation Scene that ends the opera, it is clear that there will be nothing here for tears.

First she orders the vassals to build the funeral pyre—a fine imaginative example of this composer's notorious literal-mindedness: for whereas earlier in the drama we have twice been told about the felled World Ash piled up in logs in Valhalla, waiting for the end, only now do we see them echoed in the equally doomed Gibichungs' hall. A staggeringly beautiful, drawn-out modulation changes Brünnhilde's mood from the hortatory to the elegiac. The modulation prepares a simple but very persuasive passage built out of her and Siegfried's love music.

Less persuasive is Brünnhilde's rhetoric in this passage. Many strands from earlier in the *Ring* are obsessively pulled together in the Immolation Scene, but one that is not is Brünnhilde's action in securing Siegfried's murder by Hagen—a violent enough action that we certainly remember from the last time we have seen and heard her on the stage, in the previous act of *Götterdämmerung*. Brünnhilde never refers to it, dilating instead on the paradox of Siegfried, the truest of lovers, who honored his oath to Gunther and yet "betrayed" her by marrying Gunther's sister Gutrune. Brünnhilde is of course speaking figuratively when she uses and reuses this word, for she now knows about Gutrune's magic potion; Siegfried drugged is Siegfried blameless. Though Brünnhilde has ostensibly been transformed from a Valkyrie into a loving human being, her humanity does not extend as far as accepting any responsibility for *her* betrayal of Siegfried, when she revealed that he was vulnerable to a spear thrust in his back.

Incidentally, it seems less than human of Brünnhilde to condone the humiliation, brutalization, and robbery (if not the rape) of a helpless woman on the grounds that the hero was honoring his oath and didn't know that the woman was her. An attitude more acceptable to votaries of the eternal feminine, no doubt, than to those of eternal feminism.

Next in the Immolation Scene Brünnhilde addresses Wotan:

> *Hear my accusation* [Klage],
> *great god!*
> *Through his most valiant deed,*
> *so deeply wished by you,*
> *you ordained him*
> *to endure the curse that you incurred.*
> *He, the truest, had to betray me,*
> *so that a woman might grow wise!*

Her drift seems to be that only by killing Siegfried could the gods shock her into performing the act they desire, the return of the ring to the Rhine. But while Wotan has a great deal to answer for in the *Ring*, he is not responsible for Siegfried's doom. To judge from the poem, this begins with the hero himself, who pushes his way into the

Gibichungs' lives, insisting that they fight him or befriend him and then quite consciously throwing his lot in with theirs. We are asked to find something admirable in Siegfried's inability to conceive of treachery in perfect strangers, even though he had encountered it before—and rewarded it—in his foster parent Mime.

To judge from the music, a shattering appearance of the Curse motif just before Siegfried inflicts himself on the Gibichungs works to shift the responsibility away from Siegfried's mindless "heroism" to Alberich's original curse, as transmitted by his son Hagen. Although Wotan has indeed been guilty of passing this curse along, after the curse kills Siegmund, he has been careful to remain both technically and emotionally uncommitted to the latter's son and successor Siegfried, who would never have been born at all save for the disobedient intervention of Brünnhilde. Brünnhilde does not accept responsibility for this act either.

According to her new "understanding" her task is to torch Valhalla along with the funeral pyre. Now, whatever the inclination of Wotan's much-discussed "will," his most recent wish was for Brünnhilde to save him and the world by giving up the ring. The tenderness of the superb cadence with which she promises Wotan his rest ("*Ruhe, ruhe, du Gott!*") clashes with her lethal action, just as in the parallel situation at the end of *Die Walküre*, Wotan's passionate farewell to Brünnhilde had clashed with his gratuitous action in consigning her to rape.

Emotion contradicted or unsupported by dramatic action becomes more and more sentimental the more the dramatist pours it on. Sentimental, too, is Wagner's treatment of Brünnhilde's final speech. After first demanding the complicity of her horse Grane ("in the teeth of the cult of the prevention of cruelty to animals," Adorno remarked, "she even insists that her horse should neigh with joy as it leaps into the flames"), Brünnhilde works herself into a state of ecstasy prior to her immolation. This is done with fairly extended sequences on a theme that has, quite exceptionally, never been alluded to in the drama since it was first heard in a short passage in *Die Walküre*. It is sung by Sieglinde when, in despair after the death of Siegmund, she suddenly takes a new lease on life on learning she is with child. The actual words Sieglinde sings express gratitude to Brünnhilde for telling her and saving her, so the associations of the theme include the traditional redemption by love, the origins of Siegfried, the community of womanhood, and doubtless the eternal feminine. But precisely because the theme does not recur until the end of the cycle, it recalls the scene from *Die Walküre* itself much more than any concatenation of ideas. The scene itself makes short work of Sieglinde. She is indeed electrified to hear that she is to bear a child, yet what really moves her is not that prospect, or even the prospect of bearing Siegmund's child. No Siegmund motifs are heard. What stirs her to song is Brünnhilde's information that the child will be the greatest of heroes, the Siegfried who will forge the sword and whom Sieglinde somewhat obscurely bequeaths to her benefactress. The composer himself labeled the theme accurately as "the glorification of Brünnhilde."

He needed a theme to use later and had no hesitation in upstaging Sieglinde crudely to get it. As for that later use in *Götterdämmerung*, the classic criticism is by George Bernard Shaw in *The Perfect Wagnerite*:

> There is no dramatic logic whatever in the recurrence of this theme to express the transport in which Brynhild immolates herself. There is of course an excuse for it, inasmuch as both women have an impulse of self-sacrifice for the sake of Siegfried; but this is really hardly more than an excuse; since the Valhalla theme might be attached to Alberic on the no worse ground that both he and Wotan are inspired by ambition, and that the ambition has the same object, the possession of the ring.[1]

---

1. Brentano's, 1911, pp. 97–98 and 123.

Shaw knew that this argument could be turned back on him, as surely as he knew that early in *Das Rheingold* the Valhalla motif is gradually derived from the *Ring* motif before our very ears. He knew, in short, that there will always be someone who will seize on what he called an "excuse" and cherish it as a deeper reality, and that there will never be anything to say to that person. He would also not be surprised, if he came back to check out how true this still is, to find that at a time when his prestige as a music critic has never been higher, his strictly musical judgments are seldom taken seriously:

> This particular theme of Sieglinda's is, in truth, of no great musical merit: it might easily be the pet climax of a popular sentimental ballad: in fact, the gushing effect which is its sole valuable quality is so cheaply attained that it is hardly going too far to call it the most trumpery phrase in the entire tetralogy. Yet, since it undoubtedly does gush very emphatically, Wagner chose, for convenience' sake, to work up this final scene with it rather than with the more distinguished, elaborate and beautiful themes connected with the love of Brynhild and Siegfried.

Jerome Kern comes to mind. Wagner's music, like his dramaturgy, is sometimes marvelously rich, sometimes (often, in the *Ring*) crude.

"As to the coyer subtleties of the score," wrote Shaw, "their discovery provides fresh interest for repeated hearings, giving *The Ring* a Beethovenian inexhaustibility and toughness of wear." Representative recent discoveries can be sampled in the Opera Guides series issued in association with the English National and Royal Operas.[2] These packed pocket volumes contain a libretto, together with Andrew Porter's fine singing translation (which is used at the ENO, Seattle, and

---

2. *Das Rheingold*, English National Opera Guides, edited by Nicholas John (Riverrun Press, 1985); *Die Walküre* (1984), *Siegfried* (1984), *Götterdämmerung* (1984).

elsewhere), miscellaneous essays, many illustrations, discographies, and so on. What is impressive about many of the essays—those by Robin Holloway, Anthony Newcomb, Derrick Puffett, and Christopher Wintle—is indeed the subtlety with which the authors trace the fusion of musical and dramatic effects. What is disturbing about them is a tendency to accept any musical effect that can be pinpointed or analyzed as privileged for purposes of interpretation, regardless of its aesthetic quality. Some of the authors do not even seem to find that certain of the themes in the *Ring* are crude and blatant. Other authors who do seem to, seem not to mind.

For Shaw, the emphatic use of "Sieglinda's theme" at the end of the *Ring* was one more indication of the work's artistic failure. In addition, the blatant old themes that Wagner wrote when he started the cycle in the 1850s, and then had to keep when he completed it in the 1870s, mercilessly drag down the magnificent new music of which he was then capable. Meeting up again with the Siegfried or the Treaty or the Valkyrie motifs in the middle of the Immolation Scene is rather like finding bits of yesterday's double anchovy pizza in the middle of a Chez Panisse dinner. And these blatant themes have been rumbling for a long time—since much earlier, I think, than the point in the middle of *Siegfried* to which Shaw traced his own reluctant disillusionment. *Das Rheingold*, as is often observed, is by Wagnerian standards a work of almost classical consistency. Things start grating at the latest during Wotan's Farewell at the end of *Die Walküre*.

No one has ever accused Wagner of good taste—and so these days, at the least sign of fastidiousness, a critic can expect a challenge for cause and then excuse from any jury panel for *Der Ring des Nibelungen*. But I am in fact uniquely qualified to serve, for my position is that what goes wrong aesthetically in the *Ring* does not go wrong in any of the other mature operas. In *Die Meistersinger* and *Parsifal* the trumpery themes are associated with things we can laugh at or love to hate. In *Tristan und Isolde* there aren't any.

This review started with a word of appreciation for the humanity of Gutrune. I was sorry, then, to see her represented in the 1985 San Francisco Opera *Ring* production[3] as a loopy nymphomaniac who caresses both Gunther and Hagen, drifts around the stage striking Theda Bara poses, and parks her drink glass on the plinths of big Robert Arneson–type busts that decorate the Gibichungs' hall.

Theirs is the most eccentric image, and hers the most eccentric behavior, in a strong-minded production by Nikolaus Lehnhoff. According to Alan Rich in *Newsweek*, "All told, it was a 'Ring' more for the eye than the ear," which is a fair enough characterization of a strikingly handsome, lavish production in an era that is not rich in Wagner performers. (But the Wotan of James Morris in *Die Walküre* —his first—started people dreaming of a new golden age.) The production is distinguished more for stage pictures than for stage movement. Lehnhoff has strong directorial ideas; he does not impress by a strong natural sense of the stage. His work is well exemplified by his staging of Wotan's monologue in *Die Walküre*—a staging that is patently a criticism of the famous 1976 Bayreuth production by Patrice Chéreau. No one who saw the film of the Chéreau production on PBS will have forgotten the great pendulum that swings hypnotically round and round until Wotan reaches the climax of his complaints, foresees "*das Ende, das Ende!*"—and suddenly stops it dead. Lehnhoff replaces the pendulum with a large smoking urn or brazier, which Wotan tamps down by throwing his cloak over it.

Visually, this is weaker. The brazier was never a very striking element in the scene and the audience has by now forgotten it. Wotan's action feels arbitrary and looks undignified, whereas that pendulum

---

3. *Der Ring des Nibelungen* by Richard Wagner, directed by Nikolaus Lehnhoff, San Francisco Opera Summer Festival, June 1985. Conducted by Edo De Waart, with Gwyneth Jones, Éva Marton, René Kollo, James Morris, Thomas Stewart, and others. This production was revived in San Francisco but apparently did not travel; Lehnhoff unveiled a new *Ring* at Munich in 1987 (2007).

had been growing more and more ominous—someone *had* to stop it! Wotan's action looks powerful and feels like a relief. Intellectually, on the other hand, Lehnhoff is elegant and right where Chéreau was arbitrary. What Wotan "ends" is fire, the work of Loge—and of course nothing ends, for the smoke starts up again when the cloak is removed.

The San Francisco Opera general director, Terence McEwen, promised a *Ring* production that would be "a return to romanticism" —in the broadest terms, then, a criticism of Chéreau—and so it was. But Lehnhoff's view of Wagner's romanticism is probably more clouded than McEwen's. The long period of the *Ring*'s gestation, extending from the time of the 1848 revolutions to the Franco-Prussian War; the corresponding shift in Wagner's philosophical interests from Feuerbach to Schopenhauer; the cooling of his political passions (as Shaw stressed) from a fling with Bakunin to a flirtation with Bismarck—all this dramatizes a tension in Wagner's work that is widely recognized. It is a tension between "naive" and "sentimental" romanticism, between the pure and the corrupt, between the truly romantic and what Jacques Barzun called the mechanist, Carl Dahlhaus the realist, and Theodor Adorno the phantasmagorical aspect of Wagner's art.

This tension Lehnhoff was determined to project in his *Ring* production, first of all by means of a series of sharply contrasted stage pictures. Most were freely quoted from the landscape painter Caspar David Friedrich and the architect Karl Friedrich Schinkel. They stand or fall on their own merits, for they have little force as quotations since, in spite of the attention that has been paid to these artists in recent years, neither can be said to be very well known outside his native Germany. (Schinkel is known to musicians for his designs for *The Magic Flute*. Like Wagner, he was one of those nineteenth-century artists taken up by the Nazis.) While bad taste comes through clearly enough in the Schinkel interiors and the architectural capriccio of Valhalla, the vaguer motifs of German early-nineteenth-century neoclassicism are hard to read for those who have not taken the right art-history courses. And most of the *Ring*'s natural settings are replaced by architectural ones; a columned terrace derived from Friedrich, for example, is used several times in increasing stages of ruin. Tall neoclassical portals, somewhat overgrown by vines, appear as tormenters at the sides of every scene in the cycle. This is to insist on the corruption theme with a vengeance, and it is also to frame the work of art—and distance oneself from it—in an emphatic way.

The natural scenes, designed by John Conklin and lit by Thomas J. Munn, were apt and sometimes very beautiful. As the flames die down on Valhalla, a frozen Rhine rose up to assume the form of one of Friedrich's major paintings, variously known as *The Sea of Ice* and *The Wreck of the Hope*, in which a shipwreck is barely visible in a menacing protocubist assemblage of huge ice floes. It is a form we had seen before: in the crepuscular rock of the Rhinemaidens at the beginning of *Das Rheingold*. And Lehnhoff's final image tries to suggest another frame for the *Ring*, another intellectual attempt to distance the work firmly in the nineteenth century. Loge, disconcertingly costumed in Victorian style, just as he was throughout *Das Rheingold*, returns to survey the wreckage that he had been the first to predict. Presumably, too, Loge the trickster stands for Wagner the artist-artificer doing a postmortem on his huge and hugely problematic artwork (or—so it seemed to one viewer—a satisfied Caspar David Friedrich contemplating his).

I did not mind a Victorian Loge walking through music that does not persuade me at the end of *Götterdämmerung*, but I was irritated by him in *Das Rheingold*; putting a single nineteenth-century costume (accessorized by a copy of *The Wall Street Journal*) in among a lot of ancient or fantastic ones does more than put distance between the spectator and the dramatic action, it frays the basic dramatic illusion. It makes the *Ring* hokey, silly, and laughable. Three nights later, one understood that there was an "idea" behind it, but in my view, the only bearable "ideas" in dramatic productions are those that work for the show consistently, not those that make a striking point in one scene and confuse or wreck others. (Often these ideas are, indeed, those of the original dramatist.) Likewise Gutrune's eccentric characterization in her first scene seemed to me no more objectionable than the fact that it was simply dropped in her later ones, where of course it no longer fitted as an "interpretation." When directors take strong new initiatives beyond what authors have called for, they should at least be held accountable for them throughout the drama.

It remains to say that this was reputed to be the first *Ring* ever with supertitles, and so was doubtless the first in this country at which the audience could often be heard chuckling at Wagner's rather heavy wit.

—1985

27

BAYREUTH, 2001

IN AUGUST 2001 the Richard Wagner Festival at Bayreuth celebrated its 125th anniversary. To the world (perhaps I should say, to the opera world) at large, things had been going along relatively smoothly at Bayreuth since the centennial year 1976, when Patrice Chéreau and Pierre Boulez created a sensation with their *bouleversement* of *Der Ring des Niebelungen*, and when the former director of the festival, Winifred Wagner, daughter-in-law of Richard, did likewise by celebrating her Nazi past on camera for Hans Jürgen Syberberg. For insiders, however, the interim had been marked by an intensifying struggle for the succession to the directorship, held for fifty years by Winifred's son Wolfgang. Often reported in the press, and to all appearances recently resolved, this "soap opera," as Nike Wagner calls it, forms the background for her impressive book *The Wagners: The Dramas of a Musical Dynasty*.[1] She is a great-granddaughter of the composer and has been one of the claimants.

The dramas she tells about are of two kinds, literal and metaphorical. The first half of the book consists of brief essays on the Wagner operas. The second half is a concise and caustic history of the Wagner dynasty, a series of family dramas sometimes presented

---

1. Translated by Ewald Osers and Michael Downes (Princeton University Press, 1999).

(more entertainingly than convincingly, it must be said) in parallel with tales from the Ring and the Grail. The English-language edition of *The Wagners* also includes a statement of intent that the author issued in the *Frankfurter Allgemeine Zeitung*, setting forth extensive changes she would promote to reinvigorate and modernize the festival. This was, no doubt, a final measure of desperation:

> So, a manifesto to round off a family story? It was not premeditated that it should appear, either in this form or at this point, and by the time this book is published it will already have been overtaken by events.

Indeed the new director, her more conservative cousin Eva Wagner-Pasquier, was appointed as of 2002. Has the situation been resolved? Wolfgang refuses to step down, so the soap opera may be good for a few more episodes.[2] Eva is an opera manager with solid international credentials, while Nike is described as a "music critic and cultural commentator." She has a Ph.D. from Northwestern University and has written a book on Karl Kraus. With or without manifesto, *The Wagners* must be seen as an attempt—already, I am afraid, desperate—to establish her bona fides as an intellectual rather than a theater functionary.

I approached this book (as one approaches any book by any Wagner) with skepticism, but ended up being very impressed. The opening chapters—vignettes, really, rather than actual studies—focus on one particular aspect of each opera: Romanticism in *Lohengrin*, incest in the *Ring*, the peculiar humor of *Die Meistersinger von Nürnberg*. They rely rather heavily on Freudian interpretation, and like so many of the writings about this composer, they hardly ever deal specifically with the music. That said, I would recommend them to anyone interested

---

2. Wolfgang is still in charge (2007).

in the Wagner oeuvre. What Nike Wagner writes about the *Ring, Die Meistersinger,* and *Parsifal,* in particular, is a good deal more intelligent, clear-eyed, and provocative than much else that has been turned out about these works recently.

Not that these vignettes resemble the paeans that one comes upon so very often in the literature. Nike Wagner links *Parsifal* directly to the sinister and ubiquitous tract *Geschlecht und Charakter* by Otto Weininger, well known to her from her studies of *fin de siècle* Vienna. Weininger's obsession was the corruption of Aryan manhood by the equivalent pollutants woman and Jew—Kundry, in a word, the sexual predator and female Ahasuerus who had mocked Christ and whom Wagner, in *Judaism in Music,* had consigned, after conversion, to extinction, *Untergang.* And in a chapter bluntly entitled "Disquiet about *Parsifal,*" she complains:

> The work's carefully constructed ambivalence is abandoned wholesale at the end. Everything is ultimately forced into the unequivocal unity of Christian redemption, blessed by above: this undialectical "solution" of all conflicts in universal sacred harmony is the cause of our disquiet. It suggests that we have arrived at the end of the world, with only a shadowy and discreet reminder of the horrors overcome and the evil exorcised, in the death of the victim Kundry. The reign of good—without female participation—has begun....

I can share her disquiet on musical grounds, for while *Parsifal* is admired for the special subtlety of its treatment of leitmotifs, the fact is that leitmotifs parade in the most Mickey Mouse fashion when Parsifal arrives at the end to heal Amfortas and illumine the grail ("*Nur eine Waffe taugt,*" "One weapon only serves"). It would have been trite enough if the hero came on and the orchestra presented his calling card—Debussy's characterization of Wagner's method. In the event we suddenly become aware of the old con man shaking cards out of his sleeve in rapid succession: the Grail—these classic labels are by the French musicologist Albert Lavignac—the Lance, Suffering (five times), the Promise, Parsifal, the Eucharist, Faith, the Lance again, the Cry to the Savior, the Promise, the Eucharist, and the Grail. This is more like an index to *Parsifal* than the "solution" to it that Nike Wagner is looking for.

Her chapter on "New Bayreuth as Waste Disposal Plant" should be required reading for those many critics—Bernard Williams has joined them recently,[3] and I have been there too—who see *Die Meistersinger* as apolitical. Colonialism makes a striking context for the discussion of *The Flying Dutchman*—a concept associated with a production by Nike's brother Wolf Siegfried. Many Wagnerians, I think, would have been happy to see the Bayreuth Festival in the hands of someone with the quality of mind of Nike Wagner.

However, some who admire Wagner feel considerable disquiet about the Bayreuth Festival in any shape or form. It offers a special affront, first of all, to those of us who value classical music yet detest the cult status it achieved in the nineteenth century and still maintains, to some extent, today. Temples, priests, vestments, and rites (concert halls, conductors, virtuosos, tails, standing ovations, and so on) promote submission rather than serious reception, repelling the young and many of the elderly too. More than a temple, Bayreuth's Festival Opera House was conceived as a mother church, a pilgrimage site (with the saint actually buried there) at which submission is expected and indeed exacted. Initiates sit in the dark on hard, cramped seats, their attention focused rigidly, by physical as well as psychological means, on rituals repeated, like memorial masses in a chantry, *in saecula saeculorum*.

---

3. "Wagner and Politics," *The New York Review*, November 2, 2000, p. 42. Weininger called *Die Meistersinger* "the essence of Germandom"; like Northrop Frye's ideal comedy, this work pointedly celebrates the soundness of a community threatened by *Wahn* (delusion), from which —unlike most comedies—the disruptive (Jewish) element is excluded rather than incorporated.

And at Bayreuth, of course, the cult of art was inflated into something very much like a religion, not the vague aestheticism of the concert hall but doctrine articulated in national, racial, and ethical terms. Bayreuth is to Wagnerism as Rome is to Christianity—to mention another creed which Wagner, like his contemporaries Joseph Smith and Mary Baker Eddy, meant to transform, with *Parsifal*, along his own lines. In Nike Wagner's characteristically understated words:

> Wagner regarded his theatrical revolution as both an allegory of, and a stimulant to the reshaping of German culture as a truly national art.... The continual repetition of Wagner's works, the almost incredible continuity with which they have been staged —from the days of Ludwig II, across two World Wars, to the present—signals the continuity, simultaneously disturbing and reassuring, of a particular strand of German history.

Wagner's fantasy of a national theater devoted to his own work and to his own notion of theater had indeed aroused the suspicion of German liberals as early as the mid-nineteenth century, and this turned to alarm by the time of Nietzsche's recantation. After the composer's death the festival continued under his widow, Cosima, more Wagnerian than the Master himself. Cosima not only expanded the repertory to include more Wagner operas, but also opened it up to the full ideological amplification of that "particular strand of German history." No mere house organ, like the Metropolitan Opera's *Opera News*, the journal *Bayreuther Blätter* was a primary and very vicious medium for pre-Nazi and then Nazi ideology. Haus Wahnfried, the Wagner family pile, which had played host to Gobineau for months at a time, now welcomed Houston Stewart Chamberlain, who married a Wagner daughter and came to live there and minister to them like a family chaplain. And then Adolf Hitler, who attributed the forging of National Socialism's "spiritual sword" to Chamberlain, and who "saw himself as Wagner's servant, disciple, executor," as Alex Ross has remarked pithily—Hitler would find a house at his disposal on the grounds, and later an annex built onto it to accommodate his entourage (called the Führerbau). He was the beloved "Uncle Wolf" to the children, and a special friend if not a bit more to Winifred. An indication of the awe in which Hitler held the festival is the relative freedom he allowed Winifred in managing it, though toward the end of World War II it was he who decided to keep it going, with only *Die Meistersinger* remaining in the repertory; this was for the recreation and edification of wounded veterans and the like, whether they liked it or not.

After the war Winifred was stripped of the directorship, but the festival was allowed to continue under her sons, Wieland and Wolfgang. This turned out to be a signal success for the Denazification Commission, for Wieland performed the unpredictable:

> A circular acting area [modeled on the *orchestra* of the Greek theater], the use of light to link music to movement and color, the simplification of costumes without any suggestion of a specific time or place, the transformation of characters from pseudo-human beings into symbols and the stripping away of sets and gestures inessential to the conceptual core of the work.[4]

All this was as resourceful in the face of the material shortages at the time as it was inspired. Wagner's grandson depoliticized Wagner in a coherent series of operatic productions that rank among the most distinguished and impressive (and most beautiful, perhaps; I never saw one) in the history of the stage.

So far as I can determine, nobody at the time proposed that the festival, however blatant a symbol it had become of Nazi ideology,

---

4. Frederic Spotts, *Bayreuth: A History of the Wagner Festival* (Yale University Press, 1994), p. 216.

should be discontinued—as in fact had happened after World War I. The American occupation authorities, on the contrary, saw it as just the kind of German institution they wanted to resuscitate. A new Society of the Friends of Bayreuth, in which prominent ex-Nazis were generously represented, provided financial support.[5] Wieland was one of a kind, however. After his death in 1966, with the accession of Wolfgang, productions began returning to the traditional accouterments of Valkyrie helmets, Nuremberg alleys, swans, and swords. Plenty of the Bayreuth faithful wanted to see and think about Wagner in the old ways.

Even more than Wieland Wagner's pathbreaking *Parsifal* of 1951, perhaps, the key moment for "New Bayreuth" was his 1956 production of *Die Meistersinger*. This was an essay in abstraction divested of every naturalistic detail that might evoke the Nuremberg of the 1530s —or the Nuremberg of the 1930s. The famous nationalistic speech at the end, which brought wartime audiences to their feet, was virtually defanged in Wieland's closed-up staging. For the first time, Nike Wagner tells us, boos were heard in the Festival Opera House. An emblem of today's uneasy Bayreuth was Syberberg's five-hour filmed interview with Winifred Wagner—Winifred, who kept quiet about her nostalgia for the 1930s for thirty years, until it all burst out in the centennial year 1976 like an underground river. It kept on gushing, at unpredictable intervals, until her death at the age of eighty-three a few years later.

Another cousin of Nike's, Wolfgang's son Gottfried Wagner, has harped on the issue of Bayreuth and Nazism. In his autobiography, *Twilight of the Wagners*,[6] Gottfried tells, with more honesty than self-

---

5. Spotts, *Bayreuth*, p. 205.

6. *Twilight of the Wagners: The Unveiling of a Family Legacy*, translated by Diana Couling, with a preface by Abraham Peck (Picador USA, 1999). As though driven to follow upon Richard's famous *My Life*, nearly all Wagners produce memoirs, diaries, and the like—from Cosima and Siegfried to Wieland and Wolfgang (*Acts: The Autobiography of Wolfgang Wagner*, translated by John Brownjohn, Weidenfeld and Nicolson, 1994) to Gottfried, Nike, and Wieland's sister Friedelind, son Wolf Siegfried, and widow Gertrud.

understanding or literary talent, of a wretched childhood and feckless youth crippled by Oedipal conflict. As a boy he became obsessed with the "secret" of Bayreuth's past, which needless to say was never discussed, and which he obviously (and not entirely wrongly) identified with his father. In middle life Gottfried experienced a series of conversions: a new marriage, a new religion, a new homeland (Italy), and at last a mission in life as cofounder of the Post-Holocaust Dialogue Group, one of a number of such organizations that bring children of pre-war Germans together with children of Holocaust victims. He now lectures to anyone who will hear him about Wagner's anti-Semitism and the commercial and political machinations at Bayreuth.

Though the destructive instinct of an irascible child is still recognizable in Gottfried, and he has other problems, he also has a sharp eye for backsliding and hypocrisy. A 1984 exhibit at Wahnfried on Wagner and the Jews was obviously a whitewash. In 1991 Bayreuth provided ground for a rally of neo-Nazi skinheads. He complains that one festival conductor, Daniel Barenboim, took it on himself, "in quite the Bayreuth style, to understate Richard Wagner's anti-Semitism."[7] Gottfried was conspicuously kept off the program for another hashing over of Wagner and Judaism in 1998, this time a somewhat tense conference of scholars from Germany, the United States, and Israel. Many besides Gottfried, of course, have decried the stonewalling by an increasingly Fafner-like Wolfgang, who should have given up the festival directorship years ago.

Stepping back, one can see only too easily how New Bayreuth gave the immediate postwar era what it needed, namely Wagner without Wagnerism. The sardonic words spoken by Eva in *Die Meistersinger*, "*Hier gilt's der Kunst*" ("It's art that matters here"), made an apt

---

7. "We must remember that Wagner's kind of intellectual anti-Semitism was *à la mode* in the nineteenth century, and he cannot be held responsible for the actual atrocities committed half a century later by misusing his ideas," from an interview with Carla Maria Verdino-Süllwold, *Opera Monthly*, May/June 1993, p. 10, cited in Gottfried Wagner, *Twilight of the Wagners*, pp. 255–256.

epigraph for the entire project. In another era, what many Germans are looking for is not amnesia about Wagnerism but some kind of confrontation and coming to terms with it. Both Gottfried's and Nike's books must be seen against the background of this larger project. Furthermore, while the idea of depoliticizing Wagner, or opera, or music plain and simple may have made perfect sense in the intellectual climate of the 1950s, this is certainly not the case now. *Nixon in China*, *The Death of Klinghoffer*, Solomon Volkov's book *Testimony* about Shostakovich, Beethoven and the Congress of Vienna, Ken Burns's TV series *Jazz*—these days people are sniffing out ideology and politics in music and music theater of every kind.

Bayreuth can be seen as a sort of high-level institute ("Werkstatt Bayreuth") for opera production, direction, and design in general. According to the English director Mike Ashland, who has a number of Wagner credits himself, writing in 1992:

> Key productions [at Bayreuth] have become benchmarks for production worldwide, and the stagings of Wagner himself, of Wieland Wagner, Friedrich, Chéreau and Kupfer have had far-reaching influence on the entire operatic repertory on stage. The history of Wagner interpretation *per se* became something of a testing ground for the state of opera production in general.[8]

The post-Wieland productions he had in mind were *Tannhäuser* (1972) by the late Götz Friedrich, the Chéreau-Boulez *Ring* (1976), whose importance can hardly be overstated, and the *Dutchman* (1978) and *Ring* (1988) by Harry Kupfer. Note, however, that Friedrich and Kupfer have both produced more Wagner elsewhere than at Bayreuth,

---

8. "Producing Wagner," in *Wagner in Performance*, edited by Barry Millington and Stewart Spencer (Yale University Press, 1992), pp. 46–47.

including three *Ring* cycles between the two of them.[9] Robert Wilson has done *Parsifal* in Hamburg and Houston and *Lohengrin* in Berlin and New York. David Hockney designed, and Jonathan Miller staged, *Tristan und Isolde* for Los Angeles, and Nikolaus Lehnhoff produced a *Ring* for San Francisco and one for Munich, and so on. It is a mistake, and an ideologically driven mistake, to believe that Wagner depends on the Bayreuth Festival, whether or not this is the article of faith that has always kept his fractious family from falling apart completely.

Even Nike Wagner, who has written a very skeptical book about Bayreuth, feels that the institution must be saved to save Wagner. Like any agency dedicated to the work of a single person—like the Sigmund Freud Archives, for example; or, in the music world, the Beethovenhaus and Archiv at Bonn—Bayreuth has inevitable limitations as well as obvious advantages and powers. The continuity of Wagner production and Wagner reception depends on interaction between musicians, producers, and thinkers working both inside and outside of this particular fold. As Bayreuth's director for more than fifty years Wolfgang will be remembered not for his own string of *echt*-Bayreuth productions, which include two each of the *Ring*, *Lohengrin*, *Die Meistersinger*, and *Parsifal*, but for breaking with tradition and bringing in outside directors who have been undaunted by the Bayreuth mystique. This is one thing Nike Wagner will not acknowledge, a real blind spot in a view of Wolfgang that while harsh, though no more so than that of other, ostensibly more objective observers, stands out for the effort to understand as well as judge.

The first half of *The Wagners* consists of essays on the canon, as has already been said. The second half tells the history of the dynasty over

9. And *pace* Mike Ashland, the Bayreuth *Ring* was not Kupfer's finest hour. The production was widely deplored at the time—with special acuity by Jonathan Lieberson in *The New York Review*, November 18, 1988.

four generations—those of Richard and Cosima, Siegfried and Wini-fred, Wieland and Wolfgang, and finally Nike, Eva, Gottfried, and several others born in the 1940s.

"Lavish disfunctionality" is the English Wagnerian Michael Tan-ner's term for the workings of this family. While it is clear that Nike Wagner has no qualms about washing dirty linen in public, and maybe dirtying it up some more, presumably her motives were a good deal more serious than that. Two things were incumbent on her in order to make a credible claim in the Bayreuth succession: she had to show a considered commitment to the works of Wagner, and she also had to show herself prepared to acknowledge and engage with, if not exorcise, the dark side of that heritage, the dark side of Germany. In this she may have been influenced by Gottfried, or even by his book, though hers could hardly be more different: Gottfried's *cri de coeur* is all about himself, while Nike is a mere shadowy presence in her own narrative, a dispassionate, dry account lit up by flashes of irony that could owe something to her work on Karl Kraus. While most of her portraits are dark, as I have indicated, they are far from monochromatic, and she is capable of considerable nuanced sympathy for her subjects (though love is nowhere in the picture—Gottfried is better at that). Very smartly written and excellently translated, Nike's baleful family saga is fascinating to read, well worth your time even if you hate Wagner.

That the fullest and most arresting portrait should be of her father comes as no surprise, since he is the one really significant family member after Richard. She repeats a childhood *mot* that must have haunted the adult Wieland—he wished Uncle Wolf were his real father rather than an uncle—and she takes him severely to task for the designs for *Die Meistersinger* in the traditional nationalist manner that he produced in wartime, years after he had sketched what would later be his radical, sanitized *Parsifal* of 1951. As Hitler's favorite, Wieland was deferred from military service, while Wolfgang went to the front and was badly wounded. On one occasion Hitler raved that one brother would head up "the theater of the West" and the other "the theater of the East." Wieland appears to have found out about Nazi realities only around 1944, and the information sent him into a crisis of conscience. The rest of his life was wracked by a troubled search for self-realization. This drove him more and more to the left over the next decades, which exacerbated relations with his brother and co-director, to say nothing of the festival's core constituency. For Nike, conflict between the brothers was the great cloud over her father's existence.

She remembers his productions first from dancing in several of them as a child and helping paint sets for another. She celebrates the historic *Parsifal*, which played from 1951 to 1970, though it is said the director tinkered with it so much year after year that it practically became a new production; the radically new second *Meistersinger* of 1963; the second *Ring*, and indeed the whole run of Wagner operas from *Rienzi* on—for Wieland also worked extensively outside Bayreuth and his influence extended to opera houses around the world. At his untimely death at forty-nine he was mourned, she writes,

> as the man who restored a measure of national pride in the German theater...a valuable German cultural export, whose unlikely achievement was to make Munich seem pallid by comparison with Bayreuth. More importantly still, he had made the world forget Hitler's Wagner by replacing him with Wieland's Wagner: he had abolished both the old, tradition-bound Bayreuth, and the wartime "Aryan citadel" Bayreuth, in favor of his own "New Bayreuth." Without doubt, Wieland fully discharged the task imposed on him by his personal and historical position. He both cleansed and saved the work of Wagner, and the new West Germany duly recognized his merit.

Psychoanalysis, rather than philosophy, is Nike Wagner's regular instrument for coping with dramatis personae, in life's dramas as well as those on the stage. But for language to explain her father she turns to Hegel. The individual personifies the spirit of history, which proceeds dialectically from negativity to action; personal destiny emerges from the thrust and counterthrust of the archaic laws of family on the one hand and the moral imperatives of society and state on the other. Nike reels off the negativities without mercy: Wieland's lifelong depression; his childhood tyranny over Wolfgang; his adolescent evasion of his "task" (he studied to be a painter); the practically murderous temper that flared in later years at rehearsals and elsewhere; the womanizing and the open six-year affair with Anja Silja, a very young singer in whom he found his ideal Senta; his repudiation of those who helped him most, such as his teacher Kurt Overhoff and his wife (and Hitler); and indeed his bid in 1960 to defect from Bayreuth to Berlin.

American readers are not likely to feel at ease with Nike's Hegelian terms, and we may also wonder whether Hegel would have expected to see them applied to Wieland Wagner, genius of the theater though he may have been. For his daughter, however, Wieland was not just a directorial genius. With all his negative qualities, he emerges as a tragic hero in a particular strand of German history. Perhaps for the author of this book the deepest of motivations was the abiding process of mourning:

> It may seem to us that his life was unfinished and tragic, and that there was a premature and abrupt transition from the "becoming" of an unquiet consciousness to the "being" of a quiet death. In a philosophical sense, however, this does not mean that his self-realization had not been completed to a very high degree: he had succeeded, after all, in attaching his name to a moment in intellectual history.

—2001

28

THE ART OF THE PROGRAM NOTE

IN HIS RECENT BOOK *Classical Music in America*, Joseph Horowitz devotes several chapters to "Offstage Participants," his name for people who work away from the footlights and make up the support system of musical life, as he sees it, rather than in the spots as singers, players, or conductors.[1] One from within this group who deserves our thanks, Michael Steinberg, first became known as a music critic for *The Boston Globe* and has since spent his time more peacefully as a program adviser (or "artistic adviser") for several major symphony orchestras, a lecturer, and a prolific writer of program notes. They are program notes with a difference, admired for their relaxed manner and elegance as well as their warmth and authority; Steinberg is a man who wears a great deal of learning—learned from books, scores, and especially from wide musical experience—very lightly. He has recently been expanding his program notes and collecting them in books. *Choral Masterworks* rounds out a trilogy of "Listener's Guides" with *The Symphony* and *The Concerto*.[2] The book covers music from Bach's Passions and the B-Minor Mass to John Adams's *Harmonium* and Charles Wuorinen's *Genesis*.

---

1. *Classical Music in America, A History of Its Rise and Fall* (Norton, 2001).

2. *Choral Masterworks: A Listener's Guide* (Oxford University Press, 2005).

If everything played at symphony concerts counts as a "master-work," the term has no meaning whatsoever—which is what a moment's thought would tell us anyway. Steinberg called his first book *The Symphony*, not *Symphonic Masterworks*. *Choral Master-works* as a book title is an illocutionary command, like *Masterpiece Theatre* and *Great Performances*: bow down before this music! There has to be some other way of registering that the composers of many of these works—not all, but many—took extraordinary pains with them, gave of their best and their longest.

These are outsized works, works of high ambition, composed to celebrate important public occasions, or, if not, to answer pressing and explicit personal concerns. Extra orchestral forces are mustered in them, as well as choruses and solo singers. When personal and public impulses converge the music can become highly charged, hyperbolic, almost volcanic, spilling a surplus of sonic reference beyond even the chorus-enhanced symphonies of Beethoven and Mahler and the Busoni Piano Concerto, its hour-and-a-quarter-long span relieved by the singing of bits of Goethe's *Faust*.

The *War Requiem* by Benjamin Britten, commissioned for the con-secration of the bombed and reconstructed Coventry Cathedral in 1961, is a striking case in point. Britten belonged to a generation con-vulsed by the Spanish Civil War, and at the beginning of World War II he left England as a pacifist protest, following W. H. Auden and Christopher Isherwood to the United States. Some never forgave him, but it says much for his homeland that when he returned a few years later, understanding that there was no other way to preserve his integrity as an artist, and not only as an artist, Sadler's Wells ordered an opera from him for its postwar reopening in 1945. Audiences were so moved and so amazed by *Peter Grimes* that it was seen at once as promising a rebirth of English opera.

Britten kept the promise with five new operas in the next nine years. And *Grimes* was only the most famous of a series of compositions in which he drew almost methodically on native poets and characteristic national topics: Shakespeare, Jonson, Donne, Smart, Crabbe, Tennyson, Auden, Purcell (many arrangements), medieval carols and mystery plays, Queen Elizabeth I, the English countryside and fishing coast, the Royal Navy, boy choirs.

The next milestone in Britten's career was the Coventry commission. The *War Requiem* is scored for orchestra, chamber orchestra, chorus, soloists, boy chorus, and organ—bells are also prominent—and lasts for an hour and twenty minutes. For the text Britten reached back to the antiwar poems of Wilfred Owen to commemorate two world wars, and thus an infinity of wars, in a rhetoric of pacifism superimposed on the timeless, iconic sequence of prayers for the souls of the dead that is the Catholic Mass for the Dead. Owen himself died in World War I. The English poems are sung up against or together with the Latin texts. When the text of the Offertory seeks the intercession of the Archangel Michael, according to the promise he gave in Genesis to Abraham and his progeny, Owen tells his own Abraham and Isaac story, in "The Parable of the Old Man and the Young":

> *When lo! an Angel called him out of heaven,*
> *Saying, Lay not thy hand upon the lad,*
> *Neither do anything to him, thy son.*
> *Behold! Caught in a thicket by its horns,*
> *A Ram. Offer the Ram of Pride instead.*
>
> *But the old man would not do so, but slew his son,*
> *And half the seed of Europe, one by one.*

This makes for a rough cut—Steinberg's terms are "sinister," "shocking," and "brutish-sounding"—across the grain of the Catholic liturgy, yet by using the liturgy Britten was able to acknowledge England's core faith, which it had abandoned in the sixteenth century.[3] In a further burst of symbolism, he presented the *War Requiem* to Coventry —to England—and dedicated it to the memory of friends who had died in World War II, and he wanted it sung by prominent singers from Britain, Germany, and the Soviet Union.

Steinberg sees in Britten's score the rather overt evocation of another setting of the requiem, the *Messa da Requiem* by Giuseppe Verdi, as a move by Britten "to establish a connection with the great tradition"—the masterwork tradition, the European tradition. It seems the composer was now truly at home in England and the world. The "English" pieces of his later years were outweighed by the opera *Death in Venice* after Thomas Mann, the dramatic cantata *Phaedra* after Racine, and an upsurge of untexted instrumental music. The Cello Symphony and several other pieces were written for his close friend Mstislav Rostropovich.

"My subject is War," wrote Owen in a verse taken as an epigraph in the score, "and the pity of War. / The Poetry is in the pity. / All a poet can do is warn." The Soviets would not allow Galina Vishnevskaya to sing at the première in 1961—a time of considerable tension, as Steinberg reminds us: the Bay of Pigs, the building of the Berlin Wall, and the beginning of escalation in Vietnam—and outside England it is hard to know how seriously Britten's warning has been taken. The American Symphony Orchestra League keeps statistics of hundreds of orchestras and records no more than two or three performances a year of the *War Requiem*.

Nor is Luciano Berio's beautiful elegy for Martin Luther King Jr., *O King*,[4] played more than very occasionally—and the same must certainly be said for Roger Sessions's *When Lilacs Last in the Dooryard*

---

3. The see of Coventry was moved to Lichfield in 1539, returning in 1918.

4. *O King*, a chamber music work, was arranged for inclusion as the second movement of Berio's *Sinfonia*, composed in 1968.

Bloom'd, dedicated to the memory of King and Robert Kennedy, a work that receives high praise in *Choral Masterworks*.[5] We have no musical Lincoln Memorial. The memorial that the New York Philharmonic commissioned so soon after September 11 required chorus, orchestra, and amplified speaking voices on tape, reciting distraught words from placards posted around Ground Zero and names of victims. John Adams's *On the Transmigration of Souls* registers trauma, twenty-five minutes of numbness and rage. It is one thing to respond, another to commemorate. Britten steps back from the event; Adams steps into it.

If Britten saw the Verdi Requiem as his gateway to the great tradition, he was also well aware that this work, too, was highly political and personally fraught. Written on the death in 1873 of Alessandro Manzoni, it incorporates a movement composed for a never-completed memorial for Rossini, who had died a few years earlier, thus becoming a monument to not one but two heroes of the nascent Italian state. Verdi had met Manzoni and revered him as an artist and a patriot. Verdi too was a prominent patriot, of course, an icon of Italian nationalism. Only in Italy, no doubt, could opera choruses have been taken over as patriotic hymns, and a composer swept into the country's brand new Senate.

Indeed, as Steinberg points out, the Requiem was seized on to celebrate a third national hero, Verdi himself. Its première was at a church service in Milan, but when it first traveled, to Venice, it played in an opera house, with the stage made up to look like a church. At the première in Milan the individual movements came in their traditional positions, interspersed by plainchant, as in the liturgy,

---

5. It might have been good for Steinberg to have written more about Sessions, whom he knew, but he has done that before, and handsomely, in *The Symphony: A Listener's Guide* (Oxford University Press, 1996), pp. 524–532.

but in Venice some of them were applauded and encored. Above the stage altar, instead of an image of Christ or the Virgin Mary there were cartouches inscribed with the name "Verdi" and, in smaller letters, several of his operas.

This is noted in a recent article by the musicologist Laura Basini, locating the Requiem in the broader scene of Italian music after the unification of the country in 1861.[6] A number of currents converged into a movement she calls "sacred revivalism." First, the stranglehold of opera on the music of Italy began to yield under international pressure. As operas by French composers—and indeed Wagner—began to seep into Italian opera houses, a need was felt for Italian music in other serious, imposing genres. The newly unified country set about celebrating (or constructing) national myths; these tended to form around heroes of the past such as Dante, Petrarch, Palestrina, who saved church music from the Council of the Trent, or so it was thought, and even Guido d'Arezzo, the eleventh-century cleric who invented musical staff notation. Furthermore, the new secular state stimulated a powerful reaction from the Vatican. In music this entailed, once again, a turn to the past. Unlikely as it may seem for the nineteenth century, there was a serious call for the revival of a capella church music modeled on Palestrina. The decadence of modern music was to be countered by, as a Vatican commentary put it, a new "tranquillity, peace, order, regularity, variety in unity."

The Requiem caused a problem for the revivalists, for while it followed scrupulously a Catholic text in a setting heard everywhere and acclaimed everywhere, it did so in a voice that is utterly secular—that is, operatic—at almost every moment. Donald Tovey (whom Steinberg has called "the patron saint of program note writers") remarked that "the melody of the Lacrimosa is naive enough for *Il Trovatore*,"

---

6. "Verdi and Sacred Revivalism in Post-Unification Italy," *19th-Century Music*, Vol. 28, No. 2 (2004), pp. 133–159.

not knowing that the music for this section of the Requiem actually came from a duet left over from *Don Carlos*, one of several cuts taken before the first performance. The Dies Irae movement feels like an opera that has been squeezed so hard to extrude its libretto that its rhetoric and lyricism are about to pop.

Yet other sections of the Requiem can be heard as evocations of the pure music of the past, as we learn from a fascinating address given soon after the première by a leading Catholic spokesman, Father Guerrino Amelli, at the Italian Catholic Congress in 1874. After rejecting the Requiem's emotionalism, romantic excess, "bellicose" instrumentation, and the like, Amelli lights upon one tranquil moment

> which, disdaining instrumental accompaniment almost entirely, seemed to recall with its ingenuous beauty the sublime simplicity of Gregorian Chant. Yes, the tone of that prayer [the Agnus Dei], breathing a calm melancholy, comforted by faith and hope, drew from us almost involuntarily a sigh of approval and made us exclaim: this is *real church music*. [Verdi] certainly knew the sublimity of liturgical sentiment, and also how to express it with the power of art and his genius; but perhaps he feared not being understood in a century indifferent to religion, a century which shows itself to be incapable of such high sentiment.

Steinberg has a point to make about the power of Verdi's art in the Requiem, one that is technical but easy to grasp:

> [The Agnus Dei] begins like plainsong, with thirteen measures for soprano and contralto, in octaves, unaccompanied, and famously feared for the difficulty of getting it in tune. The melody has a remarkable shape, natural and strange at the same time: a first part of seven bars (four plus three) and a subtly compressed second half of six bars (three and a half plus two and a half).

What follows is a set of five variations, the last of them spinning itself out.

The variations are very "natural," at least in one sense, and the irregular phrase lengths "strange."

Amelli, yielding to none in regard for Italy's most respected composer, found the message he wanted in an apothegm of Verdi's that was quoted everywhere, "Let us go back to the past, it will be a step forward" (*Torniamo all'antico, sarò un progresso*). And what is even more fascinating is that Verdi tapped into "sacred revivalism" repeatedly and knowingly over the rest of his life, with choral settings of a number of sacred texts. Among them are an Ave Maria and a Pater Noster in (by very generous definition) the style of Palestrina.

In any case, Verdi could take great satisfaction in the success of his Requiem, so soon after the comparable success of *Aida*. It showed he could triumph in elevated realms of music far above opera; opera was an artistic ideal for Verdi in theory, but in practice a pit of skulduggery, tawdriness, and intrigue that almost drove him crazy. He writes in high spirits to a friend:

> I feel as if I've become a solid citizen, no longer the public's clown, with a big tambourine and a bass drum, who shouts *come, come, step right up*, etc., etc. As you can imagine, when I hear operas spoken of now, my conscience is scandalized and I immediately make the sign of the Cross!!... What do you say to that? Am I not an edifying example?

How satisfactory, too, that the soprano role could be written for the singer Teresa Stolz, his lover at the time, in fact the second great love of his life. They never lost touch after their affair was broken off.

If we want to think today about the religious or spiritual quality of the Verdi Requiem, we have to remember, first, that the composer was in private a freethinker and in public a scathing critic of organized religion, notably in his three preceding operas, *Aida*, *Don Carlos*, and *La Forza del destino*. In two of these works priests are cast as villains, and in the other the characters undergo Christian religious experiences that do little or nothing to calm their souls. (It is true that Verdi softened things in his revised version of *Forza*, which is the one we know.) And second, we remember that Verdi was a dramatist and there was nothing he could not turn into magnificent theater. In the Requiem drama begins with the subdued choral utterance at the very opening. Steinberg writes:

> "Requiem aeternam" is ritual—these are words of an invisible chorus. With the pleas of "dona eis, Domine," individual human creatures become visible as four solo soprano voices detach themselves.... Next comes the prayer for mercy—"Kyrie eleison, Christe eleison"—and now single voices, assertive and full of character, are heard for the first time. Tenor, bass, soprano, and contralto—they present themselves formally, one by one, and not without a sense of competitiveness.... Verdi's correspondence makes clear that he was looking for singers with voices and taste, and beyond that, with the power and imagination to project character and situation. It is a glorious moment, this presentation of the four praying and singing men and women in the Kyrie; moreover, when these first few bars are past, we have a pretty good idea of the sort of evening we are in for.

Alerting listeners to "glorious moments" like this one is a characteristic Steinberg ploy.

And Mozart's Requiem? Here Steinberg's commentary goes beyond history, religion, and ideology into the heart of the score itself. The myth encrusted around this piece will doubtless survive all efforts to chip it away—the ominous commission, Mozart's sudden illness, his conviction that he was writing his own requiem. In any case, he had every reason to make it as impressive as possible, since he was hoping to be appointed Kapellmeister of St. Stephen's Cathedral in Vienna, a position that would have given him a much-needed source of steady income. He had produced no sacred compositions for some time but had been sketching at some as though in preparation.

So he must have jumped at the commission for a requiem mass, even though it did not come from an emissary of the Church but from an anonymous patron. (Anonymous if not, *pace Amadeus*, all that mysterious. Gossip flowed in Vienna as freely as anywhere else and Mozart probably knew all about the patron and his quirks.) When he died with the job still unfinished, it fell to F. X. Süssmayr, an unremarkable young man in Mozart's circle who may or may not have been his student, to bring it to completion. He had to fill in the orchestration and also add music of his own, with mixed results, to put it mildly. It is striking that Tovey never wrote one of his famous "essays in musical analysis" on a work he characterized elsewhere as "the most pathetic of unfinished monuments."[7]

The ending section of the Dies Irae movement, the Lacrimosa, a short, simple melody with chords in the chorus and an affecting accompaniment figure in the orchestra, poses a special problem. Inspection of the manuscript shows Süssmayr taking over after only eight bars in Mozart's hand. Tovey thought the rest was so good it had to have been dictated by the composer on his deathbed, a typically high-handed piece of reasoning—and not everyone thinks so highly of Süssmayr's continuation. A very dim view is taken by Richard Maunder in *Mozart's Requiem*.[8] The music is shot through

---

7. Donald Francis Tovey, *The Classics of Music*, edited by Michael Tilmouth et al. (Oxford University Press, 2001), p. 383.

8. *Mozart's Requiem: On Preparing a New Edition* (Clarendon Press/Oxford University Press, 1988).

with technical errors and ends with a two-chord "amen" that is excessively simple, indeed altogether vapid. Furthermore, we know that tradition called for a fugue at this place, for the end of the Lacrimosa is also the end of the entire Dies Irae movement and needs some weight. There even exists a Mozart sketch for such a fugue.

Probably none of this would much bother the unmusicological listener of today; still, Steinberg goes out of his way to mention no fewer than four efforts that have been made to replace Süssmayr's interventions with something more Mozartian and more in scale with the rest of the composition. The "amen" fugue in one modern reconstruction strikes him as "an enjoyable movement, full of energy, with no departures from the language of the 1790s, but it is in a voice that is not Mozart's." On another, more radical effort, by the Mozart scholar Richard Maunder, Steinberg does not choose to comment, but: "I vote for the fugal close."

He also likes Maunder's drastic solution for a movement Süssmayr wrote all on his own, the Sanctus: omit it and leave the Requiem a torso, like Mozart's Mass in C Minor, the one other major composition for the Church that dates from his years in Vienna. Steinberg's discussion of the history of this also unfinished piece—almost as tangled as that of the Requiem—is one of his most deft. The C-Minor Mass has also been reconstructed, at least in part, by Helmut Eder, among others, and this solution Steinberg endorses.

Program notes for concerts go back to Berlioz's *Symphonie fantastique*—admittedly, a special case—if not earlier. The writer of notes to be read before a concert performs a different function than the critic or the writer of reviews after a concert, of course. He draws prudently on musicology and cautiously on criticism. Tovey described his role as that of "counsel for the defense." Steinberg's mild manner does not and does not mean to obscure clear opinions and clear judgments. He puts in extra footnotes directing us to CDs of the various Mozart reconstructions, for example, and with certain clients, it's clear that the case in hand is not as strong as the defense would like.

Michael Steinberg steers his own middle course in these amplified program notes between the usual writer of boilerplate and the great Tovey, whose undeniable insight into the works he addresses has to contend with his hectoring tone and donnish self-satisfaction. What you read here sounds as though you have just heard it from the obviously very knowledgeable gentleman occupying the seat next to you at the Symphony, who tends to get quite talkative and even insistent during intermission. He has a way of adding personal touches to his commentary that somehow bridge the space between music and musicology, and he often seems to be enjoying the music even more than you do.

—2005

29

MARIA CALLAS (1923–1977)

ON THE UNEXPECTED DEATH of Maria Callas in 1977, aged only fifty-three, two portraits were found in her Paris apartment. One was of Elvira de Hidalgo, a leading opera singer who became Callas's teacher in Athens between 1940 and 1945 and first identified her proclivity for the bel canto repertory, taught her the technique with exemplary thoroughness, and taught her above all how to study. The other portrait was of the legendary diva Maria Malibran, who was among the first to triumph in that repertory during the 1820s and 1830s. These were icons to the professional Callas. There were no pictures of friends, relatives, or lovers.

Though certainly never the sort of person given to sentimental gestures, Callas once took a special flight to Brussels to visit Malibran's grave. In a way, she ought to have identified more closely with Malibran's rival Giuditta Pasta, the greatest dramatic singer of her time. It was of Pasta of whom it was said that with three notes she could stir an audience to the depths of its being. It was for Pasta that Bellini wrote the role of Norma, the most important as well as the most frequent of Callas's roles. But no doubt de Hidalgo spoke less of Pasta than of Malibran—another Spaniard, and a member of the formidable García family of singers and teachers to whom de Hidalgo could trace her own artistic lineage. Moreover, Malibran led what is called a "tempestuous" life, while Pasta's life was orderly. Malibran broke with her domineering father and had two husbands and two illegitimate children by the time she died at the age of twenty-eight, as the result of incautious exertions following a riding accident. Her behavior on stage was unpredictable, her appearance always hypnotic. Pasta was dumpy. It is not surprising that a dozen books have been written about Malibran and only one, it seems, about Pasta.

Malibran biographies are still being written, the most recent of them in 1979[1]: a bad omen for the bulging Callas bibliography. A dozen books about her had been produced even before her death, and that occasion signaled the preparation of many more. Arianna Stassinopoulos in *Maria Callas: The Woman Behind the Legend*[2] wrote what seemed to be designed as an official biography, bolstered by new information furnished by friends and associates, and supplemented by a fascinating collection of informal photographs. Sergio Segalini produced a conventional picture book, *Callas: Portrait of a Diva*,[3] more comprehensive if less beautiful than the picture section of *Callas*, by John Ardoin and Gerald Fitzgerald, still the best general book on the subject.[4] Steven Linakis, a cousin who fell out with her over her treatment of her mother, offered in *Diva: The Life and Death of Maria Callas*[5] little more than a hostile memoir of a woman he scarcely knew in later life. Pierre-Jean Rémy's *Maria Callas: A Tribute*,[6] on the contrary, followed in the well-trod footsteps of her many admirers and enthusiasts.

---

1. Howard Bushnell, *Maria Malibran: A Biography of the Singer*, foreword by Elaine Brody (Pennsylvania State University Press, 1979).

2. Simon and Schuster, 1981.

3. Translated by Sonia Sabel (Hutchinson, 1981).

4. Holt, Rinehart and Winston, 1974.

5. Prentice-Hall, 1980.

6. Translated by Catherine Atthill (St. Martin's, 1978).

Rémy also had a special idea about the Callas phenomenon: for him this was to be construed as a myth of woman's destruction by man. Offstage he saw her as victimized by her husband Giovanni Meneghini, her agent Eddie Bagarozy, Rudolf Bing, Aristotle Onassis, Luchino Visconti, columnists, audiences, Rémy himself. Onstage she ritually reenacted her destruction in the personae of doomed heroines such as Violetta and Tosca. That is not, however, the way the Callas performances felt, nor is it indeed the way Rémy describes them. There was another ritual in operation. Again and again a sick, furious, vocally insecure Callas faced truculent audiences and compelled their tribute. After Tosca jumped off the roof or Violetta coughed her last, the diva would return for her famous fifteen-minute ovations and flower bombardments. The fire that drove her was the fire to succeed, to triumph, to dominate. The relationship between Callas and the opera world is best described as one of mutual manipulation, and clearly this relationship offered great satisfactions to both.

The amazing thing is that a career so completely ruled by self-interest should have produced something as selfless as the revival of an entire musical repertory. Callas took the bel canto operas of Rossini, Donizetti, and Bellini with the same inexorable seriousness that she brought to her drive to success. Bel canto opera succeeded along with Callas. This revival was itself one of the main changes in the taste for classical music that took place in the postwar, early LP days, another being the flood of older music from the Baroque period and back, and another the emergence of Mahler as the favored late-Romantic symphonist. Different opinions may be offered of the relative cultural significance of these changes; what is certain is that we are still living and listening under their joint influence.

Maria Callas sang bel canto opera with a technical proficiency that few remembered having heard before, and with a dramatic conviction that no one remembered or had even thought possible. The revival must be attributed squarely to her, even though it is true she had important help: from de Hidalgo, of course, and then from the veteran conductor Tullio Serafin and Walter Legge of EMI Records. It is also true that Callas did not limit herself to bel canto singing—no doubt her voice would have fared better if she had, but her voice and her very well-being were sacrificed to that truly awesome drive to success. Some of her most unforgettable roles, such as Cherubini's Medea and Puccini's Tosca, lay outside the bel canto repertory. But *Tosca* we have with us always, like the poor, like death and taxes; it was the authority of Callas's great bel canto roles, her Norma and her Lucia di Lammermoor, that changed the working repertory of opera houses around the world. In fact nearly half of all the performances she ever sang were of bel canto works. They included some lesser-known ones (Bellini's *I Puritani* and *La Sonnambula*) and others practically unknown when she undertook them (Bellini's *Il Pirata*, Rossini's *Armida* and *Il Turco in Italia*, Donizetti's *Anna Bolena* and *Poliuto*).

There is no word in the realm of sound corresponding to "vision," yet that was the quality Callas brought to the music of Bellini and Donizetti. In the 1930s and 1940s, this music was deprecated when it was thought about at all, compared invidiously to contemporaneous German music, operatic and nonoperatic, and dismissed as fatuous for the purposes of drama. Its melodies were thought vapid, its ornamentation trivial; it was not truly heard. Here was a singer convinced of the beauty of its every gesture and its every nuance, and able to project this by means of an unfaltering attention to musical line. Much has been written about her perfectionism in sheer technique: this meant not only singing very fast and very high, but also controlling the tone quality of every note and connecting one note to another exactly as was needed to realize her unique expressive vision. Many singers command the art of molding a musical phrase. The art of this singer was not so much that of molding as of penetrating and possessing an entire melodic trajectory, an entire role, and ultimately an entire repertory.

Her accomplishment was essentially a musical one, then, though this was sometimes almost forgotten in the endless discussions of her qualities as an actress, the deterioration of her voice, and her temperament onstage and off. All of these were prodigious, but none more so than her musicianship. Only in 1954, when she seems to have faced the fact that she could not or would not husband her voice, did she begin cultivating those aspects of an opera singer's art best described as histrionic ("histrionic" rather than "dramatic," for in the deepest sense Callas's use of her voice was the most dramatic thing about her performances). After losing about seventy pounds, she emerged as a supreme singing actress in productions put on for her by glamorous directors far beneath her in artistry. Stagecraft helped to sustain her magnificently as long as she still had some voice—but no longer. In 1969 she appeared as a nonsinging Medea in Pasolini's film, and in 1973 she directed a production of Verdi's *I Vespri Siciliani* in Turin; the film was no more than a *succès d'estime* and the directorial venture a failure. Callas created character and drama with her voice, and magnificently supported what her voice created with her body. Without her voice she had no real resources.

She had no personal resources, either. The Stassinopoulos biography does not change the main outlines of the Callas story as it was known in her great days, though it adds many memorable details (e.g., La Divina refusing to pay her father's hospital bills in 1964: "I hope the newspapers don't catch on. Then I'll really curse the moment I had any parents at all. P.S. Please keep me informed and don't let him die where I might be criticized"). Stassinopoulos tells us about the retirement years, after Onassis left her and then after his death. Most of the time Callas sat around in her Paris apartment. Her favorite activity, "almost an obsession," was listening to pirate tapes of her opera-house performances supplied by devotees from all over the world.

Maria Callas was, in fact, the first great singer whose work has been preserved comprehensively, if not quite completely, on records and tapes. Therefore it is harder to write a futile book about Callas than about Malibran (though not impossible). There is even one distinctly useful book: *The Callas Legacy* by John Ardoin,[7] which goes through the 110-odd surviving recordings one by one, providing brief analyses and appreciations, comparing the seven Normas recorded between 1950 and 1965, the five Lucias, and so on. She was never filmed or videotaped in an entire opera, for although of course the technologies existed in her time, opera on film has never really caught on and opera on television has done so (with a vengeance) only recently. Perhaps it is just as well. To the extent that her collaborations with the likes of Visconti and Zeffirelli foreshadowed today's maddening fashion for utter willfulness in opera staging—

> *Director Y who with ingenious wit*
> *Places the wretched singers in the pit*
> *While dancers mime their roles, Z the Designer*
> *Who sets the whole thing on an ocean liner,*
> *The girls in shorts, the men in yachting caps*[8]

—her histrionic contribution was equivocal. Not so her musical contribution. In opera it is the music that makes the drama—even, Callas showed us, in bel canto opera. Few if any performers have so significantly expanded the range of art experienced in their own and the following generations.

—1981

---

7. Fourth edition, Hal Leonard, 2003.

8. From Auden's prescient Metalogue in *The Magic Flute*, English version by W. H. Auden and Chester Kallman (Random House, 1956), reprinted in W. H. Auden and Chester Kallman, *Libretti, and Other Dramatic Writings by W. H. Auden, 1939–1973*, edited by Edward Mendelson (Princeton University Press, 1993), p. 155.

30

CARLOS KLEIBER (1930–2004)

WHEN CARLOS KLEIBER died in 2004, at the age of seventy-four, the obituaries made it clear that the musical world had lost an extraordinary figure. What made him so extraordinary as a musician they did not say, and indeed one can hardly conceive of a pithy characterization of his distinction that would fit into a short notice. In any case there was much else to say. Carlos was the son of another major conductor, Erich Kleiber, who left Nazi Germany in protest and settled in Argentina. Carlos's repertory was highly and very idiosyncratically constrained, his recordings very few. Very large fees were required to coax him out of the seclusion of his later years. *The Compleat Conductor* by Gunther Schuller, more than five hundred pages of arduous technical matter by an eminent conductor-composer, breaks into a small paean to Kleiber as a "virtuoso with a mind," a "musician/ philosopher" in the great tradition of twentieth-century German conductors headed by Wilhelm Furtwängler.[1]

The Maestro Myth by Norman Lebrecht[2] includes both Carlos and Erich in a chapter called "The Mavericks"; it is a measure of the shallowness of this only-too-well-informed survey of modern

---

1. Oxford University Press, 1997, pp. 193–194.

2. Birch Lane, 1991.

conductors that the maverick quality adduced by Lebrecht refers to career path and personality, not musical interpretation. Kleiber's recording of Beethoven's Fifth Symphony has been said again and again, and with the greatest of conviction, to be the benchmark, even better than his father's, "must be heard to be believed" (Schuller), "as if Homer had come back to recite the *Iliad*," and so on, and I must say it bowled me over when I first heard it, in the summer of 1995—I still remember the occasion and the date. There is nothing maverick about the interpretation. It is characteristic of its time, only more intense and better (indeed fantastically) controlled. The very slight dragging of the tragic march at the end of the first movement, the clarity of the double basses and the drum in the third, the grandeur of the horn (bridge) theme in the fourth—these are things any maestro would wish for and work for. Dwelling a little longer than most conductors do on the symphony's opening wake-up call, *da da da* DA— *da da da* DA—(I would prefer both of the DAs lengthened even further) can hardly be called eccentric.

What jumps out at me as I listen again is Kleiber's remarkable legato, or long-range legato, if that is the term, the unobtrusive way he makes phrases of music flow into one another—as in the successive pair of themes that open Beethoven's slow movement, to take one conspicuous example among many. This "flowing" quality is for me the key to Kleiber the musician. It may also be unique, and it is certainly hard to analyze or describe. Yet easy and wonderful to hear! As one musical phrase follows another, phrase B seems to do more than just *follow* A, or even *follow from* A—yet it does not seem to *emerge from* A in any obvious way or *grow out of* A or anything "organic" like that. Metaphors suggest themselves from the sphere of relationship rather than teleology: B acknowledges A, alert to their mutual existence in the same force field; A creates the space for B yet it also feels incomplete without B, and by accepting that space B speaks to A's vulnerability. Whether B itself is closed or open, C will respond accordingly. So as the music goes by there is a sense that the sound sequence is earned, self-aware, and ultimately humane in an unusual way.

That Kleiber's famous Fifth is far from maverick does not mean that he shrank from individual interpretations.[3] Another of the most deeply enshrined masterworks of the classical canon, Schubert's "Unfinished" Symphony, is a case in point. The first movement begins, it will be remembered, with a hushed line in the cellos and basses, first edging up slowly and then sinking down into a long note of preparation, preparation for rustling sounds that grow more and more full and agitated. The conclusion of this passage is co-opted by French horns playing a single note, hovering in tonal space, unaccompanied—another note of preparation, now for the symphony's most famous melody, the one that has been permanently scarred for some of us by the rune "This is, the symphon-ie, that Schubert wrote and never fi-nished." Kleiber had his own idea of how this melody should go. Since the horn call makes a transition to something less agitated, almost all conductors slow the passage down at some point, and many make it sound portentous. In the present case this quality is functional; the horn call serves as a portent for his treatment of the coming melody not as a simple lyric outpouring, but something subdued and reflexive. I think the musical text will bear this reading, arresting in itself and functional, once again, in that it looks forward to the passage where various instruments toss the melody back and forth in counterpoint, a little later. Only at this point, where Schubert brings the dynamic up from *pianissimo* to *piano*, does Kleiber give the melody

---

3. Kleiber recorded symphonies nos. 4, 5, and 7 by Beethoven but never nos. 3 (the "Eroica") or 9, and it is claimed he performed No. 6 (the "Pastoral") on only one occasion, in November 1983. A cassette tape made at the time comfortably passed the test for remastering twenty years later (see *Gramofilereview*, www.gramophone.co.uk). This was the last of Kleiber's recordings to appear, issued in 2003 by Orfeo, a label which had much earlier also caught an amazing live performance of the Fourth Symphony, with the Bavarian State Orchestra.

its full lyric rein; for all its current entanglements, it now sounds direct, free, and open (not all of the melody figures here, only a fragment of it). His is therefore a notably dynamic reading. In place of the usual sequence, *sinking line—agitation—lyric melody—developments*, Kleiber gives us *sinking line—agitation—uncertainty—lyric certitude*.

In this dynamic reading the emotional climax that occurs in the middle of the movement, the development section, becomes powerful and austere, even harsh, and perhaps not to everyone's taste. It speaks for Schubert the grim balladeer of forest demons, not the lyric singer of miller-maids and wintry wanderings. The sudden appearance of sharp dactylic rhythms at one key juncture sounds like the crack of doom. The conductor does not quite vitiate the repetitious effect of the rest of the first movement; the responsibility for that rests with the composer, and all the help in the world may not be help enough. But Schubert closes the movement memorably, with something he had learned from Beethoven. He reduces the sinking theme of the opening into moaning figures repeated again and again by various instruments and instrument choirs, high and low. Kleiber makes the music swing slowly, the repetitions flowing in and out of one another, without pressure but with the inevitability of a flywheel of enormous weight. A Romantic image of depletion—and after several hammer-stroke chords have shut it down, one almost feels the motion continuing in the silence. Symphony first movements often aren't intended to end too conclusively. There are more movements to come (in this case, only one).

The second movement also ends with a passage that "liquidates" its first theme, though in a very different way. The first violins in this passage remind me of a great silent crane dropping the remnants of the theme into astonishing tonal slots with perfect precision. Nothing is silent, of course, and in Kleiber's performance the effect is, once again, altogether humane, not mechanical—tender, in fact; but I cannot get the crane out of my mind. The most routine of my metaphors, flow, owes whatever force it has to the image of smooth, inevitable, yet spontaneous forward motion, which is itself a metaphor for life (and among the many brooks in Schubert songs, even the sad ones have their life-affirming currents).

Carlos Kleiber made authorized recordings of only four operas in his whole career (*Der Freischütz, La Traviata, Der Rosenkavalier,* and the great *Tristan und Isolde* with Margaret Price, which he tried to hold back from release)—other live performances were issued on obscure labels—yet he recorded *Die Fledermaus* twice, in 1975 and 1986 (live). The music of Johann Strauss has real sparkle, without much in the way of propulsive energy, and an operetta is a long span of time to keep sparkling—a good deal longer than the typical set of five waltzes placed end to end in "The Blue Danube" or "Tales from the Vienna Woods." Strauss keeps up interest by means of many canny changes of tempo, meter, and rhythm (fast to less fast, waltz time to polka time, upbeat rhythms to downbeat rhythms, and so on). Kleiber's "fluid sense of phrase ... the naturalness of transitions, the play of relaxation and tension, the push, pull and sweep," in the words of Will Crutchfield, are a special delight in this music, the source of the sheer verve of the performances as a whole.[4] This Vienna-born, Buenos Aires–raised musician had a weakness for the popular music of his birthplace, evident when he conducted the Vienna New Years Day Concert twice, in 1989 and 1992, at a time when his reclusiveness had already set in. These treacly events had never heard the like since Willi Boskovsky and have certainly never heard the like since. Kleiber's two New Years concerts were recorded live on Sony and remain in print, the second even more brilliant than the first.[5]

—2004

---

4. "Crutchfield at Large," *Opera News*, December 22, 1990, pp. 45–46.

5. *Carlos Kleiber Conducts Strauss* and *1992 New Years Concert,* Carlos Kleiber with the Vienna Philharmonic; both are available on CD and DVD.

Sources

Chapter 1: *The Los Angeles Times Book Review*, March 20, 2005

Chapter 2: Unpublished

Chapter 3: *The New York Review of Books*, April 24, 1997

Chapter 4: *The New York Review of Books*, June 24, 2004

Chapter 5: *The New York Review of Books*, May 17, 1979

Chapter 6: *The New York Review of Books*, June 13, 2002

Chapter 7: *The New York Review of Books*, April 28, 2005

Chapter 8: *The New York Review of Books*, October 6, 1994

Chapter 9: *The New York Review of Books*, October 8, 1981

Chapter 10: *The New York Review of Books*, March 23, 2000

Chapter 11: *The New York Review of Books*, August 18, 1988

Chapter 12: *The New York Review of Books*, May 18, 1989

Chapter 13: *The New York Review of Books*, January 12, 2006

Chapter 14: *The New York Review of Books*, October 23, 1980

Chapter 15: *The New York Review of Books*, February 27, 2003

Chapter 16: *The New York Review of Books,* October 3, 1996

Chapter 17: *The New York Review of Books,* June 24, 1999

Chapter 18: Unpublished

Chapter 19: *The New York Review of Books,* July 13, 1995

Chapter 20: *The New York Review of Books,* August 4, 1977

Chapter 21: *The New Republic,* September 18, 2000

Chapter 22: *The New York Review of Books,* February 9, 1978

Chapter 23: *The New Republic,* January 10–17, 1994

Chapter 24: *The New York Review of Books,* March 4, 1982

Chapter 25: *The New York Review of Books,* December 22, 1983

Chapter 26: *The New York Review of Books,* August 15, 1985

Chapter 27: *The New York Review of Books,* August 9, 2001

Chapter 28: *The New York Review of Books,* October 20, 2005

Chapter 29: *The New York Review of Books,* April 2, 1981

Chapter 30: *The New York Review of Books,* September 23, 2004

Index

Abbado, Claudio, 271
Abbate, Carolyn, 7
Academy of Ancient Music, 192*n*
Adamo, Mark: *Little Women*, 12
Adams, John, 4, 5
    The Death of Klinghoffer, 11, 327
    Doctor Atomic, 4, 11
    El Niño, 10, 11, 12
    Harmonielehre, 4
    Harmonium, 333
    *I Was Looking at the Ceiling and
      Then I Saw the Sky*, 11
    Nixon in China, 4, 11, 327
    On the Transmigration of Souls,
      4, 337
    Violin Concerto, 4
    The Wound-Dresser, 4
Addison, Joseph: *Cato*, 91
Adès, Thomas, 17
Adorno, Theodor W., xiv, 3, 165, 170,
    187, 291, 296, 315
    *Beethoven, The Philosophy of
      Music: Fragments and Texts*,
      163*n*, 203*n*
    Versuch über Wagner, 301–305
Allanbrook, Douglas: *Ethan Frome*,
    12
Altschuler, Eric: *Bachanalia: The
    Essential Listener's Guide to Bach's
    "Well-Tempered Clavier,"* 79–85
Amadeus (film), 110, 115, 342

Amelli, Father Guerrino, 339, 340
American Symphony Orchestra
    League, 336
Andrea Chénier (Umberto Giordano),
    182
Anonymous Four, 21
Appia, Adolphe, 298–299
    *La Mise en scène du drame
      wagnérien*, 298
Ardoin, John: *The Callas Legacy*, 350
Ardoin, John and Fitzgerald, Gerald:
    Callas, 346
Arne, Thomas, 277
Arneson, Robert, 314
Arts Florissants, Les, 66
Ashkenazy, Vladimir, ix, 123, 134,
    135
Ashland, Mike, 327, 328*n*
Auden, W. H., 69, 111, 140*n*, 149,
    249, 250, 251, 334, 335
    Metalogue to *The Magic Flute*, 149,
      350
    The Sea and the Mirror, 249, 254
Audi, Pierre, 63, 64

Bach, Carl Philipp Emanuel, 70–73,
    77, 93, 94
Bach, Johann Christoph, 77
Bach, Johann Sebastian, 7, 69–77,
    87–97, 125, 128, 152, 183,
    208–209, 284

6 Organ Sonatas, 76
The Art of Fugue, 74, 88, 95
Brandenburg Concertos, 88
Canonic Variations on *Vom Himmel hoch*, 88, 97
Cantata No. 4, "Christ lag in Todesbanden," 75, 91
Cantata No. 51, "Jauchzet Gott in allen Landen," 93
Cantata No. 106, "Gottes Zeit is die allerbeste Zeit," 91
Cantata No. 115, "Mache dich, mein Geist, bereit," 71
Cello Suite in C Major, 152
cello suites, 88
Chaconne for violin solo, 75
Clavierübung, 74–75
English Suites, 74
French Suites, 74
Goldberg Variations, 74–77, 88, 93, 97
Italian Concerto, 74
Mass in B Minor, 37, 73, 74, 88, 93, 95, 333
Musical Offering, 88, 94
Partita in B-Flat, 152
Partitas, 74
Passacaglia and Fugue for organ, 75
Passions, 333
Prelude in C Major, 208
St. John Passion, 71, 88, 92, 94, 95
St. Matthew Passion, 92
"Vor deinem Thron," organ choral, 71
The Well-Tempered Clavier, 73, 79–85, 88, 208
Bach, Wilhelm Friedemann, 75, 76, 77, 82
Bach family, 157
Bach Reader, The (ed. David and Mendel), 85
Bagarozy, Eddie, 347
Bakunin, Mikhail, 315
Bara, Theda, 314
Barber, Samuel: Adagio for Strings, 3
Barenboim, Daniel, 326
Barezzi, Antonio, 261

Barish, Jonas: *The Anti-Theatrical Prejudice*, 15, 304
Barthes, Roland, 167
Bartók, Béla: Concerto for Orchestra, 3
Barzun, Jacques, 315
Basini, Laura, 338
Bauer, Bruno, 291
Bavarian State Orchestra, 353*n*
BBC (British Broadcasting Corporation), 268
Beardsley, Aubrey, 247
Beatles, 87, 223
Beaumarchais, Pierre-Augustin de, 18, 252
Beethoven, Ludwig van, ix, xiii, 2, 24, 83, 87, 97, 125, 128, 139, 151, 152, 158, 161–172, 173–183, 205, 218, 219, 239, 284, 286, 288, 302, 327, 334, 354
An die ferne Geliebte, 172, 210, 211, 212
Cello Sonata in C Major, op. 102, no.1, 172
Choral Fantasy for Piano, Orchestra, and Chorus, op. 80, 165, 190, 191, 194
Christ on the Mount of Olives, 173
Egmont overture and incidental music, 179–180
Fantasy for Piano, op. 77, 190, 191, 194
Fidelio (previously *Leonore*), 171, 173, 253, 288
Piano Concerto No. 1, 199
Piano Concerto No. 2, 188, 189, 196, 199
Piano Concerto No. 3, 169, 170, 189
Piano Concerto No. 4, 192–195, 197, 199
Piano Concerto No. 5 ("Emperor"), 23, 160, 170, 185, 190, 192, 195–199
Piano Sonata No. 17 ("Tempest"), 169
Piano Sonata No. 23 ("Appassionata"), 159–160, 170
Piano Sonata No. 28, op. 101, 172

Piano Sonata No. 29
("Hammerklavier"), 160
Rondo in B Flat for Piano and
Orchestra, 188
String Quartet No. 6, op. 18, no. 6,
163
String Quartet No. 7, op. 59, no. 1,
196
String Quartet No. 12, op. 127, 168
String Quartet No. 14, op. 131,
168n
String Quartet No. 15, op. 132,
163, 169
String Quartet No. 16, op. 135, 169
Symphony No. 3 ("Eroica"),
154–155, 156, 158–159,
173–177, 178n, 196–197, 353n
Symphony No. 4, 353n
Symphony No. 5, xiii, 124,
168–169, 175, 176, 178n, 194,
196–197, 352–353
Symphony No. 6 ("Pastoral"), 181,
196, 353n
Symphony No. 7, 353n
Symphony No. 8, 186
Symphony No. 9 ("Choral"), x,
159, 164–167, 168, 170, 176,
194, 201–204, 288
Triple Concerto for Violin, Cello,
and Piano, 198, 199
Violin Concerto, 168, 185, 192,
196, 198
Bellini, Vincenzo, 216, 217, 347
  Norma, 256, 345
  Il Pirata, 348
  I Puritani, 348
  La Sonnambula, 348
Belt, Philip, 128
Benedictines of St. Gall, 9
Benvenga, Nancy: *Kingdom on the
  Rhine*, 297
Berg, Alban, 252
  Wozzeck, 61, 251
Bergman, Ingmar, 143, 145, 146, 149,
  247, 254
Berio, Luciano: *O King*, 336
Berkeley, Bishop, 297

Berlioz, Hector, x, 21, 128, 168, 170,
  174, 207, 215, 217, 231, 251, 252
  Béatrice et Bénédict, 240, 246
  Benvenuto Cellini, 251
  L'Enfance du Christ, 240
  Memoirs, 231–235, 237, 238, 239
  La Prise de Troie, 238
  Roméo et Juliette, 216
  Symphonie fantastique ("Fantastic"
  Symphony), 233, 343
  Les Troyens, 232, 237–240,
  246–247, 251
  Les Troyens à Carthage, 238
Berlioz, Joséphine, 235
Bernini, Gian Lorenzo, 36–37
Bernstein, Leonard, 4, 14, 203
Bilson, Malcolm, ix, 120, 123–128,
  130, 132–136
Bing, Rudolf, 270, 271, 347
Bismarck, Otto von, 315
Bizet, Georges: *Carmen*, 18, 244
Blume, Friedrich, 93
Boccaccio, Giovanni, 264
Boethius: *Consolations of Philosophy*,
  31
Böhm, Georg, 72
Boito, Arrigo, 257, 269, 270, 278
Bolcom, William
  McTeague, 12
  A View from the Bridge, 12
Bordoni, Faustina, 93
Boskovsky, Willi, 355
Bossy, John, 52, 53
Boston Baroque, 138n
Boston Symphony Orchestra, 1, 2, 3
Boulez, Pierre, 11, 298, 300, 319, 327
Boyce, William, 277
Bradley, A. C., 278
Brahms, Johannes, 157–158, 160, 229
  Piano Concerto No. 2, 197
  Trost in Tränen (Consolation in
  Tears), xiii, 225, 226, 227
  Variations and Fugue on a Theme
  by Handel, xi
Breitkopf & Härtel, 195
Brendel, Alfred, 123, 133, 134,
  194–195

Brendel, Wolfgang, 149
Brentano, Antonie, 170, 171
Britten, Benjamin, 11, 251, 337
    Cello Symphony, 336
    Death in Venice, 336
    Peter Grimes, 334
    Phaedra, 336
    War Requiem, ix–x, 334, 335–336
Brody, Elaine, 291
Brook, Peter, 18
Brooklyn Academy of Music (BAM), 5, 57, 58, 66, 67
Brooks, David, 10
Brown, Howard Mayer: *Music in the Renaissance*, 43
Bruckner, Anton, 158
Büchner, Georg, 252
Budden, Julian: *The Operas of Verdi*, 267–279
Bülow, Hans von, 159*n*, 199
Burnham, Scott: *Beethoven Hero*, 173–183
Burns, Ken, 327
Busch, Hans, 269*n*
Busenello, Giovanni Francesco, 61, 62
Busnoys, Antoine, 32, 33
Busoni, Ferruccio: Piano Concerto, 334
Buxtehude, Dietrich, 72
Byrd, William, 36, 41–56
    Cantiones quae ab argumento sacrae vocantur (with Tallis), 46, 49
    Circumspice Hierusalem, 48
    Deus venerunt gentes, 44–45, 47–48
    Domine praestolamur, 47
    Gradualia, 53–56
    Haec dicit Dominus, 48
    Laetentur coeli, 47
    masses, 53
    My Lady Nevells Booke, 51
    Ne irascaris Domine, 47, 50
    Plorans plorabit, 48
    Quomodo cantabimus, 49
    Vigilate, 47

Cagnoni, Antonio, 268
Cairns, David: *Berlioz*, 231, 232, 234–236, 239, 240

Callas, Maria, 345–350
Campion, St Edmund, 41, 43–45, 48
Capell, Richard: *Schubert's Songs*, 228
Carissimi, Giacomo: *Missa L'Homme armé*, 35
Carnegie, Andrew, 2
Caruso, Enrico, 3
Carvalho, Léon, 238
Carver, Robert, 33
Casadesus, Robert, 123
Catalani, Alfredo, 274
Cavalli, Pietro Francesco: *La Calisto*, 18
Cellini, Benvenuto, 252
Chagall, Marc, 145
Chaikovsky, Pyotr Ilyich, 131, 160
    Eugene Onegin, 19, 251, 252
    Hamlet, 249
    Piano Concerto No. 1, 22
Chamberlain, Houston Stewart, 323–324
Charles the Bold, of Burgundy, 32, 34
Chéreau, Patrice, 293, 298–301, 314, 315, 319, 327
Cherubini, Luigi, 348
Chesterfield, Lord, 102
Chicago Symphony Orchestra, 195*n*
Chopin, Frédéric, 82, 83, 157–158, 206, 207, 208, 213–215, 217, 219, 220
    Berceuse, 215
    Etude in C Major, op. 10, no. 1, 208
    Nocturne in E-Flat Major, op. 55, no. 2, 214–215
    Prelude in C Major, op. 28, no.1, 208
    Sonata in B-Flat Minor, 214
Christie, William, 66
Citron, Pierre, 234
Coleridge, Samuel Taylor, 278
Collegium Musicum (Leipzig), 73, 74
Coltrane, John, xiv
Comini, Alessandra: *The Changing Image of Beethoven*, 205*n*
Conati, Marcello, 269*n*
Cone, Edward T.: "The Old Man's Toys: Verdi's Last Operas," 278*n*

Conklin, John, 316
Conrad, Peter: *Romantic Opera and Literary Form*, 243–252, 254
Cooke, Deryck, 293, 294, 304
  I Saw the World End, 284
Cooper, Barry, 171*n*
Copland, Aaron, 4, 14, 133
  Appalachian Spring, 4
  Billy the Kid, 4
  Symphony No. 3, 3
Corea, Chick, 21
Corigliano, John: Symphony No. 1, 10
Couperin, François, 87
Crabbe, George, 335
Crashaw, Richard, 92
Crookes, Nancy, 298
Crutchfield, Will, 355
Curzon, Sir Clifford, 123
Czerny, Carl, 158

da Ponte, Lorenzo, 99, 100, 108, 244
Dahlhaus, Carl, 281–284, 285, 303, 304, 315
  The Idea of Absolute Music, 186
Dale, Laurence, 67, 68
Danhauser, Josef: *Liszt at the Piano*, 205*n*
Dante Alighieri, 338
Daverio, John: *Nineteenth-Century Music and the German Romantic Ideology*, 209*n*
Davies, Peter J., 118
Davies, Sir Peter Maxwell: *Taverner*, 36
Davis, Anthony: *X: The Life and Times of Malcolm X*, 18–19
de Hidalgo, Elvira, 345, 348
de la Rue, Pierre, 33
De Waart, Edo, 314*n*
Deathridge, John and Dahlhaus, Carl: "Wagner" in *The New Grove Wagner*, 282–284, 287, 289, 292
Debussy, Claude, 183, 321
  "La Fille aux cheveux de lin," 172
  Pelléas et Mélisande, 61, 244
Dent, Edward J.: *Mozart's Operas*, 140–141

Desprez, Josquin, 33
Deym, Josephine, 171
Diderot, Denis, 70
Donizetti, Gaetano, 268, 272, 347
  Anna Bolena, 348
  Poliuto, 348
Donne, John, 335
Dryden, John, x
du Locle, Camille, 270
Duboeuf, Estelle, 232–236
Dufay, Guillaume
  Missa Caput, 32
  Missa L'Homme armé, 32, 33
Dumas, Alexandre, *fils*: *La Dame aux camélias*, 235, 249
Dumas, Alexandre, *père*, 205
Duschek, Josepha, 109–110
Duse, Eleanora, 247
Dutch National Opera, 63
Dvořák, Antonín: Symphony No. 9 (*From the New World*), 2, 4

Eddy, Mary Baker, 323
Eder, Helmut, 343
Edward VI, King, 35
Eggebrecht, Hans Heinrich: *Zur Geschichte der Beethoven-Rezeption*, 167
Eliot, T. S., 129
  East Coker, 32*n*
Elizabeth I, Queen, 35, 46, 335
EMI Records, 348
English National Opera Guides series, 312–313
Epinay, Mme d': *Letters to My Son*, 102
Epstein, David: *Beyond Orpheus*, 155, 156, 159*n*
Euripides, 232
Ewans, Michael: *Wagner and Aeschylus*, 297

Faerber, Uwe: *The Bayreuth Festival's Centenary Ring*, 298
Fellowes, E. H., 42
Ferrabosco, Alfonso (1), 36
Ferrand, Humbert, 238

Festival Opera of Walnut Creek, 19
Feuerbach, Ludwig, 296, 315
Field, John, 217
Fischer, Edwin, 125, 133
Fischer-Dieskau, Dietrich, 221, 222,
    227–229
    *The Fischer-Dieskau Book of
    Lieder*, 229
    *Schubert's Songs: A Biographical
    Study*, 221, 228
    Wagner and Nietzsche, 228–229
Fitzgerald, Gerald, 346
Fitzherbert, Thomas, 44
Flagstad, Kirsten, 3
Floyd, Carlisle, 11
    Of Mice and Men, 18
Fontenrose, Joseph: *Python*, 298
Forkel, J. N., 70, 77
Förster, Bernhard, 291
Forster, E. M.: *Howards End*, xiii, 174
Fortner, Wolfgang, 229
Frager, Malcolm, 134
Franck, César: Organ Chorales, 216
Franke, August Hermann, 90, 91
Frankfurt School, 301, 302
Frederick the Great, 70, 76, 93, 94
Freyhan, Michael, 144*n*
Friedrich, Caspar David, 300, 315
    The Sea of Ice (*The Wreck of the
    Hope*), 316
Friedrich, Götz, 327–328
Frye, Northrop, 277, 322*n*
Fulkerson, Christopher, 298
Furtwängler, Wilhelm, 351

Gadamer, Hans-Georg, 167
García family, 345
Gardiner, John Eliot, 128, 130, 135,
    190, 194
Garnet, Father Henry, 46, 54
Gay, John, 277
Gay, Peter: *Mozart*, 99, 105–106
Gellert, Christian Fürchtegott: *Lessons
    from a Father to a Son*, 102
Georgiades, T. G.: *Schubert, Musik
    und Lyrik*, 223–224, 225
Gershwin, George: *Porgy and Bess*, 15

Geyer, Ludwig, 289
Ghislanzoni, Antonio, 270
Gibbons, Orlando, 36
Glass, Frank W.: *The Fertilizing Seed*,
    296–297
Glass, Philip, 4–5
    Akhnáten, 11, 18
    Appomattox, 11
    Einstein on the Beach, 4, 11, 14
    Les Enfants terribles, 18
    Satyagráha, 11
    Symphony No. 5 "Choral," 10
    Waiting for the Barbarians, 11
Glover, Jane, 58, 66–67
Gluck, Christoph Willibald von, 148,
    231–232, 239
    Alceste, 232
    Iphigénie en Tauride, 148, 231
    Orphée, 232
Gobineau, Arthur, 323
Goehr, Lydia, 191
    *The Imaginary Museum of Musical
    Works*, 186
Goethe, Johann Wolfgang von, 143*n*,
    177–180, 210, 293
    Egmont, 179–180
    Faust, 293, 334
    "Kennst du das Land?" 199
    "Trost in Tränen" (Consolation in
    Tears), xiii, 225–227
    "Wandrers Nachtlied (Über allen
    Gipfeln ist Ruh')," 223
    Der Zauberflöte zweiter Theil, 249,
    250
Goethe Society of Vienna, 225
Goldberg, J. G., 75, 77
Gomes, Antônio Carlo, 273, 274
Goode, Richard, 134
Gossett, Philip, 269*n*
Gottsched, Johann Christoph,
    91, 92
Gottsched, Luise, 91
Gould, Glenn, 75*n*
Gould, Stephen Jay, 79
Graebner, Eric, 305
Graun, Carl Heinrich, 157
Gregor-Dellin, Martin, 258

Richard Wagner: *His Life, His Work, His Century*, 286, 288–290, 293
Grey, Thomas S.: *Wagner's Musical Prose: Text and Contexts*, 174*n*
Grimm, Baron Melchior, 102
Grove, George: *Beethoven's Nine Symphonies*, 268
Guarini, Giovanni Battista, 68
Guido d'Arezzo, 338
Günther, Ursula, 269*n*
Gutman, Robert W., 109*n*
  Mozart: A Cultural Biography, 110, 111–113

Haitink, Sir Bernard, 143*n*
Halévy, Jacques Fromental-Élie, 238
Hall, Sir Peter, 300
Hamilton, David, 228
Handel, George Frideric, 60, 71, 90, 128, 251
  Messiah, 10, 12, 82
Harbison, John: *The Great Gatsby*, 12
Harris, Roy, 3, 14
  Symphony No. 3, 4
Hart, Moss: *Act One*, 270
Hartke, Stephen: *The Greater Good*, 12
Hasse, Johann Adolph, 93
Haydn, Joseph, 109, 115, 151, 153, 160, 169, 177, 183, 187
  Mass No. 12 ("Harmoniemesse"), 160
  String Quartet in D Minor, op. 42, 152
  Symphony No. 44 ("Trauersymphonie"), 152
Hegel, George Wilhelm Friedrich, 178, 179, 331
Heggie, Jack, 12
  Dead Man Walking, 10, 11, 12
Heifetz, Jascha, 3
Helfgott, David, 24
Heller, Stephen, 239
Henry VIII, King, 53
Hepokoski, James A., 264*n*
Hess, Dame Myra, 123

Higginson, Henry, 2
Hildesheimer, Wolfgang, 117
  Mozart, 103, 104, 115, 116, 120
Hiller, Ferdinand, 236
Hindemith, Paul, 132
Hitler, Adolf, 323–324, 329–330, 331
Hockney, David, 143, 145, 328
Hoffmann, E. T. A., 169*n*, 187, 194, 207
Hofmannsthal, Hugo von, 243, 244, 247, 254, 270
  Die Frau ohne Schatten, 249
Hofstadter, Douglas R., 88
Hogwood, Christopher, 192*n*
Holland, Bernard, 21, 22
Holloway, Robin, 313
Homer, 30, 61
  Iliad, 352
  Odyssey, 65
Horowitz, Joseph, 16, 129
  Classical Music in America, 1–5, 13–14, 100, 333
  Understanding Toscanini, 3
Horowitz, Vladimir, 3, 134
Hughes, Spike: *Famous Verdi Operas*, 268
Hugo, Victor, 205
Huizinga, Johan: *The Waning of the Middle Ages*, 33
Hulme, T. E., 129
Hummel, Johann Nepomuk, 217

Ibsen, Henrik, 247
Institut de Recherche et Coordination Musique/Acoustique (IRCAM), 11
Isherwood, Christopher, 334
iTunes, 16
Ives, Charles, 4, 14

Jacobs, Robert L.: *Richard Wagner: Three Wagner Essays* (trans.), 292
Jarrett, Keith, 21
Jauss, Hans Robert, 167
Jazz (TV series), 327
Jephcott, Edmund, 203*n*
Johnson, Dr. Samuel, 148, 297
Jomelli, Niccolò, 157

Jones, Gwyneth, 314*n*
Jonson, Ben, 335
Joseph II, Emperor of Austria, 104
Jung, Carl Gustav, 87, 88, 90

Kallman, Chester, 140*n*, 149, 249, 350*n*
Kant, Immanuel, 177, 178, 187
Karl Theodor, Elector, 105
Kaufman, George S., 270
Keats, John, 278
Keller, Hans, 198
Kennedy, Robert, 337
Kenyon, Nicholas, ed.: *Authenticity in Early Music*, 128
Kerman, Joseph: *Opera as Drama*, 137
Kermode, Frank, 13
Kern, Hermann: *Through the Labyrinth*, 28, 29, 39
Kern, Jerome, 312
Keyserlingk, Count von, 75, 77
Kierkegaard, Søren, 137
King, Martin Luther Jr., 336, 337
Kleiber, Carlos, 351–355
Kleiber, Erich, 351, 352
Klimt, Gustav, 247
Knab, Armin, 229
Kollo, René, 314*n*
Kosman, Joshua, 12
Koussevitzky, Serge, 3
Koussevtzky Foundations, 3
Kozinn, Allan, 16–17
Kramer, Richard: *Distant Cycles: Schubert and the Conceiving of Song*, 209*n*
Kraus, Karl, 320, 329
Kreisler, Fritz, 3
Kronos Quartet, 5
Kupfer, Harry, 327–328

Landon, H. C. Robbins
    1791: Mozart's Last Year, 115–121
    Haydn: Chronicle and Works, 115–116
Larsen, Jens Peter, 158
Larson, Libby: *Every Man Jack*, 19

Lassus, Orlande, 42
Lavignac, Albert, 308, 322
Lebrecht, Norman: *The Maestro Myth*, 351–352
Legge, Walter, 348
Lehnhoff, Nikolaus, 314, 315, 316, 328
Leonhardt, Gustav, 129–130
Leopold II, Emperor, 118
Lessing, Gotthold Ephraim, 70
Levarie, Siegmund, 154
Levi, Hermann, 291
Lévi-Strauss, Claude, 297
Levin, Robert, 190–192, 194, 199
Levine, James, 195*n*, 271
Levine, Lawrence: *Highbrow/Lowbrow*, 15
Lichtenstein, Harvey, 5
Lieberson, Jonathan, 328*n*
Ligeti, György, 17
Linakis, Steven: *Diva: The Life and Death of Maria Callas*, 346
Lipatti, Dinu, 123
Liszt, Franz, 22, 205–209, 215, 217, 240
    "Die Lorelei," 216
    Reminiscences of Don Juan, 216
    Sonata in B Minor, 216
    Sonetto di Petrarca No. 104, 216
    Totentanz, 131
    Transcendental Etudes, 216
Livingstone, Rodney, 305
Lockwood, Lewis
    Beethoven: Studies in the Creative Process, 161
    Beethoven: The Music and the Life, 161–172
Loeffler, Peter, 299
Lortzing, Albert: *Der Wildschütz*, 18
Lott, Felicity, 143*n*
Lubin, Steven, 120, 134
Ludwig II, King of Bavaria, 287, 294, 323
Lund, Susan: *Raptus*, 171*n*

Ma, Yo-Yo, 5
McEwen, Terence, 315

Machaut, Guillaume de
  "Ma fin est mon commencement,"
    31, 32
  Missa Caput, 32
  Missa L'Homme armé, 32, 33
  Remède de Fortune, 31
Magee, Bryan, 292
Magic Flute, The (film), 143, 145,
  146, 149
Mahler, Gustav, 160, 183, 334, 347
  Das Lied von der Erde, 107
Malibran, Maria, 345–346, 350
Mallarmé, Stéphane, 250
Mann, Thomas, 288, 289, 292
  Death in Venice, 336
Manzoni, Alessandro, 337
Marchetti, Filippo, 268
Mariani, Angelo, 259
Marr, Wilhelm, 291
"Marseillaise, La," 210
Marshall, Robert L., 93
Marton, Éva, 314n
Marx, A. B., 158, 180
Marx, Joseph, 229
Marx, Karl, 87, 290, 303
Mary, Queen, 35, 44, 45, 53, 55
Mary Queen of Scots, 32n
Maunder, Richard: *Mozart's Requiem:
  On Preparing a New Edition*,
    342–343
Maupassant, Guy de: *Boule de Suif*,
  12
Mayrhofer, Johann, 224
Mazzini, Giuseppe, 262
Mazzoli, Ferruccio, 119
Medici, Mario, 269n
Mellers, Wilfrid
  Bach and the Dance of God, 87–97
  Beethoven and the Voice of God,
    87n
Mendel, Arthur, 94, 95
Mendelssohn Bartholdy, Felix, 22,
  157–158, 207, 215, 290
  Fugue in E Minor, op. 35, no. 1,
    216
  "O for the wings of a dove," 216
  St. Paul Oratorio, 216

Mendès, Catulle, 300
Meneghini, Giovanni, 347
Menotti, Gian Carlo, 11
Mercadante, Saverio, 268, 272
Merelli, Bartolomeo, 257
Messiaen, Olivier, 17
Metastasio, 19, 119
Metropolitan Opera, 300, 323
Meyerbeer, Giacomo, 217, 238, 268,
  273, 290
Michelangeli, Arturo Benedetti, 123
Miller, Jonathan, 328
Miller, Philip: *The Ring of Words*, 229
Mizler, Lorenz, 88n
Monte, Philippe de, 48–49
Montesquieu, Charles de Secondat,
  baron de, 102
Monteverdi, Claudio, 7, 57–68
  Arianna, 36, 58
  L'incoronazione di Poppea, 36, 58,
    61–65
  "The Lament of the Nymph,"
    36–37
  Orfeo, 37, 58, 64, 67–68
  Il ritorno d'Ulisse in patria, 36,
    58–61, 62, 65–66, 67
Monteverdi Choir, 190n
Moore, Douglas, 11
Moore, Gerald, 221n, 228
  The Schubert Song Cycles, 222
Morales, Cristóbal de, 33
More, Father Henry, 41
Morley, Thomas, 50
Morris, James, 314
Mozart, Leopold, 101–106, 120, 139
Mozart, Wolfgang Amadeus, ix, 21,
  60, 99–113, 151, 152, 159, 176,
  183, 187, 190, 192, 252, 343–344
  The Abduction from the Seraglio,
    107–108, 110–111, 137, 138,
    142
  Adagio and Allegro for mechanical
    organ, K. 594, 104
  Clarinet Concerto, 107, 121
  La clemenza di Tito, 19, 108–111,
    118–120, 137
  concert rondos, 124

Così fan tutte, 99, 100, 104, 108, 137, 244
Don Giovanni, 100, 104, 108, 137, 148, 216, 239, 253, 254
flute concertos, 105
flute quartets, 105
Horn Concerto No. 1, K. 412, 121*n*
Idomeneo, 137, 141, 142, 148
The Magic Flute, ix, x, 38, 59, 110–111, 116, 124, 137–149, 249, 250, 315
The Marriage of Figaro, 18, 100, 104, 108, 116, 137, 251
Mass in C Minor, 343
A Musical Joke (Divertimento for two horns and strings), 101, 120
Piano Concerto No. 7, K. 453, 192*n*
Piano Concerto No. 8, K. 456, 135
Piano Concerto No. 9, K. 271 ("Jeune-homme"), 123
Piano Concerto No. 11, K. 413, 135, 193
Piano Concerto No. 12, K. 414, 193
Piano Concerto No. 13, K. 415, 135, 193
Piano Concerto No. 14, K. 449, 121*n*, 134*n*
Piano Concerto No. 20, K. 466, 120, 124, 125–127
Piano Concerto No. 21, K. 467, 21, 126*n*, 127–128
Piano Concerto No. 22, K. 482, 191
Piano Concerto No. 23, K. 488, 121n, 133–4, 134*n*, 192*n*
Piano Concerto No. 24, K. 491, 123*n*
Piano Concerto No. 25, K. 503, 121*n*, 135
Piano Concerto No. 26, K. 537, ("Coronation") 131–132
Piano Concerto No. 27, K. 595, 104, 107, 121, 123*n*, 134*n*
piano concertos, ix, 106–107, 123–135

Piano Sonata No. 12, K. 332, 126*n*
"Prussian" Quartets, 109
Requiem, x, 110, 111, 116, 117, 341–343
Rondo in A Major, K. 386, 131*n*
Rondo in A Minor, K. 511, 125
Rondo in D Major, K. 382, 131*n*
String Quartet No. 22, K. 589, 104
String Quartet No. 23, K. 590, 104
string quartets, 109
String Quintet No. 5, K. 593, 104
string quintets, 118
Symphony No. 36 ("Linz"), 109
Symphony No. 38 ("Prague"), 109, 153, 160
Symphony No. 39, 109
Symphony No. 40, 109
Symphony No. 41 ("Jupiter"), 109, 121
Verzeichnüss aller meiner Werke, 104
Zaide, 110, 160
Mozart's Circle
  The Benevolent Dervish, 138
  The Philosopher's Stone, or the Magic Island, 138
Muck, Karl, 1
Mulcaster, Richard, 46
Munch, Edvard, 247
Munn, Thomas J., 316
Music Library, New York Public Library (58th Street), xi, xiv
Mussorgsky, Modest: *Boris Godunov*, 251
Muzio, Emanuele, 256

Napoleon Bonaparte, 175
Nattiez, Jean-Jacques: *Tétralogies—Wagner, Boulez, Chéreau*, 293, 295, 296, 298, 300, 301
Naxos (record company), 5, 16
Neighbour, Oliver: *The Consort and Keyboard Music of William Byrd*, 43
New Bach Reader, The (ed. David, Mendel and Wolff), 69
New Grove Dictionary of Music and Musicians, 282, 292

New York Philharmonic, 1, 337
Newcomb, Anthony, 285, 313
Newman, Ernest, 292
 The Wagner Operas, 268
Nietzsche, Friedrich, 284, 301, 302, 304, 323
Noble, Adrian, 65, 66
Nonesuch (record company), 5
Norrington, Sir Roger, 128
Novalis, 250

Obrecht, Jacob, 33
 Missa Caput, 32
Ockeghem, Johannes, 33
 Missa Caput, 32
Onassis, Aristotle, 347, 349
Opera Quarterly (Commemorative Wagner Issue), 284, 291
Orchestre Révolutionnaire et Romantique, 190n
Ortega y Gasset, José, 129
Osborne, Charles: The Complete Operas of Verdi, 268
Overhoff, Kurt, 331
Ovid, 30
Owen, Wilfred, 335, 336
 "The Parable of the Old Man and the Young," 335

Pacini, Giovanni, 268
Paganini, Niccolò, 205
Paisiello, Giovanni: The Barber of Seville, 18
Palestrina, Giovanni da, 2, 33, 284, 338, 340
Parsons, Robert, 36
Pasolini, Pier Paolo, 349
Pasqua, Giuseppina, 264–265
Passion (Sondheim), 19
Pasta, Giuditta, 345, 346
Paul, Jean, 207
Paulus, Diane, 67, 68
PBS (Public Broadcasting Service), 314
Peacham, Henry, 34–35
Pearlman, Martin, 138n
Pepping, Ernst, 229
Pepusch, Johann Christoph: The

 Beggar's Opera, 90
Perahia, Murray, ix, 123, 131–132, 134, 136
Persians, The (Aeschylus), 19
Persons, Father Robert, 43
Petrarch, Francesco, 338
Petre, Sir John, 51
Petre, Lady Mary, 51
Petre, Sir William, 51
Petre family, 51–52, 54
Pfitzner, Hans, 229
Phantom of the Opera (Lloyd Webber), 19
Philip the Good, of Burgundy, 33
Phillips-Matz, Mary Jane: Verdi: A Biography, 256, 258–261
Pichler, Caroline, 116–117, 265
Picker, Tobias: An American Tragedy, 12
Pipelare, Matthaeus, 33
Plantinga, Leon: Beethoven's Concertos: History, Style, Performance, 186–199
Play of Daniel, The, 19
Ployer, Barbara, 134n
Ponchielli, Amilcare, 268, 273, 274
Ponnelle, Jean-Pierre, 299
Porges, Heinrich: Wagner Rehearsing the Ring, 300–301
Porter, Andrew, 269n, 312–313
Post-Holocaust Dialogue Group, 326
Poulenc, Francis, 132
Pound, Ezra, 129
Prawer, S. S.: The Penguin Book of Lieder, 229
Previn, André: A Streetcar Named Desire, 12
Price, Margaret, 355
Prokofiev, Sergei, 131
Proust, Marcel, 249
Puccini, Giacomo, 22, 60
 Madama Butterfly, 18
 Tosca, 348
Puchberg, Michael, 101, 103, 104, 113
Puffett, Derrick, 313
Purcell, Henry, x, 335

Dido and Aeneas, 37
In Nomine à, 7, 36
Pushkin, Alexander, 252

Rachmaninov, Sergei, 3, 23
  Piano Concerto No. 2, 22
  Piano Concerto No. 3, 21–25
Racine, Jean, 336
Radant, Else, 118
Rather, L. J., 292, 297
Ravel, Maurice: Piano Concerto in G
  Major, 131
Recio, Marie, 235–237
Reger, Max, 229
Regis, Johannes, 33
Reich, Steve, 5
  Three Tales, 12
Reicha, Anton, 158
Reinken, Johann Adam, 71–72
Rémy, Pierre-Jean, 347
  Maria Callas: A Tribute, 346
Réti, Rudolph, 96, 180
Reutter, Hermann, 229
Ricci, Federico, 268
Ricci, Luigi, 268
Rich, Alan, xiii, 5, 12, 314
Richardson, Sir Ferdinando, 46
Richardson, Samuel, 102
Ricordi, Giulio, 257, 272
Ridley, M. R., 278
Riemann, Hugo, 180
Rieu, André, 3
Riley, Terry: *In C*, 182
Rilke, Rainer Maria, 163
Rodin, Auguste, 163
Rorem, Ned: *Our Town*, 12, 19
Rose, Paul Lawrence, 291
Rosen, Charles, 81, 83, 124, 232
  *The Classical Style: Haydn, Mozart,
    Beethoven*, 132, 151, 153, 155,
    157, 172, 205, 206, 211n
  *The Frontiers of Meaning: Three
    Informal Lectures on Music*,
    212n
  "Music à la Mode," 180–181n
  The Romantic Generation, 205–220
  Sonata Forms, 151–160

Rosen, Charles and Zerner, Henri:
  Romanticism and Realism, 209n
Ross, Alex, xiii, 5, 8, 12, 324
Rosselli, John, 109n
  The Life of Mozart, 99–100, 103–5,
    107, 108, 111, 113n
Rossini, Gioacchino, 193, 205, 232,
  257, 272, 337, 347
  Armida, 348
  The Barber of Seville, 18
  Il Turco in Italia, 348
Rostropovich, Mstislav, 336
Royal Opera, 312
Royal Shakespeare Company, 65
Rumph, Stephen, 167n, 203n

Saariaho, Kaija, 17
Salieri, Antonio, 119, 148
Salonen, Esa-Pekka, 5
Sammartini, G. B., 157
San Francisco Opera, 17, 18,
  314–317
Sand, George, 205
Sargent, Sir Malcolm, 126n
Sarnoff, David, 3
Scarlatti, Domenico, 90, 93
Schaden, Joseph von, 162
Schama, Simon: *Landscape and
  Memory*, 211
Schenker, Heinrich, 7, 96, 156, 159n,
  180
Schikaneder, Emanuel, 38, 110,
  138–9, 143n, 145–8
Schiller, Friedrich, 177, 178, 179,
  211–212, 246
  Don Carlos, 277
  "Ode to Joy," 159, 165–166,
    201–204
Schinkel, Karl Friedrich, 300,
  315
Schlegel, August Wilhelm, 187
  Athenaeum fragments, 209
Schmidgall, Gary, 254
  Literature as Opera, 251–252
Schnabel, Artur, ix, 123, 125–128,
  131, 133, 222
Schober, Franz, x–xi

Schoeck, Othmar, 229
Schoenberg, Arnold, 155, 156, 159n,
    180n, 284, 302, 303
    Das Buch der hängenden Gärten, 224
Schopenhauer, Arthur, 163, 193, 243,
    244, 250, 296, 315
Schröder-Devrient, Wilhelmine, 288
Schroeder, David, 104
    Mozart in Revolt, 100–101, 103,
        109n
Schubert, Franz, 117, 125, 157–158,
    183, 207
    "An die Musik," x–xi
    "Die liebe Farbe" (in Die schöne
        Müllerin) , 224
    "Der Lindenbaum" (in Winterreise),
        212, 213
    Die Schöne Müllerin, 212, 224
    songs, 221–229
    String Quintet in C, 153
    Symphony No. 8 ("Unfinished"),
        353–355
    "Tränenregen" (in Die schöne
        Müllerin), 212–213
    "Trost in Tränen," xiii, 225,
        226–227
    "Wandrers Nachtlied (Über allen
        Gipfeln ist Ruh')," 223
    "Das Wandern" (in Die schöne
        Müllerin) 224
    Winterreise, 212
Schuller, Gunther: The Compleat
    Conductor, 351, 352
Schumann, Clara, 210, 227
Schumann, Robert, 82, 157–158,
    207–208, 209, 214, 217–220, 223,
    225, 229, 236
    Carnaval, 207, 210, 218
    "Chiarina" (from Carnaval) , 218
    Davidsbündlertänze, 207, 213
    Dichterliebe, 210
    "Eusebius" (from Carnaval), 211,
        218
    "Florestan" (from Carnaval), 211,
        218
    "Im wunderschönen Monat Mai
        (from Dichterliebe)," 210

    Novelette in A Major, op. 21, no. 6,
        219
    Papillons, 210
    Phantasie, op. 17, 210–211
    Piano Concerto, 128, 210
    Sonata in F-Sharp Minor, 157
Segalini, Sergio: Callas: Portrait of a
    Diva, 346
Seidl, Anton, 2
Serafin, Tullio, 348
Serkin, Peter, 136
Sessions, Roger: When Lilacs Last in
    the Dooryard Bloom'd, 336–337
Shafer, Peter, 117
    Amadeus, 115, 116
Shakespeare, William, 69, 88–89, 233,
    245, 254, 272, 278, 335
    Hamlet, 233, 235, 249, 277, 293
    Henry IV, parts 1 and 2, 248
    The Merchant of Venice, 246
    The Merry Wives of Windsor, 248
    Much Ado About Nothing, 240
    Othello, 274
    The Tempest, 249, 251
Shaw, George Bernard, xi, 88–89,
    247, 289, 297, 313, 315
    The Perfect Wagnerite, 293, 294,
        311–312
Shine (film), 21, 24
Shostakovich, Dmitri, 11, 327
Sidney, Sir Philip, 68
Silbermann, Gottfried, 94
Silja, Anja, 331
Singer, Irving: Mozart and Beethoven,
    253–254
Smart, Christopher, 335
Smetana, Bedřich: The Bartered Bride,
    61
Smith, Joseph, 323
Smithson, Harriet, 233, 235, 236
Society of the Friends of Bayreuth,
    325
Society of the Musical Sciences, 88n
Solomon, Maynard, 166
    Beethoven, 171n, 187
    Late Beethoven: Music, Thought,
        Imagination, 201

Mozart: A Life, 105, 109*n*
Solti, Sir Georg, 300
Sonoma Opera, 19
Sony, 355
Southwell, Father Robert, 41, 46
Spanish Monks, 21
Spener, Philipp Jakob, 91
Spielberg, Steven, 298
Spitta, Philipp, 92–93, 95
Spontini, Gaspare, 232
Stafford, William: *The Mozart Myths,* 100
Stassinopoulos, Arianna: *Maria Callas: The Woman Behind the Legend,* 346, 349
Steinberg, Michael, 196, 333
  Choral Masterworks, 333, 334–341, 343–344
  The Concerto, 333
  The Symphony, 333, 334, 337*n*
Stewart, Thomas, 314*n*
Stokowski, Leopold, 3
Stolz, Teresa, 260, 265, 340
Strauss, Johann, II
  "The Blue Danube," 355
  Die Fledermaus, 355
  "Tales of the Vienna Woods," 355
Strauss, Richard, 22, 251, 270, 294
  Ariadne auf Naxos, 248–249
  Capriccio, 249
  Die Frau ohne Schatten, 249
  Der Rosenkavalier, 61, 355
  Salome, 250, 251, 252
Stravinsky, Igor, 88*n*, 129, 132, 183
Strepponi, Giuseppina, 258–261, 265
Süssmayr, Franz Xaver, 111, 113, 342, 343
Syberberg, Hans Jürgen, 319, 325

Tallis, Thomas, 36, 46, 55
  Cantiones quae ab argumento sacrae vocantur (with Byrd), 46, 49
Tanner, Michael, 329
Taruskin, Richard, 17, 33–34
  Oxford History of Western Music, 9–11, 13, 19

"The Pastness of the Present and the Presence of the Past," 128–130
Tausig, Carl, 291
Taverner, John: *Missa Gloria tibi Trinitas,* 35–36
Taymor, Julie, 145
Tchaikovsky, Pyotr Ilyich *see* Chaikovsky
Tennyson, Alfred, Lord, 335
Terfel, Bryan, 149
Theater-arbeit an Wagners Ring (ed. Mack), 299
Thomas, Michael Tilson, 5
Thomasius, Christian, 90, 91
Thomson, Virgil, xiv, 289
  Four Saints in Three Acts, 15
Three Tenors, 3, 21
Tieck, Ludwig, 187
Tinctoris, Johannes, 33
Tippett, Sir Michael, *The Knot Garden,* 38
Tolkien, J. R. R. , 298
Tolstoy, Leo, 163
  War and Peace, 248
Tomlinson, Gary, 20
Toscanini, Arturo, 1, 3, 129
Tovey, Donald, xii, 22, 24, 84, 96, 130, 132, 153, 154, 167, 338–339, 342, 343, 344
  Beethoven, 163
  "Sonata Forms," 152
Tozzi, Giorgio, 271
Treitler, Leo, 167
Turner, J. M. W. , 212
Tye, Christopher, 36
Tyson, Alan, 117*n*
  "Beethoven's Heroic Phase," 173, 182
  Mozart: Studies of the Autograph Scores, 109*n*, 118–121

Umlauf, Ignaz: *Das Irrlicht* (The Will o' the Wisp), 138
University of California, Berkeley, Symphony Orchestra, x

Verdi, Camillo, 260
Verdi, Carlo, 260, 261, 265, 266

Verdi, Giuseppe, x, 60, 244, 246, 247,
    251, 255–266, 267–279
    Aida, 257, 260, 267, 269, 271–272,
        273, 340, 341
    Attila, 274
    Un Ballo in maschera, 256, 257
    Carteggio Verdi–Boito (correspon-
        dence), 269, 270
    Il Corsaro, 274
    Don Carlos, 251, 267, 269,
        270–271, 273, 277, 339, 341
    I Due Foscari, 274
    Falstaff, 248, 257, 263, 264, 265,
        267, 269, 272, 273, 274, 277
    La Forza del destino, 256, 266,
        267, 341
    Un Giorno di regno, 257, 262
    Macbeth, 251, 268
    Nabucco, 257, 259, 274
    Oberto, 259
    Otello, 244, 257, 263, 265, 267,
        269, 270, 272–276, 278
    Requiem, x, 260, 271, 336,
        337–341
    Rigoletto, 256, 261, 263
    Simon Boccanegra, 263, 268
    Stiffelio, 256
    La Traviata, 249, 256, 355
    Il Trovatore, 256, 267, 338
    I Vespri Siciliani, 349
Viardot, Pauline, 231, 232, 237
Victoria, Tomás Luis de, 43
Vienna Philharmonic, 355*n*
Villiers de l'Isle-Adam, Count Philippe
    de, 300
Virgil: *Aeneid*, 232
Visconti, Luchino, 347, 350
Vishnevskaya, Galina, 336
Vivaldi, Antonio, 22, 74, 91
Volkov, Solomon: *Testimony*, 327
Voltaire, 102
Vulpius, C. A., 143*n*
Vulpius, Christiane, 143*n*

Wagner, Cosima, 259, 260, 287, 288,
    299, 300, 301, 323, 325*n*, 329
Wagner, Eva, 329

Wagner, Friedelind, 301, 325*n*
Wagner, Gertrud, 325*n*
Wagner, Gottfried, 329
    Twilight of the Wagners, 325–326,
        327
Wagner, Nike, 328
    *The Wagners: The Dramas of a
        Musical Dynasty*, 319–325,
        327–331
Wagner, Richard, x, xiv, 1, 2, 15,
    174*n*, 177, 183, 217, 240, 243,
    251, 255, 257, 258–259, 263,
    281–305, 319–331, 338
    music:
    The Flying Dutchman, 327
    Götterdämmerung, 247, 286, 294,
        296, 297, 308, 309, 311, 312*n*,
        316
    Lohengrin, 256, 294, 320, 328
    Die Meistersinger von Nürnberg,
        12, 286, 294, 303, 313, 320, 321,
        324–329
    Parsifal, 2, 19, 216, 247, 286, 291,
        292, 297, 313, 321–322, 325,
        328, 329, 330
    Das Rheingold, 247, 308, 312, 313,
        316
    Rienzi, 330
    Der Ring des Nibelungen, 246–247,
        286, 291, 293–301, 307–317,
        319, 320, 321, 327, 328, 330
    Siegfried, 244, 247, 289, 293, 295,
        296, 312*n*, 313
    Siegfrieds Tod, 286, 295
    Tannhäuser, 237, 256, 300, 327
    Tristan und Isolde, 216, 244, 256,
        286, 294, 304–305, 313, 328, 355
    Die Walküre, 247, 310, 311, 312*n*,
        313, 314
    writings:
    A Capitulation, 292
    A Communication to My Friends,
        287
    Gesammelte Schriften, 255, 286
    Heroism and Christianity, 290
    Judaism in Music, 290, 292, 295,
        321

Know Yourself, 290
"Music of the Future," 292
My Life (Mein Leben), 259, 281, 287–288, 301, 325*n*
"On Conducting," 292
"On Performing Beethoven's Ninth Symphony," 292
Religion and Art, 286
Wagner, Siegfried, 325*n*, 329
Wagner, Wieland, 298–301, 304, 324, 325, 327, 329, 330, 331
Wagner, Winifred, 319, 324, 325, 329
Wagner, Wolf Siegfried, 322, 325*n*
Wagner, Wolfgang, 299, 319, 320, 324, 326, 328, 329, 331
 Acts: The Autobiography of Wolfgang Wagner, 325*n*
Wagner-Pasquier, Eva, 320
Waldmüller, Ferdinand Georg, 169*n*
Walpole, Henry, 44, 45, 52
Ward, Anthony, 66n
Ward, John: *The Crucible*, 18
Waugh, Evelyn, 41, 44
Weaver, William, 269*n*
Weber, Carl Maria: *Der Freischütz*, 355
Webster, Margaret, 271
Wegeler, Franz, 162
Weill, Kurt, 11
 Die Dreigroschenoper, 244
Weininger, Otto, 322*n*
 Geschlecht und Charakter, 321
Westernhagen, Curt von, 290, 292, 293
White, Willard, 143
Wieck, Clara, *see* Schumann, Clara
Wilhelm Friedrich, King of Prussia, 109
Williams, Bernard, 322
Williams, Peter: *The Life of Bach*, 69–73, 75–76
Wilson, Robert, 11, 328
Winter, Peter: *The Labyrinth*, 38
Wintle, Christopher, 313
Wolf, Hugo, 223, 225, 227, 229
Wordsworth, William, 212
Wranitzky, Paul: *Oberon*, 138

Wright, Craig: *The Maze and the Warrior*, 27–30, 32, 33, 34, 36–39
Wuorinen, Charles: *Genesis*, 333
Wyn Jones, David: *The Life of Beethoven*, 171*n*

Zacharias, Christian, 134
Zane family, 58
Zeffirelli, Franco, 350
Zillig, Winfried, 229